LIVE AT THE FILLMORE EAST AND WEST

ALSO BY JOHN GLATT

Rage & Roll: Bill Graham and the Selling of Rock
River Phoenix: The Biography
The Chieftains: The Authorized Biography
The Ruling House of Monaco: The Story of a Tragic Dynasty

Live at the Fillmore East and West

Getting Backstage and Personal with Rock's Greatest Legends

John Glatt

LYONS PRESS
Guilford, Connecticut
Helena, Montana
An imprint of Rowman & Littlefield

Lyons Press is an imprint of Rowman & Littlefield

Distributed by NATIONAL BOOK NETWORK

Copyright © 2015 by John Glatt

British Library Cataloguing-in-Publication Information available

Library of Congress Cataloging-in-Publication Data

Glatt, John.
  Live at the Fillmore East and West : getting backstage and personal with rock's greatest legends / John Glatt.
    pages cm
  Includes bibliographical references and index.
  ISBN 978-0-7627-8865-1
1. Rock concerts—New York (State) —New York. 2. Rock concerts—California—San Francisco. 3. Fillmore East (New York, N.Y.) 4. Fillmore Auditorium (San Francisco, Calif.) 5. Graham, Bill, 1931-1991. 6. Rock musicians—United States. 7. Concert agents—United States. I. Title.
  ML3534.3.G63 2014
  781.66078'79461—dc23

                    2014027226

∞™ The paper used in this publication meets the minimum requirements of American National Standard for Information Sciences—Permanence of Paper for Printed Library Materials, ANSI/NISO Z39.48-1992.

For Gail
My sweet little rock 'n' roller

Contents

Foreword

By the spring of 1967, word came to us in New York that amazing musical and visual ideas were happening in San Francisco. At the time I was designing lights for New York discotheques of the era—such as Salvation, Arthur, Trude Heller's, and Bobb Goldstein's Lightworks—but knew I wanted something more.

That July, The Electric Circus opened on St. Marks Place in the heart of the Lower East Side. The entrepreneur behind the nightclub was Jerry Brandt. By fortunate coincidence, I'd gone to camp and was childhood friends with his wife, the late actress Janet Margolin, a relationship that gave me easy access to The Electric Circus. I went there often.

In 1967 the Lower East Side was an ethnic melting pot. Basically, Jerry had taken a 1930s Polish ballroom, inexpensively altered its shape with stretch nylon, and imported the artist Anthony Martin from San Francisco to fill the surfaces with a light show. Fill them he did and brilliantly, with colors and projections of flowing liquids. What I didn't know yet was that some artists in San Francisco, such as Bill Ham, Glenn McKay and Jerry Abrams, George Holden's Abercrombe Lights, and Little Princess 109, were doing the same thing in several similar old ballrooms. They provided illumination and powerful visual imagery behind emerging bands, mostly from the Bay Area. It seemed prudent to make a trip out to northern California to check out the whole scene, including Haight-Ashbury.

The Summer of Love (soon to be defined by major print media) was in progress.

I contacted David Denby, an old friend and also a campmate, who lived there, and flew west. Hooking up with other old friends—Iris Ratner and Fred Cohen—we took a quick tour of the San Francisco scene. In addition to the Haight, the Avalon Ballroom, Golden Gate Park, and other iconic places, we went to the Fillmore Auditorium.

My friends' connections allowed us to skip the line and go directly to the box office.

The tickets were two dollars, maybe three, all cash.

I'll always remember my first sight of the Fillmore Auditorium.

There was a basket of apples at the bottom of the stairs where we entered.

Most of the people there seemed to have a certain chill smile on their face. Perhaps it was a collective need to be part of a hip scene, a sense of expectation, a gathering of the tribes, but I still found it slightly eerie.

At the top of the stairs, near the box office was a very unusual-looking person. He was intense but not mean. Unlike the patrons, his hair was relatively short. He was dressed in a simple shirt and pants. He was exotically handsome, with large features and a strong, lean body. He was articulate and spoke with a clear baritone voice. This was Bill Graham.

Bill was clearly in charge, a sober center for a new and unfamiliar scene.

The ballroom was already full—I suspect way over capacity. As people left, Bill personally admitted an equal number of people and took their money. There was a very clear sign over the door: "No Inny-Outey."

I honestly don't remember the bands that played that night, but I do remember the ambience. In spite of the faux bliss, it was a real and powerful experience.

The light show and band music filled the space and reached deep inside me. The Electric Circus in New York was interesting, but the overwhelming feeling at the Circus was of theater, with a fourth wall always existing between the artists and participants. The Fillmore was something different and dynamic, possibly more of a "be-in"—a participatory experience rather than a business. I couldn't really define it then as much as feel it.

I returned to New York energized by what I'd seen.

A few months later, my company was hired to provide support services for a theatrical event in Toronto of all places. Toronto had a hip scene and a very traditional modern theater, O'Keefe Centre, which usually offered ballet, opera, and musicals. The Centre, aware of the coming Summer of Love, had made a deal with an up-and-coming San Francisco producer to present a week with Jefferson Airplane and the Grateful Dead. The producer was Bill Graham.

The original concept was to reproduce the ballroom scene. Bay Area light show artists Glenn McKay and Jerry Abrams of Headlights had flown in to survey the space and declared that they could do a great light show as long as the balcony was closed off to accommodate their equipment. Because we were now in a theater, the use of that space was a serious problem for box office ticket sales. Since I had been trained in the medium at Carnegie Tech drama school, it fell to me and my associates to solve the problem and find a way to stage the light show and do the concert without using any balcony space. We did this by providing an enormous rear projection screen behind the bands as opposed to the traditional way of throwing light from the balcony.

It also fell to me to "call" the stage lighting in the theater itself. This task wasn't hard, but I had to sit in the back of the house. For six performances, I was hypnotized by the combination of great music and the Headlights light show—a perfect blend of musical power and visual stimulation.

In the end I was totally addicted.

More importantly, I saw my future, at least to the degree that any twenty-four-year-old can see his future.

By December we had our first engagement as the Joshua Light Show, projecting on the same giant rear projection screen we had made for Toronto.

In January we got to play the Lower East Side at the Anderson Theater (formerly the Yiddish Anderson Theater). Our shows at the Anderson, presented by *Crawdaddy* magazine, featured the great artists of the time (Jefferson Airplane, Big Brother and the Holding Company, Frank Zappa and the Mothers of Invention, Country Joe and the Fish) and were quickly selling out all four shows every weekend.

We'd kept in contact with Bill Graham, but he was reluctant to expand to New York. I discovered later that his reservations stemmed from his stint as an unsuccessful actor in the Big Apple before striking gold as a San Francisco entrepreneur.

But finally we got him to come to New York. Bill stood on the stage at the Anderson during a Janis Joplin concert, counted the house, and within two months opened at the Village Theater (another former Yiddish theater) across the street on Second Avenue near East Sixth Street. The Joshua Light Show now had a regular gig with Bill Graham. However, the theater's previous promoter threatened to sue if the space was called the Village Theater.

So at the last minute, Bill renamed it the Fillmore East.

The rest is history.

—Joshua White, founder of the Joshua Light Show
September 19, 2014

PROLOGUE

When Bill Graham summoned his Fillmore East staff to a Saturday afternoon meeting, nobody suspected anything out of the ordinary. They were busy preparing for two sold-out John Mayall shows that night, and business had never been better.

"We just thought it was going to be another one of Bill's talks," recalled Allan Arkush of the psychedelicized liquid light show Joe's Lights, who joined the rest of the 120 staff at the front of the big theater. "He would get the staff together and give these speeches about what made a great show. He'd say a show is like a beautiful woman, and then there's Ava Gardner."[1]

Now sitting on the stage with his general manager, Kip Cohen, the tough-talking owner of rock music's two most iconic venues—the Fillmore East in New York and the Fillmore West in San Francisco—struggled to find the right words.

"As a result of my feelings as a producer," he began, clearing his throat, "but mainly as a human being, I've decided to close the Fillmore East on June 26, which is the Allman Brothers/J. Geils show."[2]

An audible gasp went through the theater. The implications sunk in immediately.

"The reason is that I'm tired personally with the artists [and] the public," he continued. "And I can't do it any more. For me the insanity is no longer endurable."

More than three years before, on March 8, 1968, Janis Joplin and Big Brother and the Holding Company had opened the Fillmore East, the shabby former Jewish vaudeville theater in the heart of New York's tough Lower East Side.

Then, three months later, Graham had opened the Fillmore West in San Francisco. Since then, the two venues had hosted legendary shows by Jimi Hendrix, Led Zeppelin, the Allman Brothers, the Grateful Dead, Jefferson Airplane, and Santana.

Like a manic circus ringmaster, Graham ran his twin operations with military precision, constantly crisscrossing the country with a double-headed watch to keep track. Yet he still found time to orchestrate the venues' transformation into a multimillion-dollar business empire, all the while giving music fans memories to treasure for the rest of their lives.

But everything changed after Woodstock, when half a million people descended on Max Yasgur's farm. The August 1969 festival—more so than previous events, like the Beatles' 1965 concert at Shea Stadium—had revealed the huge financial potential of rock 'n' roll. And Graham, well aware of the dangers Woodstock posed to him, had tried to stop it.

After Woodstock the tectonic plates of the music business shifted as musicians and managers began squeezing the promoters for more and more money. Rock superstars Janis Joplin, The Doors, and Led Zeppelin would now play one show at Madison Square Garden instead of four at the more intimate Fillmore East, for the exact same money.

Bill Graham warned that audiences would be the real losers, as these bigger venues had bad sound and distanced the audience from the concert experience. But he was secretly planning to move up to the next level of concert evolution to compete. He had no intention of laying bare such a strategy to the world or even his loyal staff.

Instead he would portray himself as the aggrieved party—an unwitting victim of greedy musicians, managers, and agents. In his V-neck sweater and rolled-up sleeves, the failed actor, who had just turned forty, gave a masterful performance, recounting to his staff his last two frustrating weeks in New York.

"It was *the* most aggravating, disappointing, unbearable two weeks of my professional career," he declared.

It had begun with a phone call, explained Graham, cancelling two upcoming Jethro Tull shows at the Fillmore East due to illness.

"Which is okay," he conceded, "but the hardships and the begging that you have to go through to get groups to replace them. . . ."

Then there had been the "fucking around" he'd received from Tanglewood Music Festival organizers. After staging two well-received "Fillmore at Tanglewood" summer shows—showcasing such acts as The Who, Santana, and Miles Davis—this year the prestigious venue wanted him only as a consultant.

"They decided they would throw us a bone," he sneered.

But the final straw came after legendary impresario Sol Hurok had invited him to present a month of shows at the Metropolitan Opera House. Hurok, Graham's boyhood hero and his inspiration to become a promoter, had rented the prestigious Met for a month of performances by the Bolshoi Ballet. But a Russian sailor had defected to America, causing the Soviet authorities to cancel everything in retaliation and leaving Hurok owing $200,000 (the equivalent of about $1,156,000 in mid-2010s' purchasing power) in rent. In desperation the octogenarian promoter had turned to Bill Graham to bail him out.

The meetings "with the old man," explained Graham, had begun "very amicably" but then rapidly deteriorated. After agreeing on which rock acts to present, Graham had explained that each would be paid $50,000 ($289,000) a week.

"His reaction was that of an old Jewish vaudeville actor," said Graham. "He couldn't understand that Isaac Stern can make $5,000 a night, which he thought was a fortune, and that an act like Grand Funk Railroad could earn $30,000 or $40,000."

Working full time to book the acts, Graham had based himself in New York, operating from his upstairs office at the Fillmore East.

"Laura Nyro said yes," said Graham. "Elton John said more than likely. Chicago said they'll try and get out of something."

Then the sensitive question of marquee billing had come up.

"And he was very blasé," said Graham. "That of course it'll be 'S. Hurok' very large and in very small letters below it would say, 'in association with Bill Graham.' I balked."

Graham explained he would be doing everything, while Hurok was only supplying the lease. After much wrangling, the old man reluctantly agreed the billing could be "S. Hurok and Bill Graham Present."

Marquee billing settled, Bill Graham pursued his dream act for the run—to book The Band for the final week of shows—feeling it would be his perfect "Ava Gardner." So he had left a message with their manager, Jon Taplin, who had returned the call at 3:00 a.m. the previous Sunday morning.

"I said, 'Jesus, what a wonderful thing, The Band and [their] music—it belongs there.' And he said, 'What's the deal?'"

When Graham offered The Band $50,000 to play six evening shows and two matinees, Taplin started laughing, saying he couldn't be serious about paying them only a "lousy fifty grand a week."

"That was the crowning blow," Graham told his staff, becoming visibly emotional. "We all have our areas which we can go, and that was mine."

After putting down the phone with Taplin, Graham said he had started listing the negative and positive aspects of running the two Fillmores on a piece of paper. On the negative side were the rude, disruptive audiences, the greedy bands and their managers, the agents, and "the personal abuse that I take."

Unfortunately, the only positive thing he could come up with was "the almighty dollar."

"Once in a while there's a good show," he conceded. "Once in a while there is a nice audience. Whereas it used to be nine good [shows], one bad one, five years ago. It's gotten to be fifty-fifty, sixty-forty, seventy-thirty against. And now it's once in a while we have a groovy evening."

At that point, he told his staff, Kip Cohen had walked into his office. "And I just threw up my hands and said, 'Kip, I've had it! I don't know how, when, where, but it's got to end.'"

Ironically, he explained, this had been the "most lucrative month" since the Fillmore East opened, so his decision was emotional.

"I'm not a good businessman," he said. "I think I'm a good booker and a pretty good producer, but not good at business."

Standing on the nape of the stage, "Uncle Bill," as his staff affectionately called him, now took them into his confidence.

"It's a frightening thing," he said. "It's a frightening thought . . . but I can't . . . I've had it. I pass. It just can't be done anymore."

Since making his decision to quit the music business, he had been crunching the numbers with his lawyers and accountants.

"[This] is the biggest moneymaker," he declared, "and it's where I'm going to decelerate . . . and begin to withdraw troops."

Closing the Fillmore East would be only the first step, as he had contractual agreements to keep the Fillmore West open until the end of the summer. And there were also his two record companies and management agency to consider.

"I'm not saying fuck you to the Fillmore East and the people that work here," he explained. "But I have to start somewhere."

He then thanked his "Fillmore Family" for their professionalism and the great job they had done.

"This theater has no comparison," he told them. "There's nothing to compare with the stage, the productions, with the way the house is run [and] the people who run it. My pride in what you people have done is incredible.

"I hope the closing of this theater, through some miracle, will melt down Madison Square Garden, will set up an invisible picket around that ugly cement factory."

After a nervous round of applause from his staff, one young male employee asked, "Do you know where we can take panhandling lessons?"

"Yes, in front of the Fillmore West, asshole," replied Graham as he left the stage.

⁓

Eleven days later, Bill Graham held a well-orchestrated press conference at the Fillmore East to announce the closing. Then, to the astonishment of reporters, he attacked the entire music industry, blaming greedy bands, unscrupulous managers, and predatory agents for his demise.

But even worse, he told the flabbergasted reporters, was that he hated his reputation as the "anti-Christ" and "capitalist pig," so he was getting out of the business.[3]

A reporter then asked if success had spoiled rock music, creating all these problems he was complaining about.

"No," he replied. "I think it's the inability to cope with success that's spoiled rock. It was the inability to cope with success that killed Janis Joplin and that killed Jimi Hendrix. It wasn't the drugs. If you spoke with them you would see that they just didn't know how to handle the adulation that was heaped upon them by the music that they created. Neither you nor I would ever know what it's like to walk on a stage and have half a million people tell you that you are a queen, that you're a goddess, and anything you do is just fine."

PART ONE

THE ROAD TO THE FILLMORES

CHAPTER ONE

The Refugee

Bill Graham was born Wolodia Grajonca in Berlin on January 8, 1931, at the start of Hitler's rise to power. The youngest child of Russian-born engineer Jacob Grajonca and his wife, Frieda, Wolodia was just two days old when his father was killed in a construction accident.

To support Wolodia and his five elder sisters—Rita, Evelyn, Sonja, Ester, and Tolla—Frieda scraped by working as a dressmaker and making costume jewelry she sold in the market. Life was a constant struggle for the close-knit Jewish family, who lived in two rooms and a kitchen in the roughest slum section of Berlin, known as "The Wedding." Eventually Frieda was forced to send her two youngest children—Wolodia and Tolla—to live in an orphanage.

As the Nazis tightened their grip on Berlin, it became increasingly dangerous to be Jewish. At school the elder Grajonca girls were expected to salute Nazi-style and cry "Heil Hitler" whenever a teacher entered the classroom. Still, they were constantly mocked by their classmates in the Hitler Youth movement.

Although Wolodia and Tolla lived at the orphanage during the week, they went home on weekends. To the sensitive little boy, his two eldest sisters, Rita and Evelyn, lived an exotic bohemian life, full of dancing and music. They were rebellious and independent, staying out late with boys and having constant arguments with their mother as she attempted to rein them in.

When Rita went to Shanghai to join her boyfriend, Freddy, and became a dancer, Wolodia dreamed of following her. After all, she was earning $150 a month ($2,500 in mid-2010s' currency).

On November 9, 1938, seven-year-old Wolodia witnessed the infamous Kristallnacht, when the Nazis indiscriminately beat up Jews, destroyed synagogues, and wrecked homes and businesses. It was a horrific experience, and one he would never forget.

In its aftermath, Frieda worried about her children's safety in Berlin, but she could not afford to move the family out of Germany. On June 5, 1939, less than three months before Hitler invaded Poland and plunged Europe into war, Wolodia and Tolla went to Paris as part of a two-week Jewish exchange program with a French orphanage. Their mother went to the train station to see them off, and it would be the last time they would ever see her.

Eight-year-old Wolodia left Germany grasping a small case containing all his worldly possessions—his yarmulke, Jewish prayer book, and a picture of his parents. And like so many other Jewish refugees from the Holocaust, he grew up feeling his only true possessions were in his pocket or what he could carry away with him.

While Wolodia and Tolla were in Paris, the Nazis banned Jewish immigration and reentry, stranding the orphans in France. Even more tragically the exchanged French Jewish orphans were trapped in Berlin.

Far from the dangers of the Third Reich, the two Grajonca children lived in the Chateau de Quincy, a beautiful old tapestry-filled mansion outside Paris. Wolodia soon settled down, forming a gang with other orphans and going on stealing expeditions to the local shops, where he often got caught. He studied at the public elementary school at Quincy and learned to speak fluent French, impressing his teachers with his love of nature.

Then in May 1940, Hitler invaded France. As the German Army marched toward Paris, Wolodia and the other children helped to build air-raid shelters. Most nights German war planes circled the French capital, and during bombing raids the petrified children hid in damp trenches. One night Wolodia was attacked by a snake, leaving him with a lifelong phobia of them.

A month later, as the German Army surrounded Paris, an International Red Cross representative arrived to escort the Jewish children to safety. Sixty-four children, including Wolodia and Tolla, were then evacuated to a farm in the Forest of Senart and Fontainebleau on the Paris outskirts. One night, armed German soldiers burst onto the farm, and the children narrowly escaped with their lives.

"This group of children has seen the Battle of Paris," wrote their Red Cross escort. "And lived through all the dangers, discovering certain cruel aspects of fighting which perhaps have left marks on their character. In the case of [Wolodia] Grajonca, however, I dare say with certainty that the moral damage is not serious."[1]

"Everybody moved south," remembered Wolodia almost fifty years later. "There were sixty-four children between the ages of eight and sixteen. My sister and I were among these. We walked, got on buses, on trains, on carts and ate what we could. When a country is invaded, that's what happens. All hell breaks loose."[2]

Heading south on foot, the children hid by day and then walked twenty-five miles every night under cover of darkness. They scrambled for safety as German planes attacked, often seeing dead bodies on the highway. They survived on berries, and all suffered severe malnutrition.

Just outside Lyon, Tolla caught pneumonia. She and Wolodia were walking hand in hand when she suddenly dropped to the roadside dead. Inconsolable, the nine-year-old cradled his sister's head in his lap, refusing to be separated from her. The Red Cross escort had to drag Wolodia away because the Germans were close behind. Tolla's body was left by the side of the road.

From Lyon the children walked two hundred miles to Marseilles, where on August 19 they were issued temporary passports by the American Consulate. Little Wulf (Wolfgang) Wolodia Grajonca, as he was listed on the passport, wore a brave smile in his photograph. It belied the terrible hardship of the four-foot, six-inch-tall boy's wretched journey across France, which had left him weighing just fifty-five pounds.[3]

At Marseilles he and the surviving orphans boarded a train to Toulouse and crossed the Pyrenees into Spain, traveling through Barcelona to Madrid, where they spent two months in a convent.

"I was living in a convent with eleven children," Wolodia remembered later. "A stray bomb that was meant for the big city next to us hit the building that I was in. Three of the children did not leave the building."[4]

The children then traveled to the port of Lisbon, where on September 10, Wolodia and the ten others—the only survivors of the sixty-four who had left Paris—boarded the ocean liner *Serpa Pinto* bound for America. After picking up more refugees in Casablanca, the vessel set off across the Atlantic for the two-week voyage to New York. During the crossing the ship was stopped and boarded by a German U-boat and then a British submarine, but it was allowed to continue on its journey.

On Wednesday, September 24, 1941, ten-year-old Wolodia Grajonca arrived at Ellis Island, undernourished and weak. His harrowing journey had been so traumatic that he would block it from his memory for years.

At the dockside to meet Wolodia and the other children was Lotte Marcuse, director of Placements for New York's German Jewish Children's Aid, Inc., who would be responsible for him until he was twenty-one. After undergoing a medical examination by seven physicians and a team of Red Cross nurses, Wolodia was fully documented by Immigration.[5]

His first American meal was a kosher one, and after being given fresh clothing, Wolodia and four other children were put on a bus to Pleasantville Cottage School in upstate New York, which served as a halfway house for young Jewish refugees until they could be adopted. Several hours later, when he arrived at the refugee reception center, Wolodia was given a bath. Then he was taken to a dormitory to spend his first lonely night in this new country.

The next morning he was examined by strangers, who spoke a language he could not understand. During his first interview, via a translator, the caseworker assigned to Wolodia was impressed by his resilience.

"Interviewed Wolodia, who is a blonde, stocky youngster with a mature and self reliant air about him," she wrote in the official report. "He responded intelligently to my questioning. Wolodia has a good deal of poise about him and although he is not a very attractive child, he has a pleasant manner and intelligence which expresses itself in a cooperative attitude and willingness to participate in whatever chores the group is expected to do."

Wolodia told the caseworker that he had an American aunt called "Schneider," whom his mother had told him about. But he had no idea where she lived, and the bureau was unable to trace her. And so each week, along with the other children, Wolodia was put on display for prospective foster parents, who would come to see if there were any kids they wanted to adopt.

After several weeks of not being chosen, Wolodia lost the poise and pleasantness his caseworker had observed, throwing a tantrum, physically attacking staff and children. His behavior so alarmed Lotte Marcuse that she requested he be transferred to a New York care center so she could keep a closer eye on him.[6]

"Wolodia is one of the children who is extremely insecure and 'cries' for individual attention," wrote the director of placements. "His reaction in the group, to children and to adults alike, is a most destructive one. He scowls most of the time and carries with him the expression of the bullying urchin. He is filthy and has no standards of cleanliness. He won't accept group action and has no feeling about disturbing adults and children alike.

"Yet yesterday, when I watched a group of children, Wolodia came along—and he had a smile, a really normal smile on his face. He had been told that in America, people 'keep smiling' and that this is a slogan that he must accept if and insofar as he wants people to like him. And Wolodia has a great need to be liked."

Yet few of the Pleasantville staff ever saw his good side. Wolodia's antisocial behavior had so alienated them that Marcuse expressed concern about his ever finding a foster home.

"Wolodia is very thin, almost emaciated looking," she noted in her report. "He has a voracious appetite and atrocious table manners. He should not be placed in a foster home in which there are children near him in age, either slightly older or younger."

For almost a month, Wolodia was rejected by all the prospective foster parents. One by one, all the other children left Pleasantville to begin new lives, but Wolodia always remained. Every night he cried himself to sleep, worrying about his mother and sisters back in Germany and wondering if he would ever see them again.

Wolodia was finally claimed by Alfred and Pearl Ehrenreich, a middle-aged couple who lived in a cramped apartment at 1635

Montgomery Avenue in the Bronx. They mainly selected him to teach their son Roy to speak German and French.[7]

Alfred Ehrenreich, an insurance salesman, showed little affection for Wolodia, who felt much closer to his new foster mother. Pearl renamed him Billy and began fattening him up with her American home cooking, rubbing him down daily with olive oil for his skin allergies.

The Ehrenreichs received $25 a month from the Foster Home Bureau toward his care, which Billy always suspected was the real reason they had adopted him.

——

Two months after Billy went to the Bronx, America entered the war. Pearl Ehrenreich enrolled him in P.S. 104, where he was placed in a class of seven-year-olds, as he knew no English. And being German, Billy Grajonca was cruelly bullied by his new classmates, who called him an "Evil Nazi" and stoned him outside school.

"To them I wasn't a Jew, I was a German," he would explain later. "I spoke German, I was a Nazi. And I used to get in more fights than I like to think about."[8]

Roy looked after his new foster brother, defending him against the bullies who mocked his strong German accent. Realizing that Billy needed to learn English fast to survive, Roy made him read the day's newspapers out loud in front of the mirror every night. And nine months after setting foot in America, Billy spoke fluent Bronx English without a hint of a German accent.

On D-Day, June 6, 1944, all Bronx schools closed early to mark the Allied major offensive, and Billy attended a special afternoon service in his synagogue to pray for the safe return of US servicemen. Although he outwardly appeared to have adapted well to his new life, Billy was deeply depressed and insecure. He developed a nervous twitch of his eyelids and was plagued with various allergies and hay fever.[9]

In mid-November, the US Committee for the Care of European Children informed Billy that his mother and sisters had probably not survived. The little boy was heartbroken and stayed in his room sobbing for hours. He also threw tantrums at school when he felt the teachers were not paying him enough attention.

"We are planning to have Billy see the agency psychiatrist," wrote his new caseworker, Marjorie Davis, in June 1943. "We want to determine whether or not he is in need of psychiatric treatment at this time."

The psychiatrist described him as "an insecure, immature child with a fear of aggression and with hostility in his associations," his bad behavior at school being caused by "personality difficulties." But psychiatric treatment was not recommended.

During the next few months, Billy's behavior deteriorated even further. He feared being left alone and would cry uncontrollably if he ever was. He hardly ever washed or combed his hair.

Citing his "peculiar personal habits," "secretive ways," and "extreme antagonisms with Roy," his caseworker advised taking him away from the Ehrenreichs and placing him with Social Services.

Ironically, it was only after he was expelled from P.S. 104 for kicking a teacher that his behavior improved. And he was allowed to remain with Pearl and Alfred Ehrenreich, whom he now called mother and father.

"Were they my parents?" he would be asked later. "She was my mother. He was never my father. He was an okay guy, but I can't say I loved him or cared deeply about him."[10]

Growing into a lanky teenager, Billy became a typical New York street kid. He played stickball or half-court ball with the neighborhood kids, spending his pocket money at Al's Candy Store.

He looked up to the older kids, who taught him street smarts, and he soon mastered the hustles needed to make extra money for candy and movies. The street became his classroom and taught him a strong moral code.[11]

"I think that's what formed my character," he later explained. "It's having to live by the book of unwritten rules, starting early on."[12]

At age sixteen, Billy joined the Pirates gang, proudly wearing their green-and-yellow jacket at clubhouse meetings. It was a matter of honor for a Pirate to have a girl by his side at the weekend meetings, and Billy was never without one.

Back in Germany, Billy's sister Ester, now age eighteen, had been liberated by the Americans from the Spandau Concentration Camp. She was now married with a young son and had started trying to reunite the family. First she tracked down Evelyn, who was living in Budapest, and then she found Sonja in Austria. But their beloved mother had perished in a concentration camp.

Ester worked at the Hanover branch of the Hebrew Immigrant Aid Society (HIAS), and she asked her boss to try to locate her little brother Wolodia when he traveled to New York for a conference.

After making a few calls, he found the boy living with the Ehrenreichs. Ester then wrote to Wolodia after her boss brought back one of the family photographs the boy had taken to America.

It was a turning point for Billy. He was overjoyed that his three sisters had survived but heartbroken to learn his mother had perished in a concentration camp. Although there were no plans for an immediate reunion, Billy started corresponding with all of his sisters.

Reuniting with his real family gave Billy a new, positive outlook on life. He was now attending DeWitt Clinton High School in the Bronx, and his first reports were excellent. He was elected class vice president and joined the school swimming team, enthusiastically competing in all school athletic events.

He found his first job delivering the *Bronx Home News* for $5 a week, which he spent on the movies. He also did errands for the local grocers and butchers and was soon giving his foster family $10.50 a week toward his board and keep.

At seventeen, Billy Grajonca found a well-paying summer job, working as an office boy and messenger. Now a seventh-term honor roll student at DeWitt Clinton, he planned to work and attend college at night after his graduation.

During his senior year, he discovered what would be a lifelong passion for Latin music, becoming a regular at the Palladium at 53rd Street and Broadway. There he saw such top Latin music stars as Xavier Cugat, Tito Puente, and Esy Morales. On Wednesday nights he would dance to the mambo music until three or four in the morning. Years later, he would faithfully re-create the feel and excitement of the Palladium with the Fillmore East. Another of his favorite places was the Apollo Theater on 125th Street in Harlem, where he saw Cab Calloway and Bill "Bojangles" Robinson.

But the late nights never interfered with Billy's schoolwork, and when he graduated he received a glowing progress report from his social worker.[13]

"Billy has grown from a distrustful, sly, underhanded, frightened little boy to a tall, good looking, outgoing, secure, warm and friendly young man with a fine sense of humor," read the report. "He has many friends and varied interests, including school, all sports, reading and socializes with other boys and girls. [He's a] well-rounded, likable young person."

On April 13, 1949, Billy Grajonca applied for US citizenship, officially Americanizing his name to William Graham. It was the surname directly preceding Grajonca in the Bronx telephone book.

The 1949 DeWitt Clinton High School yearbook contains a photograph of a smiling William "Bill" Graham, a member of the swimming team, a color guard, and a contributor to the school's *Magpie* magazine. His stated ambition was to become a physical education instructor/coach, and his graduating message was the simple toast, "To Graham."

———

At the dawn of the 1950s, six-foot-tall William Graham sought the American dream. He worked part-time for $10 a week in a neighborhood tailor shop and had been accepted by Brooklyn College on a $300 scholarship to study engineering. But the self-confessed Mambonic spent the money on fashionable suits and ties for his dancing nights out.

"The Palladium is where I went to recharge my batteries," he later explained. "Just take it and stick it in the wall. I'd come out hours later, feeling great. Get into the subway and get home maybe at four or four-thirty in the morning."

After a few months, he decided to take a semester off from Brooklyn College and get a summer job so he could afford to go night clubbing in the stylish Harlem clothes he loved. There was big money to be made at the popular Jewish resorts in the Catskill Mountains, two hours north of New York City. And the enterprising young man found a job as a busboy at Grossingers Resort Hotel. He soon learned how to charm the restaurant guests he served, ensuring good tips. At the end of the summer season, when the work ran out, he returned to New York.

Now nineteen, he quit Brooklyn College and went to work at Davidson & Sons Jewelry Co. on West 47th Street for $45 a week. He was soon promoted to assistant foreman and for a time seriously considered becoming a jeweler.[14]

In late 1950, the US Army drafted William Graham for the Korean War, with orders to report to Fort Dix in New Jersey. It was a major blow, as his American citizenship was imminent, and he was planning to bring his sisters to America. His Davidson workmates threw him a going-away party, presenting him with a gold ring bearing his initials, "BG"—which he would proudly wear for the rest of his life.

After passing a physical, he was assigned to Camp Chaffee in Arkansas for basic training. One day he had a pinched nerve and was unable to put on his backpack for the daily ten-mile hike. When his corporal ordered him to do so, Graham replied, "Fuck you, Jack!" and was promptly court-martialed for insubordination.

After basic training, Graham shipped out to Japan on a huge troop carrier. During the long voyage he joined in the nightly craps games, soon discovering that the players got hungry. The entrepreneurial young soldier organized a restaurant delivery service, charging the craps players $1.50 for sandwiches and 25 cents for fruit, which he stole from the kitchen, where he worked during the day. He was soon selling more than a hundred sandwiches a night, even hiring another soldier to help him prepare the food. After the two-week voyage, he had made a profit of $3,700 ($36,000 in 2010 dollars) in cash, which he soon gambled away.

En route to Korea, Private Graham's company was assigned to a Japanese base to prepare for action. But the aggressively outspoken young soldier soon ran into trouble.

"It was a corporal," he later remembered. "Didn't like big city guys and didn't like Jews. He and I got into it one day, and he nailed me for insubordination."[15]

Graham was then sent to the Korean town of Taegu as an artillery forward observer. And as part of a two-man team, he went into no-man's land to sight out the enemy and report their positions on a radio telephone.

Early one morning, Private Graham's reconnaissance team was attacked by four North Koreans, who shot one of his friends and beat up another. Out of ammunition, Graham fought gallantly, beating one of the enemy soldiers unconscious. Then, under full enemy fire he carried his injured friend on his shoulders three hundred yards to safety. He was awarded a Bronze Star for bravery.

Yet three days later, he found himself facing a full court-martial for refusing a direct order under fire.

"The captain sent us on a suicide mission to lay some communication lines," he later recalled. "It was obvious to us that if we carried it out we had a 90 percent chance of ending up dead, as the enemy had all the high positions. I refused a direct order because I knew it would be suicide."[16]

When Graham threatened to fight the court-martial and prove his case, the captain backed down and withdrew the charges.

"He was one of those gung-ho schmucks," said Graham, "and about a month later he was going up the side of a hill gleaming, and the enemy just popped him."[17]

A few days after Graham received his Bronze Star and a citation for holding the lines under enemy fire, Pearl Ehrenreich fell dangerously ill and Alfred requested immediate compassionate leave for his foster son. Initially the army denied the request, but when a second telegram arrived with the news she was on her deathbed, Private Graham was allowed to fly home.

He walked into the Montgomery Avenue apartment to find that his beloved foster mother had died two days earlier.

"Whatever positive things I have in me I owe to my foster mother," he would later say. "I was not an easy child to bring up. I was very angry at the world. She helped take away some of the bitterness."

Three days after his twenty-third birthday, Billy Graham officially became an American citizen. He celebrated by formally applying for his sisters to come and live in the United States. A few months later, his oldest sister, Rita, arrived with her husband, Eric. She stayed in New York only a short time before settling in San Francisco.

A year later, he met his sister Ester Chichinsky at Idlewild Airport when she arrived with her seven-year-old-son, Avi. Billy's two other sisters, Evelyn and Sonja, decided to remain in Europe.

After his army discharge, Graham enrolled in the City College of New York to study business administration. But he soon quit,[18] heading back to the Catskills to make real money. He found a job waiting tables at the Concord Hotel near Monticello, where he served breakfast, lunch, and dinner seven days a week. There he befriended another young waiter named Jack Levin, who was a couple of years older and married.

"Billy was a skinny little kid," remembered Levin. "He was funny and full of life."[19]

All the Jewish Catskill resorts had nightclubs, which were strictly off-limits to hotel staff, who were forbidden to mix with the guests. As Latin music was now all the rage in the Jewish resorts, the two waiters loved going to the clubs to hear the Afro-Cuban mambo music and dance with the female guests.

"Billy was a real ladies man, and we wound up doing a lot of things off-color," remembered Levin. "He loved Tito Puente and Machito and was a great samba dancer."

One night at the President Hotel, Billy Graham introduced himself to Latin music star Tito Puente, who was performing.

"And we hit off a great friendship," said the salsa percussionist, "since he was in love with Latin music. He was a very good dancer."[20]

On their rare days off, the two waiters would go to the Saratoga Racetrack. But whatever Graham won was usually lost a few hours later in a craps game. Soon he started running his own craps games at the Concord for the staff and guests.

"I organized the greatest craps games," said Graham, "but I made more money from shill games. I was twenty-three years old, and I loved action, from the flea races in Canada to the dog races in Miami."

He also rented a hotel room on the ground floor of the Concord, which he transformed into a gambling club, as well as operating a check-cashing service for resort employees, averaging around $300 ($2,650) a week in profits.

"Billy used to do very well," said Levin. "We'd start the game at ten in the evening and finish up about six in the morning, and then go right back to work. He supplied all the cards, and he had hot food, beer and coffee."

On a good night Graham could make up to $500 ($4,385), but usually he joined in the game and lost everything.

Many of the Catskill resorts' stars, such as Harry Bellafonte, gambled at Billy's Cabana after their show. And he became friends with Eddie Fisher, with a photograph of them together even appearing in a TV fan magazine.

One day Billy announced that he was going to become an actor and was saving his money for stage school.

"He talked about it constantly," said Levin. "That was his first love."

At the Concord, Billy dated a waitress named Patricia Kern, who was working her way through university. She became his steady girlfriend for a couple of years, serving food and drinks at his craps games.

Whenever he had a free weekend, Graham caught the Friday-night bus to New York, hitting the Palladium for the mambo dance competitions, which he would often win. Then early Monday morning he'd be back at the Concord to serve breakfast, having been up for forty-eight hours straight.

The Concord maitre d', Irving Cohen, whom Graham often compared to Captain Bligh, did not approve of his lifestyle. During his three years at the Concord, Graham was constantly feuding with his boss, who eventually fired him for trying to unionize the staff.

"He was a hippie," said Cohen, who worked more than fifty years at the resort. "He had long hair and he wanted to wear an earring. He once told me he goes to Harlem to buy clothes. He said black people are two years ahead of us."[21]

~⌒~

Back in New York, Graham found a job as a waiter at Ben Maksik's Town and Country Nightclub on Brooklyn's Flatbush Avenue, moving into a Greenwich Village apartment. He became a regular at the pickup basketball games on West Fourth Street, near his Waverly Place apartment.

He concentrated on launching his acting career and started going to casting calls and auditions. But the next few years were frustrating for Graham, with rejection after rejection.

"My heroes were Lee J. Cobb, Eli Wallach, Edward G. Robinson," he said, "the character actors who made it not because they looked good but because they *were* good."[22]

In early 1955, he drove cross country to visit his sister Rita and her husband, Eric Rosen, in San Francisco for a change of scene. He decided to stay, finding a job as a statistician and payroll clerk for the Pacific Motor Trucking Company. Then he flew back to New York to collect his things, arranging to drive an old New York yellow cab to Modesto, California, for a driveaway agency.

"That was an amazing, amazing trip across America," he recalled. "A mattress that I was schlepping for my sister tied on top, a teddy bear bigger than I was—for her son—in the seat beside me."

For the next two years he worked as a statistician, studying acting at night at the Mara Alexander School of Drama. Then he moved 260 miles north, working as chief paymaster for the Weaverville Dam Project. That job lasted just five months, and he returned to New York for another shot at acting.

He leased a tiny studio on Christopher Street in Greenwich Village, working as a waiter in a Brooklyn nightclub and driving a taxi cab at night. He also took diction lessons and enrolled in Lee Strasberg's Actor's Studio, studying in the same class as Marilyn Monroe. But his inability to remember lines proved a problem.

He joined Equity, using the stage name Anthony Graham because there was another actor called William Graham. And he had tiny roles in the movies *Breakfast at Tiffany's* and *Hatful of Rain*, as well as a string of long-forgotten "B" movies.

As he turned thirty, William Graham lacked direction, with no steady job or real acting success. So he went to Los Angeles to go all-in on becoming a movie star. But the nearest he got to fame was waiting tables at a Rodeo Drive restaurant, serving such stars as Charles Laughton, David Niven, and Lee Marvin.

In 1960, Graham was visiting his sister Rita in San Francisco when he went on a casting call to play Big Julie in the musical *Guys and Dolls*. Also auditioning for a dancing part was eighteen-year-old Martyn Buchwald—who five years later would change his name to Marty Balin and start the legendary rock band Jefferson Airplane, which Graham would briefly manage.

"And he caused this furor," recalled Balin, "just stopped the whole place because he kept telling the director how to direct his part. He had one line, and he just stopped the whole production—he was telling everybody how to work around him. The director finally kicked him out [and] we were all just sitting there watching this. He always had to be in charge." [23]

After nearly six months in Hollywood, Graham finally got a break when he was called back three times for a major role in a new TV series called *The Law and Mr. Jones*. He was even told he had the part, but at the last minute the star, James Whitmore, insisted on another actor, believing William Graham's rugged looks could upstage him.

"He quit acting there and then," said Hollywood acting coach Harold Guskin, who had become his friend. "It was a crushing blow to him. He could not take not being in control."

In early 1962, deeply depressed and feeling a failure, Graham returned to Europe and spent a year bumming around. He lived in Paris, Madrid, and Valencia but was unable to settle down. He felt insecure and began to wonder if he had any real acting talent.

"That was my lost, searching time," he later told the *New York Times*. "I was always looking for one thing that would satisfy me."

CHAPTER TWO

Carlos

As Bill Graham pondered his future in Europe, a rail-thin fourteen-year-old Mexican boy arrived in San Francisco with his parents and six siblings. Carlos Santana was born on July 20, 1947, in Autlán de Navarro, a tiny peasant town in the state of Jalisco. He had music in his blood, coming from a long line of performers.

Jalisco was the nineteenth-century birthplace of modern mariachi. A hybrid of Spanish, Mexican, and African folk music, it celebrated the triumphs and struggles of the Mexican people and was played at weddings, birthdays, and holidays.

It also has a key role in the elaborate Mexican courting ritual. In the strict Catholic countryside, where the sexes were kept apart, a young man courted a prospective bride through the *serenata*—a musical message of love delivered by a mariachi orchestra.

Carlos's grandfather Antonino Santana played French horn in the municipal band in Cuautla, four hundred miles east of Autlán de Novarro. And soon after his son José was born in January 1913, he started teaching him violin.

When the Santana family moved to Autlán de Novarro, little José showed exceptional musical talent. As a teenager he joined the local symphony orchestra and played waltzes, polkas, and tangos, eventually becoming bandleader.

By 1940, José was a famous musician in Jalisco, when he married a local girl named Josefina Barragan. Over the next few years they would have seven children: Antonio, Laura, Irma, Carlos, Leticia, Jorge, and Maria. [1]

"Everybody just loved my dad," Carlos Santana would later tell *Billboard* magazine. "He was the darling of the town. Everybody wanted my dad to play at their weddings, baptisms, whatever."[2]

From early childhood, José groomed Carlos to carry on the Santana family's long musical tradition.

"He was eight when I started teaching him [violin]," recalled José, "and we both used to sit down and study together."

Carlos grew up in Autlán de Novarro, a tiny mountainous town between Puerto Vallarta and Guadalajara. It was a throwback to the past, with donkeys and chickens running wild on dirt tracks. The houses were made of stone and dried mud, and there was no electricity or running water.

One of Carlos's earliest memories is making little paper boats during the rainy season, and then sailing them down the flooded main street.

Carlos and his six siblings grew up in a mud-brick house with music everywhere.

"My father supported [us] with his music," said Carlos. "There's something about Mexican families; they're big and they don't have any TVs or stuff in the countryside. So music was a big diversion."

From early childhood, Carlos always felt a special connection to his father, who would take him on the back of his bicycle to watch his performances in church.

"My father infected me with the virus of music," said Carlos. "I saw how the people were looking at him. All I ever wanted was to be adored the way people adored my father in this little town."

José was often away traveling with his orchestra, and little Carlos missed him terribly. On his return the father would always tell his son stories about his colorful adventures while he was traveling.

"He knew how to create tension," Carlos explained. "[It's] where I learned to build a guitar solo. Got to tell a story, man."

In 1954 José went north to Tijuana to play mariachi for American tourists. He promised Josefina that he would send for the family when he had saved enough money. But when he didn't do so after a year, Carlos's mother suspected that he was cheating on her. So she persuaded one of José's friends to drive her and her six children to Tijuana, promising that

José would pay him when they got there. Then Josefina sold all their furniture to raise gas money for the 1,500-mile journey.

Upon their arrival in Tijuana, they went to an address José had used on one of his few letters home. Then as Carlos and his siblings waited in the car, Josefina knocked on the front door. At first there was no answer, but on the third knock a young woman opened the door. When Josefina announced she was José's wife and had come for him, the woman said there was no one by that name living there and closed the door.

As Josefina sadly walked back to the car, an old man who had been sitting on the sidewalk watching everything asked who she was looking for.

"José Santana," replied Josefina.

"Yeah, he's inside. Are you guys his family?" said the man. "Knock again. He'll come out."[3]

So Josephina walked back to the front door and knocked again.

"The lady came out," Carlos would recall, "screaming 'What do you want? I told you he's not there!'"

At that point José sheepishly poked his head out of the door, seeing his wife at the door and their seven children in the car outside.

"My dad's face became like the NBC peacock rainbow," said Carlos, "turning all the different colors of surprise, frustration, anger, fear—everything."

Then he started screaming at his wife for daring to bring the children to Tijuana without his permission. When he finally calmed down, he drove them to one of the town's worst slums, dropping them off at a house without any windows or a roof. Then he drove off, leaving them there to fend for themselves.

For the next two months, Josefina and the children struggled to survive in the tough border town. Twice a week José would suddenly appear with two bags of groceries for his family, before disappearing again.

"That was the hardest time," recalled Carlos, "poverty-wise."

Eventually there was a reconciliation and José left his mistress and moved back in with his family. Then he sent Carlos and his younger brother Jorge out to hustle the tourists on Tijuana's main drag, Avenida Revolucion. Dressed in colorful mariachi suits, the two small boys would perform old Mexican folk songs, such as "Mexicali Rose" and "La Paloma."

"'Song, Mister?—fifty cents a song,'—that was my mantra," Carlos remembered.

Their father also had them selling snacks and spearmint gum to the tourists.

"My father bought us this box of Chiclets and just cracked it in half," said Carlos. "He gave half to my brother [and] half to me. He says, 'Don't come back till you sell it.'"

In July 1955, José Santana moved his family into a better Tijuana neighborhood, enrolling Carlos in the Miguel F. Martinez Primary School. Every night he attended a school of music, where his teachers wanted him to learn clarinet. Carlos refused, sticking to the violin instead.

"We always played music," said Carlos's younger brother Jorge. "We had musicians in the household, so we were exposed to music all the time."[4]

At the age of ten, Carlos joined his father's mariachi band, Los Cardinales. They played in some of the seediest bars and clubs on the backstreets of Tijuana, as well as bordellos.

"It smelt like piss and puke," said Carlos. "Being a kid I'd rather go play hide-and-seek . . . but instead I was in this place."[5]

Little Carlos was exposed to the crude, drunken behavior of the customers toward the prostitutes, who would mother him. And he came to hate the mariachi music he played with his father.

"I don't really relate to it," Carlos explained. "I don't like any kind of music that deals with lyrics about being drunk and being betrayed."

One day the little boy met an American tourist, who lured him over the border into San Diego for sex. Throughout the next two years, Carlos was repeatedly molested, and it would scar him for life. It was a deep, dark secret that he would carry for more than forty years.

"I was molested at a very young age," Carlos finally admitted in 2000. "I was seduced by toys, and I was seduced by being brought to America with all kinds of gifts and stuff."

The pedophile, who said he was from Vermont, would bring Carlos over the border two or three times a week, buying him meals, clothes, and toys and sexually abusing him.

"This person seduced a child by giving him cowboy boots and guns and a bunch of toys," said Carlos, "when I was living in the ghetto in Tijuana. And my mom couldn't figure it out?"

The abuse finally stopped in 1959 when the man became jealous when Carlos developed a crush on a girl his own age.

"And he slapped me," said Carlos. "And I woke up."

In 1960, José Santana took off and left his family again. This time he moved to San Francisco, where the earnings were higher for a mariachi musician. With his father gone, Carlos stopped going to music school, as he disliked practicing violin. Then his perceptive mother decided to show Carlos that there were other kinds of music besides mariachi.

One Sunday morning she took him to the Palacio de Municipal Park in the middle of Tijuana, where the local musicians hung out and played. Carlos was walking into the park when he first heard the sound of an electric blues guitar.

"That's when everything just changed in my life," he said. "It was like somebody kicked me in the balls, man. It was like *bang*."

The blues musician playing was a sharply dressed sixteen-year-old named Javier Batiz, who had an Elvis Presley pompadour haircut, leather jacket, and razor-pressed khaki pants. And he played the latest hits by Chuck Berry, B.B. King, Little Richard, Bo Diddley, and Freddy King.

Later that day Josefina took Carlos to Batiz's home and asked Batiz if he would teach her son to play electric blues guitar. When Batiz asked Carlos if he played another instrument, he took out his violin and played a tune.

"And it was so cute," said Batiz. "He was just a little kid."

Before they left, Batiz showed Carlos a few chords and runs on the guitar, and by the next day Carlos had mastered them all.[6]

"His Mama said, 'Carlos didn't sleep last night, he was studying,'" Batiz recalled. "I taught him one movement and the day after that he brought about ten movements, different movements. And I went, 'Wow,' because he was so hungry to learn the blues guitar."

On Friday nights, Carlos started going to see Javier Batiz and his band the T.J.'s play at the Latino-Americano club to soak up the music.

He now had little interest in his Catholic parochial school, as he was getting his musical education on the streets of Tijuana.

"I still wasn't playing," he said. "I was just sucking up the music and learning."

The first song Carlos learned was the Shadows' hit instrumental "Apache," followed by "Walk on the Wild Side" by Jimmy Smith and "Peppermint Twist" by Joey Dee and the Starliters.

When Josefina wrote José that Carlos was learning guitar, he mailed his son an old beat-up Gibson L-5 guitar, along with one pick, from San Francisco. Carlos was so delighted that he put on nylon strings, not realizing he needed metal ones since his father had not sent an amplifier.

In 1961, Josefina Santana filed US immigration papers for the family to move to San Francisco, where José was now making a good living playing mariachi. She did not want her children to spend the rest of their lives in the mean streets of Tijuana.

"My mother wanted a better life for all of us," said Jorge Santana, "by bringing us here to the United States. She was old-school in her upbringing, discipline, education, and work."

When José returned to help the family move to America, he expected Carlos to play the mariachi clubs with him again. But thirteen-year-old Carlos now had his own gig, playing blues and Top Forty songs with Javier Batiz in the rundown strip clubs of Avenida Revolucion.

"It was a conflict," recalled Carlos, "because I was already working . . . playing some real low-life stinky places where the prostitutes would be on the corner. And I didn't want to play that folk music anymore."

But when Carlos refused to play mariachi, his father was furious.

"And he says, 'Well what do you want to do?'" said Carlos. "'Do you want to play that pachuco rock 'n' roll crap music?' I said, 'Well, how can that music be worse than where I am?'"

"It was the first time I stood up to my dad. So he said, 'OK, pack up your [guitar]. You're just like your mother. You always have to have the last word. Get out of here.'"[7]

Just barely a teenager, Carlos Santana was fast gaining a reputation as one of the hottest young blues guitarist in Tijuana. Some friends had a stack of B.B. King albums, and Carlos started copying them note for note. Then he started learning John Lee Hooker and Muddy Waters songs to play at the strip clubs.

"They call it 'cut and shoot music,'" said Carlos, "because if they don't like it they cut and shoot you."

Carlos joined a five-piece band called The Strangers, who were rivals of the T.J.'s. He was the youngest member, playing a Kent electric bass and calling himself "El Apache." The Strangers played dances and small shows, but Carlos was soon fired for playing too many notes on the bass.

He was then invited to join the house band on guitar at El Convoy, one of the biggest strip clubs on Avenida Revolucion. He jumped at the chance, especially since the club provided him with a Fender Stratocaster to play, along with $9 a week.

"I would start at four o'clock in the afternoon and end at six o'clock in the morning," said Carlos, "playing one hour and then watching the hookers strip for another hour. Six hookers would strip, and then we'd play for an hour. But you learn a lot, man."

Then every Sunday morning he went to church and played "Ave Maria" on the violin.

"So I got my education really, really quick," he said, "about the spiritual and sensual being as one."

Playing at the El Convoy also provided a unique musical education for the young teenager, as the band incorporated their music into the girls' stripping routine.

"The music helps a woman to walk when she's onstage," explained Carlos, "otherwise she can look stupid. The drummer would roll whenever she was going to roll those little tassels on her breasts. I learned a lot about music and expression from places like that."[8]

Carlos was now learning from the many American black musicians, who also played the Tijuana clubs. They introduced him to soul music, including Junior Walker and The Impressions. But Carlos's favorite was James Brown, who was then inventing funk music. [9]

Consumed with music, Carlos never went to school, spending his days on the beach, reading *Mad* and hot-rod magazines.

In the summer of 1962, the Santana family's US immigration papers finally came through. José and Josefina were preparing to move the family to San Francisco's Mission District when Carlos suddenly announced he was not going.

He was now earning good money at El Convoy, and he felt going to junior high school in San Francisco seemed a big step back.

"I'm hanging around with a bunch of older guys and prostitutes," he said, "eat when I want, sleep when I want . . . to hang out with a bunch of little kids talking about bullshit stuff? No way."

During the long drive north to San Francisco, Carlos sulked, refusing to communicate with anybody.

"He was mad," said his father "He did not even say a single word during the whole trip."

And when they arrived at the family's new home in the Mission District, Carlos locked himself in his bedroom and refused to eat.

"All he did was cry, cry and cry," said his father. "He was always mad."

Finally, after three months, Josefina handed Carlos a $20 bill for a bus ticket back to Tijuana, kissing him good-bye at the bus station. It would be the last time Carlos would see his family for more than a year.

It was the night of Halloween when Carlos Santana arrived at the Tijuana bus station after a thirteen-hour ride. The streets were already full of drunken revelers dressed in skeleton costumes, celebrating the Day of the Dead.

As he left the bus station with his guitar and small suitcase of clothes, Carlos had only a couple of dollars in his pocket. With nowhere to spend the night and knowing no one, he walked to the Cathedral of the Virgin of Guadalupe, on the corner of Second Street and Avenue Niños Heroes. He had decided to pray to the Virgin of Guadalupe, who is the patron saint of Mexico, for guidance.

The huge cathedral was empty, and Carlos walked up to the front of the tabernacle, with its sacred statue of the Madonna.

"Virgin Mother," he said out loud. "I was here almost two years ago."[10]

Carlos then told her how he and his brother Tony had been there once before to do penance. While Tony had asked her for something, he had not.

"So I figure you owe me one," Carlos told the Madonna. "I just ask that you take care of my [family] who have all left Mexico to live in California. And I ask that you give me a gig tonight in this town so I can survive on my own."[11]

After leaving the cathedral, Carlos went straight to the El Convoy strip club to try to get his old job back. He walked in to find the house band playing with a new guitarist and went up to the bar. Then he handed the manager a note from his mother, giving her blessing for him to play there, although he was a minor. The note was crucial, for the club knew that the Santana family had moved to San Francisco, and the manager would not want Josefina complaining to the police about her underage son working there.

The manager told Carlos to leave, but just as he was shooing him out of the door, the owner spotted his favorite guitarist. After reading Josefina's letter he smiled and walked up to the stage, telling the new guitarist to go home.

"Carlos is going to take over," said the owner.

❧

With nowhere to stay, Carlos was put up by the El Convoy drummer at his aunt's hotel, until they were both thrown out. Then a family friend came to Carlos's rescue, renting him a room in his old neighborhood.

During the next year, Carlos had a great time in Tijuana, making good money with his nightly gig at El Convoy.

"It was a lot of fun," he'd later explain. "Checking people, doing grown-up stuff."

The musician crowd he ran with smoked marijuana in the dark alleys of Tijuana, but Carlos claims he did not start smoking until several years later in San Francisco. The tall, darkly handsome teenager had the pick of the pretty woman working the Avenida Revolucion, becoming close friends with many of them. He was empathetic to the strippers and prostitutes, seeing how tough their lives were.

"There's a certain dignity there," Carlos later explained. "They don't choose it because they like it. They do it because they have kids they need to feed."

When Javier Batiz offered Carlos a place in the new band that he was taking to Mexico City to try to make it big, Carlos preferred to stay in Tijuana.

"I thought I was already making it just playing Revolution Street and being fed," said Carlos. "I'm watching prostitutes undress for an hour. I'm a man of the world."

In early November 1963, Josefina Santana wanted Carlos back in San Francisco, feeling Tijuana was too dangerous for him. So she and her oldest son, Tony, turned up at El Convoy Club one night unannounced.

"She just kidnapped me," said Carlos. "She knew I didn't want to go, so my older brother, who was really strong, just grabbed me and said, 'Your Mama's here.'"

Carlos tried to run away, but his far bigger brother forced him into the car. Then his mother drove him back to San Francisco, where he would remain.

CHAPTER THREE

Finding Direction

In early 1963, after a year of bumming around Europe, Bill Graham settled down in San Francisco. He found a job as regional manager for the Allis-Chalmers company, which manufactured heavy industrial equipment, and was responsible for the states of California, Washington, and Colorado.

Soon after arriving, Graham interviewed a quiet-spoken brunette called Bonnie MacLean for a secretarial job. The attractive twenty-two-year-old, who wore heavy-framed black glasses, had recently moved to the West Coast.

"He had big lips and was very conservative-looking," recalled Bonnie. "That's probably my first impression of Bill."[1]

After a short interview, Graham hired her for the office secretary pool. But he soon recruited her for his pet project, to combine the two Allis-Chalmers offices into one and halve the staff.

"That was his big job at the time," said Bonnie. "He rented a bigger place and planned how it would be laid out. Apparently he did a very good job and [his boss] was very pleased."[2]

Graham now concentrated on honing his business and managerial skills, deriving great satisfaction from raising office morale while getting the most work out of his staff.

Soon after Bonnie began working there, her new boss asked her out on a date.

"It was out of the blue," she said. "I didn't see that coming, and I went out with him. That was the beginning of our relationship."

During the next few months, Bill and Bonnie enjoyed a discreet office romance. Most days after work, Bill would take Bonnie on the back of his

1956 Lambretta motorcycle through the streets of San Francisco for dinner, followed by a movie and a show.

"Which was not really my style," she explained, "but he's a persuasive kind of guy."

After almost a year of dating, Bonnie decided their relationship was going nowhere. So she quit Allis-Chalmers and moved back to live with her mother in Philadelphia and found a job. During the next few months, Bill pursued her with several letters a week but refused to commit to their future.

"Finally, it was decided that I would go back," said Bonnie. "I wasn't happy in Philadelphia, so I probably prompted it through my griping."

During Bonnie's absence, Graham had become frustrated with Allis-Chalmers. Although he was on the fast track, making $21,000 ($160,000) a year with bonuses, he felt creatively unfulfilled. He had also begun producing plays for the radical San Francisco Mime Troupe, and when its founder, Ronnie Davis, offered him $120 ($916) a year to became business manager, Graham jumped at the chance. Even though it was a massive pay cut and he would have to live off his savings, he saw it as a unique opportunity to combine his two passions of the theater and business.

After giving notice, he flew north to Philadelphia to bring Bonnie MacLean back, to be his girlfriend and secretary. He had arranged with a drive-away agency to deliver a car back to San Francisco for their return trip.

"It was a fun trip," Bonnie remembered. "We drove across the country together and alternated driving. And we went like mad and made it in twenty-four hours."

———

Founded in 1961 by Ronnie Davis, the San Francisco Mime Troupe was creating quite a stir. The ultra-left-wing group performed Italian commedia dell'arte plays in the parks in and around the City by the Bay, and they had a large following.

When Bill Graham arrived in 1964, the troupe's Howard Street loft was headquarters for the post-beatnik poets, musicians, and hippies now springing up all over the city. Surviving on handouts from wealthy admirers, the members of the troupe, who each received $5 per show, traveled around in an old truck full of threadbare costumes and props.

"We'd steal and swindle and do what we had to," said former Mime Troupe actor Peter Coyote.

Davis, who had also waited tables at Catskills' resorts, was impressed with Graham's business acumen, hiring him and Bonnie on the spot.

"I decided I'd still rather be in the world of theater even if I weren't performing," Graham later told *Billboard*. "So for the next two years I looked for gigs at schools and little theaters, made the deals, printed the posters, drove the truck, put up the lights and carried the spear."

By now, Bill Graham was a familiar sight in San Francisco, driving around on his ancient Lambretta in a three-piece suit while aggressively promoting the Mime Troupe.

"[He] was just phenomenal, very high energy," said Peter Coyote. "He was very, very different from the rest of us. Not real long on revolutionary content but incredibly smart, energetic and ambitious."[3]

Under Bill Graham's management the Mime Troupe became more professional. Now shows always started on time, and Graham introduced organization. He worked out of the back of the Mime Troupe's loft, efficiently directing operations. There was even a brass nameplate on his desk bearing the name of his hero, the famous Russian promoter Sol Hurok.

But Graham's obsessive need for control soon created problems, and his tough abrasive New York business manner grated on many. At one point he insisted that "Bill Graham Presents" be put on all Mime Troupe's posters and handbills, mimicking his mentor, Sol Hurok.

And Ronnie Davis's refusal to allow it led to many rows.

"They were quite a show," said Jim Haynie, then a Mime Troupe actor.[4] "They used to sit about three feet apart and yell at each other all day."

By the summer of 1965, the San Francisco Mime Troupe was almost broke, and Bill Graham was having little luck raising any money. The season was due to start with the sixteenth-century play *Il Candelaio* by

Giordano Bruno, about an elderly candlemaker worried about impotency. Then Graham suggested they sensationalize it with violence and swearing to provoke a confrontation with the San Francisco Parks Commissioners. He wanted the troupe to get arrested.

"Bill couldn't raise any money through his resources," said Chet Helms, who would later manage Big Brother and the Holding Company and run the Avalon Ballroom. "So the tactic was to get busted to generate publicity and money."[5]

It worked. Parks Commissioner James Lang attended the free opening performance and was disgusted by the foul language, the brutality, and an actor simulating urination onstage. The next day he called an emergency meeting of the Parks Commission, which banned the play for vulgarity.

Bill Graham was at the meeting, where he told the Park Commissioners that he had heard the same "objectionable word" one hundred and forty-seven times at a recent theater performance downtown. It came to an abrupt end when Davis stormed out shouting, "We will see you in the parks and in the courts."

Later at the Mime Troupe headquarters, Graham called for a confrontation with the San Francisco police to protest the Parks Department ban. He argued that the Mime Troupe had a duty to protect First Amendment rights, not only for themselves but for the whole of San Francisco. He was then ordered by Davis to get as much publicity as possible for the showdown.

Bill Graham immediately called all his media contacts, inviting them to Lafayette Park that Sunday afternoon for the Mime Troupe protest. So the stage was set for the troupe's most spectacular show to date, The Great San Francisco Mime Troupe Bust, directed by Bill Graham.

On Sunday, August 7, Bill Graham and Ronnie Davis led all fifty members of the Mime Troupe in full costume into Lafayette Park for the afternoon confrontation. At one o'clock the park began to fill up with police and Park Department officials. Then Mime Troupe supporters arrived with large signs saying "Mime Troupe Si! Park Commission No!" Graham had done his job well, and there were about a dozen reporters and several television crews waiting.

"We had decided that I was to be arrested for this 'showcase spectacu-lar,'" said Davis. "And it couldn't have been staged better—Sunday and a full house."

The show began with Graham debating the ban with Davis and Park Department representative James Lang. Enter stage left: the troupe's attorney, Marvin Stender, followed by a contingent of police.

Then, clipboard in hand, Bill Graham delivered an emotional address to the crowd, followed by Lang, who was booed by the excited audience. By this time the cops were becoming uneasy, fearing a riot.

Suddenly everyone went quiet as Ronnie Davis danced into the per-forming area like a fairground barker and announced:

Signor, Signora, Signorini
Madame, Monsieur, Mademoiselle,
Ladieeees and Gentlemen,
Il Troupo di Mimo di San Francisco
Presents for your enjoyment this afternoon . . .
AN ARREST!!!

On the word "arrest," Davis leapt at an astonished cop, who arrested him on the spot. Then a riot broke out, with Mime Troupe actors and supporters attacking the cops. Two other troupe members joined Davis under arrest and were driven away in the waiting police van. Two hours later they were charged with performing in the public parks without a permit and released on bail.

"I think they arranged the bust to polarize the issue," said Coyote. "The idea of publicity would not have been lost on Bill."

On November 1, Ronnie Davis was found guilty after a four-day trial and defiantly pledged to "Fight until the parks are returned to their right-ful 'owners,' the people of San Francisco."

To raise money for Davis's legal expenses, Bill Graham was put in charge of organizing an Appeal Party in the Mime Troupe's loft. One of the first people to offer their services was a new band with the unusual name of Jefferson Airplane, who regularly rehearsed in the troupe's How-ard Street loft. Poets, jazz musicians, and artists also rallied to the cause, and soon Bill Graham had an impressive lineup for his Saturday, November 6, appeal.

—⚫—

As all the pieces of the puzzle fell into place for Bill Graham, it is ironic that a peaceful hippie commune called the Family Dog, whose members despised business, would play a crucial role in his meteoric rise to success. The Family Dog included Luria Castell, a vivacious young woman who wore Benjamin Franklin wire-rim glasses and favored long "granny dresses"; Ellen Harmon, who had dropped out of her "straight" job in Detroit to come to the West Coast; and Alton Kelley, an artist who dealt marijuana. They had started the Family Dog, named in memory of Harmon's dog, who had recently died in a traffic accident, to liven up San Francisco's dull nightlife with dances.

"San Francisco can be the American Liverpool," Castell told *San Francisco Chronicle* Music columnist Ralph J. Gleason. "There's enough talent here, especially in the folk-music field. We don't have any particular group to present, just a plan to get started, to acquire knowledge, information and have fun with a rock 'n' roll sound."

Gleason, a veteran jazz critic, was impressed and thanked the Family Dog for invigorating the city's stale music scene.

The Family Dog's first event, "Tribute to Dr. Strange," was held in the Longshoreman's Hall near Fisherman's Wharf just two weeks before the scheduled Mime Troupe Benefit. It was a great success, featuring Jefferson Airplane, The Marbles, and The Charlatans. The opening act was a brand-new group called The Great Society, playing only its second performance, featuring a stunningly beautiful singer named Grace Slick.

CHAPTER FOUR

Grace

Grace Barnett Wing was born on October 30, 1939, in Illinois—although she's uncertain if it was in Highland Park or Evanston. More importantly, however, she does know it was in the Chinese Year of the Rabbit.

Her father, Ivan Wilford Wing, an Anglicization of the Norwegian name Vinje, was a successful investment banker, and her mother Virginia Barnett's ancestors had sailed to America on the *Mayflower*. Born in Idaho in 1909, Virginia had moved to Hollywood in the early 1930s to become a movie star. But she got only as far as understudying for leading lady Marion Davies, the longtime girlfriend of newspaper magnate William Randolph Hearst. Virginia enjoyed more success as a nightclub singer, appearing at the RKO Pantages Theater on Hollywood and Vine, as well as small clubs around Los Angeles.[1]

Virginia quit show business after marrying Ivan Wing, whom she had first met several years earlier at the University of Washington in Seattle, where they were both straight "A" students.

"It was looked down on for an investment banker at the time to be married to a nightclub singer," explained their daughter Grace. "[They] did what they were told."[2]

As a little girl, Grace idolized her maternal grandmother, Annie Mary Sue Neill Barnett, whom she called "Lady Sue." The vivacious old lady spun tall tales about being a champion skater, with special skates with electric lights. It would be years before Grace discovered this would have been mechanically impossible when her grandmother was a young girl.[3]

Grace's parents, meanwhile, were Republicans of the ultraconservative variety.[4]

"I think being a screwball jumps generations," Grace would later explain, "because I'm a screwy but my mother was kind of regular. She wasn't too out there."[5]

As a young child, Grace loved listening to Lady Sue's colorful tales of her illustrious family. A mixture of Celtic, Irish, and Scottish, her ancestor John Whitman had arrived in Weymouth, Massachusetts, as one of the original Puritans. The Barnett family tree also boasted the poet Walt Whitman and her musical great-grandmother Elizabeth Auzella Barnett-Whitman, a tough frontiers-woman who rode wagon trains to the Northwest Territory, with her violin and guitar.

When Grace was three, her father was transferred to Los Angeles, and he relocated the family there. Three years later, the family moved to San Francisco when the bank transferred Grace's father again.

Then Grace, whose favorite color was black, started drawing with a passion. She loved sketching the Japanese Tea Garden in Golden Gate Park and the nearby bridge. Once she drew an angel, which her parents used as their family Christmas card that year.[6]

Even as a young child, Grace was headstrong, refusing to ever take no for an answer. Her family nicknamed her "The Grouser."[7]

There was always music in the Wing home, and her mother hired a piano teacher for her daughter, who hated the lessons.

"I play by ear," Grace once explained, "so I would say to the piano teacher, 'Why don't you just play that for me one time so I can get a feel of it.' I didn't want to learn to read music. It bored me. I'd rather just play it."[8]

Her parents read her bedtime stories, her favorite being Lewis Carroll's *Alice in Wonderland*. Grace related to Alice's bitter experiences of growing up in drab Victorian England, which bore striking similarities to her childhood in the Eisenhower era.

"That's why I identify with Alice in Wonderland," she explained. "It came out of Victorian England, which was a very straitlaced time."[9]

A month before Grace's tenth birthday, Virginia gave birth to a baby boy they named Chris, who would complete the family.

Soon afterward Ivan Wing got a raise and moved the family to Palo Alto in Marin County. The Wings soon became friendly with Bob and

Betty Slick, their next-door neighbors, who had three young sons named Jerry, Darby, and Danny.

"[Grace was] a fat little girl with buck teeth and a foul mouth," recalled Darby, who was five years younger. "She took piano lessons [and] spent hours and days alone with her music and her dolls, living in magic worlds." [10]

Grace was now busy writing and starring in her own plays, as well as making the costumes and sets. Her various roles included Alice in Wonderland, Maid Marian, and Wonder Woman, which she performed for her parents and their friends, or sometimes just for herself.

Alcoholism ran deep in Grace's family. Her father was naturally shy and drank to loosen up and relax. Her mother drank constantly, although nobody ever knew, as she never showed any signs of it.

"My father was an alcoholic," said Grace, "but he was a kind one, a funny one. The trouble is he drank all the time, and it pissed off my mother."

Grace remembers walking into the living room to find her mother haranguing her father, who had passed out on the couch in his three-piece suit, complete with fob watch.

"His head was tilted to the side and he had a little drool coming out," Grace told *Vanity Fair* in 2012. "She stood in front of him and said, 'You stewbum.'" [11]

When she was ten years old, Grace had a life-changing experience when she was taken to see the new Preston Sturgis romantic comedy, *The Beautiful Blonde from Bashful Bend,* starring Betty Grable. She would later adopt Grable's character, a larger-than-life Wild West saloon singer called "Freddie" Jones, as her outlandish role model when she became Grace Slick.

"I guess Betty Grable set me up," she later explained. "I learned that a woman can defy stereotypes and do anything she wants." [12]

In September 1951, Grace began attending the David Starr Junior High School in Burbank, California. The overweight twelve-year-old decided to create a tough new image for herself in order to gain acceptance by the school's in crowd. She began smoking cigarettes and drinking hard liquor, as well as going on a diet and becoming a basketball cheerleader. But after she invited her new school friends to her birthday party and nobody came, Grace decided to rethink her popularity strategy.

Four years later, Grace made a fresh start at the Castilleja School for Girls, a private finishing school in Palo Alto. During her two years there, Grace dated and became a cheerleader for a local boy's school football team. At sixteen, she lost her virginity after her boyfriend got her drunk at his parents' house. She woke up the next morning with a severe hangover, remembering little of it.[13]

Grace was now drinking straight gin from her parents' liquor cabinet. And when Darby Slick came over to babysit her younger brother Chris, he could not believe how much she had changed.

"[She was] now thin and cute," he recalled. "Hot stuff to me."

After graduating from the Castilleja school, Grace persuaded her parents to send her to the refined and very expensive Finch College on New York's Park Avenue. In September 1957, she started her freshman year at "the easiest school in the world," and never looked back.[14]

"I wanted to see New York City," she said. "But I'm too lazy and I didn't want to work, so I figured I'd get my parents to pay for me to stay in New York for a year by going to college there."[15]

At eighteen, Grace Wing was a striking beauty, turning heads wherever she went. But she had a foul mouth and never fitted in with the refined young debutantes, who studied etiquette, learning the proper way to use a finger bowl.

At weekends she and her best friend, Celeste (Cici) Shane, who would later marry film director John Huston, would catch the train from Penn Station to Princeton. Then they would hang out on the Princeton campus, partying, before returning to Finch College on Sunday night.

Grace now mainly drank beer and popped the Benzedrine pills that students took to stay up all night and study. She found a steady boyfriend and networked her way into the historic Tiger Inn Eating Club, where she was voted Tiger Girl of the Week.

One night at a frat party, Grace and Cici got up onstage to entertain the students. Grace sang a bawdy Oscar Brand song and accompanied herself on guitar while Cici danced provocatively.

"They told us both to leave because we were being dirty," recalled Grace. "This is not the proctors either. This is the kids. So I didn't fit in too well at Princeton." [16]

While most young people loved Elvis Presley and the new rock 'n' roll music, Grace preferred the classics. She adored *South Pacific*, and her favorite classical composers were Prokofiev and Bartók.

But she and Cici also headed downtown to Greenwich Village, checking out folk music in the coffee shops and clubs. One night she went to see Odetta at a small folk club, sneaking backstage into her empty dressing room.

"I went in," said Grace. "Her goddamned guitar's sitting there. All her clothes and everything. So I sat there and played a song."

Suddenly, Odetta walked in and sat down to listen to the teenager.

"That's very nice, young lady," Odetta told her, asking her to play another song.

Then the folk superstar told Grace she was very talented, but she warned how tough the music business could be.

For her sophomore year, Grace took an arts major at the University of Miami, after hearing it had the best party scene in America. She started hanging out with the hip Jewish kids on campus and smoking marijuana in an area known as The Snake Pit.

"We'd sit around in The Snake Pit and smoke dope," Grace told *Oui* magazine in 1977. "And none of the Gentiles knew that everybody was sitting around smoking pot. That's the Fifties! . . . They figured marijuana was something you'd go to another town and lock yourself in a gas station bathroom or something."[17]

While she was at the University of Miami, Grace fell in love with the eviscerating comedy of Lenny Bruce, later writing her song "Father Bruce" as a tribute. She also frequented the tough Miami nightclubs, smoking the strong Cuban dope brought over by Fidel Castro's troops, a year before America cut ties with Cuba.

"[We'd] hang out with Castro's soldiers and smoke their dope," boasted Grace. "It was great."

On the eve of her twentieth birthday, Grace flunked out of the University of Miami and moved back with her parents in Palo Alto. After an unsuccessful attempt to break into the music business by auditioning as a singer for a record label, Grace took a few months off to decide her future.

In the summer of 1960, Cici Shane invited Grace to Beverly Hills to help her work on John F. Kennedy's presidential campaign in the Golden State. Grace accepted and soon found herself in the midst of a political operation, working alongside Cici and her friend Jill St. John to promote the charismatic Massachusetts senator. Although she had little interest in politics, Grace was soon caught up in the social swirl of political receptions and was once introduced to Kennedy.

After the campaign was over, Grace became a couturier model for I. Magnin & Co. in San Francisco. She enjoyed modeling $20,000 couture gowns for old ladies and then going home to laze around in jeans and sandals. During her five years at the luxury goods and high-fashion department store, Grace took part in numerous runway fashion shows, as well as regularly appearing in newspaper ads.

"I hated modeling," said Grace. "I don't like being told what to do at all."[18]

Now living back with her parents in Palo Alto, Grace decided to settle down and become a housewife. Although the Wings' friends the Slicks had moved away, they remained in touch. One night Grace met their oldest son, Jerry, who was a film student at San Francisco State University. The reunited neighbors hit it off, and after going on a couple of dates they were engaged within a month.

On August 26, 1961, they were married in a lavish wedding at Grace Cathedral on Nob Hill in San Francisco. Jerry's younger brother Darby was best man.

"It was like a Middle Eastern arranged marriage," explained Grace. "Only they didn't arrange it. We were the old people. We thought, 'Wouldn't it be nice for them.'"[19]

After a Hawaiian honeymoon, the newlyweds moved to San Diego, as Jerry Slick was taking a film course at San Diego State University. But

Grace disliked the city, and they moved to San Francisco after only one semester. There they rented a house in the posh Potrero Hill district, with its stunning views of San Francisco Bay, and planted marijuana in the backyard.[20]

The Slicks lived the bohemian life, hanging out in North Beach with the beatnik crowd. They listened to the new folk music being played at the coffee clubs, such as the Fox and Hounds (later renamed Coffee and Confusion) and the Coffee Gallery, where Grace's future Jefferson Airplane bandmate Jorma Kaukonen played with Janis Joplin, passing the hat for beer money. Most Sunday afternoons they took Darby to the Old Spaghetti Factory to hear live Flamenco music. It was home to a tight group of Bohemians and Flamenco artists, who called themselves Los Flamencos de la Bodega, holding weekly performances in a small room at the restaurant. Grace loved Spanish music and would later use Ravel's "Bolero" as her musical inspiration for "White Rabbit."

But after three years of marriage, there was little passion between Grace and Jerry Slick, who both started sleeping around.

"Their marriage was an open one," said Darby. "They both occasionally made it with other people."

They also turned nineteen-year-old Darby on to high-quality marijuana, pot that Jerry bought from a San Francisco cop they knew. Soon afterward they all tripped out on peyote, and after vomiting, Grace spent the next eight hours clutching a large squash.

By 1964, Grace, who was still working as a model at I. Magnin, was drinking heavily, and her unpredictable behavior alienated many.

"There was a German guy," recalled Darby, "that used to come to these parties, and she used to regularly attack him."

It was around this time that Grace composed and recorded her first piece of music, for her husband's senior thesis at San Francisco State. The forty-five-minute independent film, called *Everybody Hits Their Brother Once*, had a Spanish-influenced soundtrack by Grace, who also appeared in it. It later won first prize at the Ann Arbor Film Festival.

While Jerry was away editing his film, Darby hung out with Grace, smoking grass and improvising music. He would play acoustic guitar while she noodled around on her recorder.

One afternoon while they were alone, Grace got very drunk and tried to seduce her brother-in-law.

"Grace offered herself to me," he later wrote in his autobiography. "I had dreamed of something like this, but had not really thought that it would happen." [21]

Fearing that his brother would catch them, Darby suggested going to his parents' empty beach house, sixty-one miles away in Santa Cruz. On the way there Grace wanted more alcohol.

"I can't do this thing without booze," she told him.

After getting her a bottle, they proceeded along local streets, drinking, and smoking joints. When they got to the house they both showered and made love in the living room.

The next morning, Grace had a bad hangover and vomited. She couldn't even remember leaving San Francisco. Soon afterward, Darby left town feeling guilty and not wanting to break up his brother's marriage. He hitchhiked to New York and stayed in Brooklyn for the next few months.

—◆—

In the winter of 1964, Jerry and Grace Slick moved into a house in Tiburon in Marin County, a ferry ride across San Francisco Bay. Soon after they moved, Darby Slick returned to San Francisco and began hanging out at their house, keeping his relationship with Grace strictly platonic.

One evening he arrived to find Jerry and Grace improvising music with a friend named Jean Piersol. Darby joined in on electric guitar, and soon they were rehearsing every day. Grace shared lead vocals with Piersol, as well as playing guitar. Jerry played drums and Darby played lead guitar.

Grace, Darby, and Jerry also started writing songs, as well as playing covers like the recent Jaynetts' hit "Sally Go 'Round the Roses." One of Grace's first compositions was "Father Bruce," a tribute to her favorite comedian, Lenny Bruce, who had recently fallen out of a hotel window in North Beach.

In August 1965, while reading the *San Francisco Chronicle*, Grace Slick stumbled on an article about a hot new San Francisco rock band called

Jefferson Airplane. Accompanying entertainment critic John L. Wasserman's story was a photograph of singer Marty Balin that caught Grace's eye.

"He looked like he was Japanese or Filipino or something," she recalled, "with a Prince Valiant hairdo, which nobody had at the time."[22]

That night Grace and Jerry went to the Matrix Club to see Jefferson Airplane perform, and their lives changed forever.

"I thought, 'Wow, that would be so much better than [modeling],'" Grace would say later. "They make more money in one night than I do all week, and they can smoke and drink and hang out and only go to work two nights a week."

After seeing Jefferson Airplane, Grace galvanized Jerry and Darby to break into the blossoming San Francisco music scene. She named their band The Great Society, a sarcastic reference to President Lyndon Johnson's domestic program. She also recruited new members, David Miner on second guitar and Bard DuPont on bass and harmonica.

Grace also started going to every Jefferson Airplane gig, studiously observing their performance. She soon caught the attention of Airplane founder and singer Marty Balin.

"Grace used to sit right in front of me all the time and watch me like a hawk," he said. "I mean I used to see her at [all] our concerts."[23]

Balin later told *Crawdaddy* magazine that Grace would "stare" at him while he was performing, and he claimed she had made sexual advances, which he'd turned down.

The Great Society debuted at the Coffee Gallery on October 15, 1965—Grace's first professional public performance.

"The audience reaction was mixed," recalled Darby Slick. "Still Grace's flute playing, and our obvious jazz influence, seemed to sway them in our direction."[24]

The following night The Great Society played at the inaugural Family Dog dance, A Tribute to Doctor Strange, at Longshoreman's Hall with Jefferson Airplane, their first ever appearance outside of the Matrix Club, owned by their singer Marty Balin. Grace was overjoyed to be opening for the group that had inspired The Great Society, closely watching their pigtailed singer Signe Toly Anderson with more than a little envy.

CHAPTER FIVE

The Right Time at the Right Place

The Family Dog's first show made a healthy profit, so they immediately announced a second one, A Tribute to Sparkle Plenty. Headlining was The Lovin' Spoonful, a New York band who was riding high in the charts with "Do You Believe in Magic," supported by a local San Francisco group called The Charlatans.

After Ralph J. Gleason's rapturous *San Francisco Chronicle* review of the first dance concert, the second sold out immediately. Then the Family Dog announced that from now on they would be holding regular weekly dance concerts.

Bill Graham's big breakthrough came when the Family Dog's Alton Kelley and Luria Castell offered to stage his Mime Troupe appeal show in return for a mention on the poster. At a sit-down meeting to discuss it, the Mime Troupe's business manager asked about Family Dog's future plans.

"We told him that we had found out that the old Fillmore Auditorium . . . could be rented at only $60 a night," recalled Kelley, "and we were planning to put on dances there. He said he'd get back to us."[1]

The next day, Bill Graham slyly tracked down the Fillmore's lease-holder, Charles Sullivan, an African-American businessman who promoted R&B shows. He then negotiated a four-year option for first rights to the Fillmore, whenever it was available, for just $45 a night.

"He just grabbed it," said Kelley, "and blew us right out of the water. Bill was very smart and he had seen what was happening with our dances. He stood to get his money back in two or three weekends."[2]

Keeping his Fillmore deal to himself, Graham now concentrated on organizing his Mime Troupe Benefit. Among the artists lined up to perform were Jefferson Airplane, The Fugs, The Committee, and poets Allen Ginsberg and Lawrence Ferlinghetti.

To publicize it, Graham covered a rented Cadillac convertible with banners and drove it through downtown San Francisco on Friday at lunchtime, with costumed actors handing out flyers. The traffic-stopping parade made the five o'clock news.

Saturday, November 6, 1965, was a watershed in music history and a life-changing day for Bill Graham. Hours before the scheduled evening start at eight o'clock, there was a line stretching around the block. Earlier that day, Graham had written a tongue-in-cheek tariff on some sheetrock at the top of the stairs: $48 admission for people making over $80,000 ($600,000) a year; 16 cents entry for people living in a walkup apartment higher than the sixth floor; and if broke, people were asked to help clean up afterward.

When Bill Graham and Bonnie arrived on his Lambretta at around six o'clock, they were surprised to find so many people already there.

"There was a huge, enormous crowd," recalled Bonnie in 2012.[3]

And by the time Ronnie Davis arrived from a Mime Troupe show in Sausalito, Graham was at the front door grabbing dollar bills from the crowd and stuffing them into a green bag.

Every time the green bag was full, it would be hoisted upstairs on a rope to be emptied before being sent down again for Graham to take more money. That night he would cram more than three thousand people into the tiny loft, which legally held just six hundred.

"It was the greatest night of my life," he later recalled. "That whole world that came into that building wasn't actors, wasn't theater—it was a whole lifestyle. Everybody got bombed. There were nine measures of vodka and a drop of orange juice. This was all new—jazz and poetry or rock 'n' roll and freeform dancing. I'd never seen it."[4]

At midnight, after numerous complaints from the neighbors, several San Francisco police officers arrived to close him down.

"And we had a thousand people upstairs and thousands [more] lining around the building," said Graham. "And I kept on saying, 'You can't.

Frank Sinatra's going to help us out. Rudy Valee's coming. Harry Belafonte.' He thought I was crazy."

Then Graham tried another ploy.

"I finally said, 'Captain!' and he was only a sergeant, but the minute I called him 'Captain' everything was fine. He said, 'Yes, son.' And we came into this whole different relationship."

Then the sergeant said the show could continue as long as Graham promised to thin out the crowd.

"So we told some people to leave," said Graham, "and I ran downstairs and said, 'Ronnie, tell the people in the street we'll let them in.'"

After the police left, Graham sneaked in hundreds more people through the back, taking their dollar bills at the freight elevator.

And that was the night when Jefferson Airplane guitarist and singer Paul Kantner first met Bill Graham.

"He was busy," recalled Kantner, "simultaneously taking tickets, checking refreshments, mopping the floor and dealing with the SFPD, who had come to complain about the spillover of people from the loft."[5]

It was six o'clock Sunday morning when Allen Ginsberg brought the dance concert to a close with a chanting mantra. And after everybody had left, Bill Graham loaded all the $1 bills into his canvas knapsack and threw it on his back. Then he drove Bonnie to Mel's Drive-In for a celebration breakfast. Back at their apartment they carefully counted the night's takings, which came to $4,200 ($31,000 today).

"He emptied the bag on the floor," explained Bonnie, "and we'd just separate the bills in piles. He saw the opportunity. The opportunity light bulb really went on."

———

The next day, Bill Graham announced a second Mime Troupe Benefit for Friday, December 10, at his newly acquired Fillmore Auditorium. He booked Jefferson Airplane, The Great Society, The Mystery Trend, and the John Handy Quintet to play, as well as a light show like the one Family Dog used.

"So Bill discovered rock 'n' roll," Ralph Gleason told KSAN radio in 1972. "The only music [up to then] he was interested in was Latin music—I mean he was a Mongo Santa Maria freak and Tito Puente."

Several days before the second benefit, Bob Dylan, who had just released "Like a Rolling Stone," happened to be holding a press conference at the KQED-TV studios to publicize an upcoming show. Graham and Bonnie arrived early, sneaked in through a side door, and placed a handbill on every seat. Graham then handed a poster to Dylan when the folk star arrived.

Later when a reporter asked about the poster he was carrying, Dylan replied: "Yeah. It's a poster somebody gave me. It looks pretty good—and I would like to go if I could, but unfortunately I won't be there."

He then read out on camera all the acts performing at the Fillmore benefit, giving Graham a publicity home run, which was immortalized in the D. A. Pennebaker documentary *Don't Look Back*.

A fireball lit up the clear San Francisco night sky as Bill Graham arrived for his first show at the Fillmore Auditorium. Although he raised the admission price to $1.50, by nine-thirty that night there was a double line of people waiting outside the beige brick building on the corner of Geary and Fillmore Streets. More than 3,500 people came that night, 500 more than fire regulations allowed.

In his column on Monday, Ralph J. Gleason wrote: "Inside, a most remarkable assemblage of humanity was leaping, jumping, dancing, frigging, fragging, and fruggling on the dance floor to the music of the half-dozen rock bands.

"The costumes were free-form Goodwill-cum-Sherwood Forest. Slim young ladies with their faces painted à la *Harper's Bazaar* in cats-and-dogs lines, granny dresses topped with huge feathers, white Levi's with decals of mystic design; bell-bottoms spilt up the side! The combinations were seemingly endless."

When Luria Castell ran into Bill Graham on the steps of the Fillmore, he pretended not to recognize her. The Family Dog leader then angrily accused him of stealing the venue from her.

"She says, 'You stole my idea!'" Graham told his friend Ralph Gleason. "'What was that?' I said. 'Throwing dances.' I looked at her and I said, 'That's 4,000 years old. The Egyptians. You didn't start that.'"[6]

Inside the auditorium, Graham's sister Ester Chichinsky served her matzo ball soup and salad at a concession stand. Only soft drinks were available this time, as Graham, who did not have a liquor license, did not want to take any risks.

Jefferson Airplane lead guitarist Jorma Kaukonen was fascinated and impressed as he watched Graham with his clipboard backstage, making sure everything went according to plan.

"I remember him as being outspoken and mercurial," Kaukonen said. "He was ten years older than us [and] so different from most of the people we would have dealt with at the time. He certainly got things done."[7]

As everybody filed out of the Fillmore early Sunday morning, the big question on their minds was when the next dance was going to be held. Graham, having made nearly $6,000 ($44,500) from his first Fillmore show, could hardly wait.

The very next day Graham quit the Mime Troupe and started a new company called Bill Graham Presents, although he agreed to hold one final Mime Troupe Benefit on January 14.

"Bill ran away with the cash box," said Ronnie Davis. "I don't think he was committed to anything but [his] ego and money in the bank."[8]

The third Mime Troupe Benefit featured The Great Society and Sam Thomas and The Gentlemen's Band. Listed at the bottom of the bill were the Grateful Dead, who had only just changed their name from The Warlocks. It was the first time they had played under their new name.

The Grateful Dead dated from the early 1960s, when guitarist Jerry Garcia met drummer Bill Kreutzmann in a Palo Alto music store. They immediately bonded, and when Garcia started giving guitar lessons at the store, sixteen-year-old Bob Weir became one of his first pupils.

Garcia, Kreutzmann, and Weir began playing around the Bay Area as Mother McCree's Uptown Jug Champions. A fifteen-year-old blues singer and harmonica player named Ron McKernan (better known as Pigpen) then convinced them to go electric. They renamed themselves The Warlocks, adding Phil Lesh on bass.

In the fall of 1965, The Warlocks became the house band for Ken Kesey's legendary LSD-fueled parties, which evolved into the Acid Tests.

But after Lesh discovered there was another band called The Warlocks, they decided they needed a new name.

It was Jerry Garcia who stumbled upon the phrase "Grateful Dead" in an old *Britannica World Language Dictionary*.

"It hit me like a hammer," Lesh later recalled. "It seemed to describe us perfectly."

The newly minted Grateful Dead debuted at Bill Graham's third and final Mime Troupe Benefit, which Garcia would fondly remember as the beginning of everything.

"It just sort of evolved into the rock 'n' roll palace trip [when] Bill Graham took over the idea," he remembered in 1975. "In those days our audience wasn't an audience in the concert sense. Our audience was all dancing and they were all high too during this formative period. The fact that we were the band didn't mean anything to anybody. We were just there to supply music at a party." [9]

Sitting on the edge of the stage that night was Grace Slick, who watched the Grateful Dead aghast. The Great Society were playing next and the model, always fastidious with cleanliness and makeup, was disgusted by the dirty, scruffy-looking musicians.

"We'll have to wipe the mikes off after they play," she reportedly told a friend. [10]

～～

In early 1966, Bill Graham began to weave his name into the very fabric of San Francisco. His trademark "Bill Graham Presents" would soon be everywhere around the city on posters, on the radio, and in the newspapers. All his life he had been waiting for this opportunity, and he seized it with both hands.

"He never much talked to me about what he was doing," said Bonnie MacLean. "He just did what he wanted to do and I went along for the ride, because it was an exciting time." [11]

While preparing to stage his first "Bill Graham Presents" show at the Fillmore Auditorium, he hired out his services to Ken Kesey to stage the three-day Trips Festival at the Longshoreman's Hall for a percentage of the profits.

It was billed as a "Non-drug re-creation of the psychedelic experience," and it would be San Francisco's most ambitious multimedia event to date.

On Saturday night the newly formed Big Brother and the Holding Company, still five months away from discovering Janis Joplin, played their second public concert. Then the Grateful Dead performed as part of what was billed as "The Acid Test."

The Dead's psychedelic space music was accompanied by flashing strobes and ultraviolet lighting. The hall was awash in Day-Glo paint and pulsating with electric energy. At one point a young woman ran up on the stage and stripped to the waist to dance, before being led away.

Everyone was tripping from the LSD-dosed ice cream . . . everyone except Bill Graham, who was running around with his clipboard, barking orders and screaming at anyone who got in his way.

At one point, Big Brother and the Holding Companys guitarist Sam Andrew asked for a free pass for the band's then-drummer, Chuck Jones.

"Bill started yelling and screaming and generally terrorizing us," said Andrew. "I just thought, 'What is he doing here? We're supposed to be in the Aquarian Age and everything's supposed to be beautiful and he's terrorizing everybody.' So I leaned into Bill's ear and said, 'You're a motherfucker.' And he just exploded. I thought he was going to kill me."[12]

When Jerry Garcia came onstage after a break, he found his guitar bridge smashed, with the strings hanging limply.

"He was just staring at it and absorbing the news when [Bill Graham], wearing a cardigan sweater and carrying a clipboard, showed up," recalled Charles Perry in his book *The Haight Ashbury: A History.*

" 'What's the matter?' he asked.

" 'Well, my guitar . . . the bridge . . .'

"Without another word, Bill was down on the guitar with his customary furious energy, trying to fix the unfixable the same way he'd been trying to keep track of the incomprehensible all night."

A young student named Jann Wenner, writing his very first piece for Berkeley's *Daily Cal* under the nom de plume mr. jones [*sic*] later penned a piece on the Trips Festival, singling out Bill Graham for special mention.

"The Festival's 'producer,' i.e., the man-who-was-in-charge-of-thebusy-work, was a total drag," wrote the student who would go on to found

Rolling Stone. "Mr. Bill Graham of the Mime Troupe, seemed opposed to having a good time, relaxation, and producing general ease. His extreme up-tightness put the rent-a-cops up-tight, and the rent-a-cops put quite a few other people up-tight."

After the Trips Festival, Bill Graham recruited Mime Troupe actor Jim Haynie to manage the Fillmore Auditorium.

"It was pretty obvious Bill had, as my daddy used to say, a bird's nest on the ground," said Haynie, "and it was going to make him a rich man. He had a hall that would hold 3,000 people and he only had to pay $45. What an opportunity."[13]

At the end of January 1966, the Fillmore Auditorium's leaseholder, Charles Sullivan, offered it to Graham permanently, but not efficiently. When Graham approached the owner about taking it over, he said he did not want to be bothered, as he was off on a fishing trip. Graham then hounded him with letters until he finally gave in and made him the Fillmore Auditorium's sole leaseholder.

Things were also happening for Grace Slick and The Great Society. Influential San Francisco DJ and club owner Tom Donahue had heard them play at the Family Dog dance and liked them. He booked them for a two-week run at his club, Mother's, as well as arranging studio time to record a demo album.

Ralph Gleason penned a glowing review of one of their performances in his *San Francisco Chronicle* music column, singling out Grace's song "Father Bruce" for special mention.

"I have a strong feeling that they will make a reputation for themselves," he wrote.

His review attracted the attention of several record company scouts, including Decca, who expressed interest in signing the band. While their new manager, John Carpenter, sifted through the offers, the band worked on their demo at the Golden State Records Studio. A local disk jockey named Sylvester Stewart, still a year away from founding Sly and the

Family Stone, was hired to produce it, but he immediately clashed with Grace Slick.

"There was kind of an adversarial relationship right from the beginning," said Darby Slick, "which was unfortunate."[14]

While they were in the studio, Darby wrote "Somebody to Love" while coming down from an acid trip and depressed about his cheating girlfriend. The Great Society recorded it on November 30, 1965, with Sly Stone at the controls, and everybody knew it was something special.

A few days later, Grace composed "White Rabbit" late one night on her battered old four-string guitar, after listening to Miles Davis's *Sketches of Spain*.[15]

"[It took] about an hour," she recalled. "There were two influences there. I loved the bolero used by Miles Davis and Gil Evans on their 1960 album. I also had a long-standing affair with *Alice in Wonderland*."[16]

The song was aimed at parents who read their children *Alice in Wonderland* at an impressionably young age and later told them not to take drugs.

"It is a drug song," Grace explained. "The things you learn between zero and five are supposed to be the most important and stick with you. They read us things like *Alice in Wonderland*, in which [Alice] has taken five or six different drugs [and] runs into a caterpillar sitting on top of a psychedelic mushroom. She takes things that say 'drink me' and literally gets high."[17]

Grace was now also developing her unique stage persona, utilizing Betty Grable's six-gun-toting character from *The Beautiful Blonde from Bashful Bend*. But instead of bullets she used rhetoric.

"Grace really fired her performance at the audience," said Darby. "She would get a little drunk, and use that part of her in-your-face personality to virtually attack the audience. She swore like a truck driver, unusual in 1965, and swaggered and posed onstage in ways that had been, hitherto, masculine."[18]

She had a magnetic stage presence, standing as still as a statue as she sang into the microphone, using her voice like an instrument to improvise.

"Then she would run suddenly to the edge of the stage," said Darby, "and bend forward to deliver the next phrase right at a particular person."[19]

At one show, Grace and Jerry Slick met a wealthy chemist in his early twenties named Brian who introduced them to his self-manufactured high-grade LSD. He worked for the Shell Oil Company and had made a fortune from inventing an industrial glue used for roadways. He was also very eccentric, tooling around San Francisco in an antique Rolls Royce.

"He was a chemical genius," said Grace, "and he looked sort of like a pansy, because he had real pink cheeks and white skin. And he was big around the middle. Very strange." [20]

But before he allowed them to drop his acid, Brian insisted they read books about hallucinogenic drugs and have a straight guide there to look after them.

Soon, Grace's morning regimen included scraping a little acid off a pill with her fingernail, giving her a nice mellow high for a few hours.

"Just a little tiny bit," she said. "It was very pleasant. Taking 600 mikes every day . . . doesn't work. But with that powder form it was very nice. You can take care of business."[21]

CHAPTER SIX

The Saloon Keeper

Although he had now tied up the Fillmore Auditorium, Bill Graham was still viewed as an outsider by the tight-knit San Francisco music community. Knowing little about the city's bands or their music, he needed help. And his unwitting guide would be a tall, young, bearded Texan hippie named Chet Helms.

An aspiring promoter himself, Helms also managed Big Brother and the Holding Company, and he had formed an alliance with The Great Society manager John Carpenter to start booking shows. They had already signed up the Jefferson Airplane for their first show, but then they lost their venue at the last minute. Now in desperation they turned to Bill Graham, offering him free future shows by their bands in return for using the Fillmore for their first.

Graham readily accepted the partnership. Helms and Carpenter were two of the best-connected managers in the San Francisco music scene, after all, and the networking possibilities were promising. Cunningly, Graham also proposed they produce shows at the Fillmore on alternate weekends, while splitting the profits.

"Graham needed us to bring the bands and the audience to him," said Chet Helms in 1992.[1]

The deal was sealed on a handshake over Coca-Colas, and it was agreed that Helms and Carpenter would hold their shows under the established Family Dog banner, although the original dance concert pioneers were now out of business.

At the beginning of February 1966, Bill Graham held his first weekend of shows at the Fillmore Auditorium with Jefferson Airplane as the headliners. Bonnie MacLean took the tickets and worked the concessions with Bill's sister Ester. As patrons arrived and walked up the stairs, there was a large barrel of apples with the sign, "Take One or Two."

Graham seemed to be everywhere in bursts of frenzied activity, clutching his clipboard and issuing orders to his new manager, Jim Haynie.

The first Family Dog show at the Fillmore, "A Tribal Stomp," was held on February 19, 1966, again featuring Jefferson Airplane and a pre–Janis Joplin Big Brother and the Holding Company. The next Family Dog show, "King Kong Memorial Dance," had Big Brother sharing the bill with The Great Society.

Flushed with success for their third show in late March, Helms and Carpenter booked the virtually unknown New York–based Paul Butterfield Blues Band for a weekend of shows, paying them a record $2,500 ($18,000).

"We were paying Jefferson Airplane only $500 ($3,600) for a weekend," said Helms, "so it was very aggressive of us. Graham fought us a lot on that."[2]

The Butterfield weekend was a triumph. More than 7,500 people paid $2.50 a ticket, grossing the trio $18,750 ($133,000), a huge sum in those days. After the final show on Sunday night, Graham divided the takings with Helms and Carpenter as they discussed a plan to rebook the Butterfield Blues Band for April.

Bill Graham had other ideas. And they did not include his two partners. At six o'clock on Monday morning, he called Paul Butterfield's manager, Albert Grossman, in New York, buying out all the band's San Francisco dates for the next two years.

Helms and Carpenter were livid when they learned of the deal, asking their partner to explain himself. But Graham was unapologetic, simply telling them that he had woken up early.

"Graham had this New York–style of doing business," said Helms, "where anything you can get away with is OK, as long as you didn't break your word."[3]

Soon afterward, Graham dissolved the partnership. Then Chet Helms secured the Avalon Ballroom, eight blocks east of the Fillmore on Sutter Street, and began staging his own shows in direct competition with Bill Graham.

By spring 1965, Bill Graham faced a community backlash accusing him of corrupting the city's youth. There had been extensive media coverage of the wild dance concerts at the Fillmore, amidst rumors of drugs and sex orgies on the ballroom floor. Anxious parents now pressured the San Francisco Police Department to clamp down on this evil.

The Musicians Union also had their sights trained on the Fillmore. Though Graham deliberately billed his shows as dance concerts, the union insisted that he hire ten of their union members for a three-band show at full rate, otherwise there would be trouble. One night a deputation of cops and union leaders arrived at the Fillmore to confront Bill Graham.

"Bill held them off at the head of the stairs and really laid into them," recalled Alton Kelley, who had been in the original Family Dog. "He told them that he'd come out of the Nazi concentration camps, and he wasn't going to take any shit from them. He played hardball, and that was the last we ever heard from the union."[4]

But the San Francisco Police Department was not so easily dealt with. At a City Hall permit hearing to review his application for a Dance Hall Keeper's license, a police patrolman presented a petition against it being granted, signed by twenty-eight store owners.

Then Graham put on his best suit, accessorized with as much charm as he could muster, and visited each of the store owners, arguing persuasively that his concerts drew people to the area, which meant bigger profits for them.

At his appeal, the sole opposition came from the beat officer and a local rabbi, who claimed that people were urinating on his wall. While they awaited a decision on his license, the San Francisco Police Department started enforcing an obscure 1909 city ordinance forbidding minors to attend public dances without an adult.

On Friday, April 22, police officers raided the Fillmore Auditorium during a Quicksilver Messenger Service concert, after a Gleason editorial in the *San Francisco Chronicle* accused the police of harassing Graham. With a paddy wagon outside, cops burst into the Fillmore, checking IDs and arresting minors on the dance floor. Finally, Bill Graham was arrested at three in the morning and thrown in jail for allowing underage patrons inside the Fillmore.

At a bail hearing in front of a judge, Graham threw a tirade and had to be calmed down by his attorney. In the following day's *San Francisco Chronicle*, Gleason condemned the San Francisco Police Department's brutish behavior.

"The only reason I would not allow my own teenage daughters [in the Fillmore] without me now," he wrote, "is for fear that they would be treated like criminals by the police for being under 18."

On June 7, Bill Graham finally got his Dance Hall Keeper's license for the Fillmore Auditorium, after the city introduced a new provision allowing under-eighteens to attend dances where special rules prevailed. Exactly what were the special rules was—famously—never clarified.

◆

Bill Graham's profits were immediate. He had an instant cash flow at every concert. In the beginning, headliner acts such as Quicksilver Messenger Service or the Grateful Dead were getting only $200 to $300 for a show. With minimal outlay and practically no overhead, Graham could gross $25,000 ($180,000) in one weekend in tickets and concessions—far more than he had been earning a year as an executive at Allis-Chalmers. And as the Fillmore never dispensed tickets, it was untraceable income.

"Bill's profits were enormous," said manager Jim Haynie. "We knew he was stuffing thousands of dollars away every week, and I thought he was sending it to Swiss bank accounts. I never knew for certain."[5]

◆

On July 1, 1966—three weeks after Bill Graham's license came through— Janis Joplin made her debut at the Fillmore Auditorium with Big Brother and the Holding Company. Opening for Quicksilver Messenger Service, Janis's raw emotional performance took Big Brother to a new level and blew everyone away.

"It happened the first time," she would later say. "I just exploded."[6]

CHAPTER SEVEN

Janis

Janis Lyn Joplin was born on January 19, 1943, in Port Arthur, Texas. Her parents, Seth Joplin and Dorothy East, had first met on a blind date around Christmas 1932, nearly seven hundred miles northwest in Amarillo. Seth, a handsome engineering student, was something of a playboy. During the last months of Prohibition, he made bathtub gin for his college parties, and he smoked marijuana, then legal in Texas.

Dorothy was a gifted singer with a beautiful operatic voice. A Broadway director had once invited her to travel to New York, where he promised to launch her singing career. But she had declined, opting to go to Texas Christian University in Fort Worth after winning a scholarship in a singing contest.[1]

When her teacher decided she was unsuitable for a classical opera course, Dorothy returned to Amarillo to work at a local radio station. She became a flapper, cut her hair into a bob, and started smoking.

After a four-year courtship, Seth and Dorothy married on October 20, 1936, moving to Port Arthur, where Seth went to work as an engineer for the Texas Company, which would later become Texaco. In 1901 "The Lucas Gusher" had erupted at Spindletop in nearby Beaumont, launching the petroleum age and bringing Texas untold wealth. Gulf Oil and the Texas Company had then moved into Port Arthur, building refining facilities and making it the hub of the Texas oil boom. By the early 1940s, when Janis was born, Port Arthur had become hot and smoky, with the refineries spewing sulfurous gas into the air, day and night.

Oil-company executive Seth Joplin was so happy to become a father that he wrote Dorothy a congratulatory note complimenting her on the "successful completion of [her] production quota."[2]

Growing up in the rigidly conservative, narrow-minded town would scar Janis for life. Her parents lived in a nice house at 3130 Lombardy Drive, an affluent middle-class neighborhood. Thanks to oil, Port Arthur was safe and well kept, with some of the best schools in the country for its sixty thousand residents.

Right from the beginning, it was obvious that Janis was a gifted child. Highly intelligent and inquisitive, the little girl loved to paint and write poetry. But it was her singing voice that really made her stand out. For her sixth birthday, her mother bought her an old upright piano and began teaching her some tunes. But after a thyroid operation ruined Dorothy's singing voice, the piano disappeared, as she couldn't bear hearing little Janis singing her own favorite tunes.

In 1949, Dorothy Joplin had another daughter they named Laura, followed by a baby boy, Michael, four years later.

Even before she had entered school, Janis was a voracious reader with a library card. By the end of her first year, she was so far ahead of her classmates that she skipped second grade altogether. From then on she would always be a year younger than her classmates, and while mentally equal to them, she was emotionally inferior.

In September 1954, Janice entered Woodrow Wilson Junior High School. An excellent student, she was also quite popular and *the* star in the First Christian Church choir. Though she was soprano lead vocalist in the school glee club, her real passion was art, and her mother had arranged for her to have private art lessons.

Like Grace Wing, Janis wrote and performed her own plays. Seth Joplin built his daughter a puppet theater in the backyard so she could stage them for an audience of friends and family.

The young girl had an insatiable curiosity and quickly saw Port Arthur's huge inequalities. The thriving petroleum port had a revolving door of sailors coming in and out of the town. And to cater to their needs, scores of brothels and gambling clubs existed in plain view, alongside the Port Arthur's strict churchgoing morality.

"The city was on the one hand very straitlaced," said Janis's high school classmate and lifelong friend Tary Owens, "but on the other hand absolutely wide open. The hypocrisy just glared." [3]

At fourteen, Janis moved up to the Thomas Jefferson High School and everything changed. During puberty, she had put on weight and developed such severe facial acne it required sanding.[4] Self-conscious and embarrassed about her appearance, Janis fell into a deep depression.

Then, Janis began her outrageous rebellions. She dyed her hair orange in junior year and started drinking beer and screaming obscenities in the high school corridors.[5] But even worse by Port Arthur standards, she spoke out in class about segregation and the inequalities suffered by African Americans, who made up 40 percent of the town's population. Such outspokenness did not go down well with her bigoted classmates.

"Integration was a major issue then," explained Owens, "and we were still in segregated schools. The racism was just horrid, and Janis spoke out about that in class. And that was just the beginning of the reactions against her."

Her classmates spat on her and threw stones, calling her "Nigger Lover," "pig," and "whore." She then gravitated toward a small group of more enlightened students and started hanging out with them.

"We all had some things in common," said Jim Langdon, who became her friend. "I would say everybody was darn bright. We had a sense of adventure . . . and [were] interested in the arts in some form or another. We were decidedly not in the mainstream of high school social life."[6]

Janis's behavior also caused problems at home, where her conservative parents put her into psychological counseling so she could fulfill their dream of becoming a school teacher.

"There were lots of arguments in the house between my parents and Janis," said her sister, Laura. "Trying to help her change her approach, so that life wasn't so challenging for her."[7]

Janis and her new set of friends rushed out to buy Jack Kerouac's novel *On the Road* as soon as it was published in September 1957, and they discovered a kindred spirit.

"[We] were blown away by it," said Langdon. "It was a new voice and I think we were all rebels at heart. So that's how we identified."

Janis also started listening to such folk groups as The Kingston Trio, as well exploring the musical roots of Lead Belly, Odetta, and Woody Guthrie. And they began driving fifteen miles east across the state line into Louisiana to hear the local blues bands play. They hung out in road-houses, such as the Big Oak Club and Louanne's, where underage teenagers could smoke and drink alcohol with no questions asked.

"Everybody else was going to drive-ins and drinking Cokes," Janis later told *Time* magazine, "and talking about going across the tracks to go nigger knocking."[8]

By her senior year of high school, Janis's classmates found out about her trips to Louisiana and branded her a loose woman.

"Every guy in our class claimed that he'd been to bed with Janis," recalled Owens, "and the truth was probably she was still a virgin."[9]

Although Janis relished her reputation as an outlaw and still had excellent grades, she suffered from low self-esteem and felt socially inadequate. And in the safety of her bedroom, she would paint her nails and worry about her weight.

When no one invited her to the senior prom she was devastated. Further humiliation followed when she was barred from attending the Black and White Ball.

"There was nobody like me in Port Arthur," she later explained. "It was lonely. I was just 'silly crazy Janis.' Man, those people hurt me."[10]

In 1960, seventeen-year-old Janis graduated. She enrolled at Lamar State College of Technology in nearby Beaumont for an art degree. Her bad reputation from Jefferson High had preceded her, and once again she found herself an outcast. She roomed with another female student and took a course at Port Arthur College, learning to punch keys on business machines. But she soon started cutting classes, spending most nights across the Louisiana state line with her friends, listening to music and drinking hard liquor.

"We spent from midnight until dawn just prowling in and out of the clubs," said Jim Langdon, "and hearing blues players [and] jazz players. Just digging the music and drinking. Janis loved it, and I think that was sort of a beginning as far as the kind of life she was going to pursue."[11]

One time, after telling her parents she was spending the night with a girlfriend, Janis drove their car to New Orleans. On the way back, one of her friends crashed the vehicle and Janis was questioned by the police, although no one was ever charged.

"It was things like that that solidified Janis's reputation as a bad girl," said Langdon. "A really bad girl."

Soon after starting her own stint at Lamar State College, Frances Vincent met Janis in the student union.

"My first impression was I didn't like her," recalled Frances. "She felt so bristly and hostile. As I got to know her I realized that she really was a vulnerable, fragile soul; under all that armor. And I became very fond of her."[12]

Janis ran off to Houston without telling her parents, hanging out at The Purple Onion Coffee Shop and getting ill from drinking too much alcohol on an empty stomach. Back home she had to be hospitalized for kidney trouble, later telling friends she had suffered a nervous breakdown.[13]

Some time around her eighteenth birthday, Janis started becoming serious about her singing. At parties she began imitating her musical heroes, Bessie Smith, Big Mama Thornton, Big Maybelle, Odetta, and Joan Baez, with uncanny accuracy.

"I had this voice," she said in 1970, "and I found that every time I started singing it kind of just broke down a bunch of walls."[14]

In the summer of 1961, Janis Joplin bought an autoharp and left home, heading to Los Angeles to become a singer. For a few weeks she lived the beatnik life on Venice Beach, playing at the Troubadour Club's "Hootenanny Night" and the Gas House on Venice Beach.

She then hitched north to San Francisco, buying a sheepskin jacket and hanging out in bohemian North Beach. She frequented the coffeehouses and went bar hopping, having indiscriminate sex with male and female strangers.

"I met her at the Coffee Gallery," recalled Nick Gravenites, who would later become a close friend. "She was playing autoharp and singing country stuff at the time—country blues, country music in particular."[15]

That winter, Janis returned to Texas, refusing to talk about her time on the West Coast. She later explained that she had been "at a very young and fucked up stage."[16]

Janis spent the holidays at Jim Langdon's house, and he persuaded her to play at a New Year's Eve party at the Halfway Coffee House Club in Beaumont. Then, in early January, she returned to Port Arthur and moved back in with her parents.

In the spring of 1962, Janis enrolled at the University of Texas in Austin, majoring in art. Working part-time as a waitress in a bowling alley, she befriended a group of Austin hipsters living in "The Ghetto," a small building west of campus. To Janis it was an oasis with a rotating cast of musicians, artists, and political activists. They saw themselves as a little island of intellectuals in a sea of rednecks, and Janis became a regular at their parties, singing a cappella and strumming her autoharp.

Six years before his ill-fated partnership with Bill Graham at the Fillmore Auditorium, Chet Helms was a handsome young student at the University of Texas. He first met Janis in a student's meeting room and was immediately struck by her distinctive country blues singing. It was the beginning of a close friendship that would set Janis on the path to superstardom.

"We all sat around on these cushions," recalled Helms. "People put jugs under their coats and would take turns playing. It was pretty loosely organized. Janis was very shy until she'd had a fair amount of alcohol. And then she could be cajoled, persuaded to sing. And then once she'd let go it would be fantastic." [17]

That July, Janis joined the Waller Creek Boys with fellow students Powell St. John on harmonica and guitar and Lanny Wiggins on guitar. Janis sang and strummed autoharp.

They began playing an Austin folk club called Threadgills, an old service station owned by a folk enthusiast named Kenneth Threadgill, who had converted it into a music venue. On Wednesday nights, Janis and the Waller Creek Boys soon became the house band.

"Janis just knocked everybody out right from the beginning," recalled Jim Landon. "They loved her."

One night at a Threadgills after-party, Janis played a Bessie Smith–influenced song she had just written called "What Good Can Drinking

Do?" The song was captured on reel-to-reel tape, and it is probably the earliest recording of Janis Joplin singing.

"This is a song," she told her audience, "that I wrote one night after drinking myself into a stupor."[18]

On July 27, the nineteen-year-old freshman student was profiled in the student newspaper, the *Daily Texan*.

"She dares to be different," was the headline on the story, written by campus life editor Pat Sharpe. "She goes barefoot when she feels like it, wears Levi's to class because they're more comfortable, and carries her autoharp with her everywhere she goes so that if she gets the urge to break into song it will be handy.

"Her name is Janis Joplin and she looks like the type of girl a square (her more descriptive term—a 'leadbelly,') would call a 'beatnik.' 'Jivey' is what Janis calls herself, not 'beat.' She leads a life that is enviously unrestrained."

The article noted that although Janis's voice is "untrained," she "sings with a certain spontaneity and gusto that cultivated voices sometimes find difficult to capture."[19]

<hr />

With her long unkempt hair, torn jeans, and bare feet, Janis Joplin certainly stood out on the University of Texas campus. She looked nothing like the regular prim-and-proper white-bloused, bobbysoxer Texas coeds, who favored beehive hairdos and penny loafers. And many were openly hostile to Janis.

"Janis wore blue jeans, work shirts and no bra," recalled Chet Helms, "and she swore like a sailor."[20]

At the end of the 1962 fall semester, Alpha Phi Omega held its annual Ugliest Man on Campus Contest to raise money for charity. Each fraternity donated $5 to nominate one of their members, and Janis was elected Ugliest Man. When she found out, she was devastated, bursting into tears.

"She was profoundly hurt," said Powell St. John. "I'd long ago written off those people as irrelevant . . . but Janis wasn't able to do that. She took their criticisms to heart and it really hurt her very deeply."[21]

Soon afterward, Janis wrote a song called "It's Sad to be Alone," recording it at a friend's house. Accompanying herself on autoharp, she sings, "The dusty road calls you. You walk to the end. It's sad, so sad to be alone."[22]

——◆——

In January 1963, Janis quit the University of Texas after Chet Helms persuaded her to hitchhike to San Francisco with him so he could launch her musical career.

"I thought Janis will knock people's socks off," said Helms, "if I can get her to California and [they] can hear her sing."[23]

Janis looked up to the intense charismatic young man, viewing him as a worldly sophisticate. He had told her about the blossoming North Beach folk scene that he had discovered on a visit a year earlier. Now he promised to use all his contacts to help her get established.

They set out on a cold winter's night, after Janis's regular Wednesday spot at Threadgills. In Fort Worth, Chet brought Janis to his mother's house to spend the night. But the devout fundamentalist Baptist took one look at Janis, who was wearing pink sunglasses and a low-buttoned blue denim shirt with no bra, and refused to let them stay. Chet's younger brother John then drove them to the highway outside of town, where they started hitching.

They made it to North Beach in just fifty hours, and Chet immediately took Janis to the Coffee and Confusion Club on Grant Street. It had recently changed from a beatnik hangout to one of the new North Beach folk clubs. During the next few days, Chet also introduced her to the regulars at the nearby Coffee Gallery, including Jerry Garcia, Jorma Kaukonen, Paul Kantner, David Crosby, and David Freiberg.

"Anybody could play," explained Helms. "None of the performers were paid and if you wanted to go and strut your stuff you'd just put your name on the list."[24]

Everybody loved Janis's raw country blues songs, and she was soon making $50 a night from passing the hat, with as much beer as she could drink.

"I played with Janis briefly in 1963," recalled Jorma Kaukonen, still two years away from joining Jefferson Airplane. "The Janis that I knew fairly well was the folky, bluesy Janis."[25]

Word soon got around North Beach about this plump Texan girl with bad skin and tattered clothes who had an amazing voice. But when her future Big Brother and the Holding Company bandmates Peter Albin and Jim Gurley came to see her play, they were unimpressed, thinking her too weird.

＊＊＊

When they had first arrived in San Francisco, Janis and Chet Helms crashed at a friend's apartment, but Janis soon moved in with a girl named J.J. She collected unemployment and had several short-term jobs to augment what she made in the coffeehouses.

Janis soon started injecting speed and heroin and hanging out at the Amp Palace on Grant Avenue and a lesbian bar called the Anxious Asp.[26] Although she found a boyfriend who went by JP, she was sexually adventurous with both men and women. She also tried to become a hooker, but with little success.

"We did so much dope," recalled Helms. "We walked right into a speed crowd."[27]

One night Bobby Cohen, who would later become Helms's partner in the Avalon Ballroom, saw Janis singing at a coffeehouse and decided to record her.

"She was one wild lady," he said. "Drank a lot, sung incredible and was just a very fun person. I told everyone there was going to be a big party at my house, dragged Janis over and recorded her." [28]

That summer Janis's career seemed to be taking off. She played the Monterrey Folk Festival and sang live with the Dick Oxtot Jazz Band on Berkeley's KPFA-FM *Midnight Special* radio show. In May 1964, she moved to New York to try to break into the flourishing Greenwich Village folk scene. Janis took an apartment on the Lower East Side, spending the summer shooting speed and reading Nietzsche and Hermann Hesse. At night she sang at Gerde's Folk City and an East Village bar called Slug's, accompanying herself on an old guitar.

By the fall, she was back in San Francisco and seriously addicted to speed. After being beaten up by a gang outside a North Beach Bar, she crashed her Vespa motor scooter and hit rock bottom. She even tried to check herself into a psychiatric ward at San Francisco General but was refused admission.

"She was freaking out a lot of her friends," said Helms, "and became very aggressive."[29]

By summer of 1965, Janis weighed just eighty-seven pounds and had ugly track marks up and down both arms. Concerned that she would die if she didn't get off the streets, her friends threw a bus ticket party and sent her home to Texas.

Reunited with her family in Port Arthur, Janis vowed to clean up her act. She underwent psychiatric counseling and returned to Lamar College to finish her art course.

"She went into a complete makeover," said Jim Langdon. "She wore her hair up in a bun and it was just really a kind of charade. I think she was honestly trying to go straight [because] that [San Francisco] experience had really scared her."

Soon after returning, Janis threw a homecoming party at the Joplin home, only inviting her straight and sober friends. At the party she proudly announced she was now engaged to Peter de Blanc, a wealthy young man she'd met in San Francisco.

On August 21, de Blanc duly arrived in Port Arthur to formally ask Seth Joplin's permission for his daughter's hand in marriage. Seth and Dorothy both approved, thinking him very refined with some potential.

During the next few months, Janis would write her fiancé sixty love letters, even sending him home-cooked pralines. She enthusiastically wrote of filling up her hope chest, about shopping for a wedding dress with her mother, and the Texas-style quilt she was making for their marriage bed.

But by winter, de Blanc had broken off the engagement and jilted her.

That Thanksgiving, Janis Joplin channeled her heartbreak into her music, playing at the Half Way House Club in Beaumont. Old friends found her almost unrecognizable, with her neat dress and her brown hair piled up in a bun, as she sang Bessie Smith songs mixed in with some folk blues.

Jim Langdon, who now wrote a music column for the *Austin American-Statesman*, was in the audience that night and much impressed. He could not believe how far Janis's singing had come in the two years since he had last seen her. He arranged for Janis to play the next weekend at the Eleventh Door Club in Austin and used his column to champion her.

"Janis just absolutely took the place down," recalled Landon, "and she was wonderful."

The next day he wrote a glowing review, calling Janis Joplin the "Best white female blues singer in America."

"Of course nobody knew who she was," he said. "She'd never cut a record."[30]

In Janis Joplin's absence, Chet Helms had been busy establishing himself in the San Francisco music scene. He now managed Big Brother and the Holding Company and had launched the Avalon Ballroom to compete with Bill Graham's Fillmore Auditorium. By early 1966, Big Brother was starting to get known in San Francisco, and Helms decided Janis Joplin would be the ideal vocalist for them. Up to this point all the vocals had been shared by bassist Peter Albin and guitarists James Gurley and Sam Andrew. Helms believed the band sorely needed a female singer.

"Early in the game I had suggested the band try out Janis," said Helms. "I knew she was in Austin and maybe we could get her."[31]

But Albin and Gurley, who had seen her perform three years earlier, were against the idea. Finally, after months of auditioning girl singers, it was agreed that Janis should be given a tryout, and Helms dispatched his friend Travis Rivers to Port Arthur to collect her.

On June 4, 1966, Janis returned to San Francisco after a monthlong affair with Rivers. She had initially been reluctant to come back, not wanting to be exposed to hard drugs again. But Chet Helms promised her a bus ticket back to Port Arthur if things did not work out.

"So I told her in truth that most of these people were totally cleaned up," said Helms. "She said, 'How will I live?' So I agreed to pay her basic rent for five or six months while she sorted it out."[32]

The night she arrived, Helms brought her to Big Brother's rehearsal room at 1090 Page Street, where drummer David Getz and guitarist Sam Andrew both had visions of the beautiful goddess that Chet Helms had told them about.

"And in comes Chet with this real scraggly-looking girl," recalled Andrew. "And she was kind of tough. She was kind of scrappy. It would be like if you went out and got a cat out in the alley and dragged [it] in. She has her claws out."[33]

But as soon as Janis started singing, everybody knew she was a perfect fit.

"When she opened her mouth," said Getz, "it was apparent that she was *the* one. That she was *the* singer for this band."

CHAPTER EIGHT

The Pieces Come Together

Janis Joplin first performed with Big Brother and the Holding Company at Chet Helms's Avalon Ballroom in late June 1966, opening for the Grateful Dead and Quicksilver Messenger Service. A week later, she played the Fillmore Auditorium for Bill Graham.

She was an instant sensation with her raw, earthy blues vocals, which seemed to come straight from her heart. Like Grace Slick, Janis had her own unique style and voice. But whereas Grace was always well groomed, favoring a pantsuit or a sexy black leotard, Janis went braless in oversize men's shirts and faded Levis.

When they first met backstage at the Avalon, Janis and Grace became instant friends, finding common ground as the only female rock singers in San Francisco.

"You're so pretty," Darby Slick remembered Janis telling Grace, as Big Brother was about to take the stage. "How do you make your hair look like that?"

Grace laughed, saying she had no idea but just messed it around with her fingers and sprayed on lacquer. Then The Great Society singer started sipping champagne from a brown paper bag as Janis brought out a bottle of Southern Comfort and took a slug, offering the bottle to Grace.

"Want to try some of this?" Janis asked. Grace "cringed" as she refused, telling Janis with a smile that she preferred champagne.[1]

Bill Graham initially disliked Janis. His rival Chet Helms managed her, after all. He would mockingly call her "That screaming witch," only allowing Big Brother to play benefits at the Fillmore. So they mainly played at the Avalon, where they soon became the unofficial house band.

That first year Bill Graham ran the Fillmore Auditorium on a shoe-string, using all his management skills he had honed at Allis-Chalmers. His girlfriend, Bonnie MacLean, was his "lady Friday," answering phones and keeping the books. She also listed the bands coming to the Fillmore on chalkboards at the top of the stairs. And before long, with Graham's encouragement, she did some of the first Fillmore posters, as well as over-seeing local artists Wes Wilson and Alton Kelley, whom Graham paid a pittance.

His only other regular Fillmore employees were Jim Haynie and his cleaner/security guard, John Walker.

"Bill called me his right-hand man," said Haynie, who was then twenty-six, "and I had a number of hats to wear. I ran all the concessions and I introduced the bands. I was in charge of all the technical shit."[2]

Bonnie now rarely saw her boyfriend outside of the Fillmore, as he worked late every night and was up early the next morning, calling the New York agents to book bands.

"Oh my God he was driven," recalled Bonnie. "He was working all the time. There was a hell of a lot of screaming going on. He was the boss. He yelled at me once and I slammed my hand on the tabletop, and told him not to talk to me like that. And he never did it after that."[3]

Although the Fillmore Auditorium had a legal capacity of just a thou-sand, Graham regularly crammed twenty-five hundred people inside. After every show Bonnie would help fill his canvas knapsack with cash, taking it back to their apartment on his old Lambretta. He was at his most affection-ate as they counted the night's takings, piling it in stacks of $1, $5, and $10 bills. Then early Monday morning, Graham put a loaded handgun into his side pocket and took many thousands of dollars to the bank.

That summer, as the money rolled in, he splashed out $8,000 on a brand-new green Mercedes.

"That was a big deal," said Bonnie, "because he was very frugal about what he wanted for himself. But he wanted that nice car and felt he could spare that money."[4]

Many music-scene observers saw Bill Graham as a capitalist pig who was growing rich on the backs of the Love Generation. In an early issue of *Rolling Stone*, publisher Jann Wenner referred to him as "The burgeoning

Howard Hughes of the dance scene," leading to a bitter long-term feud between them. That accusation hit a raw nerve. And from then on even the suspicion of a negative whisper behind his back would unleash a torrent of Graham's anger and abuse, followed by the culprit being physically thrown out of the Fillmore.

———

Among the regulars at the Fillmore Auditorium was fifteen-year-old Carlos Santana, who would sneak past Bill Graham to get in for free. He went every week, seeing blues legends B.B. King, Muddy Waters, and Otis Rush play.

"The Fillmore was a real education," Carlos would later explain. "If you hung out at the Fillmore for a week, you didn't have to go to the Berkeley School of Music if you really listened and learned."[5]

Carlos Santana had now been living in the Mission District for three years and had his own blues band. But when he had first arrived, Carlos was so angry with his mother for kidnapping him that he had locked himself in his room and refused to eat.[6] When he finally came out, Josefina Santana enrolled him in the James Lick Junior High School, where he learned English. But he found little in common with his classmates after his time at the El Convoy strip club.

"The stuff they were talking about was silly-ass corn shit," he told *Rolling Stone* in 2000. "I'm hanging around a bunch of old guys talking about Ray Charles and the blues."

Soon after arriving in San Francisco, Carlos checked out a guitar store that his mentor Javier Batiz had told him about while he had been back in Tijuana. He was enthralled, gazing longingly at the displays of gleaming Gibsons, Fenders, and Epiphone guitars.

"To me that was like what kids do with *Playboy* magazine," recalled Carlos. "I was like, 'I wonder what she smells like? I wonder what she feels like? I wonder what she sounds like?'"[7]

As he was eyeing the guitars, some sailors started screaming racist remarks at him, calling him a "Pancho Villa, chili-beany motherfucker."

"I'm just a kid," he said, "and I turned around and realized they were screaming at me. I was angry because I started feeling the sting of racism, the sting of ignorance directed straight at me."[8]

Life was tough for the Santana family, with seven children sharing just two bedrooms. Carlos found an after-school job at the Tic-Toc drive-in diner on Third Street. He washed dishes and scrubbed potatoes, saving enough money to put down the deposit on a Gibson Les Paul.

Tragedy struck when a friend of his big brother Tony accidentally sat on the guitar and destroyed it. A fight ensued, and Carlos hit his brother and gave him a black eye.

The following night Carlos, who shared a bed with Tony, was expecting a beating. Nothing happened. But when Carlos came home from school the following afternoon, he found a brand-new white Les Paul and an amplifier waiting for him.

It would be the same guitar that Carlos Santana would play at Woodstock five years later, the instrument that would make him a star.

In fall 1964, Carlos Santana had enrolled at Mission High School and started a band called The Dynamics. They rehearsed in a garage, playing blues songs and Top 40 covers at weddings and bar mitzvahs. A year later, The Dynamics entered a local radio station's "Battle of the Bands" at the Cow Palace, backing up soul singer Joyce Dunn and making it to the final three. Unfortunately, they got drunk at the final to calm their nerves and were eliminated.[9]

Most days, Carlos arrived for attendance at Mission High School before disappearing to jam with other musicians. He also discovered the Hungarian jazz guitar virtuoso Gabor Szabo, who would become a huge influence on his music.

"I didn't hang out with my race," he later explained. "Your race is like a fence, you know. I always tend to hang out with the people who are more soulful—or at least not always thinking about quads and carburetors and chicks and parties."

In late 1965, Carlos Santana graduated from Mission High School and left home. It would be more than two years before his family heard from him again. He crashed on friends' floors and slept rough in the park, busking around Haight-Ashbury for spare change and playing street fairs and parties.

"You used to see him walking down the street dragging his amplifier," said percussionist Richard Segovia, who also lived in the Mission. "He was really quiet and reserved and he came out of his shell [later]."[10]

Carlos became close friends with a student barber named Stan Marcum, whose father owned a clothing store on Mission Street. Marcum, who was a couple of years older, loved music and had a great record collection. He introduced Carlos to his friend Ron Estrada, and the three of them got an apartment together.

During the next few months, Marcum became Carlos's mentor, turning him on to LSD and jazz musicians, especially Miles Davis and John Coltrane.

In early 1966, Marcum started taking Carlos to Bill Graham's new Fillmore Auditorium. They soon became fixtures, soaking in all the new San Francisco bands, as well as the black blues artists Graham was starting to book. Then Carlos would go home and practice what he'd learned.

"I used to see him every time we played in the city," recalled Jerry Garcia. "[He'd be] right down in the front, watching me play at the shows that we did at the Fillmore and the park."[11]

Carlos loved going to the Fillmore and was usually tripping on LSD, mescaline, or magic mushrooms.

"They were expanding my consciousness, expanding my goals" he later said. "I wanted to try everything, just like a little child. You put him in front of a TV set and he wants to see what this knob does. It took me a long time to find out the difference between getting loaded and getting high."

On August 15, 1966, Jefferson Airplane's first album, *Jefferson Airplane Takes Off*, was released and the band was in big trouble. Singer Signe Toly Anderson, who had a three-month-old baby daughter, was refusing to leave her child to play dates outside San Francisco. So the rest of the band had a meeting and voted to replace her. But the question was with whom?

"There were only two other girls singing in town," explained Marty Balin. "One was Grace and one was Janis. And I said, 'You know I can't see Janis doing our thing. Grace . . . is a good singer but she's got her own band.'"

Then bassist Jack Casady left the meeting to invite Grace to join Jefferson Airplane.

"And that night she was at our rehearsal," said Balin. "She had left her band The Great Society—her husband and her brother—and joined up with us. And she brought "Somebody to Love" and "White Rabbit" with her. And the rest is history. Boom!"[12]

In fact, Grace had already decided to leave The Great Society, realizing the group's musical limitations. She had long dreamed of joining the far superior Jefferson Airplane, which she had seen many times.

Her husband, Jerry Slick, gave her his blessing, but the other band members learned she had left only after playing the Fillmore Auditorium on September 11. It would be The Great Society's final show. As they were packing up the equipment to go home, Jerry told his brother Darby and bassist Peter Vandergelder that Grace had quit.

"I felt completely betrayed," said Darby. "How could she quit? She was just another showbiz asshole, me, me, me. Fame and riches, and fuck everybody else. We had done our last show."[13]

<hr />

Most weekends that summer, you could find Janis Joplin and Big Brother and the Holding Company either playing or hanging out at the Avalon Ballroom on Sutter Street and Van Ness. The San Francisco music scene was now exploding, and Janis loved checking out the bands; she was fascinated by their "bizarre names." Although Bill Graham gave the members of Big Brother a free pass for the Fillmore, they far preferred the Avalon, where they felt more comfortable.

Janis often held court in the upstairs snack bar, usually dressed in an antique cape and sipping a Coke or standing near the stage, listening to the music.

"She would laugh and cackle and joke around with you," said Peter Albin. "She was fun to be around and smiling. She wasn't under a cloud."[14]

Soon after Janis joined Big Brother, Chet Helms rented her a room on Pine Street. She was determined to stay clean and warned the other band members never to do drugs in front of her, or she was leaving.

One day she came home to find her roommates fixing mescaline.

"She was just screaming and she threw them out of the room," said David Getz. "And just the idea of needles had such a fear-attraction thing for her that she couldn't stand it."

Country Joe McDonald first met Janis in a shared dressing room, when his band Country Joe and the Fish played a gig with Big Brother in Berkeley. He was tripping on acid and found an immediate rapport with her.

"Janis and I started talking," he said, "and really seemed to enjoy each other's company. We were laughing and carrying on. We were both Capricorns and kinda leaders of the bands we were in."[15]

Soon afterward, Big Brother moved into a communal house in Lagunitas, Marin County, and Janis began falling off the drugs wagon. She was now having an intense affair with Big Brother's lead guitarist James Gurley, and his wife, Nancy, had no problem with it. She even took Janis under her wing and gave her a gypsy look, dressing her in swirling brightly colored scarves, underslips worn as dresses, and dozens of bangles and rings.

But Nancy and several others at the new house were shooting speed, and Janis soon joined in.

"She started injecting drugs again," said Sam Andrew. "Probably about the time we moved into Lagunitas."

Before long Janis and the Grateful Dead's singer Pigpen hooked up. The Grateful Dead lived in a commune just down the road, and Janis was a frequent visitor. Janis and Pigpen both eschewed pot and LSD in favor of hard liquor, and Janis often spent the night in Pigpen's cabin, spending her time drinking, playing the blues, and making love.

"I turned her onto Southern Comfort, man," Pigpen told *Rolling Stone* in 1970. "I told her one day, 'Tex, try some of this.' She said, 'Oh man, that's *good*.' We used to get drunk and play pool together. She beat me 80 percent of the time."[16]

In late summer 1966, Big Brother fired Chet Helms, as he could no longer devote enough time to them because of the Avalon. They replaced him with Julius Karpen, who had once measured the LSD doses for Ken Kesey's acid tests. It was only then that they began playing the occasional show at the Fillmore Auditorium.

"Graham never hired us until we fired Chet," explained bassist Peter Albin, "and then we started working slowly at the Fillmore."

The first week of August, Paul Rothchild of Elektra Records saw Big Brother perform at the Avalon Ballroom. After the set, he came into the dressing room and invited Janis to lunch. On the menu were recording opportunities.

"She met with him the next day," said Peter Albin, "and he wanted to start a supergroup with Taj Mahal and Ry Cooder."

Rothchild, now on a roll after producing the Butterfield Blues Band's breakout album *East-West*, promised to make Janis a star, complete with a home in the Hollywood Hills and a Cadillac.

When she told her bandmates about his offer, they were livid, as Big Brother was about to leave for their first out-of-town booking in Chicago. So they ordered her then and there to make up her mind to leave or stay in the band.

"She broke down in tears and was very emotional," recalled Albin. "And she said, 'This is everything I ever wanted.' He had promised her lots of things and we really had to persuade her to continue with the band."[17]

The Chicago trip was a disaster, as their new manager had made no hotel reservations. They band was reduced to pushing their amplifiers and instruments from hotel to hotel, as one after another said there were no rooms available for the long-haired musicians.

Peter Albin's uncle, who lived in a Chicago suburb, finally came to their rescue, allowing the band to stay with him. The monthlong booking at Mother Blues Club, where Jefferson Airplane had played several weeks earlier, was a catastrophe. Although they had been promised a thousand dollars a week, the manager told them they could play for door money, and few people came.

At the end of the month, Big Brother and the Holding Company found themselves stranded in Chicago, without the fare back to San Francisco. Bob Shad of Mainstream Records then offered the musicians bus money home in return for signing a record deal and recording an album. Desperate for money, they reluctantly agreed and recorded some tracks before being told there would be no advance and that they were on their own.

Big Brother finally stuffed all their equipment in a drive-away Pontiac and started the long drive cross-country back to San Francisco.

———

In mid-May of 1966, a New York City band called the Velvet Underground had flown to San Francisco to play two nights at the Fillmore Auditorium. The experimental band, which was managed by Andy Warhol and featured a gorgeous German chanteuse named Nico—who had appeared in Fellini movies—was getting a lot of attention with its Exploding Plastic Inevitable Show. When Bill Graham had learned about the band, he immediately hired them on the same bill as the Mothers of Invention. He billed the show as "Pop-Op Rock."

The Velvet Underground, led by Lou Reed and John Cale, were the antithesis of the California flower-power acid movement. Where the San Francisco scene was all about peace, love, and LSD, the New York scene was far more hard-core, with S&M, speed, and heroin.

"We had vast objections to the whole San Francisco scene," explained Lou Reed. "It's just tedious. They can't play and they certainly can't write."[18]

Reed especially disliked San Francisco's two most popular bands, Jefferson Airplane and the Grateful Dead.

"Just look at them physically," he sneered. "I mean how can you take Grace Slick seriously? It's a joke! The kids are being hyped."

Bill Graham took an instant dislike to the Velvet Underground, and vice versa. As the biggest promoter in San Francisco, he felt the Velvet Underground should show him more respect, but they went out of their way to avoid him.

Graham's feelings were especially hurt when the Velvets ridiculed his light show during a rehearsal, saying it did not compare to theirs back in New York.

"That's one of the reasons Graham really hates us," said guitarist Sterling Morrison. "Right before we went on, he looked at us and said, 'You motherfuckers! I hope you bomb.'"[19]

When their set finished to deafening applause, Reed started smashing up Moe Tucker's drum kit, as a big "fuck you" to Bill Graham. During the violent commotion, a cymbal hit Lou Reed in the forehead, covering him in blood.

After they came offstage, Graham rushed to their dressing room to give them a dressing down, but he left as soon as he saw Reed's wound. Later, the Velvet Underground would speculate that he had not wanted to jeopardize his insurance.

In his book *POPism*, Andy Warhol recounts how filmmaker Paul Morrissey, who was traveling with the band, deliberately antagonized Bill Graham while they were watching a Jefferson Airplane show.

"'Why don't they take heroin?' Paul asked. 'That's what all the really *good* musicians take.' Graham didn't say anything, he just fumed. Paul knew he was driving him good and crazy so he kept it up. 'You know, I think I'm really all for heroin, because if you take care of yourself, it doesn't affect you physically.' He took a tangerine out of his pocket and peeled it in one motion, letting the peel fall on the floor. 'With heroin you never catch cold—it started in the United States as a cure for the common cold.'"

But what really upset Graham was Morrissey's dropping tangerine peel over the floor of his ballroom.

"Graham stared down at the peel," wrote Warhol, "and he got livid. I don't remember his exact words, but he started yelling—things like, 'You disgusting germs from New York! You come out here with your disgusting minds and whips.'"[20]

That would be the first and last time the Velvet Underground would ever play for Bill Graham.

CHAPTER NINE

Moving Up

Grace Slick's first show with Jefferson Airplane was at the Fillmore Auditorium on October 16, 1966. Several days earlier, Bill Thompson, the Airplane's road manager, had fired Signe Anderson after buying out Grace's recording contract for just $750. But Signe was still contracted to perform a three-night run at the Fillmore with the Airplane.

Exactly a year to the day after her first show with The Great Society, Grace was in the wings, still learning the Airplane's set. But when Anderson failed to show up on the second night, Grace was ordered on instead. As the set started, Grace was petrified. Jefferson Airplane played far louder than The Great Society, and as stage monitors were a couple of years away from being invented, Grace could hardly hear herself. But her first performance was a triumph, followed by a performance she really nailed on the last night.

With Grace aboard, everything came together for Jefferson Airplane, setting the stage for their huge international success.

"Nobody sounded like her and it coalesced the band," said Jorma Kaukonen. "It gave us a unified vision and a drive we didn't have before."[1]

Grace also brought her songs "Somebody to Love" and "White Rabbit" with her, which would soon give the Airplane their only two top-ten hits.

"They were performed differently," explained Grace, "in the sense that the . . . Great Society were not as good as the Airplane."[2]

And Grace brought a new edge to the music, much harder than the style of Signe Anderson, who had come out of the folk music scene.

"When Grace came into the band the harmonies changed," explained Jack Casady. "And it was actually rougher because she sang in the same range as Marty and the harmony structure of the songs changed. It allowed us to move ahead . . . and explore different directions."[3]

On October 30, Grace went on a short tour with Jefferson Airplane, and her effect on audiences was astonishing.

"She was stunning," said David Crosby. "With Marty she was like a bullfighter with a bull. She would circle him and dart at him and pull from him and electrify him and touch him with bare wire. And Marty rose to the occasion."[4]

During the brief tour, which included shows at the University of Santa Barbara and Grinnell College, Iowa, Grace easily found her place in the band.

"She was just like we were," explained Balin, "drugged-out, drinking, free and ballsy and outrageous."[5]

Grace was so delighted to be in Jefferson Airplane that she wanted to thank Jack Casady for bringing her in.

"So Grace was thinking about how can I reward Jack," recalled Thompson. "He's got the best pot in the world. Alcohol he didn't drink. So what did she do? She fucked him. Just one time. It was a nice reward."[6]

On October 5, 1966, Janis Joplin gave an interview to a small mimeographed newsletter called the *Mojo Navigator*. Asked to compare the Avalon and the Fillmore ballrooms, Janis said the Avalon was where the San Francisco in-crowd went for a good time, while the Fillmore was where drunken sailors went to get laid.

When Graham, who had already banned the *Mojo Navigator* from the Fillmore, read the article he went ballistic, swearing revenge. Several weeks later, Janis arrived at the Fillmore stoned on crystal meth for a B.B. King show.

"Bill met her at the top of the stairs and just pointed to the door and said, 'You're not coming in here,'" recalled Big Brother drummer David Getz. "Then he started screaming as he threw her [down the stairs]."[7]

"You're no damn good," he bellowed, as the people waiting on line for the show looked on in amazement. Janis burst into tears and ran out onto Geary Boulevard.

Realizing that he may have gone too far by publicly humiliating Janis, Graham sneaked into the backstage dressing room and hid in a closet to eavesdrop on what the other musicians would say about the incident.

"Bill Graham was the Sam Goldwyn of the rock 'n' roll business," said Nick Gravenites, who was playing the Fillmore that night with Electric Flag. "He would hide in places just to hear what was being said about him in his empire. I was in the backroom when I heard Janis had been thrown out and I exploded. Went right off the handle. So here Bill is hiding in the closet with all these irate, pissed-off musicians putting him down, using every conceivable epithet to describe his meanness."

With the show about to start, the musicians' attack on him showed no signs of abating. Due onstage to announce the first band, Graham was trapped in the closet with no means of escape.

"So I was ranting and raving about Bill Graham," said Gravenites. "Then he finally came out and was standing behind me, where I couldn't see him. Michael Bloomfield pointed at the back of the room and I turned round and there was Bill. I knew that he had heard everything that I had said about him, so I continued, 'And, Bill, that's not all, there's more!' I just cussed him up and down."[8]

Graham barely responded, but his eyes went cold.

"I'll get you for this," he hissed and walked out of the dressing room.

In early November 1966, Jefferson Airplane went into the RCA studios in Los Angeles to begin recording their second album, *Surrealistic Pillow*. Grace Slick and the other band members stayed at the Tropicana Hotel on Santa Monica Boulevard in $12-a-night rooms, complete with a kitchenette. During the next four nights, the band laid down six tracks, including a new version of Grace Slick's "White Rabbit," which would soon become *the* anthem of the Sixties and turn Grace into a rock icon.

Jerry Garcia hung out in the studio, helping to arrange "Somebody to Love," as well as playing guitar on several other tracks. He would be credited on the album as the band's "musical and spiritual advisor."

"We were pretty stoned all the time," recalled Marty Balin. "We felt good about ourselves . . . and it was a real fun time."[9]

After flying back to San Francisco to play the Fillmore Auditorium on November 6, the Airplane returned to Los Angeles to finish the album.

That Thanksgiving, Jefferson Airplane celebrated the completion of *Surrealistic Pillow* with another show at the Fillmore, the first of seven sold-out nights they would play there during the next month.

Bill Graham was now taking a special interest in Jefferson Airplane, indisputably the biggest band in San Francisco. With the Fillmore running smoothly, Graham wanted to expand into other areas of the San Francisco music scene. So he started courting Jefferson Airplane, with a view toward managing them. First he offered them the Fillmore as a rehearsal space, and then he started socializing with Grace Slick and the other members of the band.

"We got to know the Airplane pretty well," said Bonnie MacLean, "because they were the principal group that played the Fillmore. He schmoozed them so that he could get them at the price that he wanted, and behaved in a way that would make them want to do for him."[10]

But although Bonnie liked the rest of the band, she did not approve of Grace or her morals.

"She had an all-right voice," said Bonnie, "but beyond that I think she was a terrible person. She was an alcoholic. She was a slut [and] went with all the guys in the group. I'm not used to that crap."[11]

That winter, Jefferson Airplane rehearsed every day at the Fillmore Auditorium, working on new songs for their third album, *After Bathing at Baxters*.

"I watched [Bill Graham] on a daily basis put the Fillmore shows together," said Jack Casady. "We rehearsed at the Fillmore and we watched him in action in his office and how he would deal. And we got an appreciation for his ability, his knowledge and his work ethic. He oversaw the total experience."[12]

During this time, Bill Graham edged closer and closer to the band, seeking their advice about whom they thought he should book for the Fillmore.

"He'd pick our brains," said Casady, "about the kind of musicians that influenced us. And I would have long talks with him and show him my record collection."

Jack Casady introduced Graham to Chicago blues and jazz. He played him records by Buddy Guy, Muddy Waters, James Cotton, and Little Walter, as well as jazz artists Eric Dolphy, John Coltrane, and Roland Kirk. Throughout the next few years, Bill Graham would book many of them for his legendary eclectic shows.

"One of his real geniuses was to put an important mix onstage," said Casady, "so that the audience would see a great poet, hear a great jazz musician mixed with a great blues musician. Then he might mix a great rock 'n' roll guy with a great R and B guy. That would all be presented onstage at the same time."[13]

Paul Kantner also recommended artists for the Fillmore Auditorium.

"We helped him along," said Kantner, "and suggested all the people that he brought in like B.B. King and the jazz artists. And to his credit he would look into it . . . and have three complete disparate acts."[14]

Years later Graham would acknowledge the enormous debt he owed the San Francisco musicians for his musical education.

"I relied so much on Paul and Marty from the Airplane and Garcia and Weir," he told KSAN Radio in 1972, "who'd say, 'Bill, you should listen to this group.'"

Bill Graham also befriended Jorma Kaukonen, recounting his war experiences to the Jewish musician.

"He was a Holocaust survivor," said Kaukonen, "and as a Jew myself . . . there was that cultural sort of thing. He was so different from most of the people we'd know."[15]

As Graham schmoozed the band, his only obstacle was that they already had a manager. Matthew Katz was a middle-aged businessman from old-school Tin Pan Alley. Under his direction, Jefferson Airplane had become the first San Francisco band to secure a major record contract with a $20,000 advance from RCA Victor. And some band members felt they owed Katz for this, but Graham was determined not to let that stand in his way.

He arranged a meeting with Katz to discuss Jefferson Airplane becoming Fillmore regulars. It took place in Katz's bedroom, as he was feeling unwell, with his insurance broker present.

For four hours, Graham listened patiently and silently as Matthew Katz lectured him on the music business. Finally, when Katz demanded an exorbitant price for Jefferson Airplane to play, Graham started walking out of the bedroom.

"I had a lot of chutzpah, already," he explained later.

When Katz ordered him to come back, Graham realized that what Katz really wanted was someone to listen to him and any negotiation was just incidental. Ultimately, Katz agreed to Graham's opening offer of $500 a night or $1,000 for a weekend, a real bargain for the most popular band in town.

Graham's opportunity to get rid of Katz came soon afterward when he discovered that it was illegal for a manager to bypass an agent and book his own band. He then took Katz to court, accusing him of soliciting gigs for Jefferson Airplane and his other bands, It's a Beautiful Day and Moby Grape, and won the case.

"We had a bad manager at the time," said Paul Kantner. "[Bill] helped us shed him."[16]

In retaliation, Katz sued Jefferson Airplane, enmeshing the group in a landmark case that would take twenty-two years to resolve, and that still impacts entertainment law to this day.[17]

⌒

On October 16, 1966, Carlos Santana and Stan Marcum were at the Fillmore Auditorium for the final night of a Jefferson Airplane/Butterfield Blues Band run of shows. A superjam was planned later for members of the two bands, as well as members of the Grateful Dead and Quicksilver Messenger Service.

When Paul Butterfield failed to turn up after taking too much LSD, Marcum asked Bill Graham if his guitar-playing friend from Tijuana could join in the jam. Graham said it was okay with him as long as Butterfield lead guitarist Michael Bloomfield agreed. When Carlos asked his guitar hero for permission to play, Bloomfield graciously handed him his guitar and pointed to the stage.

"So I grab his guitar," said Carlos, "and I waited my turn when he said to play. The next thing I know is that I got a reaction because Bill says, 'Have you got a band?' I said yeah, I got a band.'"

In the audience that night was a young rhythm guitarist named Tom Fraser, who was dazzled by Santana's unique lead guitar style. As soon as he got back to his home in Palo Alto, he called his friend Gregg Rolie, who played keyboards in a band called William Penn and His Pals, saying he had just seen this amazing new guitarist he must play with.

Two days later, Fraser tracked Carlos down at the Tic-Toc Diner and offered to drive him straight to Mountain View to meet Rollie so they could jam together.

Carlos agreed, and after finishing his shift, he drove with Fraser across the bridge to a farmhouse in Mountain View, where Gregg Rolie was waiting. Then after smoking some strong weed in the garage, Carlos set up his equipment and started jamming with Rolie and Fraser.

"We were playing," recalled Rolle, "making all kinds of racket and smoking. Pretty soon the cops came. I looked around and said, 'We've got to get out of here.' Because we heard the sirens. I looked over at Carlos and he was already about fifty yards down the road. He was way more hip than I was. We jumped and hid in a tomato patch, and that's where I met him."[18]

In November, Janis Joplin saw Big Mama Thornton play at a small club. After the show she went backstage to ask the blues legend for permission to use her song "Ball and Chain" in Big Brother's act. Big Mama not only gave permission but also insisted on writing down the lyrics on a sheet of paper.

A month later Otis Redding played three nights at the Fillmore Auditorium. Bill Graham had flown to Macon, Georgia, to persuade him.[19]

Janis arrived early to all the shows, claiming a prime position front and center of the stage. Janis, who idolized Otis, watched each performance like a hawk, soaking up everything he did. With his hard-driving twelve-piece band behind him, Otis blew the musical roof off the Fillmore, which was only half-full, as the young white kids had not discovered soul music yet.

"Janis told me she invented the 'buh-buh-buh-*ba-by* . . .' after seeing him," recalled Country Joe MacDonald. "She wanted to *be* Otis Redding."[20]

Bill Graham was also knocked out, later saying it was one of *the* best shows he ever did.

"Otis is by far the greatest thing I've ever seen on any stage," said Bill Graham. "I don't know how much more can be said other than that. He was beautiful to look at, beautiful to listen to. He moved like no other man I've ever seen. I loved to watch him move."[21]

CHAPTER TEN

1967

One year after taking over the Fillmore Auditorium, Bill Graham had become wealthy beyond his wildest dreams. To celebrate, he held a New Year's Eve concert with the Grateful Dead and Jefferson Airplane. Graham, who loved theatrics, had Jim Haynie make a grand entrance at the stroke of midnight dressed as the New Year's baby with a homemade diaper and a sparkly banner.

"I was completely whacko-stoned," Haynie recalled. "I had taken my acid about an hour before."

At five minutes to midnight, eight Fillmore security guards carried him into the Fillmore on a litter, to a trumpet fanfare.

"I looked around as if I was just waking up," said Haynie, "and the crowd roared its appreciation. Then I got up on my knees and threw flowers to people. When we hit the stage Bill did his countdown to 1967, and the Grateful Dead started their set by playing 'The Midnight Hour.'"[1]

From then on, Haynie would always be the Fillmore's New Year baby. Several years later, Bill Graham began dressing up as Old Father Time, complete with a long white beard and robe, to ceremoniously hand over the New Year to Haynie.

＊

As Jefferson Airplane's new manager, Bill Graham became the most powerful player in the San Francisco music scene, a man with the city's top ballroom and number-one band. He also briefly managed the Grateful Dead, but they soon got rid of him when he tried to lay down the law.

"Bill Graham was the straightest person that we knew," said drummer Mickey Hart. "We fired him after twenty minutes. 'You want to be macho? Okay cool.'"[2]

Bill Thompson, now appointed the Airplane's assistant manager, remembers Jerry Garcia slugging Bill Graham one night backstage at the Fillmore.

"[Jerry] said, 'You fucking asshole,'" said Thompson. "Punched him in the face after an argument about band stuff."[3]

Bill Graham's timing in the City by the Bay could not have been better. In December, *Newsweek* ran a major story about the San Francisco music scene that focused on Jefferson Airplane. During the next few months, a string of major features would follow, as well as a national profile of the band on the *Bell Television Hour*. All this publicity would lure thousands of young people to San Francisco for the Summer of Love.

Graham's management deal with Jefferson Airplane had been sealed on a handshake, with nothing in writing. It gave him an equal financial share with the band members, as well as a vote at band meetings. But their new manager had definite ideas about how the band should dress and behave, which were not popular.

"He talked about band uniforms," recalled Jorma Kaukonen. "The fact that somebody wanted to control how we presented ourselves was anathema to us."[4]

Graham also wanted to exploit the band's success with a full-scale national tour. Band meetings often became acrimonious, as Grace and the other members preferred to stay in San Francisco, playing the odd show or party.

"It was very difficult," Graham admitted, "and there was a great strain between us sometimes. I came from the business community and it was my job to act realistically."

⌐⌐⌐

On January 8, 1967, *Surrealistic Pillow* was released, catapulting Grace Slick and the Jefferson Airplane to fame and fortune. It was a worldwide hit, going gold on the *Billboard* chart, peaking at number 3.

"It changes your life," said Marty Balin. "You can't walk down the street. We couldn't leave our homes. They thought we were gods or something."[5]

After an East Coast promotional tour, the band went on a three-week hiatus in March when Grace had surgery on her vocal chords. Then Bill Graham sent them off for another round of shows to promote the album.

To cope with all the extra work managing Jefferson Airplane, Bill Graham hired a young woman named Marushka Greene as his new secretary. Her husband had taken the cover photograph for *Surrealistic Pillow*.

Graham also brokered a deal with Levi Strauss & Co. for the band to create a series of radio advertisements. They recorded four in the studio, including one written by Grace, somehow linking Levi's jeans to whiskey and cactus. But the band soon pulled out of the deal when radical activist Abbie Hoffman accused them of selling out.

That spring, as he prepared to take Jefferson Airplane on a short publicity tour, Graham asked Jim Haynie to look after his girlfriend, Bonnie, while he was away.

For the last several years, Bonnie and Jim had worked closely together in the cramped upstairs office at the Fillmore. They had long been attracted to each other, and after work one night they went back to Bill's apartment in the Richmond District.

"We had a one nighter," said Haynie, "and it was sweet and wonderful."[6]

A couple of days later, they were both at the airport to meet Bill Graham off his New York flight.

"He sensed something right away," said Haynie. "His antennae were up."

Graham then called them into his office for a meeting.

"And he said just one thing," recalled Haynie. "'Don't let this happen again, but the main thing is do you love her?' And I said, 'Yeah, I do.' He said, 'That's all I require. It's between Bonnie and me now.'"

After the meeting, Jim Haynie asked Bonnie to leave Bill and move in with him, but she declined, as she wanted to stay in the relationship.

"It was an issue [with Bill] for a while and we discussed it," said Bonnie. "He wasn't happy about it, but after all he let it happen."[7]

After he had cooled down, Bill Graham asked Bonnie to marry him, but she refused to commit herself.

"Well he begged and begged," said Bonnie, "because I wasn't sure I wanted to marry him. We'd been living together for quite a while, but he was always leaving me alone. So I took my time."[8]

— ◁▷ —

After their close call with the Mountain View police, Carlos Santana and Gregg Rolie started to put a band together with rhythm guitarist Tom Fraser and the bassist and drummer from Carlos's old band The Dynamics. Carlos also recruited a young conga player he had met at a jam session, Michael Carabello. They called themselves The Santana Blues Band.

They began rehearsing in a garage on Potrero Hill, with Rolie hitching up to the city for rehearsals. They started playing weekend gigs at the Matrix Club in San Francisco and the Ark across the bridge in Sausalito.

A few weeks earlier, the Fillmore Auditorium had started holding weekly auditions for new talent every Sunday afternoon. And Stan Marcum, now acting as their manager, called Fillmore Auditorium manager Jim Haynie for an audition spot for the Santana Blues Band.

"Bill Graham had given me the job of finding new talent," recalled Haynie. "I said, 'Well you can be on the Sunday show.' They were a high school band basically."[9]

On a Sunday afternoon in late January, The Santana Blues Band set up their equipment on the Fillmore stage and played.

"We were playing songs like 'Mary Ann' by Ray Charles and 'Misty' and 'Taste of Honey,'" said Santana, "only with Latin percussion."[10]

Bill Graham, who was in the audience along with some mothers and their children, who had each paid a dollar to get in, was impressed by Carlos Santana's distinctive guitar style and the band's Latin sound. When they came offstage he congratulated them, saying he wanted to book them at the Fillmore. He then started using them as a fill-in band for acts that didn't show.

"They sounded great," said Haynie. "They were my first major find."

One day while Carlos Santana was washing dishes at the Tic-Toc Diner, the Grateful Dead pulled up outside in two limousines.

"I had my apron on," Carlos recalled, "full of hamburger pattie, peeling potatoes and shit. My shoes were funky from cleaning floors with hot water and bleach."

Jerry Garcia walked in with the other members of the band, and they sat at the counter and ordered burgers and french fries.

"I never talked to the Dead that day," Carlos said. "I just looked at them. But something in me just said, 'Man, you can do . . . what they do.' I walked up to the owner of the Tic-Toc and said, 'Man, I quit. I'm outta here.'"

Grace Slick moved in with Jefferson Airplane drummer Spencer Dryden, although they were both married to other people. They'd first hooked up in a New York motel during a short East Coast promotional tour for *Surrealistic Pillow*. Both hard drinkers, they viewed themselves as "outsiders," as the rest of the band preferred pot and acid.

The two massive hits Grace had given Jefferson Airplane had changed the whole dynamic of the group. Founder and leader Marty Balin now found himself overshadowed by Spencer Dryden, who used Grace's growing influence to try to control the band.

"Whoever slept with Grace had the power in the band," Balin later said.[11]

At the end of May, when Jefferson Airplane returned to Los Angeles to begin recording *After Bathing at Baxter's*, Balin found himself virtually shut out. Although he'd written some of the most memorable songs on *Surrealistic Pillow*, "Come Up The Years" and "Today," his sole composition on *Baxter's* was "Young Girl Sunday Blues," cowritten with Paul Kantner.

During the recording of their new album, the band moved into a $5,000-a-month luxury mansion in the Hollywood Hills, with their record company RCA Victor footing the bill. Meanwhile, sales of *Surrealistic Pillow* had now hit about one million, giving the band huge leverage. Bill Graham sent Jim Haynie to Los Angeles to keep an eye on things and report back.

"He was pretty busy with the Fillmore," explained Haynie. "The guys in the band were staying in a big house in Hollywood up on the hill and they worked on the album at night."

During the day the band and their entourage hung around the large pool and skinny-dipped, getting stoned and socializing with the band's new Hollywood friends, Rip Torn and his wife, Geraldine Page.

"I was running around butt naked," recalled Haynie, who joined in the fun. "Grace was a Scorpio. She was very into her position on things. And she was sassy."[12]

Jorma Kaukonen's marriage to his Swedish wife, Margaretta, was tempestuous, and the two were constantly fighting about his cheating on the road. He wrote "The Last Wall of the Castle" on the *Baxter's* album about his marital problems.

"Jorma was fucking around on the road," said Bill Thompson. "He used to stay with a woman and give her a guitar and the band paid for all [of them]. There's probably five hundred women about now that have a guitar."[13]

On one occasion when the lead guitarist saw strangers in the pool, he took out his pellet pistol and began shooting at the water. Things were no less crazy inside the studio, where Kaukonen liked to ride his powerful motorcycle. The band also installed a tank of nitrous oxide for their communal amusement. The cost of studio time went into the stratosphere, as some band members insisted on jetting in every day from San Francisco, causing many delays.[14]

<hr />

In early 1967, Janis Joplin—who had been living in Lagunitas—moved back to San Francisco, renting an apartment in the Haight-Ashbury district. All the recent publicity about the new music scene and youth revolution in the city had drawn thousands of runaways to the Haight. LSD was everywhere, and the streets were a carnival of color as the idealistic young people swirled around the streets.

Janis soon became a familiar sight in Haight-Ashbury, walking her collie, George, down Haight Street or driving around in her Sunbeam convertible. Big Brother and the Holding Company now played regularly at the Avalon as well as performing free shows around San Francisco.[15]

Janis was now having a great time. Just six months after being voted the University of Texas's "Ugliest Man on Campus," she became a pinup girl after posing nude for photographer Bob Seidemann. The sexy shot, with just a string of beads hanging over Janis's breasts, soon became a best-selling poster.

Janis and Grace now lived about a block away on Washington Street, and they saw much of each other. One day photographer Jim Marshall photographed them together for a *Teen Set* magazine feature called "Two Queen Bees of San Francisco."

"That morning I went over to Grace's house and then had to leave and pick up Janis," Marshall wrote in his book *Not Fade Away*. "Janis wasn't in the mood to do any pictures that day, but I begged her and she came along. Everyone always thought there was a huge rivalry between Janis and Grace, but they were dear friends. This is the only time they were ever photographed together. And, by the end of the session, we were all getting pretty silly and clowning around."

"They were like fire and ice," said Big Brother guitarist Sam Andrew. "Grace came from the upper middle class and was a model; Janis actually [did] too but she more or less disowned it. She went into the lower part of society, if you will. She sang their songs. Janis had this famous phrase about country club chicks coming in their pantie girdles, so they can barely move in their seat. And in a way that's who Grace was. I never got a sincere feeling about her music-making."[16]

Most days, Janis rehearsed in a dingy warehouse with Big Brother and the Holding Company, playing around the city at weekends. Their new manager, Julius Karpen, hired Barbra Streisand's singing coach, Judy Davis, to work on Janis's singing. At her first lesson, Davis told Janis she had the "worst voice she had ever heard," reducing her to tears.

Soon after moving to Haight-Ashbury, Janis hooked up with Country Joe MacDonald after they shared a bill at the Avalon.

"We wound up dancing together," wrote Country Joe in his blog. "We were just caught up in flirting and being attracted to each other. That night I went home with her to the flat she shared in the Haight."

For the next three months, they carried on a passionate affair. They would stay up late drinking herbal tea and listening to the *Larry Miller Show* on KMPX Radio, calling in to request a song from Country Joe's new EP.

When Janis got a new apartment in Lyon Street in the Haight, Country Joe moved in.

"We took those posters of her nude and put them up . . . all over one wall," he recalled. "It was my idea."

That spring, Dorothy Joplin came to visit and Janis couldn't wait to show her mother her new life.

"She was so proud of that," said Country Joe. "She wanted to make chow mein."

One day while Janis and Country Joe were making love in a sauna, her hand suddenly became paralyzed.

"It started to freak me out," he recalled. "She said not to worry about it."

Janis explained that she'd had this paralysis since her days as a speed freak, but it was only temporary.

"A few minutes later she got back movement in the hand," he said. "I did not share . . . her life with speed and heroin." [17]

Their brief affair was very tempestuous, as they were also sleeping with other people. One night they were sitting by their apartment window while screaming at each other.

"And people would walk by and tap at the window," said Fish keyboard player David Bennett Cohen, asking, "'Hey. How are you doing? Where are you playing?'"

When they broke up, Janis asked Joe to write a song about her.

"So Joe wrote this song called 'Janis,' which is on our second record," said Cohen. "He actually wrote it for Big Brother and the Holding Company to do, but they didn't know what to do with it and we did it really nicely." [18]

Their affair finally ended after Country Joe failed to arrive for a meal Janis had cooked for him. According to Peggy Caserta, who would eventually become her lover, Janis burst into tears and ran down Haight Street, screaming, "Joe stood me up!" [19]

Fish bass player Bruce Barthol fondly remembers the time the band spent with Janis.

"She was very friendly and a very warm person," he said, "but Janis was into hard drugs and Joe bailed on the relationship." [20]

Jerry Garcia first saw Carlos Santana play in Golden Gate Park.

"They were called the Santana Blues Band," Garcia recalled. "I watched them and listened to them play and [thought] this kid is really good. He's got a great feel and I knew right away he was going to be happening."[21]

True to his word, Bill Graham had booked the Santana Blues Band to open for the Steve Miller Band and Howlin' Wolf. But in early April, everything was put on hold after Carlos was hospitalized with tuberculosis.

For the next three months he lay in a TB ward at Mission General Hospital, watching people die. Fortunately, the doctors soon had it under control by giving him massive amounts of streptomycin.

"They shot me so full of holes in my butt," he said, "that I couldn't sit for a week."

While he was in the hospital, the authorities arranged for a private tutor, and Carlos graduated while hospitalized. Other friends would come in with various drugs to cheer him up.

"They'd bring me a couple of joints and LSD," Santana told *Rolling Stone*. "And I'm taking LSD like a dummy."

On one acid trip he started watching *The Four Horsemen of the Apocalypse* on television and freaked out.

"I'm inside the bed with my sheets over my head, going, 'Oh, shit.'"

Eventually Carlos became so fed up with the hospital he had a friend bring him in some clothes and discharged himself. [22]

In spring of 1967 Jefferson Airplane went out on the road, earning up to $15,000 ($105,000) a night. Bill Graham had organized a booking agent for them so he wouldn't run into the same legal problems as Matthew Katz had.

There was a huge demand for the band, who reveled in its new success. It soon turned into one long drug party, with Paul Kantner and Marty Balin throwing handfuls of Owsley's Orange Sunshine acid into the audience at shows.

"I was almost always [tripping]," said Kantner, "as was the audience. So it sort of blended in and meshed it inside."[23]

The band also delighted in spiking backstage drinks and food with LSD, and they had an ongoing competition with the Grateful Dead to be the first to dose Bill Graham.

"They were always trying to get Bill to do acid," said Bonnie MacLean, "but I don't know that they succeeded. He wasn't taking drugs at all in those days. That came later."[24]

Being the adult and trying to bring some order into Jefferson Airplane was a constant uphill battle for Graham. He now went behind their backs, secretly corresponding with their parents, hoping they would exert some influence on the unruly band.

On June 2, 1967, on the eve of "White Rabbit" being released as a single, Graham wrote to Jorma Kaukonen's mother, Beatrice, care of the the American Embassy in Stockholm, where his father worked for the US State Department. The letter was written on the band's official notepaper, which carried the header "Jefferson Airplane Loves You."

> *Dear Mrs. Kaukonen:*
>
> *Sorry to have taken so long in answering your note of May 20— as always things are frantic in a nice way. The group is on "American Bandstand" June 3 and will be on the "Smothers Brothers Show" again June 5. We are releasing White Rabbit as a single June 7. If all goes well, we should have an album ready in early August along with two or three singles—Things are going nicely.*
>
> *If all goes as planned, I hope to get the group to Europe in mid-August for at least four to six weeks stay. My main concern now is to get some more records done so that when we are away we are still here record-wise.*
>
> *Jorma is playing extremely well and in a sense has somewhat taken over the musical leadership of the group. I only wish he had done it months ago.*
>
> *Hope all is well with you and Mr. Kaukonen; hope to see you while you are here.*
>
> *Best*
> *Bill Graham*

The following day, a national television audience saw Jefferson Airplane lip-sync "White Rabbit" on Dick Clark's *American Bandstand*. On its release, "White Rabbit" would become the band's second *Billboard* top-ten hit.

After Dick Clark had Grace introduce the band, he asked her about all this new music coming out of San Francisco.

"I think part of it is the promoters gave us the freedom to write our own material," replied Grace.

"Let me skip along," Clark continued. "Older people worry. They see the way you're dressed and they hear your music. They don't understand it. Do parents have anything to worry about?"

"I think so," replied Paul Kantner. "Their children are doing things that they didn't do and they don't understand it."

Then America's oldest teenager asked Jorma Kaukonen what was going to happen in San Francisco this summer.

"I couldn't even begin to tell you in about an hour," he said, "but there's going to be a lot of people there."

———

On Sunday, June 11, 1967, Bill Graham married Bonnie MacLean at their home on Sacramento Street, San Francisco. Bonnie's cigar-smoking mother flew in for the ceremony, which was officiated at by a Unitarian minister. A mambo band played at the wedding reception, performing Bill Graham's favorite Latin music.

"Bill was dancing," recalled Bill Thompson. "He liked Latin dancing and he was a good dancer, too."

Graham was too busy for a honeymoon, so he took his new bride to the Monterey Pop Festival the following week, where Jefferson Airplane was headlining.[25]

CHAPTER ELEVEN

Monterey

On May 13, 1967, a catchy song called "San Francisco (Be Sure to Wear Flowers in Your Hair)" was released. Written by John Phillips of the Mamas and the Papas and sung by his friend Scott McKenzie, it became a huge international hit and the unofficial anthem of The Summer of Love.

It was written to promote the Monterey Pop Festival, an event that Phillips and record producer Lou Adler were organizing to exploit the booming San Francisco music scene. The festival was to be held at the small coastal town of Monterey, 120 miles south of San Francisco. The film rights had already been sold to the ABC network for $600,000 when the organizers approached the leading San Francisco bands about playing. But the San Francisco musicians were wary, suspecting the slick LA music establishment of exploitation.

"There was a definite rivalry and antagonism between the L.A. and San Francisco camps," wrote John Phillips in his autobiography, *Papa John*. "We had trouble even getting them to talk to us."

Former Beatles PR man Derek Taylor was hired as festival publicist and goodwill ambassador, traveling to the Fillmore Auditorium for a meeting with the San Francisco musical community.

"The conscience of the movement was seen to be in San Francisco," explained Taylor. "Bill Graham, Chet Helms, Ralph Gleason, and the Grateful Dead all had to be convinced that we were not charlatans. Bill was extremely hospitable when we met in his upstairs office at the Fillmore. He kept quite a salon and I was very impressed."[1]

Bill Graham thought the festival was such a great idea that he secretly invested $10,000 in it, agreeing to act as a go-between for the LA organizers and the local music community. He wasn't the only one with great expectations for Monterey. Representatives from every major record company, including Columbia Records president Clive Davis, flew to the West Coast with blank checks to sign up the new San Francisco bands. Bob Dylan's manager, Albert Grossman, also came to Monterey, to see his band The Paupers play and to find new acts to sign.

"The real action of Monterey took place backstage, in the makeshift green rooms and private bar areas where record companies made their deals," wrote Marc Eliot in his book *Rockonomics*.

The three-day festival, which drew ninety thousand fans, soon turned into a cattle auction for the major record companies desperate to sign up as many new San Francisco bands as they could. Monterey was officially a charity event, with the bands getting traveling expenses only. And there was immediate trouble when the San Francisco bands were handed a release to sign that gave the filmmaker D. A. Pennebaker worldwide rights to the festival concert special. It was only after much arguing that the bands signed, with the exception of the Grateful Dead and Big Brother and the Holding Company.

On Saturday afternoon, Janis Joplin and Big Brother played a historic show-stopping set that made her a star. Wearing a silver knit pantsuit, she mesmerized the audience for the five-song performance, climaxing with a devastating rendition of "Ball and Chain."

"I was knocked out by Janis Joplin, who wasn't known on the East Coast," said music critic Robert Christgau, who was reporting for *Esquire* magazine. "A fantastic stage presence. Her left nipple erect under her knit pantsuit, looking hard enough to put out your eye, she rocked and stomped and threatened any moment to break the microphone or swallow it." [2]

As Janis left the stage to tumultuous applause, Clive Davis rushed over and offered Big Brother a major contract with Columbia.

"Her performance was incendiary," wrote Davis in his 2013 autobiography, *The Soundtrack of My Life*. "I experienced a personal epiphany . . . I've got to sign this band." [3]

But he was stunned when Janis told him that Big Brother had already signed with the indie label Mainstream Records for a meager $100 the previous year. When Davis told Albert Grossman about his dilemma soon afterward, he promised to help.

Grossman also wanted to sign Big Brother, moving in after discovering that their manager, Julius Karpen, had not allowed Big Brother's set to be filmed. Grossman knew that if Janis's astonishing performance ever made it to network television, it would be a sensation. So he took Janis aside and offered to make her and Big Brother into stars if they let him represent them. After Grossman found loopholes in the Mainstream record contract, the band agreed to overrule Karpen and perform again the following night, so they could be filmed.

"We needed [Albert's] advice," said Sam Andrew. "And he was a lot of help and matter-of-fact and not excitable. He really supported us, so we started talking to him about managing us." [4]

Albert Grossman was now on a roll, also signing up Steve Miller and Quicksilver Messenger Service. He then agreed to buy out Big Brother's old Mainstream contract for $100,000, demanding Davis pay him a $100,000 advance for recording rights to Big Brother, Steve Miller, Quicksilver, and Electric Flag.

While Davis and Grossman were negotiating, Capitol Records slyly bought up record rights to Quicksilver and Steve Miller for six figures apiece, acing out Grossman.

After Janis Joplin's second incendiary performance on Sunday night—which was filmed—Grossman doubled Big Brother's price to $200,000, and Clive Davis accepted.

"We sat on the stage after Monterey and I remember our feet were hanging over the edge," said filmmaker D. A. Pennebaker. "[Janis] seemed very excitable. She was still coming down and she poured out some Southern Comfort. And I thought . . . nothing better was ever going to happen to her."

~⌒~

After Janis and Big Brother played, newlyweds Bill and Bonnie Graham watched from the side of the stage as Jerry Garcia introduced Jefferson Airplane as "a perfect example of what the world is coming to."

"Monterey Pop was absolutely perfect," recalled Grace Slick. "The weather, the way it was arranged. And you could actually get to a bathroom within about four minutes. Even the cops were good. So that was the best of any of the festivals I played."[5]

Backstage that night, a Texan dealer introduced Paul Kantner to cocaine, which would become the new drug of choice for many of the band members.

On Sunday night the Airplane watched Jimi Hendrix play for the first time. Just before Hendrix took the stage, Jack Casady gave him two strong hits of Owsley acid.

"That's when he started fucking his guitar," said Bill Thompson.[6]

Grace Slick and Janis Joplin were backstage together watching in amazement, as Hendrix set his guitar alight during "Voodoo Chile."

"We'd never seen anybody set fire to a guitar before," said Grace. "And we were just appalled by this guy. He was just amazing."[7]

━━━

Back in San Francisco later that night, the Santana Blues Band was booked to open for The Who at the Fillmore. It was the big break they had been looking for.

"And we were late," said Carlos Santana. "Bill Graham was screaming at me and he asked me what kind of fuckin' band we had, 'cause these other cats were late, just blowing it, putting cologne on themselves and all that shit."

Carlos then fired everyone in the band except for Gregg Rolie, and Stan Marcum started recruiting new musicians. He found bassist David Brown, who had toured with the Four Tops, playing in a small club in North Beach and invited him to join. Then he discovered a conga player named Marcus Malone, who had been born in Memphis. To complete the group he found drummer Bob "Doc" Livingston.

"The band didn't embrace the Latin thing until Gregg Rolie and I started hanging out with Marcus Malone," said Carlos. "Marcus was a street mutt, just like Santana's music."[8]

━━━

The week after Monterey, Jefferson Airplane headlined a week of shows at the Fillmore Auditorium, with the Jimi Hendrix Experience opening. To capitalize on the Summer of Love, the Fillmore Auditorium would now be open six nights a week.

In July, Jim Haynie quit to become road manager for the Butterfield Blues Band. Bill Graham had never treated him the same after his brief affair with Bonnie, and he was relieved to go.

"I think Bill held a grudge," explained Haynie. "I was never properly paid and when I asked for a raise he would say, 'Not right now. Business is kind of tailing off.' Bullshit."[9]

In his place Graham hired a straight businessman named Paul Baratta, who knew little about the new rock music.

That summer, as Jefferson Airplane became stars, their relationship with Bill Graham was disintegrating. Although he disapproved of the band's hedonistic lifestyle, he could do little about it. But when *Time* magazine profiled the band in June, Graham was furious when Grace and the other band members urged young Americans to take LSD and make love on it.

"The stage is our bed," Marty Balin was quoted as saying, "and the audience is our broad. We're not entertaining, we're making love."

Grace Slick, described as "a striking former model who gives the Airplane go-power with her big, belting blues voice," explained how "White Rabbit" was "aimed at the twelve-year-old junkies."

"It doesn't matter what the lyrics say, or who sings them," she said. "They're all the same. They say, 'Be Free—free in love—free in sex.'"

In mid-July, on the eve of the band's first major US tour, their frustrated manager wrote another letter to Jorma Kaukonen's mother, complaining about her son's behavior.

> *Dear Mrs. Kaukonen:*
>
> *Sorry to be so late in answering your note of July 1. As always, life with the Airplane is hectic.*
>
> *The album is doing well over here—it's 4 or 5 on all the charts. We released White Rabbit four weeks ago and it is already #12. Presently working on next album—sorry to have to tell you problems are setting*

in. Don't want you to mention this to your son, of course, but the "ego egg" is hatching. The group in general is getting just a bit too demanding in their general demands of society; but more on that when I see you.

Also sending copies of recent publication and photo of your son that I thought you might like to have.

Best to you and yours.

Sincerely, Bill Graham.[10]

In late July, Bill Graham took the Summer of Love on the road. He staged a week of shows at the O'Keefe Centre in Toronto, starring the Jefferson Airplane and the Grateful Dead. It was designed to re-create the Fillmore experience in different cities across America, becoming the blueprint for the Fillmore East a few months later.

To make it happen, Graham hired a small New York–based company called Sensefex, run by a group of ex–drama students. Their only previous concert experience had been staging disco dances with strobes and flashing lights (a few years in anticipation of the disco craze that took over America). As soon as Sensefex lighting director Joshua White and his partners, John Morris and Kip Cohen, arrived in Toronto to start work, they were briefed by Bill Graham.

"Bill was the most insane human being I had ever met in my life," remembered Morris. "The first thing I remember is his face, which is not the most beautiful thing in the world. But the strength and passion of that face."[11]

For the next forty-eight hours, White and Graham discussed transforming the O'Keefe Centre, with its seats, balcony, and a stage, into a replica of the far smaller and more intimate Fillmore Auditorium.

"Although we were total opposites," said Joshua White, "we understood each other instantly. Our love of the theater was the basis of our relationship in the beginning."[12]

To publicize the O'Keefe shows, Graham helped John Morris organize a free concert in Toronto for the Jefferson Airplane and the Grateful Dead, drawing 52,000 people.

The opening night at the O'Keefe Centre was a triumph, with 2,400 people dancing in the aisles.

"The legend of Haight-Ashbury, San Francisco, is part of the appeal of the Airplane," wrote Barrie Hale in the Toronto *Telegram*. "The Airplane come onstage to the sound of a piston-driven plane in full snarl giving way to the high wail of a jet. There is Grace Slick, the lady Airplane, dark hair, fierce voice, beautiful smile. And from sticks burning on Grace's piano, the smell of incense fills the air."[13]

After the week of Toronto shows, the Sensefex team decided to leave disco behind forever and move on to staging rock'n'roll shows.

"I was just sucked in," said White. "I was sucked into the music of the Airplane and the Dead. I was sucked into the light show. I looked at it and said, this is good but I could do this better. And all the people who were part of my disco company felt the same way."[14]

After the final show, Bill Graham asked John Morris to move to San Francisco and restructure the business side of the Fillmore Auditorium. Morris agreed and spent a few weeks living with Bill and Bonnie Graham in their new Washington Street house, unraveling the tangled Fillmore finances.

"There was no organization," said Morris. "He was running it with cash out of his desk. It was pass them in, pass them out. It wasn't done that way to bury tons of cash. It was done because that was the way it was done."

Morris then helped Graham start a corporation to run the Fillmore Auditorium and his other business interests. He also became one of Graham's closest friends and trusted associates.

One night they were walking home after a show, with Graham carrying that night's box office takings in a plain brown paper bag that he called his "Polish briefcase." Suddenly a man leapt out of the shadows brandishing a gun and demanded the money.

"Bill just told him, 'Fuck you, get outta here,'" remembered Morris. "Wouldn't even give the guy a quarter. The guy was stoned and he just turned tail and ran."

After eating breakfast at Zims diner, it was about three in the morning when they returned to Graham's house and went to sleep. About an hour later, a naked Bill Graham burst into Morris's bedroom, screaming that he'd left all the money back in the diner.

"We got dressed at 900 mph, hopped in the car and drove to Zims," said Morris. "The same waitress was there and she pulls the bag out from behind the counter. She had no clue that there was about $60,000 in that bag. Bill was so relieved he pulled out a $100 bill and gave it to her."[15]

—⁓—

After John Morris finished putting the Fillmore organization onto a business footing, Bill Graham asked him to become Jefferson Airplane's tour manager. He was put in charge of the band's first national tour, as a buffer between Graham and the band.

"Jefferson Airplane's whole thing was, 'Yeah, let's stay loose and stoned and high and have a great old time,'" said Morris. "But somebody's got to watch out for the business. 'Oh, Bill will do it.'" But when Bill started saying, 'Oh you're screwing up, you're doing this,' they didn't want to listen. That would frustrate the hell out of Bill."

In Cincinnati, Grace Slick walked off stage at the end of the set, refusing to sing her current top-ten hit "White Rabbit" for an encore.

"She said, 'I'm not singing it,'" recalled John Morris. "'I've done it five thousand times and I'm not doing it again.'"

So Morris opened the dressing-room door to the stage and told Grace to listen to the audience screaming for "White Rabbit."

"And she said, 'Okay, I'll do it,'" said Morris. "I said, 'Good, because it's the only way we're getting out of here alive.' So she went out and sang it one more time."[16]

At another show, a drunken Grace suddenly turned on the audience, screaming obscenities.

"[Grace] was one of the most interesting, attractive and wonderful people you could ever be around," said Morris. "She was also as crazy as a hoot owl when she wanted to be."[17]

—⁓—

While John Morris was chaperoning Jefferson Airplane around America, Bill Graham flew to London to sign up new English bands for the Fillmore. He soon realized that there was a goldmine of talent across the Atlantic waiting to be discovered by American audiences.

"That was the first time I went over to England," he said. "I caught the Cream and then agents would start to send me tapes and records. And there were other people who were extremely helpful [like] Pete Townshend."[18]

While Graham was in London he visited the UFO Club, where he saw a new act called The Crazy World of Arthur Brown, and loved them.

"Bill was doing a band-finding mission," said Arthur Brown in 2013. "He saw us and he loved all the drama and theatrics. A few months later he brought us to America."[19]

At the end of August, Graham flew Cream to San Francisco for two weeks of shows at the Fillmore Auditorium. He paid the English supergroup—comprising Eric Clapton, Jack Bruce, and Ginger Baker—just $500 a night. And on the opening Saturday night he packed in more than 3,500 people—more than three times the Fillmore's legal fire limit.

Jefferson Airplane flew in for the Cream show by private plane after their own show in Bakersfield, California. And when the pilot ordered Paul Kantner to put out a joint during the flight, the guitarist opened the plane's door and threw it out.

The Cream's run of six shows was a huge success, grossing Bill Graham more than $80,000 as well as another $60,000 from concessions—almost $1 million in current purchasing power.

After the final show, Bill Graham benevolently presented each member of the group with an engraved Rolex pocket watch.

"It meant so much to Eric, Ginger and Jack," said Chris Brooks, who was the Fillmore publicist, "because nobody had ever done anything like that for them before."[20]

In fact, Graham brought the knockoff watches from Japan in bulk.

"They were plentiful and they were given out," said Chip Monck, who would later work closely with Graham. "He was very gracious." [21]

CHAPTER TWELVE

Hiring and Firing

After the Monterey Pop Festival, Janis Joplin's relationship with Big Brother and the Holding Company would never be the same. Journalists were only interested in talking to Janis, as if the other band members didn't exist. And they soon started resenting it.

"Monterey was really the beginning that separated Janis from the band," said drummer David Getz. "It made her a star. It made her a diva, an icon."

In November 1967, Big Brother finally fired Julius Karpen and looked for a new manager. They initially approached Bill Graham, who was now courting Janis to start playing the Fillmore as often as possible after her Monterey breakthrough.

"Janis had actually asked Graham to manager them," recalled John Morris. "[We] were together in the Pan Am building in New York, when he phoned her back and sent her to Albert Grossman."[1]

After Janis called Grossman in New York, he took the first plane out to San Francisco, meeting Big Brother in Peter Albin's apartment. Grossman offered to manage the band in return for 20 percent of their profits, as well as his expenses. Then he asked how much money they wanted to make next year. Big Brother had earned around $25,000 that year, so David Getz said he would like to triple that to $75,000.

Grossman guaranteed they would earn at least $75,000, if not more, promising to tear up the contract if they did not. After agreeing to terms, the portly, gray-haired manager said there was just one proviso to his managing them. He explained that his first wife had died of a heroin overdose, saying he refused to deal with anybody who took it.

"He called it 'schmack,'" recalled Albin. "He said, 'You guys don't do that?' I can still see everybody crossing their fingers behind their backs, saying, 'Oh, no.'"[2]

⁓

While Jefferson Airplane toured America, Bill Graham kept adding extra dates to keep up with the high demand. Finally, there was a show-down in a hotel room when Graham wanted them to play new shows toward the end of the tour, and the band just wanted to go home. At the meeting Spencer Dryden lashed into him, saying his brain was made of money.

"I'll never forget what you just said, Mister," came Graham's angry reply as he stared the drummer straight in the eye.

Grace Slick and Spencer Dryden both disliked Bill Graham, who was constantly on their case for drinking too much.

"He was not [Grace's] idea of a manager," said Bill Thompson. "He was tough, a strict guy who wanted them to work, work, work. He wanted them to tour, which they really didn't want to do."[3]

There were other issues, too. When Graham wanted to release Grace's rousing new song "Two Heads" as the next single, she vetoed it, saying she didn't want everyone to think she was band leader.[4] Instead, they released "The Ballad of You and Me and Pooneil," which only reached number 42 on the charts.

When Bill Graham demanded the band sign a formal management deal with him, they refused. He then arrived at a band meeting at the Landmark Hotel in Hollywood with a pile of contracts for them to sign. Jorma Kaukonen stormed out first, saying he was hungry, followed by the others.

"Bill was a great businessman," said Kaukonen, "but one of the strengths and weaknesses of the Jefferson Airplane was that we don't like to be told what to do."[5]

On October 20, the band was in New York to play Hunter College. The afternoon of the show, Grace Slick asked John Morris to take her to the Upper East Side to see Finch College, where she had studied a decade earlier.

"So we went," said Morris, "and we wandered around and somebody finally recognized her. So she signed some autographs and we went on our way."

Then they went shopping and Grace bought a couple of expensive Pucci gowns.

"She looked fabulous," Morris recalled. "When she showed up to play that night in fatigues, I said, 'What the hell are you doing?' and threw her back in the limousine and made her go change." [6]

That night, Jefferson Airplane was playing two shows, and the band held a press conference before the first.

"Miss Slick calmly pulled what appeared to be a chrome-plated hand grenade from a lunch box and lit her cigarette from it," reported John Kifner in next morning's *New York Times*. "Elder, non-McLuhanesque reporters with hang-ups about linear thought appeared baffled." [7]

After playing the first show, the band returned to the dressing room and refused to play an encore.

"Bill came [in] and said, 'Do an encore! Do an encore!'" recalled Bill Thompson. "And Grace said, 'We don't do encores.' And he started to go nuts at the band. 'Who do you think you are?'"

Then Thompson took Graham to one side, warning him to cool it, or they might refuse to play the second show that night.

"I said, 'Bill, they're playing New York City,'" said Thompson. "'I wouldn't bum them out and make them feel bad.'" [8]

Despite the absence of an encore, Kifner wrote an ecstatic review of the show, headlined: "Jefferson Airplane Electrifies Hunter Audience."

"Miss Slick," he wrote, "a tiny former model who is reputed to have once been a student at Finch College for young ladies, can lean easily against a mike stand and belt out the lyrics of 'Don't You Need Somebody to Love' over the assembled din like a cross between Dinah Washington and Mick Jagger."

***

Grace Slick and Spencer Dryden were furious when their manager refused to supply them with a bottle of Southern Comfort before each show, as they had demanded.

"Grace didn't like that the fact [Bill] wouldn't give them money for booze," said Bill Thompson. "She had brought in 'Somebody to Love' and 'White Rabbit,' which were two huge hits, so she called the shots."[9]

Bill Graham also alienated other members of the band when he refused to buy Jack Casady an amplifier he needed to get a new sound.

"Bill wouldn't hand over the bread," one anonymous band member told a reporter. "He didn't believe we needed it. You always have to prove things to Bill, fight to convince him of everything. It's a drag."[10]

On Sunday, December 3, Bill Graham and the Jefferson Airplane arrived an hour late for two shows at the Sheraton Park Ballroom after their equipment got lost in a snowstorm. Then Graham complained about the way a local disc jockey had been promoting the concert. After he refused to let the DJ announce the band, a "shouting match" ensued backstage.

"I can't stand the way disc jockeys come on," he told Mary Ann Seawell of the *Washington Post*, "'Hey there, kids, here's that way-out psychedelic group you've all been hearing so much about.' I just want a simple straightforward announcement."

Before the Airplane even took the stage, a small peace demonstration and an announcement of an upcoming protest against the Vietnam War were greeted by loud booing and hissing.

"Then Grace Slick," wrote Seawell, "showed her feelings about being in Washington by playing a markedly off-key version of 'The Star Spangled Banner.'"

On November 27, *After Bathing at Baxter's* was released. It had cost more than $80,000 ($560,000) to record, more than ten times as much as *Surrealistic Pillow*, and would sell a million fewer albums. After RCA Victor nixed the original album title *Good Shit*, the band settled on naming it after their code name for LSD—"Baxter."

When album sales failed to match those of *Surrealistic Pillow*, Bill Graham's I-told-you-so appeals for more commercial material for the next album fell on deaf ears.

Grace Slick was feeling anything but commercial. Her song "Rejoyce"—the last track on side one of *Baxter's*—is a homage to James Joyce's *Ulysses*.

"I was paraphrasing some of the stuff in *Ulysses*," she explained in 2012, "but it's said with such sarcasm and darkness. So I didn't write anything that you could say, 'Oh, isn't that beautiful.'"

On December 31, 1967, San Francisco's two biggest bands, Jefferson Airplane and Big Brother and the Holding Company, played the Winterland Ballroom. The New Year's show, billed as "The Fillmore Scene at Winterland," had tickets costing $6 for the far larger 5,400 capacity Winterland, which Graham now used for his bigger shows. That night, according to his official ledger, Graham sold 7,800 tickets to make $20,604 ($144,000), with an extra $165 ($1,500), from coat check.

"That was certainly a memorable gig for me," said John Cooke, who had just been appointed Big Brother's road manager by Albert Grossman. "I thought this is it. This is amazing. This is rock 'n' roll."

In the dressing room, Graham had laid out a long table filled with sandwiches, fresh fruit, and soft drinks.

"I'd never seen anyone treat the artist like that," said Cooke. "[Soon] bands began putting in their rider what kind of food and drink had to be provided backstage, but Bill, in my opinion, originated that."[11]

Janis Joplin had already played a sensational set with Big Brother when a diapered Jim Haynie made his second appearance as the New Year baby.

Then at the stroke of midnight, as hundreds of balloons were released into the audience, the sound of jet engines filled Winterland to announce the Jefferson Airplane.

"At 7:00 a.m. the music stopped a while," said Bill Graham, "and I served a catered breakfast for 4,000 people. See, I wanted to have it be gay and festive but still make a statement . . . that the main theme of the New Year should be peace."[12]

The first week of 1968, Jefferson Airplane was nominated for a Grammy Award for the Best New Artist of 1967. And *Rolling Stone* magazine publisher Jann Wenner gave *After Bathing at Baxter's* an excellent review, calling the Airplane "*the* best rock and roll band in America today."

But as their career soared upward, the band's relationship with Bill Graham deteriorated even further. Jack Casady and Jorma Kaukonen were furious when they discovered that their manager owned the Geary Temple—where they rehearsed—and then billed them rent. And there was significant opposition to Graham's booking them for as many shows as he could.

"He definitely wanted us to play out more," said Casady, "and there were certain elements within the Jefferson Airplane that didn't really want to do that. We wanted to make all our own decisions and move our career forward ourselves. We felt it was a little too much having a decision-maker as our manager."[13]

In mid-January 1968 at a band rehearsal, Grace Slick announced that she and Spencer Dryden had received an offer from another record company and were leaving unless Bill Graham was fired.

"It's either me or Bill Graham," she told the band. "If he remains the manager I'm quitting."

The other members of the band agreed. After all, Grace was not only *the* star of Jefferson Airplane but also of the entire San Francisco scene.

"And we really didn't have a choice," said Paul Kantner, "because he was threatening to take Grace away from us if we didn't fire Bill Graham."[14]

So Marty Balin and Bill Thompson were sent over to the Fillmore to give Graham his marching orders.

"And we told Bill, 'We have to fire you,'" said Thompson. "'You really have to go.'"

The next morning, Graham telephoned Thompson, who had now been appointed manager, and accused him of stabbing him in the back.

"He goes, 'Mister,'" recalled Thompson, "'You don't ever get a Jewish kid in the gutter.' I said, 'Bill, I'm a hippie living in the Haight.'"[15]

Kantner now regrets firing Bill Graham, calling it a big mistake.

"Our drummer got pissed off at him," said Kantner, "and he was along with Grace at the time. He drank too much and Bill complained about it and wanted him to back off a little. He threatened to leave if we didn't fire Bill Graham, so we gave into that unfortunately from my point of view. And I was never good friends with [Dryden] since."[16]

The next issue of *Rolling Stone* carried the front-page headline: "Airplane Flies!—Leaves Manager, Battles RCA." The article said that the Airplane, along with the Grateful Dead and Quicksilver Messenger Service, were now planning to handle its business affairs as a cooperative and were renegotiating their record contract with RCA Victor.

"The Jefferson Airplane have 'divorced' themselves from the personal management of Fillmore Auditorium manager Bill Graham," said the article. "We might get other management," Thompson was quoted as saying, "then again, the earth might split open."

A few days later, Jefferson Airplane announced a partnership with the Grateful Dead and Quicksilver Messenger Service to open a new San Francisco ballroom to compete with Bill Graham. Each band would own a 10 percent stake in the new venue they named The Carousel Ballroom, which was above a car dealership on the corner of Van Ness and Market Street.

"The Airplane and the Grateful Dead broke away from Bill Graham," explained Bill Thompson, "and said, 'We're going to do our own shows.' The coolest guy in the middle of it all . . . was Jerry Garcia. He'd say, 'Hey, it's us against them. We're empowered and we've got to stay together.'" [17]

The Carousel Ballroom opened on January 17, 1968, with a Grateful Dead show. Neither the Dead nor Jefferson Airplane would ever play the Fillmore Auditorium again.

PART TWO

THE MUSIC NEVER STOPPED

CHAPTER THIRTEEN

Birth of the Fillmore East

January to March, 1968

On Saturday, February 17, 1968, Janis Joplin made her much anticipated New York City debut at the Anderson Theater. A week earlier, she had flown in during a heavy snowstorm, checking into the Chelsea Hotel on West 23rd Street.

In the seven months since Monterey Pop, Janis's career had taken off, but Big Brother and the Holding Company was falling apart. The other members disliked all the attention now being lavished on Janis, accusing her of being on a "star trip" and using them as her backup band.

Things had gone downhill rapidly after signing the management contract with Albert Grossman.

"The first thing Albert told her was to get rid of Big Brother," said singer/songwriter Nick Gravenites, who was also managed by Grossman. "Instead of splitting the money five ways, he and Janis could work out the percentages between the two of them." [1]

Initially, Joplin resisted his demands out of loyalty, but Grossman kept up the pressure. He promised a $250,000 record deal if she went solo, saying Big Brother were amateurs and she needed more professional musicians.

At Christmas, Janis had found herself pregnant, with no clue who was the father. She spent the holidays back in Port Arthur, Texas, with her family and threw a party for old friends. Then she secretly drove to Mexico and had an abortion on January 19, her twenty-fifth birthday.

"The experience was gruesome," wrote her friend Myra Friedman in her book *Buried Alive*, "but the emotional trauma was far more severe. Her reaction was one of moral horror." [2]

Now a month later, Janis regretted her decision and was drinking heavily, feeling the pressures of the band's all-important New York opening.

In the days leading up to the two Saturday shows, Janis spent hours ensconced with Grossman at his smart Gramercy Park town house. The charming bon vivant, who resembled Ben Franklin with his round spectacles and long curly gray hair, spun her colorful tales of his days as a club owner on Chicago's tough North Side. He wined and dined her lavishly, impressing her with his knowledge of the finer things of life. But there was always an underlying message that she must cut Big Brother loose to become the rich superstar she had always dreamed of becoming.

Several days after they arrived, all the band members met in Grossman's corporate offices at 75 East 55th Street. During the meeting, Janis was asked what image *she* wished to project for marketing purposes. It was only then that the rest of Big Brother realized they played no part in their new manager's future plans.

"It was as if the band didn't exist," said David Getz. "He was only interested in Janis."

To prepare for the make-or-break Anderson Theater shows, Grossman had rented the band an East Village loft for daily rehearsals. But they rarely went, sidelined by all the distractions of the vibrant big city.

Janis, who loved antique clothes, hit the thrift stores of the West Village, hunting for old dresses, trinkets, and jewelry. Few then could have predicted that her unique gypsy style, encompassing thrown-together bangles, feathers, and colorful loose clothing, would still be imitated by cutting-edge fashionistas nearly half a century later. Meanwhile, the other band members bought heavy Afghan coats and fur hats to keep warm during the freezing temperatures.

"It was real cold," recalled Sam Andrew. "We'd go into these army surplus stores and find these old coats."[3]

The band made the Chelsea Hotel their headquarters for the next six weeks. It was favored by all the San Francisco bands, as they were free to smoke dope and play loud music all night.

"The Chelsea had a reputation for being lenient that way," explained Jack Casady. "It was also an artist's hotel and a musician's hotel, so when the word got around, 'Hey, where would you like to stay?' People like Janis, Jorma, and I would stay there."[4]

Jorma Kaukonen, who would later write a song about the hotel, "Third Week in the Chelsea," loved its mystique and history.

"That was our home base," he explained. "The Chelsea Hotel already had a history of artists and poets and writers. It was like we've got to stay there. And of course it was delightfully funky."[5]

Janis Joplin adored the Chelsea, decorating her room with a Persian rug and hanging her favorite retro jewelry from the mirrors. One night she ran into Canadian poet and singer Leonard Cohen in the hotel elevator. She took him back to her room for a blow job, which he later immortalized in his song "Chelsea Hotel #1."

Janis also frequented the El Quijote Restaurant next door, where she went on the prowl for attractive young men.

"She'd be downstairs in El Quijote just hanging out," said Peter Albin. "Her word for young guys that she wanted to make it with was 'coward.' 'Where's the young coward?' she'd ask. 'Well Janis, I don't know.'"

Each night, Big Brother and the Holding Company trooped out of the Chelsea Hotel onto West 23rd Street and hailed a Checker Cab in search of a good time. One night, Albert Grossman arranged a visit to Max's Kansas City to introduce Janis to the city's fashionable elite. Opened in December 1965 by lawyer Mickey Ruskin, the Park Avenue South club was then at the height of its decadent fame. Andy Warhol and his Superstars famously held court between midnight and dawn in its infamous backroom, a block away from The Factory. They would sit around a large round table bathed in red light, socializing with the likes of Mick Jagger, Salvador Dali, Allen Ginsberg, and Bob Dylan.

"Albert Grossman told me he was bringing this group in," said Ruskin. "I remember Janis certainly."

For his ingénue's dramatic entry, Grossman gave Ruskin a tape of Country Joe's song "Janis," along with instructions to play it as she walked in.

"Max's was packed," recalled Big Brother roadie Mark Richards. "We entered all in a line, having a great time. Everything stopped. Not a word was spoken as we walked the length of the bar, all the way to the backroom, and sat down at a big roundtable. Max's immediately became our New York home."[6]

Janis then joined Andy Warhol and singer Tim Buckley at the celebrated roundtable, where they were duly photographed by Elliott Landy.

Janis soon became a regular at Max's, with her own private booth, and she may well have been served by future Blondie singer Debbie Harry, who was waitressing there at the time.

"I remember her very, very well," said Max's manager, Robbin Cullinen. "She used to walk around Max's holding a bottle of Southern Comfort by the neck. She was always walking around talking to people at tables. I felt she was lonely."

On several occasions after Janis had had too much to drink, the manager had to step in.

"I used to drag her out of there when she was falling down drunk," he said. "I've put her into a cab more than once."[7]

Janis partied hard in New York, reveling in her new celebrity status. Big Brother's new road manager, John Cooke, the son of the legendary BBC broadcaster Alistair Cooke, introduced her to his old school friend Bobby Neuwirth and actor Michael J. Pollard and they became close. They took her to a tough Lower East Side bar on 6th Street, where her pool skills won her the title "Eight Ball Champion."[8]

That week, Janis also hung out at Steve Paul's The Scene nightclub on West 46th Street and Eighth Avenue. It was popular with rock musicians, who often showed up unannounced to jam on its tiny stage. It was around midnight on Wednesday night when Janis arrived at the dingy basement club to find Jimi Hendrix jamming onstage. Hendrix, who had just played three record-breaking nights at the Fillmore Auditorium, was trying out new material for his *Electric Ladyland* double album he would soon record.

Also there was Jim Morrison of The Doors, staggering around with a drink in his hand. During one long and intense blues jam, Morrison suddenly leapt onstage, grabbed the microphone, and began improvising some obscene lyrics. He then fell to his knees and embraced Hendrix's legs.

When a furious Hendrix kicked Morrison away, he crawled off the stage, upsetting a table of drinks over Janis's lap. She exploded and jumped on the stage screaming, "I wouldn't mind if he could sing!" before physically attacking him. Then security moved in to separate them.

Behind the scenes, Albert Grossman had been busy. Viewing Saturday night as Janis Joplin's New York coronation, he had personally invited all the city's leading rock journalists and key music business players to come and see her play.

The Big Brother show was being presented by John Morris and Joshua White, who had worked on Bill Graham's week of Toronto shows the previous year. After finishing up road managing the Jefferson Airplane tour, Morris had decided to stay in New York and try his hand at concert promotion.

He and White had rented the decrepit Anderson Theater on the Lower East Side for a series of shows, culminating with Big Brother and the Holding Company. But first they had to negotiate their way through the druggy, violent Lower East Side, along with its dubious power brokers.

In early 1968 the East Village was a war zone controlled by the Hells Angels from their Third Street clubhouse. The mean streets were dangerous, with muggings commonplace and murders very nearly so. Hippies lived alongside Ukrainians and Russians, with a smattering of disapproving older people who deplored the area's decline.

Morris and White were booking the Anderson through Tony Lech, a self-styled tough guy who owned a string of gay bars. Sporting curly red hair and glasses, he reportedly kept a loaded gun behind the bar.

"It was East Village '68 anarchy," explained Morris. "[The Anderson] was a really hairy operation and done on a shoestring."[9]

At that time all major New York rock concerts were held in the 5,000-seat Madison Square Garden, which had terrible acoustics. There were also two medium-sized venues on Second Avenue—the Anderson

Theater, which held 2,000, and the Village Theater, holding 2,645, which sporadically presented rock shows.

A rash of smaller clubs and venues also dotted the city. Howard Soloman's 375-seat Café Au Go Go on Bleecker Street had first introduced Jefferson Airplane and the Grateful Dead to New York, as well as presenting Jimi Hendrix, Cream, Joni Mitchell, and the Mothers of Invention when they were unknowns.

In July 1967, Jerry Brandt's Electric Circus had opened to great fanfare on St. Marks Place. The 740-seat club presented a slew of rock bands, including the Velvet Underground, the Grateful Dead, the Allman Brothers, and Sly and the Family Stone.

But the hottest rock club at that time was Steve Paul's The Scene, which attracted Manhattan's young jet-setters, Broadway dancers, motorcycle riders, and various rock stars, including Janis Joplin, who soon became a regular.

John Morris saw a huge void in the New York market for a regular concert venue like the Fillmore Auditorium. He decided to do something about it; he would persuade Bill Graham to come and open one.

"There were two reasons to get Bill to New York," he explained. "One, selfishly, working with Bill was just so exciting and it was so interesting. Secondly, Bill had a financial, monetary base that most rock 'n' roll [people] didn't have at that point.

"So I got on the phone and told him, 'Bill, you're out of your goddamned mind if you do not come [here]. Look you're a New York guy. You've *got* to do this. It's in your blood.'"[10]

After failing to make it in New York as an actor, Graham was reluctant to risk another disappointment. He also questioned the wisdom of moving east, as everything was going so well in San Francisco.

"Well he was a big fish in a small pond," explained Bonnie Graham. "It was easy for him in San Francisco, but he wouldn't be able to do that in New York."[11]

Morris cleverly played on Graham's enormous ego and gambling instincts, slowly wearing him down.

"It was a big scary city," said Kip Cohen. "[Bill] knew it well. He lived there. But it was anything but the lifestyle of San Francisco, and he really had to be convinced that it could work."[12]

Finally, Graham agreed to fly in for the Big Brother concert on a reconnaissance mission, with a view toward taking over the Anderson Theater and expanding his operations east.

———

Around one in the morning on Sunday, February 18, 1968, while Big Brother and the Holding Company prepared to take the stage for the second show, John Morris and Joshua White escorted Bill Graham backstage. They filed past Janis Joplin's dressing room, where she was being photographed for *Creem* magazine by Linda Eastman, who would marry Paul McCartney the following year. The first show had gone well, and Janis was now confidently preening and posing, swigging Southern Comfort in preparation for the second.

To lure Graham to New York, Morris and White had devised an elaborate stunt. During the interminably long set changes, a curtain of deep blue light would be projected straight onto the audience, to keep things flowing. Although these calming lights masked the frantic backstage set changes, the audience was perfectly visible from the stage.

They then led Bill Graham out on the stage as the roadies were setting up Janis and Big Brother's equipment.

"We raised the screen and threw down the lights," said White, "and Bill could see the house was packed to the rafters. He turned around and took a look at the house. As only a great promoter can do, he just went *brrrrm!* And he *counted* the house. From that point in his mind, he was convinced he could make a go of it. I was there. I saw the *click* in his eyes. I saw him realize this is *do-able*. Because here were these sleaze-buckets promoting Janis Joplin with two-thousand people in the house. So why wasn't *he* doing it?"[13]

———

That night Janis Joplin became a star. Despite the lack of rehearsals she was in top form, thrilling the sold-out audience with the powerful songs Big Brother would soon release on their chart-topping *Cheap Thrills* album.

Janis strutted out onstage and up to the microphone for the first show.

"Well, New York," she told the screaming audience, "we're finally here you know."

Then as David Getz counted her off, they launched into "Combination of the Two."

"And the place levitated," said Allan Arkush, a young New York University film student in the audience that night. "She was electrifying. It was every bit as exciting as we thought it would be."[14]

Janis wore a slinky low-cut, dark sleeveless dress and fishnet stockings, with a dozen different colored necklaces of love beads twisted around her long neck. Her raw vocals filled every inch of the Anderson Theater, as the swirling colors of Joshua White's light show pulsated behind her on a giant screen.

With her hair flying around wildly, Janis gripped the microphone hard for "Ball and Chain." The song seemed to come from the very depths of her soul. Her unearthly voice soared and dived through "Down on Me," and "Light Is Faster Than Sound." But the highlight of her performance was her deeply moving version of George Gershwin's "Summertime," perfectly suited to her scratchy vocals.

Finally, after several encores and a five-minute standing ovation, a triumphant Janis left the stage drenched in sweat, having conquered New York.

Back in her dressing room, Janis held court for the journalists, wittily fielding questions while swigging Southern Comfort from the bottle.

"I'm a juicer," she declared unapologetically.

Frustrated at the lack of attention they were receiving, the rest of the band left Janis with the reporters and went back to the Chelsea Hotel with various groupies to celebrate. There was supposed to be a rehearsal after the show for the new album, but when Janis showed up there was nobody there.

"We didn't leave her on purpose," explained Sam Andrew. "It was a misunderstanding."[15]

At around three Janis left the theater alone, walking out into the freezing cold on a deserted Second Avenue. She was angry at the band members for abandoning her, and so—feeling lonely and isolated—she walked into the nearby R.O.K. Bar and ordered a drink. A rowdy crowd of Ukrainians came over, with no idea who she was. They invited Janis to their table, and she started buying rounds of drinks and began to cheer up.

As Janis become drunker and drunker, she started berating the rest of the band, calling them "fuck-offs" for not bothering to come to rehearsal. It was almost daylight when she was finally rescued by one of Albert Grossman's assistants, who took her back to the Chelsea Hotel in a taxi for a few hours of sleep.

A few blocks away to the west, Bill Graham was eating breakfast at the Tin Angel Cafe on Bleecker Street, which Joni Mitchell would immortalize the following year on her album *Clouds*. John Morris had arranged a meeting with Tony Lech and his associate Jerry Pompili to discuss a partnership in the Anderson Theater before Graham returned to San Francisco. But not everyone had been told the purpose of the get-together.

"Tony had no idea who Bill was or what he wanted," said Pompili. "Bill came in. We all shook hands. Bill ordered some soup, and he started talking. Tony never looked up from his plate."

Graham proposed a partnership to present shows at the Anderson.

"Tony . . . started screaming," said Pompili, "like he was doing a bad Jimmy Cagney impression from a third-rate gangster flick. 'Who da fuck do you think you are coming into town and telling me that we're gonna do business together?' Bill never batted an eye."

After Lech finished his rant, Graham stood up from the table, put his legal pads and other papers into his leather case, and thanked Lech for his time.

"He shook my hand very politely and said, 'Good-bye,' and he left," recalled Pompili. "I turned to Tony, who was still ranting and raving, and said, 'Something tells me you just made a mistake dealing with this man the way you did.' Tony said, 'Fuck him. Who needs him?'"[16]

With the Anderson Theater now off the table, John Morris suggested going after the semivacant 2,645-seat Village Theater, right across from the Anderson. The building exuded the faded glamor of a 1920s movie palace, with a grand proscenium arch, red velvet walls, and painted murals with a gilt chandelier hanging above the double balcony.

"It was like the movie theater I had gone to every Saturday as a kid in the Bronx," said Bill Graham.[17]

During the next several days, Graham visited the Village Theater numerous times, casting his expert promoter's eye over its possibilities. He looked for ease of access for bands trucking heavy equipment in and out and checked out the stage and dressing-room spaces.

Finally, Graham decided to buy it and told his lawyer to start negotiations.

"I knew I was taking a risk," said Graham. "But I never minded the risk factor. I still knew that if it all went down, I could go back to being a waiter."

— ✦ —

On the morning of Monday, February 19, 1968, the *New York Times* carried a rave review of the Big Brother show, headlined, "Janis Joplin Is Climbing Fast in the Heady Rock Firmament."

"Miss Joplin made her New York debut Saturday night," began the piece by music critic Robert Shelton. "The lines can start forming now, for Miss Joplin is as remarkable a new pop-music talent as has surfaced in years."

If anyone was under illusions, Shelton wrote that the "excellent pop show" had featured Janis with her group.

"They used to call vocalists of such rare talent as Janis Joplin 'a great jazz singer,'" he wrote. "Because the music has changed and the scene has shifted, the 25-year-old dynamo from Port Arthur, Tex., is what one would call nowadays a great rock singer . . . a white stylistic sister of Aretha and Erma Franklin."

The influential *Village Voice* was equally ecstatic.

"A star rises quickly," wrote "Scenes" columnist Howard Smith. "New York's golden ears came out ringing from the Saturday evening performances of Janis Joplin. The two shows were the East Coast premiere of Big Brother and the Holding Company—long the favorite group of the San Francisco dance halls—but it was all Janis. Outside of soul, no girl has emerged with the sexual pizazz of male singers like Jim Morrison and Jimi Hendrix. Now with Janis, all this is over. Although not beautiful in the usual sense, she sure projects. Janis is a sex symbol in an unlikely package."

A few hours after the *New York Times* review appeared, Big Brother and the Holding Company arrived at the Columbia Records headquarters on Sixth Avenue to sign a record deal. After the official signing ceremony, the band stunned CBS Records president Clive Davis by stripping naked in his office and changing clothes for a downtown press conference to publicize the Anderson show.

Janis then propositioned the suave thirty-five-year-old record boss for sex, a gesture she suggested would seal their new recording deal.

"For her, it was the event of a lifetime," Davis later explained. "The culmination of her professional dream. For a mere signature to be taking place between the two of us seemed an inadequate expression of the event."

Davis politely declined her offer, settling for a kiss instead.[18]

That night, Albert Grossman threw a press party at a Greek restaurant on 57th Street called Piraeus: My Love. After Robert Shelton's ecstatic review, the space was packed with press who wanted to interview Janis.

Howard Smith of the *Village Voice* got there early and met Janis for the first time.

"It was mostly press and close friends," he recalled in 2013. "And Grossman wasn't there yet and [Janis] was nervous. And he showed up and said, 'We did it. Isn't that everything you've wanted?' And she was so happy and jumped in his arms. That was one of the few times I ever saw Albert Grossman publicly emotional, because he was Mr. Cool."[19]

After Janis Joplin's breakthrough at Monterey, Bill Graham had suddenly welcomed her to the Fillmore Auditorium, courting her with charm and flattery, his cruel public humiliation of the singer apparently forgotten.

As soon as Graham committed himself to New York, he booked Janis to launch his new venue.

"Oh, [Bill] likes us now," Janis later quipped. "He's good to any group that's made it."

But Graham still needed financing to buy the Village Theater.

The asking price was $400,000, so with John Morris's help and contacts, Graham set up a cartel of music business investors to raise the necessary cash. These moneymen included Albert Grossman, his partner Burt Block, promoter Ron Delsener, and the building's broker, Mike Rogers.

At their first meeting, Graham demanded 75 percent of the shares for himself, with the remaining quarter being divided among the other partners.

"We had lots of meetings deciding how to do it," said John Morris, who had already been appointed as general manager.

At one marathon investment meeting in Delsener's Upper East Side office, Bill Graham became emotional as he set out exactly how his new theater would work.

"Delsener was listening carefully but kept very quiet," recalled Morris. "Then in a very gentlemanly way he said, 'I have just come to a decision. I was here before you guys came with this project, and I think I will probably be here afterwards. So if nobody minds, I think I'll back out.' I think Ron suddenly saw the egos involved that were going to make his life miserable and he stepped back from it."[20]

The remaining partners agreed to put up $40,000 each, leaving Graham to raise the rest. Later, Graham would claim not to be able to remember where his share of the down payment had come from.

By the beginning of February 1968, after the contracts were signed, Jerry Pompili jumped the Anderson Theater ship to work for Bill Graham, taking along the rest of the competitor's staff.

From then on it was a race against time to ready the theater for the March 8, 1968, opening night.

On the southwest corner of Second Avenue and Sixth Street, the Village Theater had begun life in 1925 as a Yiddish vaudeville playhouse called the Commodore. It was one of eleven lining Second Avenue from Houston to 14th Street. The "Jewish Rialto," as the area was then known, was the center of Jewish cultural life in New York, with vibrant cafes and bookstores.

In the Thirties it was taken over by the Loews Corporation, who turned it into a movie theater, renaming it the Loews Commodore. In the Fifties it became the Village Theater, reverting back to live music and comedy, before being abandoned. By 1968 it was being used only for the occasional rock show.

When Bill Graham first set foot inside the venue, its condition could only be described as terrible. As he had now announced it would open on March 8, there were less than two weeks to have it up and running. Work needed to be done, and fast.

"The derelict building," said future manager Kip Cohen, "was actually converted into the Fillmore East in twelve unbelievable days."[21]

Bill Graham leased a cheap $90-a-month apartment on East Seventh Street to oversee the renovation. Then John Morris, Joshua White, and Kip Cohen got down to business, bringing in Chip Monck as lighting director. Everything came together.

"It was in a bad state," Monck recalled. "I went up to measure the ceiling and the joists, and through a hole in the wall comes this wonderful lanky character called Chris Langhart. He said, 'What the fuck are you doing in my ceiling?'"[22]

Langhart was professor of stagecraft, lighting, and sound at the NYU Tisch School of the Arts Theater Program, which shared a wall with the Village Theater. Within a couple of days Professor Langhart and most of his class of "college student theater buffs" had signed on with Bill Graham at $2.50 an hour.

"There was a bunch of us who were pretty tight," said Bob See, who was in the NYU theater program, "so it flashed [around] pretty quick what was going on."[23]

But their first task was clearing out all the rubbish and debris from the theater.

"There were just piles of dead seats and all manner of crap lying in the thing," recalled Langhart. "And we would just go out to St. Marks Place and flag down kids and say, 'Here, you're going to come and move some junk.'"[24]

Enlisting Professor Langhart and his students was a masterstroke of luck by Bill Graham, as they were all trained in the theater.

"You had people with great theater skills and no theater to work in," explained Joshua White. "So you ended up with a workforce that was well skilled beyond what they were doing. I mean playwrights and filmmakers were working as stagehands."[25]

From the outset, Bill Graham wanted a state-of-the-art sound and lighting system, so bands would not have to bring in their own. With three acts playing two shows a night, it was vital to streamline the operation and prevent bands from parking forty-foot trucks outside and lugging heavy equipment in and out of the building.

"So Bill sensed correctly that in this venue," said Kip Cohen, "he could say, 'I don't care what you do in Detroit or in St. Louis, but when you come here it's our lights and our sound. And that's the way it's going to be.'"[26]

Graham then hired pioneering sound technician Bill Hanley to create a sound system for his new rock theater.

"I designed and engineered it and installed it," said Hanley. "My job was to make his place sound good."[27]

The "Hanley Sound System," as it became known, cost $35,000, and Graham only leased it from Hanley, who retained ownership. It consisted of twenty-six speakers, including some manufactured for civil defense alerts, strategically placed around the theater with a total power source of 35,000 watts. There were professional-grade mixing consoles, as well as a two-ton center cluster speaker system, suspended over the center of the stage using a series of fly weights especially designed by Chip Monck and Chris Langhart.

The sound level could often break the 100 decibel level, and the cluster had to be perfectly positioned, aiming the sound into the audience so there would be no echoing.

"We were basically inventing stuff," explained John Morris. "The lighting started out as being theatrical lighting off the shelf, and then became lighting that we built and designed and put up. We built a rigging system. We built big dollies so that we could have three bands, each on a dolly, and slide one in and let them play and then take them out and let someone else play, and then put someone else in. And it cut the equipment set-up time for the audience."[28]

Chris Langhart and sound engineer John Chester even constructed an anechoic chamber above the theater dome to test out sound systems and microphones. The mathematically precise room was completely lined with absorbent material to screen out all outside noise and echoes to be acoustically pure. In it they would scientifically analyze the causes of distortion to design revolutionary multimixing boards, providing the Fillmore East with recording-studio sound quality.

Another innovation was using rear projection for the Joshua Light Show. All previous light shows had projected light from the back of the theater onto a large screen across the stage.

White and his light show colleagues operated the elaborate light show from projectors set up on two platforms that were suspended on the back wall of the theater. His equipment included three film projectors, ten slide machines, and four overhead projectors, as well as an array of color wheels, mirrors and spot lamps, and other devices White designed.

The improvised images would then be projected twenty feet onto the back of a huge screen across the stage. Audiences would see only the stunning psychedelic patterns coming through the screen, but none of the complex equipment that created them. As the light show artists were on the other side of the screen, separating them from the band and the audience, they could see only shadows.

Joshua White, then twenty-six, had signed a long-term contract with Bill Graham. It paid him $1,000 per show, plus an extra 10 percent if the weekend sold out, with a guarantee that all bands had to perform in front of the light show. The name "Joshua Light Show" would also permanently be on the marquee, giving it rock-star status.

Meanwhile, some of the problems faced by the Fillmore East renovators were more prosaic. For years the Village Theater had illegally been tapping into the electricity supply from Rattner's Jewish Restaurant next door. So Chris Langhart had to rewire the whole theater, which was a huge undertaking.

"It was a really dangerous job," said John Morris. "It was probably 880 volts for all the power in the building, so we could actually pay a bill to Con Edison.[29]

On February 29, 1968, during the height of the theater's transformation, the first advertisement appeared in the *Village Voice* for the Big Brother and the Holding Company opening at Bill Graham's Fillmore East. And the box office was now open for the reserved-section tickets, selling for $3, $4, and $5 dollars. Bill Graham had initially wanted to turn the Village Theater into a ballroom, but that proved too expensive. So he kept the 2,645 seats and introduced reserve seating, in the manner of a Broadway theater.

In the days leading up to the opening, Bill Graham shuttled between New York and San Francisco. His wife, Bonnie, was now pregnant, but he was far too busy to spend time with her.

"During the time that I was expecting," said Bonnie, "I wasn't paying much attention to what was going on in the business. I couldn't care less at that point."[30]

The week of the opening, Graham presented a run of Cream shows at Winterland and the Fillmore Auditorium, many of which he attended. The eight West Coast shows grossed $107,000 ($720,000).

While in New York, Graham either micromanaged the preparations for the Fillmore East opening or schmoozed the key East Coast music business power brokers, such as Albert Grossman, Ahmet Ertegun of Atlantic Records, and agent Frank Barsalona.

"Bill used to hang," said Lee Blumer, whom Graham had hired as his personal assistant. "When Bill would come to town that's where he would go to sit at the feet of the masters and absorb as fast as he could."[31]

After Albert Grossman's February 19 press party, Janis Joplin and Big Brother left for a short East Coast tour prior to the Fillmore East opening. They played Boston, Providence, and the Grande Ballroom in Detroit on March 1, where they began recording a live album with Columbia

Records producer John Simon. It was a disaster. Big Brother, who was always very loose onstage, were intimidated by all the recording equipment and played badly. Always the perfectionist, Janis railed at them.

"That Detroit concert sounded really awful," said Sam Andrew. "The band almost broke up right there."

After the show the band commiserated in a diner, where one of them accidentally dropped a packet of heroin, which was duly reported to Albert Grossman.

Several days later, Janis and Big Brother listened to a tape of the abysmal Detroit show in their manager's New York Office. Grossman then announced he would hire a session drummer and bassist to go into the studio and record the album.

"I [told him] that's just the way we are onstage," said Peter Albin. "We're really a live act and it's difficult to record us."[32]

After they refused to bring in any new musicians, Grossman agreed that they would go into Columbia's Black Rock studios with producer John Simon at the helm.

"And it was a serious moment," said Sam Andrew. "So we say, 'Okay, we're going to have to make it in the studio.' And even that was really hard."[33]

On Friday afternoon, March 8, a nervous Bill Graham and his team were still frantically putting the final touches to the Fillmore East. His newly recruited team of ushers had just arrived for a final briefing, and they were given their green-and-gold football uniforms—replicating Graham's old neighborhood gang—the Pirates. One of them was a young photographer named Robert Mapplethorpe, who would go home the next morning and tell his girlfriend, Patti Smith, that Janis Joplin was going to be a big star. [34]

"Guys were still painting gold leaf in the lobby," recalled John Morris. "Still testing the sound system and Bill Hanley was onstage with a solder gun in his hand hooking the sound up. We weren't ready."[35]

When Big Brother and the Holding Company arrived for the afternoon soundcheck, they were livid upon seeing the marquee sign, which read "Big Brother/Janis."

"And I had to take it down," said Joshua White, "because Big Brother and Janis wanted to be considered 'Big Brother,' and she was the vocalist. But all of us knew it wouldn't be long before she was back on her own."[36]

Inside, while they were rehearsing, Graham noticed that a spotlight on the bridge, forty feet above the stage, was out of focus. He went berserk.

"Janis is rehearsing for opening night," recalled Chip Monck, "and Bill is literally pounding on the [ladder] to get the fuck up there and focus it or he'd do it." [37]

Monck duly climbed up the ladder and fixed the light.

A few hours later, a smartly dressed Bill Graham arrived to find John Morris and Chip Monck in his office having their hair cut by a hairdresser friend from Vidal Sassoon.

"I thought Graham was going to have a fit," said Morris, "because it was happening in the office. The two of us were totally filthy from head to toe, but they were nice haircuts."[38]

—~ ~—

Bill Graham had invited the cream of the New York music industry to his opening, planning a show that would triumphantly announce his Big Apple return. But just hours before the opening, he discovered that eight hundred counterfeit tickets had been printed by a competitor bent on sabotage.

"Some spiteful bastard wanted to screw up the first show," said Kip Cohen. "It made some people uncomfortable." [39]

Graham then stationed himself at the entrance, personally inspecting everyone's ticket, looking for forgeries.

Vincent Fusco, who worked for Albert Grossman, and his pregnant wife arrived early, with backstage passes. They were surprised to see the box office was still being painted and the new marquee sign was being set up.[40]

When the Fillmore East doors opened for the first time, everybody surged in like a tidal wave. No one had thought about crowd control, and celebrities, including Judy Collins and Elektra Records president Jac Holzman, were crushed on the way to their VIP seats.

"It was absolute pandemonium," remembered Kip Cohen. "I remember seeing some very highly placed people literally being crushed into the lobby walls, trying to get in. It all worked out but it was a little tense for a while."[41]

Backstage, Janis Joplin was nervous as she sat drinking Southern Comfort from the two cases Albert Grossman had sent over earlier.

"Janis was terrified," said John Morris. "This was New York and this was the big time."[42]

At one point blues legend Albert King, who was opening for Big Brother with Tim Buckley, came into the dressing room to chat.

"He was getting really chummy with Janis and asking her questions," said Peter Albin. "I said, 'Are you related to B.B. King?' He said, 'All us Kings are brothers.'"

After the first show, a young teenager named Nils Lofgren, who would later play guitar with Bruce Springsteen's E Street Band, came into the dressing room and asked if he could play a tune.

"Nils came to see us at that show and he was just a kid," recalled Sam Andrew. "Just the way he was playing and the questions he asked, I thought, 'This guy's going to be incredible.' And we got to know him backstage at the Fillmore East that night."

Upstairs in his office, Bill Graham entertained a succession of top music industry executives.

"It was all business," said Chip Monck, "and he changed colors like a chameleon . . . ingratiating every agent and band manager that could possibly be found. He wasn't a great actor but he sure knew his business."

It was around two in the morning as Janis Joplin and Big Brother took the stage for the second show. They did not disappoint.

"When I saw her live at that Fillmore opening I was blown away. I mean blown away," said *Village Voice* columnist Howard Smith. "It was one of *the* most riveting performances."[43]

But although Janis received several standing ovations, she came offstage uncertain about her performance. Sam Andrew reassured her that everything had gone well.

"Janis was so extremely insecure," he said. "She was going, 'How was I? Did I sing well? It wasn't too bad, was it? Did I look okay?' One question after another for half an hour. I said, 'It was great. Now let's talk about something else, Janis.'"[44]

The Fillmore East opening was a sensation, enthusiastically acclaimed by the New York music establishment and the press.

"It's making waves ten foot high," one music industry "A"-lister told *Rolling Stone*. "Looks like an enormous money-maker," said another.

Bill Graham had returned to New York, and neither he nor the city would ever be the same.

CHAPTER FOURTEEN

Up and Running

April to June, 1968

The spring of 1968, Bill Graham bounced between New York and San Francisco several times a week, relishing his new bicoastal operation. He even had a double-faced watch custom made so that he always knew the time at both his Fillmores. It would become his personal trademark.

He delighted in flying first class to New York on a red-eye and then putting in a full day's work. He functioned on pure adrenaline, often working twenty-hour days.

"Bill invented the shuttle and he loved every minute of it," said his Fillmore East manager, John Morris. "Whoosh. . . . I'll be here one minute and there the next. The man's energy was phenomenal in good ways and bad."[1]

On Friday, March 22, The Doors headlined the first weekend of sold-out shows at the Fillmore East. At the Friday early show, Jim Morrison introduced a new song called "Unknown Soldier" before seguing into an extended "Celebration of the Lizard."

The late show began with the band onstage but no sign of Morrison. Then, as keyboardist Ray Manzarek played the haunting first notes of "When the Music's Over," the leather-clad singer appeared, launching himself over the drum kit and grabbing the microphone just in time to scream the opening line.

That night Jim Morrison pulled out all the stops. During an extended version of "Light My Fire," he swung the microphone over the heads of the audience lariat-style, letting it out a little more with each circle. A worried Bill Graham then tore straight into the audience at the front of the stage, frantically waving at Morrison.

"I could see that sooner or later he was going to lose it," Graham recalled in 1985, "and I didn't want it to hit anybody. I was standing maybe ten people back, waving my arms trying to catch his attention, and then he loses it. And out of two thousand people in the hall, it hits me right in the head."[2]

Back in the dressing room after the show, Graham nursed his injured head and joked about it. The next time The Doors played for Graham, the singer brought him a pith helmet for protection.

On Saturday night, The Doors had such a good time playing that they didn't want to leave the stage after the second performance.

"Bill Graham has been putting on some beautiful, well-run concerts at his Fillmore East," wrote Howard Smith in his *Village Voice* column, "but even he couldn't have planned what happened Saturday night at The Doors' last show. After one encore, wise in the ways of rock, part of the audience left, but to those who cheered on, Graham announced that The Doors had themselves requested to keep playing if the audience wanted it. They did and The Doors played for another full hour."[3]

In the audience that night was a twenty-two-year-old bookstore assistant named Patti Smith, who was given a free pass by her usher boyfriend, Robert Mapplethorpe. That night at the Fillmore East, she was inspired to become a rock star.

"I felt, watching Jim Morrison, that I could do that," she later wrote in her autobiography, *Just Kids*. "I can't say why I thought this. I had nothing in my experience to make me think that would ever be possible."[4]

As Big Brother and the Holding Company began recording their new album in New York, Peggy Caserta flew in and moved into Sam Andrew's room at the Chelsea Hotel. Caserta, who had a steady girlfriend back in San Francisco, had a crush on the guitarist, which wasn't reciprocated. After a night of passionless sex, Andrew was taking a shower when Janis Joplin knocked on the door, surprised to see the beautiful owner of the San Francisco boutique where she bought her clothes.

As Sam Andrew came out of the shower, Janis invited Caserta to move into her room. Caserta declined.

If things were awkward at the Chelsea, the Columbia recording sessions were not going well, either. Producer John Simon, who had worked with Simon and Garfunkel and The Band, had little rapport with Big Brother. He would later describe the sessions as "mind-blowing brutal," complaining that Big Brother was incapable of playing a complete tune together in the same tempo.[5]

"It wasn't working well," recalled Sam Andrew. "There was tension. We were playing very badly and Janis always knew her stuff. She could do it in one take."[6]

Janis became more and more frustrated in the studio while watching her band going through countless false starts and takes without nailing it down.

"She came to me about wanting to leave [the band]," said Andrew. "I talked her out of it."[7]

One night, looking for diversions, Janis invited Peggy Caserta to the studio and proceeded to get drunk on Southern Comfort. She became so drunk that Albert Grossman asked Caserta to take Janis back to the Chelsea. With the help of a member of staff, Caserta managed to get Janis outside, where they hailed a cab.

After throwing up in the back seat, Janis demanded to be taken to a bar. Caserta talked her out of it and they went back to her room at the Chelsea.

"I pulled off her dress and panties," Caserta wrote in her book *Going Down with Janis*. "When she was completely naked she began groping at me, but she was so drunk . . . she kept missing my face."[8]

The next night they did get it together, and Caserta moved into Janis's room for the rest of her stay in New York.

"We were young and wild and interested in each other," said Caserta in 2000. "We had a lot of fun. We made a lot of love."[9]

On Thursday, April 4, *Village Voice* music critic Richard Goldstein officially welcomed Bill Graham to New York, saluting his "hip professionalism" and wishing him every success.

"Bill Graham is in town," wrote Goldstein, "and the manifestation of his arrival—the Fillmore East—may yet transform this city into the only place on the East Coast with a genuine San Francisco–style live rock scene."

Goldstein applauded Graham for the Fillmore East's "superb acoustical system," making it "one of the best sound-boxes in the city."

"Outside the new Fillmore," he wrote, "someone has scrawled, 'Bill Graham is our businessman.' To which I say, 'Amen.'"

That night Martin Luther King Jr. was gunned down in Memphis, sparking riots all across America. There were real fears of violence in the East Village, and Bill Graham, who was in San Francisco, told John Morris that he would have to decide whether to go ahead with a scheduled weekend of The Who shows.

Morris then met with Pete Townshend and The Who's manager at the Fillmore East.

"Pete was talking about violence and the stupidity of it," said Morris, "and how he was not going to smash amps or anything anymore."

It was decided the shows would proceed as planned. The Who's first set on Friday night began on a restrained note, reflecting all the tension after the assassination.

"Pete was just about halfway through the set and he just lost it," said Morris. "And he turned around and attacked these amps."[10]

Morris stood behind the amps, which were dangerously close to the $6,500 Joshua Light Show screen, to keep them from being damaged.

"And my hands were up there," said Morris, "so I was moving them to keep from getting smashed fingers. And he looked over the top and went, 'Oh, sorry Guv.' And then poked the speaker and smashed it."[11]

At the end of the show, a dazed-looking Townshend threw his white Stratocaster to a kid in the front row and walked off the stage.

On Friday, May 3, Jefferson Airplane debuted at the Fillmore East. It was their first show for Bill Graham since his firing, and they were wary. There was also the fact that they were now competing with him in San Francisco with their own Carousel Ballroom.

"He was just another promoter to us," said Airplane road manager Bill Laudner. "As long as he was forthcoming with his part of the show requirements, then we got on fine."[12]

Since their divorce, Jefferson Airplane had hardly slowed down. Their new manager, Bill Thompson, had ambitious plans. But the band members were breaking into different factions that would ultimately tear them apart.

Grace Slick and Spencer Dryden now kept their own company, with their drunken behavior becoming more and more outrageous. With Bill Graham gone, there was no one to rein them in.

"They were always on alcohol tears," said Thompson. "But what can you do with Grace? I mean there was nobody who could replace her. She's too good. Too great."

At one outdoor concert, Grace ripped off her blouse when it started raining and performed the rest of the show topless, to the audience's delight.

"She couldn't stay away from the booze," said Thompson. "And when she'd get drunk she couldn't stop drinking. It cost us a lot of money."[13]

At another show, Grace and Dryden got into a drunken argument backstage that turned violent.

"Spencer got a knife out and put it by Grace's throat," recalled Thompson. "And our road manager Bill Laudner said in a very stern voice, 'Now Spencer, I don't want to hurt you. Put that knife down!' Everything ended peacefully."

In Fort Wayne, Indiana, Grace's behavior put the band's future in real jeopardy.

"Grace was drunk onstage," said Thompson, "and she says to the audience, 'Which one of you guys has the biggest cock?'"

The Bible Belt promoter was so disgusted with Grace's "foulmouthed behavior," that he wrote to his colleagues all over the country calling for a concert ban on Jefferson Airplane. But as the band was such a huge draw, nobody paid much attention.

Grace was on her best behavior though when Senator Robert Kennedy flew Jefferson Airplane to Washington, DC, in a government Lear jet for a fund-raising telethon.

"His kids really liked Jefferson Airplane," said Thompson, "so we were the only band invited."

It was at the height of the Vietnam War, and Grace insisted they perform her antiwar song "Rejoyce," to make a strong political statement.

Before they went on, Bill Thompson asked Pierre Salinger, who had been John F. Kennedy's press secretary, to sit in with the band on piano, knowing he was an accomplished pianist.

"He didn't know the song was 'Rejoyce,'" said Thompson, "which had a line, 'War's good business so give your son, but I'd rather have my country die for me.'"[14]

Although some at the telethon were "outraged," Salinger took it in his stride.

The next day, the band attended a lunch at the Kennedys' private compound in Hickory Hill, Virginia. Other guests included Lauren Bacall, Tommy Smothers, and Andy Williams. That afternoon, Grace Slick and several other band members had a private audience with Senator Kennedy, whom they admired.

Later, they took a stroll around the grounds, finding a cottage belonging to the young Kennedy children, complete with a jukebox.

"It had 'White Rabbit' on it," recalled Thompson. "It was a great weekend."

⎯ ⎯

Soon afterward, to cash in on Grace Slick's name, Columbia Records released an old 1966 live performance by The Great Society at the Matrix. Entitled *Conspicuous Only in Its Absence,* it featured the original versions of "Somebody to Love" and "White Rabbit."

In March, the Jefferson Airplane bandmates were back in Los Angeles to work on their fourth album, *Crown of Creation.* This work would feature two new Grace Slick compositions—"Greasy Heart" and "Lava," a tongue-in-cheek song about Spencer Dryden turning thirty. The album was released in April but only reached number 98 on the *Billboard* chart.

On Tuesday, April 30, Jefferson Airplane flew to New York to appear on the *Tonight Show with Johnny Carson.* While they were waiting in the green room, they skinned up and started smoking some strong dope.

"[It] smelled like Tijuana," said Bill Thompson. "Carson was pissed off at the band and he shot us some dirty looks."

During the show the band lip-synced "Somebody to Love," standing on a stage set with a merry-go-round of carousel horses.

"Grace sat on the back of a carousel horse and sang the song to Johnny Carson," said Thompson. "At the end of the song she took the microphone and shoved it up the horse's ass. Carson almost fell off his chair."

The next night, the band went to see Traffic, who was playing at The Scene. Jimi Hendrix was also there and invited Jack Casady and Steve Winwood back to a studio, where they recorded the legendary live version of "Voodoo Chile."

On May 4, Jefferson Airplane played the first of two nights at the Fillmore East, where they would soon become the unofficial house band.

"New York was a big deal," explained Jorma Kaukonen. "We worked a number of venues before the Fillmore East opened but when [it] did it was absolutely a home away from home."[15]

The Fillmore East audience loved Jefferson Airplane, and the band would appear there more than any other musical act. They always played in front of Glenn McKay's Light Show, who were considered part of the band and given special dispensation by the Joshua Light Show to perform there.

Opening for the Airplane on May 4 was The Crazy World of Arthur Brown, whom Bill Graham had discovered in London a year earlier. It was the band's first stop on its first US tour, and Arthur Brown was suffering from jetlag and lack of sleep.

Before they went on, manager Chris Stamp handed Brown a powerful black bomber speed pill, saying it was what Keith Moon took to combat jetlag.

To allow the "God of Hellfire" to make a dramatic entrance, the Fillmore East technical staff had run a cable from the balcony to the stage. Brown was then attached to a winch and his helmet set alight as his band started to play "Prelude to a Nightmare."

"He actually flew himself in from the balcony into the deck for his performance with his hair on fire," said lighting director Chip Monck.[16]

But as Brown landed on the stage to thunderous applause, the speed started taking effect.

"The stage started to spin around," he said. "I was still able to sing, so it didn't interrupt the act, but I was concentrating on staying upright."

The stage was bathed in half-light and somebody had left a trapdoor open by mistake. Brown fell right through it.

"I had the sensation of falling through space," he remembered. "The next thing I knew the music was coming from a long way away."

Realizing what had happened, he sobered up fast and managed to climb back onstage.

"The audience thought it was really good fun," said Brown. "They saw me crawling out of a hole in the stage and thought, 'Wow! Great Theatrics.' I damaged my knee and it's never fully recovered."[17]

Reviewing the show for the *New York Times*, music critic Robert Shelton advised The Crazy World of Arthur Brown to pay "more attention to music and less to hokum."

Then turning his attention to Jefferson Airplane's performance later, Shelton applauded Grace Slick's "striking" vocals.

"Grace Slick is the star here," he wrote, "for her luminous and fluent alto voice is one of the ornaments of the group. She was soaring and poised on this occasion and the harmonization of Mr. Balin and others was especially effective."[18]

On Sunday, May 5, Bill Graham organized a free concert in Central Park with Jefferson Airplane, the Grateful Dead, and the Paul Butterfield Blues Band. The bands all set up their equipment on a flatbed truck at the back of the bandshell, powered by portable generators. And an estimated ten thousand people turned up to see the afternoon show.

"Bill Graham's Fillmore East has been . . . a revelation for New York audiences starved for quality rock," observed the *Village Voice*, "but until Sunday something was missing. The bands knew it. Bill Graham knew it. So they got together and turned Central Park into the Panhandle. The coasts linked, and my head is still buzzing."

After the concert, everybody went to the Sheep Meadow for an impromptu game of football. Bill Graham played quarterback, sporting a number 60 shirt to lead his Fillmore East Team to victory against a team fielded by the Grateful Dead. [19]

That May, Jefferson Airplane purchased a massive three-story mansion at 2400 Fulton Street, across the street from Golden Gate Park. The seventeen-room Victorian mansion, which they renamed the Big House, would become an integral part of Jefferson Airplane folklore. Built in 1901, the structure reportedly offered refuge to opera legend Enrico Caruso during the night of fire after the 1906 earthquake.

Bill Thompson bought it from a ninety-three-year-old rancher, putting down a $20,000 deposit for the $73,000 mansion. At first the band members thought Thompson was crazy for buying such a large place, but they soon warmed to it.

"It was a beautiful old house," said Grace Slick, "and we painted it black just to be kind of offensive."[20]

It became the band's headquarters, with the basement serving as a rehearsal space with a four-track recording studio. On the first floor was a games room with a Ping-Pong table and pool, leading into a dining room complete with a medieval torture rack used as a dining table.

Their resident martial arts instructor/cocaine dealer, who supplied the band with Merck Pharmaceutical cocaine, even had his own office in the basement. Inside were two huge nitrous oxide tanks with six spigots, so band members could get high together.

Grace had commissioned the wooden torture rack, complete with chains, winches, and screws, as well as an electric chair, which she placed alongside the Louis XIV couches and fancy furniture. On one occasion a stoned David Crosby was strapped onto the rack, and somebody turned the wheels until he screamed in pain.

"I had the macabre items specially made," explained Grace, "because the juxtaposition of happy dining and instruments of death tickled my dark fancy."[21]

Every couple of months, the Airplane would throw a lavishly catered banquet, complete with gourmet dishes, vintage wines, and acid-spiked punch.

"We had some of the great parties of all time there," Bill Thompson fondly recalled. "Most of the members of the band lived there at one point."[22]

Grace Slick and Spencer Dryden shared a room on the second floor, alternating between there and Grace's house in Sausalito. Paul Kantner lived on the third floor, with its own private bathroom.

"That's the best deal we ever made," said Bill Thompson, who had found the house. "We used that 2400 Fulton Street for about twenty years."[23]

On Friday, May 10, the Jimi Hendrix Experience and Sly and the Family Stone debuted at the Fillmore East with two sold-out shows. Despite sound problems, Hendrix played a long and blistering second set, including an amazing version of "Hey Joe." The audience went crazy, bringing the Jimi Hendrix Experience back for an encore of "Wild Thing."

"He was just staggering," said John Morris, who was watching from the side of the stage. "And he was wearing a pair of velvet pants when he did his famous drop to his knees thing."

Suddenly, Morris heard the distinctive sound of Hendrix's skin-tight blue velvet pants ripping apart at the back seams.

"And he wasn't wearing underwear," he said. "The look on Jimi's face—I mean he literally turned pink. And I thought, 'Oh shit!'"

Thinking fast, Morris grabbed a towel and waved it at Hendrix, who was still playing his solo.

"And he sort of played his way into the wings," said Morris, "and I wrapped it around him and tied it around his waist. And then he went back on and finished the set with a towel on. He was so cool. It was early Fillmore."[24]

Soon after the Fillmore East opened, one of the sound technicians secretly fed a wire from the mixing consul out of the Fillmore to an upstairs apartment to record all the shows in two-track stereo on ten-inch reel-to-reel tapes.

"It was all set up," said Amalie Rothschild, who would become the Fillmore East house photographer, "and there was always somebody up there monitoring the tapes and changing the reels."

Many years later, these priceless recordings of hundreds of Fillmore East shows would become part of the Bill Graham Archives, later to be bought by Wolfgang's Vault and made available to the public.[25]

From the beginning, *Village Voice* music critic Robert Christgau knew that something special was happening at the Fillmore East. He lived just a few blocks away on Eighth Street and Avenue B with Ellen Willis, who was then art critic of the *New Yorker*.

"So we were like the big rock critic couple," he explained in 2012. "We went [to the Fillmore East] every week. It was our ritual. We would go to the late show, have friends over and get stoned."

Christgau viewed the new rock theater as a "ritual space," where rock 'n' roll, politics, and bohemia all collided, creating something far bigger than the sum of its parts.

"The confluence of hippies, rock 'n' roll and bohemians achieving both commercial success and popular renown," he said, "was to us an incredibly big fucking deal. And it was the place where you could see that happening."[26]

And by mid-May, the Fillmore East was also making waves in the fashion world.

"In fashion terms a Fillmore East opening deserves as much coverage as the Philharmonic Galanosed Galas," stated the *Village Voice* in its *Outside Fashion* column. "With some tribal differences it's a scene-making pageant whether they're seeing Lenny at Lincoln Center or Jimi at the Fillmore. Both audiences have their peacock strutting groupies, who could be classified ad infinitum."

When Bill Graham, who favored baggy white shirts and jeans, was asked to comment, he was glib.

"I'm a functionalist," he declared, "and I'm working constantly during every performance, so I can't be hung up on beads and Nehru jackets. I'd probably choke to death on all those damn necklaces, just running up and down the aisles with the folding chairs. Besides I just don't have the balls to wear them."[27]

Janis Joplin also claimed to have little interest in fashion, although young girls all over America were starting to copy her new "got together" style.

"The Total Janis Look," explained the *Village Voice*'s Stephanie Harrington, "is wearing everything and anything from her gypsy cape to her antique lace tablecloth bellbottoms to her rabbit fur Cossack hat which she made herself."

Janis told the *Voice* that she "really don't give a damn about clothes" and was "an absolute slob" as an art student.

"I groove on my clothes now because I have to," she said. "I'm entertaining in front of an audience and I have to care how I look, regardless how I really feel."

Janis said she collaborated with friends on her styles, and most of her outfits consisted of separates, bellbottom pants, and tops with low square necklines and long sleeves.

"[So] I can give my body the most freedom while I'm singing," she explained. "Anything that interferes with my thing, baby, forget it."

Janis also revealed that her stunning glass beaded necklaces and belts were her own creations.

"Bead stringing is a real thing with me," she said. "It's like therapy." [28]

After playing the West Coast, Janis Joplin and Big Brother and the Holding Company returned to New York. It was early June, and the pressure to deliver an album was mounting. There were already huge advance orders for the new album, certifying it gold before it was anywhere near finished. And CBS chief Clive Davis wanted to release it immediately. So the band went back into the studio for more grueling sessions.

Producer John Simon discovered that Janis was anything but spontaneous while recording, working hard at perfecting her vocal phrases.

"Whereas a blues artist would sort of scream from the soul with whatever scream came to mind at the moment," said Simon, "Janis would try out different screams and say, 'How do you like this scream?' 'How about this scream in this place?' So it was all very calculated. It wasn't sincere."

Sam Andrew believes it came down to Janis's insecurity, and he would also see her practice outrageous lines in front of the mirror before delivering them word-for-word at interviews.

"She wasn't really much of a star from day one," said Andrew. "She would practice these things to say in interviews and riffs to sing onstage. She always did that. She was this powerful person who was really insecure."[29]

While Big Brother were recording, top fashion photographer Richard Avedon shot Janis for a *Vogue* photo spread that came out in June, anointing her the "leading woman" in rock.

"Janis assaults a song with her eyes, her hips and her hair," read the accompanying story. "She defies key, shrieking over one line, sputtering over the next, and clutching the knees of a final stanza, begging it not to leave."

A feature on Janis in *Time* magazine soon followed, as well as numerous newspaper and magazine interviews. But none mentioned the other members of the band.

"And this eventually had an effect," said John Cooke. "They would be resentful. I think the focus of the press on Janis was wearing over time. Some reviews in the press would basically suggest that Janis was good enough to do whatever she wanted to do."[30]

During that short period, the marquee, posters, and billing changed drastically. It went from "Big Brother and the Holding Company" to "Big Brother and the Holding Company featuring Janis Joplin," to "Janis Joplin with Big Brother and the Holding Company."

"I'm sure that made her heart beat faster," said John Cooke. "How can it not?"

And all the time Albert Grossman was pressuring Janis to ditch the band and go it alone.

"Grossman started hitting on her really heavy," said Peter Albin, "telling her the band was not up to her quality."

◆━◆

Janis and several of her band members started using heroin at the time of their recording sessions in New York.

"[Heroin] was easier to get in New York than San Francisco," said Peter Albin, who avoided hard drugs. "It was a problem for us . . . and also the downfall of the band."[31]

Janis later told the *New York Times* that she thought New York made everyone uptight and aggressive.

"San Francisco's different," she said. "I don't mean it's perfect, but the rock bands there didn't start because they wanted to make it. They dug getting stoned and playing for people dancing. What we have to do is learn to control success."

In mid-June, the album was finally finished, after John Simon had quit and insisted he not be credited as producer. There were now more than two hundred reels of tape in the can, but none that Simon considered usable.

Columbia house producer Elliot Mazer was then brought in to edit and mix all the recorded tapes into an album. Janis insisted on being there with him to ensure quality.

Big Brother had wanted to call the album *Sex, Dope and Cheap Thrills*, but Clive Davis refused, warning it would be too controversial for many record stores to carry. Instead they compromised and called it, simply, *Cheap Thrills*.

———

In July, Clive Davis flew Big Brother and the Holding Company to Puerto Rico for the annual Columbia Records Company Convention. After playing a stunning showcase set for executives, Janis was disappointed when they displayed little reaction. But afterwards she enthusiastically networked on the convention floor, oozing "Texas Charm."

"It's the sort of thing that many artists, particularly the hipper ones, have a difficult time doing," recalled Davis, "but Janis enjoyed it. 'Oh you're going to be selling my album? I hope you like it,' she'd say to one salesman with a girlish sweetness. To another, she'd declare, 'I hope you can sell the shit out of my album, man!'"[32]

Soon after the convention, Big Brother flew to San Francisco to play Bill Graham's Winterland Ballroom. The opening band was The Crazy World of Arthur Brown, and they met backstage.

"Janis had a bottle of Southern Comfort in one hand," said Arthur Brown, "and some other stuff in the other. She was quite rip-roaringly raucous and bossing the band about."[33]

While in San Francisco, Big Brother also played several shows at the Carousel Ballroom, which was now losing money. The Jefferson Airplane/ Grateful Dead joint venture was based on a community mind-set, and the musicians held regular meetings to discuss what was going wrong. Janis turned up at one, bearing a bottle of liquor, a loaf of bread, and a sausage.

"Well what is it?" she cackled. "Music or money?"[34]

On June 16, Big Brother and the Holding Company had headlined the Fillmore Auditorium for a benefit for the Matrix, with a hot new opening act named the Santana Blues Band. During the last six months, Bill Graham had quietly nurtured Carlos Santana and guided his career. After Graham's firing by Jefferson Airplane, Santana and Stan Marcum had invited Graham to manage their affairs. On a handshake deal he became their de facto manager, taking 10 percent instead of the usual 15 percent commission.

"I never asked for papers from anyone," Graham later explained. "Because I felt, I'm good and you're good. If we get along why have a marriage license. I'd rather live together."[35]

That spring, Graham provided Santana with a rehearsal space and started booking the guitarist's band around the Bay Area through his new company, Shady Management. He also had them open at the Fillmore Auditorium whenever there was a hole in the program. He wanted them to gain more experience and find their chops before they were ready to headline.

"Bill Graham just adopted us," said Carlos Santana. "He loved to play salsa music, but he only called it Afro-Cuban music. And so we were the closest to that because we played blues with congas."

One day Graham had a serious talk with Carlos and the other band members, telling them they had something really special.

"He said, 'You guys got something different,'" said Carlos, "'Something that makes the pelvis move in a different way. Your music is two things that should never be separated; spiritual and sensual. So stop fighting it.'"[36]

Santana Blues Band was paid $600 for the Matrix Benefit and were at the bottom of the bill, but their spirited set made a big impression. In the signed contract for the benefit, Carlos Santana is listed as the leader of the band, which now consisted of Carlos on guitar, Gregg Rolie on keyboards, Bob "Doc" Livingston on drums, Marcus Malone on congas, and David Brown on bass.

A couple of days after the benefit, the band decided to change its name simply to "Santana," and everything started coming together.

"But the idea of calling it Santana," said Herbie Herbert, whom Bill Graham had just installed as road manager, "was probably a big mistake."[37]

—◆—

Back in New York, the Fillmore East was taking off as audiences flocked to see the eclectic bills that Bill Graham now presented. In May, Country Joe and the Fish had played shows at the Fillmore Auditorium and Winterland in San Francisco before making their debut at the Fillmore East a week later. The two opening acts were Pigmeat Markham, who had just had a huge hit with the novelty song "Here Comes the Judge," and Blue Cheer, probably *the* loudest band to ever play there.

"I remember how excited I was at the prospect of playing with Pigmeat Markham," recalled lead guitarist Barry Melton. "He put on a wig like an English barrister with black robes and stuff. He was a showman. Blue Cheer were loud. You had to be in a certain mood to appreciate them."[38]

The night before, Indian sitar virtuoso Ravi Shankar had played the Fillmore East, and Bill Graham had wanted to make him feel at home.

"Bill was not a star fucker, he was a star honorer," explained his assistant Lee Blumer. "And I remember before Ravi Shankar, we had gone out and bought three hundred carnations and put them on the stage. That was very beautiful and was like a welcoming gesture. It wasn't in somebody's rider."[39]

Graham had also had an employee check out the neighborhood's best Indian restaurants, and after soundcheck he offered to send out for an Indian meal. Shankar thanked him but declined, saying he'd much prefer a couple of cheese Danishes from Rattner's.

The Jewish dairy restaurant next door had been about to close for lack of business before the Fillmore East arrived. But once the Fillmore opened, it thrived. Bill Graham used it as a suboffice, holding business meetings there and listing it on his cards as his business address. And it also became an aftershow ritual for Graham and many of his staff to eat an early-morning breakfast there.

"You'd see half the stage crew at Rattner's getting breakfast or lunch," said Allan Arkush, an NYU film student who moonlighted as a Fillmore East usher. "Then after the show we'd go there and sometimes the bands actually paid for food."[40]

On the weekend of June 14, 1968, the Grateful Dead played the Fillmore East for the first time. Former Yardbirds' guitarist Jeff Beck opened for them, with future Rolling Stone Ron Wood and his then-unknown singer Rod Stewart, making his American debut.

That weekend, as the Dead played his venue, Bill Graham secretly flew to Ireland to try to wrestle control of their Carousel Ballroom away from them. Due to the ineptitude of the Dead and the Airplane's cronies in running the ballroom, it was now heavily in debt. Graham saw an opportunity to seize it.

In the wake of the Martin Luther King Jr. assassination, elements of San Francisco's black community were harassing Graham's predominantly white audience. Ticket sales were down, as many fans were too scared to go out. To survive, Graham knew he needed a new venue in a safer part of town.

"The Fillmore neighborhood became a battleground in the streets," said Graham, "[with] black and white [and] racial issues. And I was ready to lose my business."[41]

Situated on the busy corner of Van Ness and Market, the Carousel was owned by Bill Fuller, who was in Ireland on business.

Knowing his competitors would also be bidding for the Carousel, Graham flew across the Atlantic and tracked Fuller down to a construction site near Shannon. Over breakfast and a bottle of bourbon, the two men then hammered out a deal for the Carousel. An overjoyed Graham left with a five-year lease on the Carousel, just in time to catch an early plane back to the States.

＊＊＊

On Saturday, June 22, after a Georgie Fame show, Bill Graham closed the Fillmore East for a month so that Chris Langhart could rebuild the ancient air conditioner from scratch. It was a brutally hot summer, and audiences had been sweltering. The old movie theater air conditioner was constantly breaking down.

"It was a serious business," said Langhart. "We put a new cooling tower on the roof—just hired a crane and up it went."[42]

CHAPTER FIFTEEN

The Fillmore West

July to September, 1968

The final show at the Fillmore Auditorium was on Thursday, July 4, 1968, two and a half years after Bill Graham had opened it, igniting the San Francisco music scene. The last marquee bore the words "Nothing Lasts," and headlining the emotional closing was a new East Bay band called Creedence Clearwater Revival, currently riding the Top 40 with an eight-and-a-half-minute cover of the Fifties classic "Suzie Q." At the end of the night, Bill Graham led a chanting conga line a mile downtown to his newly acquired Carousel Ballroom—now renamed Fillmore West.

"It was a historic gig," recalled Graham. "It was very, very hectic and madness. We were being a little tearful about leaving that place, but being very happy because we were going into a better neighborhood."[1]

The very next night, without missing a beat, Graham presented a sold-out weekend at the new Fillmore West, with the Paul Butterfield Blues Band, Ten Years After, and Fleetwood Mac.

A former ballroom turned car dealership, the Fillmore West building had a large parquet wooden dance floor. It was more than twice as big as the Fillmore Auditorium had been, holding 2,800 people. But soon Graham was defying the legal capacity and letting many more people in.

In deference to the fire marshals, Graham would stand at the top of the stairs, collecting tickets in a small basket. But he didn't tear them. And as soon as the basket was full, he'd race back down to the booking office to resell the same tickets. If they were ever raided by fire marshals, he would swear he had only sold the legal number of tickets.

Even while he was across the country in New York, Graham obsessively worried that his Fillmore West staff were not packing enough people in. Jim Haynie, now back at the Fillmore West after a year on the road with the Paul Butterfield Blues Band, was left in charge while Graham was away.

"Bill called me at least five times a night to see how many people had come to the show," said Haynie. "I told him the fire marshals had been 'round to check on us and were still on the premises. Bill got angry and said, 'Damn it! You've got to do better than that!'"[2]

Soon after opening the Fillmore West, Graham erected basketball hoops on either side of the large parquet wooden dance floor for his beloved Tuesday-night games. He named his team the Fillmore Fingers, with an aggressive logo of a clenched fist with a finger sticking up sewn on their purple uniforms. His star players were his six-foot, four-inch nephew Avi Chichinsky and Jim Haynie, who was just an inch shorter.

"And of course Bill was the nob and Avi and I were the underneath guys," recalled Haynie. "We played the Grateful Dead and other teams from radio stations."[3]

Barry Melton of Country Joe and the Fish often played basketball against the Fillmore Fingers.

"Bill was a vicious basketball player," said Melton. "He was mean. He hit you. He kicked you. I mean he'd get in close and he would hurt you. It was more than a game to Bill, because he was *so* competitive."[4]

On July 1, The Band released its landmark album *Music from Big Pink*. Up to then, Bob Dylan's former backing group had never played their own live show. Bill Graham was determined to be the first to present them. To court The Band, he took his six-months-pregnant wife to spend the weekend at their manager Albert Grossman's spread near Woodstock, in upstate New York.

While they were there, Graham was at his most charming while trying to persuade The Band to play some shows for him.

"He kept talking about how we owed it to 'the people' to play," recalled guitarist Robbie Robertson. "So I just said, 'Bill, how do I meet these people you speak of?' And he said, 'The best place would be in the Winterland, in San Francisco—that's where there's the most love—and then at the Fillmore East, in New York.'"[5]

Also discussed was Bob Dylan playing the Fillmore East, with The Band backing him up. At the end of the weekend, Albert Grossman refused to commit to anything concrete.

"They told me they weren't thinking about performing live," Graham later explained. "So I said, 'But there are so many people who wanna hear you.' What I hadn't realized was that they weren't entertainers, they were players."

On July 16, Big Brother and the Holding Company played the first of three nights at the new Fillmore West that would gross a total of $33,843 ($226,000). With the release of *Cheap Thrills* less than a month away, Big Brother hit the road to promote it. And the tension in the band got thicker and thicker as the stakes got higher. It seemed all work and no play, leaving little opportunity for the band members to blow off steam.

"Life on the road [when] we released *Cheap Thrills*," said Sam Andrew, "consisted of motels, the soundcheck and then playing the gig. It was too insane."[6]

On July 27 they played the Newport Folk Festival, and the eighteen-thousand-strong audience adored them. Janis wore a sexy minidress with a neckline plunging down to her navel, and she was brought back for two encores, receiving a huge standing ovation for her stunning performance of "Ball and Chain."

A triumphant Big Brother left the stage at one o'clock and found Albert Grossman and his wife, Sally, waiting in the wings. Grossman then "dragged" bassist Peter Albin and drummer David Getz into a tent behind the stage, complaining that their rhythm section just did not make it.

"I said, 'What are you talking about?'" recalled Albin. "'They just went nuts over the band. This is the way we play.'"[7]

The next *Rolling Stone* carried an eviscerating critique of Janis's Newport performance by Jon Landau, who would go on to manage Bruce Springsteen. When Janis read it she was gutted.

"From my point of view Big Brother was not very good," he wrote. "And then there is Janis. Talent, yes. A fantastic voice, yes. A great singer, no. To me her melodrama, overstatement and coarseness are not virtues. They are signs of a lack of sophistication and a lack of security with her material. Janis is a little too obvious for my tastes."

Landau then castigated Big Brother for their weak musicianship and criticized Janis for overusing her "gimmicks" to the point of becoming a "bore."

"Judging from their performance here," he wrote, "the rhythm section never really happens. The whole band drags her at every turn."[8]

Soon afterwards *Time* magazine profiled Janis and Big Brother under the headline, "Passionate and Sloppy."

"When I go onstage to sing," Janis explained to the *Time* writer, "it's like the 'rush' that people experience when they take heavy dope. Sex is the closest I can come to explaining it, but it's more than sex. I get stoned from happiness. I want to do it until it isn't there anymore."

Playing down her musical ambitions, Janis told *Time* she was not a "dispassionate professional."

"We're passionate and we're sloppy," she declared. "I'm untutored native folk talent—I like that phrase, it's so pretentious."

She also boasted of drinking so much Southern Comfort that "I may own that company some day," saying her only regimen was not drinking cold beer before a performance.[9]

～⌣～

After having its air-conditioning system installed, the Fillmore East reopened on Friday, July 19, with a weekend of Jefferson Airplane shows. Kip Cohen had now been appointed managing director, as John Morris had taken a leave of absence to organize the upcoming European tour of the Airplane and The Doors.

Bill Graham, who wanted to repair his frayed relationship with Jefferson Airplane, ordered Chip Monck to come up with something really special to start the band's set.

"It was really important to Bill to impress the Jefferson Airplane," said Joshua White. "It was truly a love/hate relationship."[10]

So the Fillmore East technical staff constructed a giant model airplane, which would take off from behind Spencer Dryden's drum kit while accompanied by a recording of a Boeing jet engine. The airplane was actually two hollow ones inside each other. They were made out of paper and stretched wire, with five-foot wingspans, bright headlights, and red taillights.

As Jefferson Airplane prepared to go onstage, the Joshua Light Show projected stock footage of a runway on the screen while the sound crew played a tape of jet engines revving up.

The model airplane had been attached to a fishing line running out of the lobby, through the candy counter, and out onto Second Avenue. And for its takeoff, the Fillmore staff stopped the traffic outside so Chip Monck could reel in the fishing line from the other side of Second Avenue.

Then the model plane took off from behind the drum kit, flying just over the heads of the gasping audience and up to the balcony. Then it dramatically split in half, one side continuing on to the back of the balcony, while the other flew to the rear of the orchestra. To make it even more authentic, the smell of kerosene was pumped into the theater.

The stunt was a huge success, and Jefferson Airplane was impressed.

"Bill's an absolute maven," said Jorma Kaukonen. "This gigantic quarter-size airplane zoomed across the audience. What a guy." [11]

On July 31, Jefferson Airplane manager, Bill Thompson, wrote Bill Graham a thank-you letter.

> *Dear Bill,*
> *On behalf of Jefferson Airplane, I would like to thank you very much for the nice way we were treated by the entire staff of the Fillmore East, and by yourself, during our visit to New York.*
> *The group enjoyed playing Fillmore East, and thought that the wooden airplane was a real gas.*
> *Be talking to you soon …*
> *Peace, Bill Thompson.* [12]

At the beginning of August, Big Brother was in New York for a weekend of shows at the Fillmore East. Soon after arriving, Janis met her heroin dealer at the Chelsea Hotel and went on a binge. After all the bad reviews, Albert Grossman had finally persuaded her to dump Big Brother, and she was now trying to summon up the strength to tell them.

Ten Years After and The Staple Singers were opening for Big Brother at the Fillmore East, and Sam Andrew was late for the first show.

"Bill was so furious," remembered Andrew. "He screamed, 'You fucking amateur! God damn you!'"

At the first show, Janis watched Mavis Staples in awe from the wings.

"I'll never be able to sing like that," she whispered to her friend and publicist, Myra Friedman. A few minutes later she was brought onstage by Pops Staples to join them for a song.

Big Brother's final shows at the Fillmore East were among their best. In the *Village Voice*'s "Riffs" column, Annie Fisher wrote that Big Brother "sounds better to me this time. And the selection of material has improved—more variety in texture and tempo."

At the end of the second show on Saturday night, the packed house audience were on their feet, screaming for more.

"The band had come back onstage and I looked into the wings for [Janis]," wrote Fisher. "It was a moment frozen in time. She stood back there, pulling herself together for one more time, and her evident exhaustion was raw and frightening. I'd like to forget that look, but I won't for a long time."[13]

After the show, Bill Graham threw a champagne reception in the band's dressing room, which he had painted purple, Janis's favorite color. During a party, Friedman noticed a "tall, curly-headed" stranger hand-slip a small package of heroin to Janis, who was swigging Southern Comfort.

"Janis's drinking served to distract the public from an awareness of her drug use," said Friedman. "With the bottle as a talisman, she floated in and out of Holiday Inns and backstage at hundreds of concerts without arousing the slightest suspicion."[14]

On August 12, *Cheap Thrills* was released and sold more than a million albums in the first month, eventually reaching number 1 on the *Billboard* chart. Clive Davis also released an edited version of "Piece of My

Heart" as a single, which went to number 12 and helped drive sales of Big Brother and the Holding Company's album.

Although presented as a live album with a concert introduction by Bill Graham, the only actually live track was "Ball and Chain," which had been recorded at the Grande Ballroom, Detroit. The striking Robert Crumb album cover falsely credited "Live material recorded at Bill Graham's Fillmore Auditorium."

"It was an artifact," said Sam Andrew. "All the other songs were manufactured in the studio and made to sound as if they were live. So the whole thing was an illusion."[15]

Bill Graham was so delighted at the Fillmore name-check that he thanked Janis and Big Brother in a letter he penned on August 9.

"I want to thank you sincerely for your generous consideration," he wrote, "in giving the Fillmore Auditorium credit on your album cover. This is no bullshit. It gives me a very warm and personal feeling. You won't need my spiritual push, but I wish you much, much success with the album."[16]

New York Times music critic William Kloman certainly wasn't fooled, savaging the album in his review.

"*Cheap Thrills* is in effect a stereophonic minstrel show," he wrote, "and probably the most insulting album of the year."

Accusing Big Brother of being middle-class white kids pretending to be black, Kloman labeled it "a bad parody," even lacking the humor of an old Amos 'n' Andy show.

"Every cut on the album rings false," he wrote. "The falsity would be excusable if so much of the music weren't boring and second-rate."[17]

Soon after its release, Janis summoned the band to her room at the Chelsea Hotel. She announced she would be leaving Big Brother in early December, after completing their remaining tour dates.

"Then Peter Albin started screaming," recalled Sam Andrew. "Nobody else said anything . . . we were completely silent. But Peter was upset and angry and he was screaming. So then the meeting broke up."[18]

As Sam Andrew was leaving the room, Janis called him back, inviting him to join her new band that Albert Grossman was now recruiting.

A year later, Janis would explain why she had fired Big Brother, whom she had once seen as family.

"It was . . . time for each of us to start growing in another direction," she said. "Like you grow together [in a] certain way and you exhaust the good you can do for each other."[19]

Peter Albin felt betrayed by Janis and was convinced that Albert Grossman had put her up to it.

"She didn't break down or cry," said Albin. "She was a tough egg breaking it to us. 'I've made this decision for my career. I want to go on my own.'"[20]

The next day, Albert Grossman's office issued a press release announcing an "amicable split" between Janis and Big Brother. It ensured that the last dates of the tour would sell out.

"We weren't growing together any more," read Janis's words in the statement. "It should be good for their heads as a band not to be dominated by a chick singer any longer, and as for me, I hope I will be able to develop further as a singer along the lines I have in mind."[21]

— ⁓ —

When they went back on the road, bad feeling toward Janis and Sam Andrew was oozing from the rest of the band.

"So that was a tough little tour to do," said Albin. "I mean she'd already quit. Obviously she looks for some remnant of her past and she wants somebody to do drugs with."[22]

Sam Andrew agreed that Janis's insecurity was the main reason she wanted him to stay.

"One thing's for sure," he said, "she and I started doing a lot of drugs together when we left."[23]

On August 18, Janis and Peter Albin almost came to blows during a show at the Tyrone Guthrie Theater in Minneapolis. The bassist became infuriated when Janis, near the end of the first set, suddenly stopped dead in the middle of a song and began panting into the microphone.

"It was very obvious that she was milking the crowd," said Albin. "This is like phone Hollywood bullshit. So I made the crack, 'Well, after Janis's Lassie impression we'll go onto the next song.' And she immediately hit her microphone and said, 'Well, fuck you!'"[24]

Two songs later, when they came offstage, all hell broke loose.

"Janis just started ranting and raving," said Albin. "I said, 'If you want to talk like a sailor, you'll be treated like one. Bring it on!' And that was threatening to her. I didn't raise my fists or try and punch her or anything. But just the fact that the word Lassie was used, which is the name of a dog. Women don't like references to dogs or bitches."[25]

A week later, Big Brother and Jimi Hendrix headlined the Singer Bowl at Flushing Meadows, New York. Ed Sullivan had personally taken Janis to the concert in his limousine, as he wanted to book her for his top-rated *Ed Sullivan Show*.

The Chambers Brothers and Soft Machine opened the sold-out show. It was dark by the time Janis took the outdoor circular stage with Big Brother. Previously, it had been agreed with the promoter, Shelly Finkel, that the bright stadium lights would be turned off for Big Brother's set.

"So Janis goes out and hits the stage," recalled Vinnie Fusco, who worked for Albert Grossman, "and she's waiting for the lights to go out and [they] don't."[26]

A visibly uncomfortable Janis then started the set under the blinding glare of the stadium lights, but it threw her and she sang badly.

"She never gets with it," wrote Annie Fisher of the *Village Voice*, "and it's a mediocre set. Something's missing—the fire. It's not her night. Not her house."

Janis came offstage furious that the stadium lights had been left on for her performance. When Fusco asked Finkel why they had not been dimmed, he replied that the Parks Commissioner had insisted they remain on.

As Fusco drove Janis back to Manhattan, the lights were finally turned down and Jimi Hendrix took the stage for what would be a great performance.

"That the house is Jimi Hendrix's is clear the minute he comes in sight," wrote Fisher. "He wipes his nose with a Confederate flag. The monster lights are finally dimmed. Groovy."

After dropping Janis off at the Hilton Hotel, where she was staying instead of the Chelsea like the rest of the band, Fusco drove home. A few hours later, he received a frantic phone call from Janis in a midtown bar.

"She calls for help," said Fusco, "and says she'd OD'd and dying."

Fusco jumped in his car and drove to the bar, where he found her wearing just a nightgown under her Lynx coat. When he brought her back to the Hilton, the hotel staff would not let her in, as she had lost her key and had only a California library card for identification. Fusco told the front desk manager that she had the number-1 record in America and could die if she didn't get back to her room.

"He said, 'Let her die in the street,'" said Fusco, "so I punched him."

Fusco then went and bought a suitcase, loaded it with phone books, and checked her into a room at the Americana Hotel in Times Square (now the Sheraton).

A few days later, Fusco discovered that Jimi Hendrix had ordered the stadium lights to remain on during Big Brother's set so Janis would not upstage him.[27]

———

In mid-August, the Grateful Dead played three sold-out shows at the Fillmore West, the first time they'd played there since Bill Graham had snatched the Carousel Ballroom away from them. During one of the band's lengthy space jams, Bill Graham was in the wings with his house manager, Paul Baratta, when he noticed a beautiful, exotic-looking girl dancing below. He could not take his eyes off her as she danced, whipping her waist-length hair around and twirling around the floor. She reminded him of a young Ava Gardner, his favorite movie star. Then he went over and introduced himself, thanking her for adding color to his ballroom.

Although sixteen-year-old Diane LaChambre was less than half his age, and Bonnie was home eight-months pregnant, Bill Graham was love-struck. That night the young Tahitian-American, whose parents ran a bar in the Mission, had taken some PCP and her girlfriend had to explain that Bill Graham—whom Diane had never heard of—owned the Fillmore. The schoolgirl was flattered by the older man's attention, accepting his invitation to be his guest at the following night's Grateful Dead show.

When she came back, Diane was dressed to kill, wearing a tight, clingy black frock with a slit up the side. When she arrived at the box office she was given a free pass, and Bill Graham went over to welcome her back.

He stayed close that night, flattering her and telling her how beautiful she was. Three days later he seduced her and they embarked on a wild passionate affair. [28]

— ◆ —

On August 21, Jefferson Airplane flew to Brussels for their much-anticipated European tour with The Doors. They brought along an entourage of fifteen, including Glenn McKay's Headlights and more than five tons of equipment. After spending the night at the five-star Hotel Metropole, they flew to Stockholm for the first show. Before takeoff, Jorma Kaukonen was listening to music on his headset when the stewardess told him to turn it off.

"Jorma refused," recalled manager Bill Thompson. "The pilot, a big bald man, came out and ordered Jorma to turn off the music or he would have to throw him off the plane."

By this time everybody in the plane was aware of the trouble, and they were encouraging the pilot to throw Kaukonen off the plane.

"I ordered Jorma to turn off the music," said Thompson. "I told the pilot that we were a rock & roll band, and had not gotten much sleep in the last few days. We were allowed to travel to Stockholm."

But most of the airline staff Jefferson Airplane met during their travels were only too pleased to look after the band.

"We used to hang out with the stewardesses," said Grace. "We'd go on these huge 747s that had little bubbles on top which was like a bar. We'd go up there and the stewardesses would snort coke with us . . . and the guys would screw them or whatever. I mean it was really fun to fly."[29]

After co-headlining shows with The Doors in Stockholm, Copenhagen, Hamburg, and Dusseldorf, the Airplane flew to London. They spent a week in the city, sightseeing in a red double-decker bus.

On August 31, they played the Isle of White at three o'clock in the morning in frigid temperatures. And five days later they played a free concert on a rainy afternoon in Parliament Hill Fields, with Fairport Convention opening.

"What is wrong with you people?" Grace asked the crowd. "It's raining. Go home."

The next weekend's two shows at London's Roundhouse were hotly anticipated by the English music press. It was the first time any of the new San Francisco bands had played England.

"The biggest freak-out since Babylon is likely to erupt at London's Roundhouse next weekend," wrote the *Melody Maker.*

The two Roundhouse shows, with the Airplane and The Doors alternating as headliners, were critically acclaimed and would firmly establish Jefferson Airplane in the U.K.

One night in London, Grace sneaked out of the hotel room she shared with Spencer Dryden to seduce Jim Morrison.

"I hit on him," said Grace in 1998. "I went to his door and knocked. I was so nervous."

When Morrison opened the door and Grace said, "Hi," Morrison didn't reply. Then he just sat on his bed and watched her, without saying a word. Not quite sure how to proceed, Grace picked up a bowl of frozen room-service strawberries and stuck her finger in them. Morrison followed suit, picking up a strawberry and squeezing it in his hand until the juice ran out through his fingers. He began to laugh and started squeezing more strawberries. Feeling more relaxed, Grace started squeezing some, too.

Soon they were both crushing the strawberries into the white bed sheets with abandon. Then they fell into each other's arms and made love on the wet strawberry sheets.

"Yeah he was good," said Grace, who would later call him well-endowed. "And I said, 'Well, if you ever want to call me up again.' But he never did."[30]

Two weeks later, Jefferson Airplane and The Doors played the Concert House in Amsterdam. Grace was still recovering from laryngitis she'd contracted in London. The afternoon of the show the two bands went out on a shopping expedition together.

"And drugs are legal in Amsterdam," said Grace. "So we're walking down the street [and] the kids know who we were. And most of us would say, 'Oh, thank you.' If it's marijuana we'd have a toke or something. Or if it's hash, 'Oh, thanks very much and you'd put it in your pocket, I'll save it for later.' Or heroin or whatever it was.

"Jim sat down on the curb and did everything that was handed to him. That's in the daytime. We had to play that night."[31]

And that night it was the Airplane's turn to open the show. They were in the middle of "Plastic Fantastic Lover" when Morrison, having just washed down an ounce of blonde hashish with a twelve-pack of Heineken, suddenly leapt onstage.

"He looked like a spastic windmill," recalled Grace. "His arms are flailing around and he's doing all this stuff. His band is just looking at him like, 'Oh God.'"

Morrison promptly passed out and the paramedics carried him out in a stretcher to a waiting ambulance, which drove him to the hospital to have his stomach pumped. The three remaining Doors played two sets that night, with keyboardist Ray Manzarek doing the singing.

"Yeah, but The Doors without Jim Morrison," said Bill Thompson, "was a lot like watching paint dry."[32]

After the Amsterdam show, Grace Slick and Spender Dryden flew to the Caribbean for a week's vacation in St. Thomas. A couple of days later, Paul Kantner flew in with a girlfriend to join them. Grace's relationship with Dryden had become increasingly strained, and after finding a cockroach in their bed she flew back to San Francisco alone.

Santana was now regularly playing the Fillmore West, fast building a devoted following. At the end of August, Santana was third on the bill to the Staple Singers and Steppenwolf. Three weeks later, Santana had moved up to second on the bill to Janis Joplin and Big Brother and the Holding Company. And by the end of December, Santana were headliners in their own right.[33]

"It started to get weird with the Santana [audiences]," said Michael Wilhelm of The Charlatans, who regularly played the Fillmore West. "They were real loud and low-lifes . . . from the Mission. You'd think you see acid heads and pot heads, but they had a following of downer freaks . . . the opposite of what Santana represents."[34]

In mid-August, Carlos Santana contacted his parents for the first time in two years, inviting them to the Fillmore West to see him play.

"I had never gone to one of those places," said José Santana. "We saw a bunch of lights and a lot of strange things in that place. We saw many hippies, too."

But when the veteran mariachi musician saw his son's Latin rock band, he was not impressed.

"They were still not playing too good," said José. "You could tell by listening to them."[35]

— ⌒ —

On Tuesday, September 17, Bill Graham flew Diane LaChambre to New York for Traffic's debut at the Fillmore East. He had several business meetings lined up, and he asked his twenty-one-year-old personal assistant, Lee Blumer, to look after his new mistress.

"He had me babysit," said Blumer. "She was young and very pretty and kind of ethereal. Stoned. I assumed he was having a relationship with her."[36]

While Graham was away on Fillmore East business, Diane stayed at Blumer's apartment. Diane was fascinated by her collection of Fillmore posters, and they called out for Chinese food. Then around eleven in the evening, Graham arrived to take Diane back to his Lower East Side apartment to spend the night.

A couple of days later, Bonnie Graham went into labor and was taken to the hospital, where she was cared for by her sister-in-law, Ester Chichinsky. Although Bonnie would have liked Bill to be there for the birth of their first child, she understood how busy he was running the two Fillmores.

"That he wouldn't be there when [our baby] was born was unfortunate," said Bonnie, "but I thought, 'OK, he's busy.' I always accepted the fact that he was going here, there and every other place."[37]

Bill Graham was in his Fillmore East office, going over details of the Friday night Traffic show with Kip Cohen, when he learned he had become a father.

"He got the call from Bonnie at the hospital that [his son David] had been born," recalled Cohen. "Was he touched and moved? Yes. But I also remember it was just one of a barrage of phone calls that went to agents and managers. It was just another phone call."[38]

That night Graham celebrated the birth of his son with his young girlfriend back in his apartment. The next morning, he asked Lee Blumer if she had sent flowers to Bonnie. Lee replied that she had, but she had signed the card with her name and not his.

"I didn't think to send flowers for him," she said. "That night his wife yelled at him for not sending her any flowers, so he almost killed me for that."[39]

For Saturday night's show, the Fillmore East technical staff had hung an old English traffic light over the stage, just out of view of the audience. Before Traffic went onstage, the Joshua Light Show showed films of traffic in various cities, accompanied by a specially recorded soundtrack of street sounds.

Then, as Steve Winwood and the rest of the band were tuning up, the illuminated traffic light was slowly lowered by a wire, stopping about six feet above the stage.

"We had the whole thing timed," said Bill Graham, "and all I said was, 'On drums, Jim Capaldi, on sax, Chris Wood, on organ, Stevie Winwood—Traffic.' First the light was red, on yellow I introduced them. At the word 'Traffic,' the light went green. Music, up! The kids screamed. It did something for the set."[40]

After Traffic's final encore, Graham was led out onstage to a round of applause as a photograph of his newborn son, David, just flown in from San Francisco, was projected onto the giant light show screen. It was his very first look at his son, and he shared the moment with his Fillmore East audience.

<hr>

A few hours earlier, *Life* magazine hit the streets with another candid interview with Janis Joplin, headlined "Singer with the Bordello Voice." Writer Al Aronowitz had interviewed Janis at the El Quijote Restaurant next to the Chelsea Hotel on a recent afternoon, where she was knocking back screwdrivers for breakfast.

"If [Janis] wasn't so feminine, she might have become a lady wrestler," wrote Aronowitz. "She's pop music's only broad, and whether she's singing or talking it's with all the sound of a Hells Angels exhaust pipe. Like Mae West, she could be the greatest lady who ever walked the streets."

The article also observed that just a week after *Cheap Thrills* was released, Janis had sent the rest of Big Brother back to San Francisco, while she "shopped around" for a new band.

"I want a bigger band with higher highs," she told Aronowitz, "a bigger ladder and I want more bottom—I want an incredible amount of bottom. I want more noise. When I do a rock tune I want it to be so HUGE."[41]

<hr />

Back in San Francisco after their European Tour, Jefferson Airplane threw a housewarming party at 2400 Fulton Street. Long banquet tables stretching the entire length of the first floor—from the billiards room to the great hall—were laden with stuffed birds, racks of lamb, and a suckling pig, prepared by GUSS (The Grand Ultimate Steward Service). At each place setting was a perfectly rolled joint of the best marijuana. Fine vintage wines were served by uniformed waiters, and the punch bowl was overflowing with Owsley's latest batch of LSD.

On Sunday, September 29, the Airplane made its second appearance on the *Ed Sullivan Show*, signaling their mainstream success in America.

"The number one rock group in the country," went Sullivan's introduction. "For the youngsters, let's hear it, the Jefferson Airplane."

Jefferson Airplane then lip-synced to the newly released "Crown of Creation," with swirling psychedelic patterns projected behind them on a blue screen. As the band arrived in blue jeans and refused to change, they appeared to disappear from the waist down. Ed Sullivan was angry and they were never invited back.

The following day they played another free Bill Graham concert in Central Park, supported by Country Joe and the Fish, Ten Years After, and Buddy Guy.

"There were forty thousand people there," recalled Barry Melton of Country Joe and the Fish. "It was huge and in the middle of our dates at the Fillmore East. And I remember climbing on top of the thirty-foot towers of speakers in the middle of some guitar break. I almost killed myself."

The next day, Graham's Fillmore East football team challenged the New York City Police Department to a game in Central Park. Graham invited Melton to play wide receiver for him.

"So I took a bunch of drugs that put you up for a football game and showed up," he said. "I was good, man. The guys were throwing to me and I was getting hit. I mean this was a bruising exercise. Bill played."

The New York cops easily beat the Fillmore East team.

"They smashed us to smithereens," said Melton. "It was awfully hard contact [with] no padding or helmets. You just went out there and got hurt."[42]

⬥

Graham's passionate affair with Diane LaChambre was now an open secret among the staff at both Fillmores, but no one dared challenge him on it.

"And it wasn't for me to comment as to what was proper and what wasn't," said Kip Cohen. "I understood . . . but it had its consequences—his marriage and his relationship with his son."[43]

Diane now became a fixture backstage at the Fillmore West, and Graham proudly showed her off to his friends.

"I met her backstage a couple of times at the Fillmore West," recalled Bill Thompson. "Bill used to always say, 'She's got the greatest butt.'"[44]

After a brief visit to San Francisco to see Bonnie and hold their baby David for the first time, Graham took Diane for a three-day vacation to John Morris's luxury home in the Virgin Islands.

"He came down with her," recalled Morris, "and it wasn't done well. If Bill was going to have an affair, even if he was going to have it three thousand miles away from Bonnie, he didn't have the instincts. He didn't have the thoughtfulness. He didn't have whatever it took to keep it a quiet, secret affair."[45]

A couple of months later, Graham boasted to the *New York Times* about his recent dream vacation, staying in a big house with its own private beach.

"It was *Holiday* magazine but *real*," he gushed. "I never knew that world existed. I never have time to discover those things. I work too hard making money to spend it."[46]

Soon afterward, Graham told John Morris that Kip Cohen was now running the Fillmore East and Morris was out.

"I was fired," said Morris. "Kip Cohen had wheedled his way into my position. Bill said to me, 'I don't think we're a suit anymore. Kip can run the theater.' And I thought, 'I've just been fired.'"[47]

In late September, Janis Joplin bought an oyster-white 1965 Porsche 356C Cabriolet from a Beverly Hills dealer for $3,500 ($24,000). After the car was delivered to her San Francisco home, she had her friend Dave Richards paint it in a stunning psychedelic design, with an image of her and the members of Big Brother and the Holding Company on the left fender.

Janis and her psychedelic Porsche soon became a common sight driving through Haight-Ashbury. It became one of her most treasured possessions.

CHAPTER SIXTEEN

Catching Fire

October to December, 1968

With her two-year relationship with Spencer Dryden disintegrating, Grace Slick hit the bottle with a vengeance. On Thursday, October 3, the Jefferson Airplane played a fund-raising evening at the Whitney Museum in New York, for the same kind of WASPy society crowd she had grown up detesting in Palo Alto.

"They didn't know what to make of us," said Grace, "the women in minks and diamonds, and they're really straight in their beehive hairdos. Each weekend they have a new performance group and I guess they were trying to be cool and have new stuff."[1]

The evening got off to a bad start when the security guards barred Jack Casady from entering until one of the organizers came down to explain who he was. Grace had brought along a bottle of Southern Comfort, and she proceeded to down it before they went on. By the time classical pianist Raymond Lewenthal had finished playing his opener—pieces by Scriabin and Liszt—Grace was bombed.

The band had been waiting in an upstairs room in the Whitney, and Grace had been given a wireless microphone to use. It was the first time she had ever seen one.

In the elevator, going down to the great hall, Grace started mocking the audience, unaware that every word she was saying was coming through the PA system.

"I had this wireless mike and I'm talking," she said. "And the band was going, 'Oh Jesus, we haven't even gone on yet, Grace.' By the time we got to the stage the audience was completely nonplussed."

As they began playing, Grace startled hurling insults at the rich audience wearing tuxedos and evening gowns.

"Hello, you fools," she told them. "You got Rembrandts on the mantel and a Rolls in the garage, but your old man still wouldn't know a clitoris from a junk bond, if you had the guts to show him your twat in the first place."

During one song she slurred into an incoherent monologue, calling the Whitney patrons of the arts "filthy jewels," which many of them misheard as "filthy Jews."

Then she went on to insult the curator's wife, demanding to know if she ever slept with her husband or only saw him at fund-raisers. The rest of the band carried on playing, well used to Grace's unpredictability onstage.

The *Village Voice* was there to witness the "out of wack" show, and Annie Fisher's negative review appeared in her next "Riffs" column.

"Grace was at her most abrasive," it read, "stalking around with a wireless mike, spattering her own, in her anti-properness. Someone who shall remain nameless here said later that she should be told she's a marshmallow and just come off it, baby. Grace Slick, stockbroker's daughter and Finch dropout, is not, in the farthest stretches of anyone's imagination except her own, funky. And funny and cheap are polarities. I would like to hear what she can do besides sing off-key. Off-color, she just don't make it man."

Manager Bill Thompson witnessed many crazy scenes going down over the years when Grace went on a three-day bender.

"[It] was always an adventure," he said. "Given the combination of Grace and drink and a full moon and when Grace was having her period, it was a very dangerous time. She didn't just drink a little—she'd drink everything she could lay her hands on."[2]

At the end of October, Jefferson Airplane headlined the Fillmore West for three nights with the Ballet Afro-Haiti and a Milwaukee blues band called AB Skhy. The plan was to record all the shows for a live album, and the Lee Conklin poster for the show carried the enticing side banner, "recording Live" on it.

One of the Airplane's main problems was that their records failed to deliver the band's raw energy they had when playing live. They had been trying to capture their electrifying performances on tape for two years without success.

"The first time we recorded ourselves live it was so awful," explained Spencer Dryden. "We'd play the tapes and it was a contest to see who could listen all the way through and not have to leave the room. It was just shit."[3]

This time it would finally work. The subsequent *Bless Its Little Pointed Head* live album, which would be released the following February, would have six tracks from the October Fillmore West shows. The rest would be recorded at the upcoming Thanksgiving shows at the Fillmore East.

"The Fillmores were our home ground," said Paul Kantner. "They were a large garden party and tribal gathering. They were our tribal stomping grounds."[4]

On November 1, Grace Slick was on every front page in America after performing in blackface on the *Smothers Brothers Comedy Hour*. At the end of her performance of "Crown of Creation," she raised her fist in a black power salute, showing solidarity with the radical Black Panthers.

Bill Thompson says Grace got the idea a couple of weeks earlier after watching the Mexico City Olympic Games, where US sprinters Tommie Smith and John Carlos gave the salute during the medal ceremonies.

"That's why Grace wore a blackface in sympathy with them," said Thompson. "She's forgotten why she did it, but I remember."[5]

Paul Kantner said he never saw what all the fuss in the media was about.

"It was just Grace being Grace," he said. "I mean it was another thing to do. We got away with stuff like that and we didn't consider it daring. It was just something to do."[6]

———

In mid-October, Bill Graham presented the Jimi Hendrix Experience for two shows at Winterland, while Country singer Buck Owens and his Buckeroos played across town at the Fillmore West.

"And it was a disaster," Graham told journalist Howard Smith. "So I advertised it. One poster said 'Jimi Hendrix at Winterland,' and we did monstrous business. And then we had 'Bill Graham Presents the Buck Owens Country and Western Show at Fillmore West.'"

Graham said his big mistake was mentioning the Fillmore West, as it put off Buck Owens's straight country fans.

"The Fillmore for the straights has a certain dangerous air about it," he explained. "You know that's the place where they 'smoke dope,' do those strange things and wear those funny clothes . . . in that never, never land. I realized after that that if I had said, 'Bill Graham Presents Buck Owens at the Hoochie Club,' we would have filled up."[7]

In the late Sixties it was standard for a headline act to take 60 percent of the gross and be responsible for all the promoter's local expenses. Promoters paid a guarantee of $10,000 and split the gross sixty/forty, with the band paying its touring expenses. Once the deal was signed, the promoter assumed all risk for the show.

"All promoters are gamblers," said Bob Grossweiner of *Performance* magazine. "The highest rollers at the poker table are the promoters and they don't care if they win or lose. In the concert situation the promoters are the only ones at risk. Everyone else has a guaranteed salary."[8]

In order to survive, promoters needed to know the sales potential of any given act to use as a starting point in their negotiations with the performers' agent.

The profits to be made were enormous. A typical Fillmore East program ran for two evening performances on Friday and Saturday. Tickets were $3, $4, and $5, and a full house for all four shows would gross Graham $45,000 ($300,000). Set against the operating expenses of running the Fillmore East and paying the musicians, Graham could clear $17,000 ($115,000) profit on a good weekend. The Fillmore West made him $6,000 ($40,000). This gave him the potential to earn $832,000 ($5.6 million) a year from just staging concerts, without taking the larger Winterland or any of his other interests into account.

Bill Graham's conspicuous success was unpopular with many counter-culture activists, who accused him of exploiting the community. He now drove a green convertible Jaguar XKE that he had won in a crap game, and he and Bonnie had moved into a luxurious apartment in Pacific Heights. He also liked to boast about his new trappings of success in interviews.

His constant presence on Second Avenue standing outside the Fillmore East, taking tickets and yelling orders at people, made him many enemies.

"Once the Fillmore was established and very successful," said New York journalist and broadcaster Howard Smith, "there was going to be some backlash in the community about if you're giving enough back to the community. That was always the cry. And they started to target the Fillmore."

The fuse was lit by the underground newspaper the *East Village Other*, whose staff had became his tenants when he bought the Fillmore East. In early October, the paper cruelly attacked Graham in an editorial, wishing he had followed his family into the Nazi concentration camps. When Graham read it he stormed into the editor's office, turned over his desk, and threw him out into the street.

Soon afterward, a revolutionary street gang called the Motherfuckers (short for "Up Against the Wall, Motherfucker"), who were looking for a cause, fixed their sights on Bill Graham. And in the name of the people, they demanded that the Fillmore East be open to the community one night a week.

"[The Motherfuckers] were out of their fucking minds," said Smith, who covered the story in the *Village Voice*. "And they loved disrupting things just for the sake of it."

Motherfuckers' spokesman Ben Morea told *Rolling Stone*, "The Fillmore's interests are not our interests, and that's the conflict. They're into making money and we're into living."

In an attempt to avoid a possible community boycott, Graham agreed to their demands to "liberate" the Fillmore for one free night a week.

But there was trouble when the Living Theater staged their play *Paradise Now* at the Fillmore on one of the first free nights. When an actor suddenly announced that the people were going to liberate the Fillmore, Graham dashed onstage to defend his theater. Quickly overpowered, he was tied to a chair on the stage, where he remained for the next six hours, arguing and screaming at the rioters.

"It was their drama and Bill's drama but in retrospect it was hysterical," said Lee Blumer, who hid in the sound booth during the takeover.

"Bill battled the Motherfuckers," said Joshua White. "They were demanding that the theater should be free and accused us of stealing money from the community. Bill told them, 'It will be free when the musicians play for free, and the airplanes fly them here for free, and the limousines are free.' His argument was pretty tight."9

The next day, an angry Graham told the *Village Voice* what he thought of the Fillmore takeover.

"Those rotten pieces of shit," he said. "I'm so sick and fucking tired of listening to that 'rip off the community' shit. I told those pieces of shit, you get the musicians, and you get the equipment and you pay my stage people, and I'll let you have this place on Wednesday. For all I care, this community can fucking shrivel up and die if they continue to let themselves be represented by that bunch of cheap-ass chicken-shit punks."

Yet within a few days, Graham backed down and agreed to allow the Motherfuckers the use of the Fillmore every Wednesday night.

However the first free Wednesday after the *Village Voice* piece was a disaster, attracting Bowery bums, winos, and speed freaks from St. Marks Place, who vandalized the Fillmore. Then the police stepped in, ordering Graham to stop the open drug taking during the free nights or risk losing his operating license. Graham replied by circulating an open letter to the community, appealing for order. It cited, "Incidents of physical confrontation, and the blatant use, distribution, and sale of drugs on the premises— obviously illegal" and urged "intelligence, understanding and grace."

The Motherfuckers replied with a letter of their own. In the radical black-and-white rhetoric of the times it read: "Situation: Pigs and Bill Graham stop free night. Why? They say we smoke, they say we take dope, but we know it's because they are afraid of us. Afraid that we'll get together there to destroy their world and create our own. The pigs threaten to close Graham down unless he stops our free night. He doesn't have to worry about the pigs. We'll close him down. No free night, no pay night."

Then Bill Graham—to the anger of many—canceled the free nights and kept the Fillmore closed on Wednesdays.

At the beginning of November, the Grateful Dead finally dosed Bill Graham with LSD. It was during a weekend run at the Fillmore West, and although Graham and his staff at both Fillmores never ate or drank anything unless they'd brought it themselves, the Dead's so-called "Assassination Squad," finally hit their number-one target.

"That was . . . during my 7Up era," Graham later explained. "We'd put plastic barrels full of soda and ice in the dressing rooms. And they took the 7Up cans on top of these barrels and used a hypodermic needle. To put in their goodies."

The Grateful Dead figured that eventually "Uncle Bill," as they called him, would drink one of the doctored cans.

"I picked up a can of 7Up," he said. "Just about the time they were going onstage, it hit. Rather heavily."

As a smiling and very stoned Bill Graham stood in the wings digging the powerfully psychedelic Grateful Dead music, drummer Mickey Hart invited him onstage to join them, handing him a cowbell.

"I spent the next four and a half hours onstage with the Dead," said Graham. "I just had one of the great evenings of my life."[10]

The following weekend, Country Joe and the Fish headlined the Fillmore East. They were in New York recording a new album, and their record company, Vanguard, wanted photographs of the band playing naked for an album cover.

"So we went to the Fillmore East," recalled keyboard player David Bennett Cohen, "and we took off all our clothes and played."[11]

While onstage playing, a photographer shot still photographs, but Joshua White was also there secretly recording the action on 16 mm film.

"I was the only person that didn't have an instrument in front of them," said Country Joe McDonald. "So I'm completely just frontal nudity there."

Although there were strict instructions not to go into the theater, all the female staff sneaked in to watch the naked band. At Country Joe's next Fillmore East show, they were in the middle of the "Fixin'-to-Die Rag," when McDonald noticed that members of the audience were staring up at the Joshua Light Show screen behind them.

"And I remember turning around," he said, "and seeing the projected image of us playing naked."[12]

On Tuesday, November 19, Jefferson Airplane band members were in New York to shoot a scene for the film *One American Movie*, being made by French New Wave director Jean-Luc Godard. In bitterly cold conditions that afternoon, road manager Bill Laudner set up the band's equipment on the roof of the Schuyler Hotel at 57 West 45th Street. One floor below, the film's stars, Rip Torn, a close friend of the band, and Paula Matter, were perched dangerously on the sill of a bedroom window, to be woken up by the sound of the live music.

Directly across the street from the window of D. A. Pennebaker's studios, Godard called "Action," and his crew started filming.

"Hello New York!" screamed Marty Balin, as the rest of the band in heavy winter coats were tuning up. "New York! Wake up you Fuckers! Free music! Get some free Love!"

Jefferson Airplane then launched into a menacing version of "The House at Pooneil Corners," as heads started appearing out of nearby office windows to see what was happening.

Soon a large crowd had gathered in the street below, and they were shouting for more. Then, as the band started playing a new song, "We Can Be Together," a New York City cop appeared on the roof and ordered the music to stop.

"Neither playing nor filming stopped," reported Renata Adler in the next morning's *New York Times*, "and the policeman retired to a place in the background of the shot."

Several minutes later, more police arrived and ordered the Airplane to stop playing. Again, no one took any notice and the filming across the street continued. Finally Rip Torn and Paula Matter, wrapped in a white sheet, came out onto the roof for their next scene, as the Airplane struck up "Somebody to Love."

"There were some angry words and some pushing," wrote Adler. "Mr. Torn [was] placed under arrest. The filming continued."

Godard would eventually shelve the project, though it was completed by D. A. Pennebaker and shown briefly in art houses.

Just two months later, the Beatles—well aware of Jefferson Airplane's rooftop gig—would play their final show on the roof of their Apple offices in Savile Row, London, a performance that was filmed for their 1970 documentary, *Let It Be.*

—◆—

The night before Thanksgiving, Bill Graham threw a private dinner for the key players in the San Francisco music scene. After his staff served a roast turkey buffet inside the Fillmore West ballroom, Graham came onstage to a round of applause, to introduce the evening's musical entertainment.

He proudly announced to his guests that his new Millard Booking Agency would be representing Santana and It's a Beautiful Day, who were the entertainment that night, and the next wave of San Francisco music.

It's a Beautiful Day played first, with "White Bird" climaxing their ethereal set. Then Bill Graham introduced his protégés—Santana.

"Then these hard asses from the Mission came on," wrote Jim McCarthy in his book *Voices of Latin Rock.* "No one then realized they were the spike of this huge cultural revolution."[13]

After the show, Bill Graham caught the red-eye back to New York for the Jefferson Airplane and Buddy Guy's Thursday to Saturday run of Fillmore East Thanksgiving shows. Once again the Airplane would be recording the performances for a live album.

"We recorded the shows at both Fillmores," explained Jack Casady. "We wanted the recording of the East Coast aspect as well. I remember thinking at the time that we played as a band really well outside of our own environment. When you're at home sometimes you get kind of hung up because it's home. And out on the road there's a certain kind of aggressive attitude in the musicians' part . . . and we enjoyed that."[14]

As another stunning set-piece to open the Jefferson Airplane show, an NYU Film School student suggested projecting the final scene from the 1933 *King Kong* movie onto the Joshua Light Show screen.

"And that was our cue to go on," said road manager Bill Laudner. "That [became] a regular feature."

Then with the movie's final words, "Ah no . . . It wasn't the Airplane. It was beauty that killed the beast," Jefferson Airplane launched into "Three-Fifths of a Mile in Ten Seconds."

"Bill Graham had a bit of that Cecil B. DeMille thing going," said Laudner, "where he wanted to have these grand productions."[15]

Those sold-out Thanksgiving shows were a huge success, and some of Jefferson Airplane's best shows ever.

"That album recording," said Jorma Kaukonen, "was done in my opinion at the peak of the Jefferson Airplane's live performance career. We did it when we were hot. Thank God it was recorded then and as a result it lives on."[16]

The next morning, Graham laid on another Thanksgiving dinner for all the bands in town, key agents, bookers, and his Fillmore East staff. It was served buffet style on a long trestle table in the Fillmore East lobby.

"The Thanksgiving show—I mean what a concept," said Kaukonen. "And of course nothing could compare with a Thanksgiving Dinner."[17]

Later, in the dressing room before going onstage, Paul Kantner gave Joshua White his first snort of cocaine.

"It was in a 16 mm film can and it was completely filled," recalled White. "He paid about $400 for it. If I had that film can now, I could retire."[18]

On December 2, *New York Times* music critic Mike Jahn penned a glowing review of the Thanksgiving shows.

"Jefferson Airplane flies on stronger than ever," he wrote, "nearly two years after the San Francisco hippie scene that launched it was abandoned for lack of interest."

Although the Airplane performed Grace's two "superhits," "White Rabbit" and "Somebody to Love," Jahn said the band was never "simple and obvious."

"Always it is complex and dreamy," he wrote. "Sometimes it is nightmarish, rather like a Fellini movie."

And Grace Slick's life was also beginning to resemble a Fellini movie. On the last night of the Fillmore East run, a drunken Spencer Dryden grabbed a groupie out of the audience and brought her back to the hotel with Grace in their limo. When they got to their room, Dryden and the girl went inside, leaving Grace standing alone in the hallway.

The next morning, she flew back to San Francisco with the rest of the band while Dryden remained in New York. When he finally came home, he discovered Grace was in Los Angeles and their apartment had burned down. Dryden then moved into 2400 Fulton Street, where he took up residence.

—◦—

Prior to the Thanksgiving festivities, Janis Joplin and Big Brother and the Holding Company played at Hunter College. It would be their final New York performance. After several months on the road, everybody in the band was on edge that Friday, November 15. Janis and Sam Andrew had now distanced themselves from the rest of the group, spending their time shooting speed, writing songs, and making plans for their new band.

Several weeks earlier, Grateful Dead drummer Mickey Hart had approached Janis about forming a new supergroup with him, Jerry Garcia, and Jack Casady. Janis turned him down flat.

"Can you imagine me turning around and seeing you guys behind me?" she quipped.

The Hunter College show was a hot ticket. Myra Friedman, who was doing Janis's public relations, was swamped with requests for press passes, and a local TV station wanted to film the concert.

The night before the show, Janis, who had been up speeding for days, took two Seconals to try to get some sleep. But they didn't work and she was awake all night. By Friday morning she was in a terrible state, convinced that she had a throat infection and wouldn't be able to perform.

Three hours before she was due out onstage, a doctor examined her and could find nothing wrong with her throat. Back at Hunter College, Janis started drinking Southern Comfort and felt a little better. She and Sam Andrew even worked on a new song on a backstage piano, as Rick Danko and Richard Manuel of The Band watched.

That night, Janis rose to the occasion and sung her heart out. By the end of the show, the audience was dancing in the aisles.

"Janis was astounding," Friedman later said. "Seconal, speed, and God knows what else all pumping through her system, she lacerated that hall with notes that flew up from her dancing feet, spiraled from her pumping hips, and gushed from her throat."[19]

Janis was having such a good time onstage that during David Getz's drum solo, when the rest of the band left the stage, she walked out carrying a gaudy tiger-skin drum as a joke. Getz, who had dropped acid before the show, was furious and kicked the drum across the stage. Thinking that he'd kicked it at her, Janis screamed "Fuck you!" and stormed offstage.

After the show, Janis laid into Getz and accused him of humiliating her in front of the audience, when she was just trying to be nice.

"You fucker!" she told him. "You embarrassed me in front of three thousand people."[20]

The next morning, Janis was rushed to the hospital with acute bronchitis. Still, she must have felt vindicated about leaving Big Brother, after reading Mike Jahn's review of the Hunter College show.

"The band was severely disjointed," he wrote. "Miss Joplin was fine. Big Brother may be coming to an end, but Janis Joplin is just beginning."[21]

—◆—

After New York, Big Brother's farewell tour snaked through Houston, Denver, Seattle, and Vancouver, before the ultimate show on December 1 at a Family Dog benefit at the Avalon Ballroom.

Over the last few weeks, Albert Grossman had put out the word that he needed musicians for Janis Joplin's new backup band. Canadian pianist Bill King was playing a small Greenwich Village club when he heard Grossman needed a keyboard player. After auditioning for Grossman with his drummer friend Roy Markowitz, King was appointed Janis's musical director and keyboardist. He and Markowitz were then flown to San Francisco to start rehearsals.

They were put up in an apartment in North Beach, where they met Canadian bassist Brad Campbell, who would also be in the band. Soon after arriving, Janis invited them to the Noe Street apartment she was now sharing with Nick Gravenites's ex-wife, Linda.

"As soon as I walked in through the front door she handed me a joint and a Seagram's 7," recalled King. "I didn't drink or smoke anything, and she started laughing when I told her. She got a kick out of it."

Janis told them she was looking for a Memphis rhythm and blues–type sound, somewhere between Sam and Dave and Otis Redding.

"This was the big move," said King, "and she loved Stax records and that whole sound from the South. She wanted to get away from the Big Brother thing and go somewhere else."[22]

As they were leaving, Janis invited them back later for dinner, saying there were some friends of hers they should meet.

"When we arrived [that evening]," said King, "it was apparent a party was brewing in a nearby room. As we reached the dining room Janis charged in."

Over the next hour, a succession of heavily-tattooed denim-clad bikers arrived, as the three musicians became more and more uncomfortable.

"[We] looked like choirboys at a prison picnic," recalled King. "Janis journeyed from lap to lap kissing and hugging each man. Eventually . . . she introduced us as her new handpicked band, and the men in denim as the Oakland Chapter of the Hells Angels."[23]

After the hard drugs and liquor started flowing, the three musicians made their excuses, telling Janis they would see her tomorrow.

—◆—

The rehearsals for what was being called "The Janis Joplin Revue" were held at the old Fillmore Auditorium. The band had now been supplemented by Marcus Doubleday on trumpet, Tony Clemons on tenor sax, and Sam Andrew on lead guitar. Whereas Big Brother had always been a straight five-way split, Andrew was now a salaried employee, making $150 a week.[24]

Bill Graham was a constant presence at the rehearsals, as his new acts Santana and It's a Beautiful Day were also rehearsing at the old Fillmore.

"We all became friends," said King. "After we got done rehearsing, we'd run down and listen to Santana, who were miles ahead of our newly assembled unit."

At the beginning, Sam Andrew taught the new band members all the Big Brother crowd favorites, like "Ball and Chain" and "Piece of My Heart," but he felt a little out of his depth musically.

"These musicians were trained and had been around the block," said Andrew. "I was kind of 'wow, these guys are really different than Big Brother.'"

And Janis, with no idea of how to be a bandleader, was spending hours on the phone with Albert Grossman every day, asking for advice.

With the new group booked to play their first show at the Second Stax Volt Christmas Show in Memphis in just five days time, a nervous Grossman asked Mike Bloomfield and Nick Gravenites to take over the rehearsals. Soon afterward The Band's Levon Helm arrived to join them.

"The whole thing [was] not coalescing," said John Cooke, who had stayed on as Janis's road manager. "Mike Bloomfield did as much as anybody to try and make that band."[25]

Each day after rehearsals, Janis would hang out with her new band, drinking and playing pool. One night she took Bill King to see a Small Faces show at the Fillmore West.

"We caught the set and we were blown away by Rod Stewart singing," recalled King. "So afterwards she says, 'Let's go back and say hi to the band.'"

When Janis went backstage, Stewart and his guitarist Ron Wood kept their distance.

"They were really cold," said King. "And Janis just flipped out and said, 'You British guys are all alike. Fuck you!' and stormed out of the dressing room."[26]

Years later, Rod Stewart would reveal why he and Ron Wood had given her the cold shoulder.

"Janis Joplin was always chasing me and Ronnie around the place," he explained in 2013, "trying to shag one or the other of us, though without success. We were terrified of her and would hide."[27]

Soon afterward, Janis managed to deflower Fleetwood Mac's original guitarist Danny Kirwan, who was still a virgin.

"Janis suffered from a reputation of eating men alive," said Mick Fleetwood. "Danny . . . looked like a little English choirboy with blond hair. Janis basically summoned him to her room. And Danny at that point I don't think had had sex with anybody. So he turned up the next morning [having] been ravaged by Janis. He had fingernail marks all over him, of which he was quite proud. She was one hell of a girl."[28]

On Friday, December 20, Janis Joplin and her new band flew into Memphis to prepare for the Stax Volt Christmas Show. During the limousine ride from the airport to the Lorraine Hotel, where they were staying, Janis announced that she needed a drink. When the limo driver got lost trying to find a liquor store, Janis screamed at him.

But during that same ride, Janis saw a billboard for the Christmas show with a huge photograph and her name in large letters, far bigger then her Stax heroes, who were also on the bill, Rufus and Carla Thomas, Booker T. and the M.G.'s, and the Bar-Kays.

"Janis was flabbergasted," said King. "The thought of headlining amongst such prestigious talent sent her into an apologetic rant."

When they finally arrived at the hotel—where Martin Luther King had been gunned down a few months earlier—they were welcomed by Mike Bloomfield, who was holding a garbage bag full of marijuana.

That afternoon, there was a final rehearsal at the Soulville's USA Studios, with Bloomfield and Albert Grossman in attendance. Then they headed to the Mid-South Coliseum, where the concert would be held Saturday night.

"The soundcheck was a disaster," remembered Bill King. "You would have assumed the promoters would have spent decent coin to rent adequate amplification. Enough wattage for a sermon but not enough to carry the power of a raucous singer."[29]

The next night, Janis waited nervously backstage as a procession of Stax/Volt stars performed. The Bar-Kays opened the show and did the pony and boogaloo. Then Albert King, who had opened the Fillmore East with Big Brother nine months earlier, played. The last act before the intermission was Rufus and Carla Thomas, who dazzled the audience, leaving Janis shaking her head in the wings.

After a short break, Booker T. and the M.G.'s came onstage, followed by Eddie Floyd, who was presently enjoying a huge hit, "Knock on Wood."

Then the Janis Joplin Revue were announced. They had planned to do three new songs and encore with "Ball and Chain" and "Piece of My Heart."

Half the audience were African Americans who had never heard of Janis Joplin. The remaining white people who were there to see her did not want to hear any new songs. She started the set with Eddie Floyd's "Raise Your Hand," which received little applause. Things went downhill from there, and an encore was scrapped.

"We were intimidated by being there," explained Sam Andrew, "and we didn't play very well."

"Janis Joplin died in Memphis," wrote Stanley Booth in the next edition of *Rolling Stone*. "A few people went backstage, where everyone from the Revue was in shock. [Albert Grossman and Mike Bloomfield] tried to tell Janis that she was not to blame for what had happened. She had sung well and the rest had been beyond her control. But she was having none of it."[30]

Bandleader Bill King remembers a fan coming backstage after the show and handing Janis a gift that might have helped to erase any of her disappointment, at least for a while.

"She opens it up and it's six needles with syringes," said King, "and she's just so excited about it. I thought, 'Oh man, this is too weird.'"

Later that night, Grossman escorted Janis to a Christmas cocktail party at the home of Stax Records' president, Jim Stewart. Also there were Isaac Hayes and M.G.'s Steve Cropper and Donald "Duck" Dunn.

"All the great Memphis musicians were there," said King. "Janis was in an effervescent mood. She joked, laughed, poured drinks and talked music. All of us were swept away by her sincerity."

The following morning, during the limo drive to the airport, Janis told King how she and trumpet player Marcus Doubleday had shot heroin after the party and passed out.[31]

On December 15, the *New York Times* magazine ran a major profile on Bill Graham, headlined, "The Producer of the New Rock." The front page showed the smiling promoter in his Fillmore West office alongside another photograph of an appreciative Fillmore East audience.

"I dream about doing the Beatles," Graham told writer Michael Lydon. "I wake up in the middle of the night and I can see the show."

Graham said he would present the Beatles for nothing, conceding he would probably turn it into a closed-circuit TV show to offset his costs.

"For Bill Graham," read the article, "master of the Fillmores West and East, to mount a Beatles concert would be an almost orgasmic consummation of his ambitions."

Calling him "a classic American success" despite his "underground commodity," the article said his two Fillmores were "small mints" that had made him rich. His coast-to-coast Fillmore empire was an extension of himself.

"Am I good producer?" he asked. "You're right, I'm a good producer! Do I do it to feed my ego? Yeah, but it's a real ego, respect and pride. I wanna be the best; I want that Oscar every night."

Graham said he worked too hard to enjoy any of his money, admitting he did not spend enough time with his family

"His wife and their three-month-old son, David, live in a big apartment in plush Pacific Heights, San Francisco's Upper East Side," wrote Lydon, "but he pads around as he didn't quite fit in."[32]

When Bill Graham read the article he was furious. He fired off a letter to the editor of the *New York Times*, complaining that he had been falsely caricatured as "a raving Scrooge McDuck."[33]

———

Soon afterward, Chip Monck's wife told Bonnie that Bill had been cheating on her.

"She had the kindness to come and tell me," said Bonnie, "because I hadn't known."[34]

When Bonnie asked Graham's secretary Marushka Greene if it was true, she told her to ask Bill. When Bonnie confronted her husband, he initially denied it, before breaking down and admitting everything.

"I can still remember the conversation," said Bonnie. "He was in the bathtub and I was sitting next to him telling him all the reasons why he's making a big mistake. He's picking her over me and what's going to happen here [is] I'm leaving."[35]

Graham swore that he loved Bonnie and their new son David more than anything, vowing to break up with Diane immediately. But that would be easier said than done.

The day after Christmas, the Motherfuckers threatened to burn down the Fillmore East when Bill Graham refused to give them free tickets for an MC5 show. The *Village Voice's* Howard Smith was there when the Motherfuckers started disrupting the show.

"They started yelling things like, 'Burn down the Fillmore!'" said Smith. "So it was getting kind of dangerous. The ushers were spread out and they didn't know whether to intercede or not."

Even the radical MC5, whose patented battle cry was "Kick out the jams, Motherfuckers!" ignored the Motherfuckers, saying they did not want to get involved.

"David Peel and the Lower East Side opened the program, but the real show was the pressure and tension inside the hall," reported *Rolling Stone*. "Although most of the seats were filled, the crowd outside the theater wanted in—and the people inside supported them with cries of 'Open the doors! Open the doors!'"[36]

Bill Graham, transported back to his childhood and the horror of the Nazis, came out to face the angry mob and ordered them to leave.

"They came into the lobby," said Graham, "and said to me, 'You know we can come in by force.' And I said, 'Well I can't tell my staff to fight you, because that's not why they're hired, but I'm gonna stand in front of the building and if you try to come in, I'm gonna try to stop you.'"[37]

The mob's vicious reply was delivered with a chain, lashing across Graham's face from behind. It broke his nose, which started pouring blood.

"It hit him really, really hard," said Smith. "He staggered for a second and it was a shock. Then he stood up on the seats . . . above everybody. I was afraid he was going to be killed. It was a mob scene."

Graham then gave an impassioned speech, telling them how he had fought the Nazis in Europe as a child and survived, and if they wanted to burn down the Fillmore East they would have to take him down first. He then challenged them to fight him, saying he was ready.

"I've got to tell you that look [of his] was very ferocious," said Smith, "and it froze everybody. Not just what he was saying, it was the look in those eyes that you knew he might kill you."

Nobody came forward to fight him. The place went silent.[38]

"A strange thing happened," said Kip Cohen. "The minute they saw the blood on Bill's face, there was a strong reaction from the crowd, and these hundreds of people who had been swarming on top of him backed away."[39]

Many people were disgusted by the chain attack on Bill Graham and left. But now inside the theater the Motherfuckers went on a rampage, causing hundreds of dollars of damage. They broke an usher's arm with a metal bar and stabbed a young Puerto Rican boy. The asbestos stage curtain, which had been lowered to protect the backstage area, was slashed with a knife.

"And it was completely scary," said usher Allan Arkush, "and we were told, 'Take off your Fillmore jerseys and put on your street clothes.' It turned really ugly."[40]

———

After Bonnie discovered his affair, Bill Graham offered Diane LaChambre $10,000 to leave San Francisco and get out of his life. But she refused, saying she loved him regardless of money. Graham came to his senses after his lawyer warned him that a messy divorce with a teenage Lolita could ruin him. In fact, it could even get him arrested, as Diane was underage. Finally, it was agreed that Diane would take a trip to Tahiti at Graham's expense to see her father until things had quieted down.

But Diane did not leave town. On New Year's Eve, she arrived at Winterland, talking her way backstage. When Bill Graham found out he was livid, as Bonnie was also there to see the Grateful Dead, the Quicksilver Messenger Service, and Santana perform.

Graham asked Diane to leave immediately, but she refused, saying that she could handle any confrontation with Graham's wife. A few minutes later, when Bonnie walked in, the teenager brazenly introduced herself.

"Suddenly there she was," said Bonnie. "She wanted to be best buddies with me for some reason."[41]

When Bonnie said that she knew exactly who she was and she was going to Tahiti, Diane said she had changed her mind.

At midnight, Bill Graham welcomed in 1969 as Old Father Time and announced the Grateful Dead. And backstage, during the long Dead set, Bonnie and her young rival started drinking wine and talking.

At one point Diane asked why they all couldn't be friends and carry on as before. Bonnie was shocked at the suggestion.

"She thought we would be a ménage à trois or something," said Bonnie. "But she was just a child for God's sake. She was sixteen at the most and at the time I thought she was even younger than that."[42]

CHAPTER SEVENTEEN

The Sunshine Makers

January to March, 1969

On Saturday, January 4, 1969, Bonnie Graham was backstage at the Fillmore West when Diane LaChambre came over and greeted her like an old friend. Bonnie, who had had a couple of drinks, was furious that her husband's mistress was "getting in my face."

Later, as the Grateful Dead played, the women started arguing at the top of the stairs. Then it became physical as they fought on the floor to the astonishment of the people walking by.

"Well, she was on my turf," explained Bonnie. "and I took exception to it. I then had a few drinks which made it worse. So we actually got into a physical fracas at the top of the stairs of the Fillmore West, and there were plenty of witnesses around. It was *the* low moment in my life."

A security guard was trying to break them up when Bill Graham arrived on the scene. He promptly ordered them both out of the building and into his Mercedes. He then drove Diane to her grandmother's house, saying that the relationship was over and he never wanted to see her again. Then he drove Bonnie back to their apartment.

"I argued fiercely in the car," she recalled, "and it got a little wild. I was so upset. I was just venting. Having had two drinks made it easier to do."

Graham swore he would never see Diane again, but within days he had secretly moved her into his summer home in the Santa Cruz Mountains.

One afternoon a few days later, Bonnie took their son, David, to the Fillmore West to see his father. They were waiting in his office when LaChambre casually strolled in.

"She was wearing a see-through blouse with nothing underneath," said Bonnie. "It was like what's this nerd doing in my face? I had David with me and she wanted to see the baby. I thought, 'Get away from me you awful person.'"[1]

Bonnie was heartbroken, finding it hard to comprehend how much Bill had changed in the four years since he had entered the world of rock 'n' roll.

"He had been a very straight arrow," she explained. "And I kept that image of him for a long time. It took years for me to understand that he had become something different. Sex, drugs and rock 'n' roll is not the best way to live."

On Thursday, January 9, 1969, Led Zeppelin made their San Francisco debut at the Fillmore West as the opening act for Country Joe and the Fish. Bill Graham paid Jimmy Page's new band $2,500 ($17,000) for four nights. Within three months Graham would be paying them five times as much when they next played on the West Coast for him again.

"We were an opening act on the first tour," said Led Zeppelin road manager Richard Cole. "We did such good business that [Bill Graham] gave us a cash bonus."[2]

Soon after Led Zeppelin first played the Fillmore West, Bill Graham sent Santana into the studio to record some tracks. He asked his friend David Rubinson—who had worked with Latin musicians before—to produce the songs in an effort to score a record deal.[3]

Then Graham suggested a three-way partnership between him, Rubinson, and his lawyer Brian Rohan to set up two record companies—Fillmore Records and San Francisco Records, which would be distributed by CBS and Atlantic Records, respectively. Rubinson agreed and moved his family to San Francisco to run both of Bill Graham's record companies.

To get Santana a record deal, Graham first invited Atlantic Records founder Ahmet Ertegun to the Fillmore West to see them play.

"Ahmet sees the band take the stage," said Santana road manager Herbie Herbert, "and the place is sold out and the crowd loves them. But Ahmet says, 'There's nothing there. I've got conga players on fucking St. Marks Place on the Lower East Side that can smoke that guy.'"[4]

Later, Carlos Santana would claim to have deliberately thrown the Atlantic audition. He dreamed of being on Columbia Records.

"They had Miles Davis, The Electric Flag, and Bob Dylan on their roster," explained Carlos later. "I had heard stories about Atlantic from The Young Rascals and other people who weren't happy with the distribution or the royalties."[5]

When Santana next played the Fillmore West, Clive Davis of Columbia Records was there at Bill Graham's personal invitation. He loved them.

"You didn't need to be a rocket scientist to know that Carlos was a virtuoso guitarist," said Davis. "They were feisty. They were real. They looked good. You were dealing with the real deal. So I operate from the gut and I said yes, right on the spot."[6]

A few days later, Santana signed with Columbia Records and went into the Pacific Recorders Studio in San Mateo, California, with David Rubinson producing. But the sessions did not go well.

"There were a lot of internal problems," explained Rubinson. "They had reformed."

Santana's conga player, Marcus Malone, had recently been arrested for murder, and drummer Doc Livingston had been so drunk at the New Year's Eve show at Winterland that he'd fallen off his stool during the set.

A few weeks later, Livingston was fired by the band during a studio rehearsal. And as he walked out of the studio, he passed a nineteen-year-old drummer named Michael Shrieve, who was hustling free studio time.

The young drummer was a longtime fan of Santana. He had first seen Carlos several years earlier, playing a church hall near his home in Redwood City, California.

"I just stumbled onto them at some church hall," Shrieve remembered, "and I really enjoyed them so much I told my brother, 'I really want to play with these guys.'"[7]

Then in September 1968, Shrieve was at the Fillmore West for a Super Session with Michael Bloomfield, Stephen Stills, and Al Kooper and sat in on drums for a couple of songs.

Backstage, Santana's manager, Stan Marcum, was impressed, telling the teenager they needed a new drummer and even taking his number.

"But I never heard from them," said Shrieve, "but when I walked into a recording studio when they had a falling out with their drummer, [they] remembered me from that night."

Carlos Santana then invited him to jam with the band to see how he fitted in.

"We played for hours," said Shrieve, "and at the end of that period they pulled me into a room and asked me to join the band."

Carlos and Gregg Rolie then drove him back to his parents' house in Redwood City.

"I woke up my parents and said, 'See you later,'" said Shrieve. "I packed a few things, got in the car with them and drove up to the city to Bernal Heights and took my place on the couch. That's how I got in the band."

When Shrieve joined Santana they stopped recording, instead beginning an intense couple of weeks of rehearsals and gigs.

On February 13, Santana headlined four nights at the Fillmore West and introduced their new drummer. Michael Shrieve, who had hung out at the Fillmore as a fan for years, was nervous when he walked onstage to loud boos.

"The first show at the Fillmore was a huge thing for me," said Shrieve. "I remember the people booing because they were a popular group and their drummer was gone. I thought, 'Oh, boy. This is not how I want to be greeted at the Fillmore.'"

But after playing a mesmerizing drum solo on "Soul Sacrifice," the Fillmore West audience warmed to him.

"I got a standing ovation," he said, "and after that it was fine."[8]

Each day, Santana would rehearse in the studio before going to the Fillmore West to hear music. Michael Shrieve soon bonded with Carlos Santana and the other members of the band.

"Santana as a group was no hippie love thing," explained Shrieve. "This was like a street gang, but the weapon was music. If you messed up they were all over you. It was pretty serious."[9]

When they went back into the studio for another attempt at recording, producer David Rubinson was unhappy with the results, which failed to capture the Santana magic.

"It wasn't great," said Rubinson. "I was very disappointed in the recordings."

When they finally finished the album and gave it to Columbia Records, Clive Davis rejected it, saying it was no good.

"They blew it off," said Herbert, "and the band broke up right there on the spot."

After Janis Joplin had bombed at the Stax Christmas Show, Mike Bloomfield came in to tighten up the band. At the beginning of January, musical director Bill King fled to Canada to avoid the draft, with trumpeter Marcus Doubleday quitting soon afterward. So their replacements had to learn the Janis Joplin set from scratch, while Janis and Sam Andrew wrote new material.

With the pressure now squarely on her shoulders, Janis was taking more and more drugs to escape into oblivion.

"She had to become a businesswoman and she was afraid of that," said Sam Andrew, who often joined her on binges. "There was no brake on her as far as drugs go. She took a lot more drugs when she left Big Brother. It was just a natural progression . . . just becoming more of a superstar."[10]

On January 19, Janis celebrated her twenty-sixth birthday with a crate of Southern Comfort and an orgy.

"Me and Linda and two guys for two days, man," she later boasted. "The best party I ever had."[11]

At the beginning of February, Albert Grossman booked her into a tiny off-the-beaten-track theater in Rindge, New Hampshire, for what was officially being called "a sound test," to avoid any further humiliation. The next day she played "a preview" at the Boston Music Hall in preparation for her big Fillmore East debut as a solo act in early February.

"The pressure is on," said John Cooke. "She's decided to go off on her own and she doesn't want to fail."[12]

By the beginning of 1969, Bill Graham's Fillmore East and West were running like clockwork and the money was pouring in. His marriage falling apart, Graham was now spending more and more time away from San Francisco, running his ever-expanding operation.

"The Fillmores are now what the Savoy, the Paramount and the Apollo used to be," declared the *New York Times*, "great stages on which anyone who counts appears; to make it on them is to make it with the whole youth market."[13]

Graham now split his time 70/30 between San Francisco and New York, leaving Kip Cohen in charge of running the Fillmore East. It was fast developing its own personality, one distinct from its West Coast sibling. The Fillmore West was more laid back, with a ballroom for dancing, while the Fillmore East was virtually a Broadway theater, with ushers to escort patrons to their assigned seats. It even had perfume dispensers in the ladies' bathrooms and Candy Chicks running the concession stands.

At the end of 1968, ushers had started handing out programs to patrons at each concert. These pamphlets contained performers' biographies, editorials, public service announcements, and even a guide to other music events around town.

Bill Graham was also branching out with eclectic bills, pairing artists from all over the musical spectrum and introducing them to his young rock audience. On January 17, veteran jazz drummer Buddy Rich and his orchestra headlined the Fillmore East, with the Los Angeles rock band Spirit opening.

"Buddy Rich played for me in New York," said Graham proudly. "He broke the kids up, and now every Joe College promoter wants him. The Fillmore likes you, you're a smash."[14]

Bill Graham knew he could even risk booking lesser-known jazz greats like Woody Herman or Charles Lloyd, who wouldn't be able to headline at either of the Fillmores, as long as he had a big draw like Led Zeppelin or the Jimi Hendrix Experience.

"Everything is based on draw," he told Howard Smith. "I cannot have a bill with Archie Shepp, Miles Davis and Dizzy Gillespie—great music. One of them can fit in with a Creedence Clearwater. Isn't it incredible that Miles Davis plays for X dollars a week and Creedence Clearwater plays for X dollars a night. Why is that? Not because one is better than the other. One sells eight million records and appears on the *Ed Sullivan Show*. That's not knocking them. It's just what life is about."[15]

But when Graham launched a series of eight Sunday-night jazz concerts at the Fillmore East, it bombed. He canceled the program after only three shows when nobody came.

The Joshua Light Show was now an integral part of the Fillmore East experience. As well as providing an exciting visual accompaniment to the bands, it had also started screening cartoons and funny captions between changeovers.

"It was the Sixties so everyone has been smoking pot or whatever they did to go to those shows," said Allan Arkush, who was now working on the stage crew. "They're a captive audience and you've got them sitting in the dark. Even though it was a fast changeover—fifteen minutes—you want to keep them occupied, so we came up with the ideas of bringing cartoons."[16]

The Light Show staff would also pair film clips with the bands; like Walt Disney's *Alice in Wonderland* for Jefferson Airplane and Alfred Hitchcock's *The Birds* for The Byrds.

A particular audience favorite was a trippy 1935 cartoon called *The Sunshine Makers*, featuring elves who bottled beams of sunlight. In the piece, the bottles would be given out to people, who then drank from them, which caused each imbiber to start singing and dancing.

"*The Sunshine Makers* was a huge success," said Arkush. "We'd run it before the Grateful Dead."

In the beginning, Bill Graham turned a blind eye to open drug taking at concerts. It was mainly marijuana and LSD in those days, and many of his staff were getting high along with the audience. When the Grateful Dead played the Fillmores, there was always plenty of LSD backstage, and often a jug of spiked apple juice would be passed into the crowd.

At the Fillmore East, a special room off the mezzanine had been set aside for people suffering bad trips. And manager Kip Cohen hired four young doctors and gave them permanent passes to be on call during concerts.

"It became known as the Bummer Palace," said Cohen. "We furnished it very comfortably with soft couches and a select group of rather more sensitive ushers would babysit the people who were freaking out and having bad trips with drugs."[17]

On Friday, January 24, The Doors played Madison Square Garden, becoming the first band to graduate from the Fillmore East to play the far larger venue. Instead of playing four shows for Bill Graham, they opted to play just one at the Garden for the same money. Graham felt insulted.

"I was the one who put The Doors into the Fillmore in San Francisco before they had a hit," he raged to Doors' manager Bill Siddons. "I gave them their first break."[18]

Graham had always detested Madison Square Garden, referring to it as a "cement factory," with none of the good vibes of the Fillmore East.

Annie Fisher of the *Village Voice*'s "Riffs" column, agreed.

"The sound system is abominable," she wrote. "The Doors and the promoters got lots of money, and money is really all these monster events, indoor and out, are all about. The music? Who knows?"[19]

After playing the show, Jim Morrison arrived at the Fillmore East, gloating about how much money he had made that night. While walking around, he spotted the bosun's chair that Chip Monck used to ride sixty feet up to the lighting bridge. Morrison boasted that his father was a Navy admiral, so he knew all about bosun's chairs, asking if he could go up in it.

"So we put him in the bosun's chair and took him up," said John Morris, who was there that night. "We then tied him off in the chair and left him to go next door to Rattner's for breakfast. We could hear him screaming through the walls because Rattner's was on the other side. When we finally let him down we said, 'So, play for us next time.'"[20]

Two weeks later, Led Zeppelin debuted at the Fillmore East, opening for Iron Butterfly, currently enjoying a huge hit with "In-A-Gadda-Da-Vida." And all the Fillmore East ushers wanted to be stationed by the stage for a better look at the new Yardbirds.

"I certainly remember the first weekend of Led Zeppelin," said Allan Arkush. "And the excitement. It was incredible."

On Friday night, Led Zeppelin upstaged Iron Butterfly with an extended "Dazed and Confused."

"At the late show on Saturday night Iron Butterfly decided they were going to take an earlier flight," said Arkush, "so Led Zeppelin got to close. It was an epic concert. Epic."[21]

⁓

Soon after the fire in the apartment he shared with Grace Slick, Spencer Dryden started an affair with a beautiful twenty-year-old groupie named Sally Mann, moving her into 2400 Fulton Street. The runaway daughter of the mayor of Houston, Mann recently had been featured in a *Rolling Stone* special on groupies. A divorcée with a baby boy, she was collecting $150 a month on welfare.

"Sally is a good girl," Dryden told *Rolling Stone*, "and the way you can tell is that the other girls here dig her."

Mann explained that there was an unwritten rule among the girls at the Airplane Mansion, "about balling more than one guy in the band at a time."[22]

By the time Grace Slick returned from Los Angeles, where she had been helping Paul Kantner mix the new Jefferson Airplane live album, Dryden had installed Sally Mann as the band's new housekeeper. Grace then found an apartment in Sausalito, having her husband, Jerry Slick, move in as her roommate.

Grace got on well with Sally Mann, and for a time they shared Spencer Dryden in a love triangle.

"There were lots of bizarre evenings," Mann explained. "The three of us would be up real late, drinking."[23]

In late January, Grace went into the hospital for a second operation to have nodules removed from her throat. By coincidence Lydia Pense, the singer of the band Cold Blood, also managed by Bill Graham, was there for the same procedure.

"Gracie and me were in the same hospital," recalled Pense. "We had our nodes in our throats scraped. Back then they scraped them."[24]

In early February, Jefferson Airplane's live album *Bless Its Pointed Little Head* was released to great reviews, with *Rolling Stone* calling it "an LP of astonishing power."

A month later, the Fillmore East's playbill's "Your Mother Should Know" column applauded the LP, which had been recorded live at both Fillmores.

"All the energy that the Airplane's giant wall of sound creates," wrote editor Mark Spector, "becomes part of everyone's living room. Furthermore, the group is at its best, giving us the finest Jefferson Airplane you can get in an onstage situation. This is an era of live, visual music and hopefully other groups will follow quickly in the Airplane's footsteps."[25]

With Grace and Spencer Dryden estranged, the other band members met to decide who was now going to look after the beautiful rock goddess.

"We had a meeting," said Marty Balin," to try and figure out who would go with Grace and take care of her, because she always needed a guy to talk for her. Jorma didn't want the job and Casady had tried it and didn't like it, and I didn't want the job. Paul was actually elected, damned straight."[26]

In mid-February, when *Rolling Stone* ran its special issue about the new breed of groupies, the backstage action at the Fillmore East and West was featured prominently. Along with Spencer Dryden's new girlfriend, Sally Mann, Bill Graham's twenty-nine-year-old Fillmore West publicist, Chris "Sunshine" Brooks, was profiled.

"Few groupies have been as active as long as Sunshine, who originally started with jazz players," it read. "Now she is the senior partner in a group of five girls ... who travel in a pack in quest of rock bands. Sunshine is both a groupie and more than a groupie."[27]

Soon after the article appeared, Brooks, whom Bill Graham had recently appointed his national director of publicity, received calls from many of the bands she worked with at the Fillmore West.

"That article made me famous," she said, "and I got phone calls from Ten Years After and all the bands that I worked for, 'Chris, I didn't know you were a groupie. Are you busy Friday night?'"

Brooks, the mother of twins, says that part of her job involved setting up girls for the visiting English bands who played the Fillmore West.

"I was a pimp for my English mates," she explained, "by virtue of the fact I was a publicist. Because of my seniority at the Fillmore West, I surrounded myself with a bevy of beautiful birds, who I knew were clean and fun and would show the guys a good time on the weekend and not bother them at home. That's where the pimping came in. It was all part of the job."

During her years working for Bill Graham, Brooks became good friends with many top bands, including The Who and Led Zeppelin, whom she supplied with beautiful willing girls.

"Most of the bands I worked for were proper Englishmen away from home," she explained. "It would be a matter of Roger Daltrey saying, 'Chris, you know that Chinese bird over there with the big Bristols?' And I'd say, 'Yes, I do.' 'Could we have an introduction please?' And they were always properly introduced."[28]

She would also set up Jimmy Page with nice clean women, as well as warning him about the more unsavory ones.

"There were two contingencies of San Francisco groupies," she said. "One was very nice and then there was Miss Harlow. I remember Jimmy Page looking at her when she was coming onto him. And he said, 'God, one night with her and it'd be two weeks in hospital.' She was very grungy with all her Twenties get-up and Jimmy never went for that type anyway. He liked to do the hitting."

On one tour, Led Zeppelin drummer John Bonham caught the clap from a Fillmore West groupie and went home and gave it to his wife. The next time he played the Fillmore West, Bonham had Brooks "babysit" him, so he wouldn't be tempted by any groupies.

Fillmore East general manager Kip Cohen was also interviewed for the *Rolling Stone* piece, saying his security men stopped groupies from going backstage unless they were with a band.

"We don't have that many problems," he said. "One of our security guards was once offered a free fuck on the fire escape, if he would let the groupie in afterward. But this sort of thing rarely happens."

Cohen said that the English groups were "the worst," because they attracted the most exotic-looking groupies.

"There's definitely a run on black groupies this season for some reason," he said.[29]

Howard Smith said dozens of groupies would congregate outside the Fillmore East before shows, offering sex for free tickets.

"And one night this particularly cute groupie," he recalled, "was begging and begging because I had an extra ticket. I said, 'Here, you can have it but we'll have to sit next to each other.' She said, 'No, no, no. I'm going to blow you.' I said I wasn't interested in trading sex for a ticket."

———

There was a great deal at stake when Janis Joplin and her Band, as they were now billed, played two sold-out nights at the Fillmore East on February 11 and 12. Opening for them were the Grateful Dead, who would record part of their landmark *Live Dead* album that weekend, with the rest being recorded a few weeks later at the Fillmore West.

A crew from CBS's *60 Minutes* came to film a segment on the Fillmore East. And along came reporters from *Time, Life, Look, Newsweek,* and the *New York Times,* who all wanted to profile Janis. Albert Grossman was snowbound in Woodstock, unable to come to the show. And Myra Friedman only discovered at the last minute that Mike Wallace and the *60 Minutes* crew wanted to film Janis's performance for an upcoming segment entitled "Carnegie Hall for the Kids."

Earlier, while the band had been setting up, Janis was interviewed by Mike Wallace for *60 Minutes.* She was stoned, telling the veteran newsman to just scream "fuck" if she said something he didn't like, so it couldn't be used on the air. She promised to do the same if he were to ask a "dumb" question.

When Wallace asked if a white woman can sing the blues, Janis looked straight at the camera and said "Fuck."[30]

———

The four hotly anticipated shows had been sold out for weeks, and ticket scalpers outside on Second Avenue were charging exorbitant prices for seats. The Grateful Dead played first, launching into "Good Morning Little Schoolgirl" and not stopping for more than an hour.

One hard-core Janis Joplin fan named Ronnie Finkelstein sat through the Grateful Dead set while waiting patiently for Janis.

"I found them original and satisfying," he explained to a reporter. "I wanted Janis, though. I rushed back when Bill Graham—the dirty capitalist!—introduced my girl."[31]

Her new band came on first and played without her for a few minutes before Janis strutted out wearing a black pantsuit and delivering a fine performance.

Later, as she held court to the press in her dressing room, Janis was insecure and sought reassurance.

"Don't you think I'm singing better?" she asked one reporter. "Well, Jesus, fucking Christ, I'm really better believe me."[32]

There was mixed critical reaction to Janis and her new band. Ellen Willis of the *New Yorker* was sympathetic to Janis for putting herself on the line with a new band and a new sound.

"I hoped she would do well," she wrote, "but I knew *I'd* like her anyway. The show I saw wasn't a flop. And though it wasn't great, either, at this point the deficiencies can be attributed to growing pains. What was missing was a sense of authority; Janis did not know exactly where she was going, and she was not completely at home with her band."[33]

Mike Jahn in the *New York Times* called it "an improvement."

"Miss Joplin had been limited by Big Brother's strict adherence to psychedelic music," he wrote in his review. "Miss Joplin has never been better, even though her new group sounds as if it is just getting to work well together, it still is very good."

———

After the Fillmore East shows, Janis Joplin and her band did a short East Coast tour before heading back to New York for the *Ed Sullivan Show*. While they were on the road, she hooked up with her new organist, Richard Kermode, for a few weeks, but he soon tired of her heroin use.

"The junk didn't dampen her enthusiasm for sex," he said later. "It was like she'd want to go on forever, but not *feeling* anything. I couldn't get into it. It was weirdness."[34]

On March 15, *Rolling Stone* published a devastating profile, headlined: "Janis: The Judy Garland of Rock?" Joplin was in New York when it came out, and she was so upset that she canceled an interview with Howard Smith for his show on WNEW-FM.

The feature, by writer Paul Nelson, put Janis under the psychological microscope, finding her lacking the necessary mental armor required to survive stardom.

"Janis seems that rare kind of personality," wrote Nelson, "who lacks the essential self-protective distancing that a singer of her fame and stature would appear to need."

Nelson ended the article saying it was too premature to pass definitive judgment on Janis and her new band, and that although her Fillmore East opening wasn't a success, it wasn't a disaster either.

"One wishes nothing but good things for her," he wrote. "It would be tragic if she were allowed to become the Judy Garland of rock."[35]

— ~ —

In late March, Janis Joplin played three sold-out nights for Bill Graham at the Fillmore West and Winterland, grossing $75,447 ($480,000). After the first night's show, Janis went downstairs to a garage to collect her beloved psychedelic Porsche, only to discover it stolen.

"She was in tears," recalled Graham. "She really loved that car. That was her escape into faraway places."

Graham took charge, using his contacts on San Francisco radio stations and going on air himself to appeal for listeners to help find Janis's car.

"We put out an all-news bulletin," he said. "[Janis] was just sitting all night long. Just a little lady who'd lost something precious to her."[36]

At seven o' clock the next morning, they received a call that the Porsche had been found abandoned in Oakland and the thief arrested.

And the shows went on. In reviewing them, *San Francisco Chronicle* critic Ralph J. Gleason noted that the audience at Winterland had not even brought her back for an encore.

"Her new band is a drag," he wrote. "The best things that could be done would be for her to scrap this band and go right back to being a member of Big Brother . . . If they'll have her."[37]

When Janis read his review she was mortified, scoring some heroin with Peggy Caserta on the street outside the Fillmore West to dull the pain.

On March 28, former US President Dwight D. Eisenhower died, bumping Janis off the cover of *Newsweek*, which she had been looking forward to. Later, when she was shown the discarded cover photo of herself, she threw a tantrum.

"God-dammit, you motherfucker!" she screamed in anger. "Fourteen heart attacks and he has to die in my week. In my week."

Two days later, Janis left for a European tour with her still-unnamed band, hoping things would be a little calmer across the Atlantic.

At the beginning of March, Jefferson Airplane rented a castle in Hawaii while they played a show at the Honolulu International Center. Grace and Spencer Dryden were now making a final attempt to salvage their two-year relationship, but the drummer mainly stayed in their hotel room, drinking himself into a stupor.

One afternoon, Grace left him and went down to the pool, where Paul Kantner gave her some orange sunshine acid. During their trip, the two realized they were in love, although nothing happened at that time, as Kantner had brought a girl with him.

When they returned to San Francisco, Jefferson Airplane began rehearsals for their next album—*Volunteers*. One night after Grace cooked him dinner, Paul Kantner invited her upstairs to his bedroom to share a bottle of champagne. The next morning, Bill Thompson arrived at the mansion to start work.

"And Grace came down from the third floor smiling from ear to ear," said Thompson. "That's when they started."[38]

CHAPTER EIGHTEEN

Go Ride the Music

April to June, 1969

In early April 1969, Bill Graham received a registered letter stating that he would have to vacate the Fillmore West building by January 1, 1970, as it was being demolished to make room for a Howard Johnson's hotel. When he had signed a five-year lease with Bill Fuller nine months earlier, he believed it was airtight. But it had a "demolition" clause, which allowed the landlord to serve him nine months' notice if he decided to tear down the building.

"I had no reason to believe this would happen," Graham later wrote in an editorial in his Fillmore East program. "However, even before I signed the lease, and unbeknownst to me, he was negotiating for the sale of his lease to a large corporation. I just wish he could have been upfront with me when I signed the lease."

Graham wrote that his Fillmore West meant a lot to the San Francisco community, and it would be a tragedy if it were replaced by a giant hotel.

"This will be the 583rd Howard Johnson's in America," he railed. "I don't like their hotels, and I never liked their foods, but the transaction was legally correct."[1]

Graham appealed to the San Francisco community to stop Howard Johnson's razing the Fillmore West to the ground.

"A Fillmore is important," he said. "A place that can present the kinds of shows we've put on. It doesn't make any difference whether *I'm* running it or somebody else. The scene needs this focal point—the

Fillmore has more connecting points to the electrodes of the scene than any place else."[2]

Soon afterward, Graham brought in Keeva Kristal, an old friend from his Catskills days as a waiter, to manage the Fillmore West and his other West Coast operations. Kristal knew nothing about the music business and was disliked by the staff from the beginning.

"Keeva was the guy who ran the coffee shop at the Concord," said David Rubinson. "And he was the quintessential penny-pinching, money-grabbing Catskills fuck."[3]

———

Six thousand miles away in Europe, Janis Joplin and her new band were finally jelling. Away from the intense scrutiny and pressure of the American critics and audiences, Janis was more relaxed and delivering some of her finest performances. Her new brass section, consisting of saxophonists Snooky Flowers and Terry Clements and Luis Gasca on trumpet, were a perfect foil for her unique vocal style.

"That's when we played our best," said Sam Andrew. "We really hit a good gear and that's when you sense, 'Oh yeah, now Janis is really becoming this big star.'"[4]

The early April shows in Amsterdam, Frankfurt, Paris, Stockholm, and Copenhagen were all triumphs, receiving rave reviews.

"Everything came together in Europe," said John Cooke. "The band was good. The concerts were good. It showed everybody what [the band] could be, but nobody saw it but us and the European audiences."[5]

The third week of April, Janis arrived in London for a sold-out show at the Albert Hall. There was huge anticipation in England to see Janis, and reportedly a pool of musicians vied to be the first to sleep with her.

Prior to the performance, Janis met London *Evening Standard* music writer Ray Connolly in a bar for an interview. She told him she had been drinking Gordon's Gin all day, after Mick Jagger had snubbed her concert, saying that if he wanted to hear black singing, he'd listen to black singers.

"She's cut to the quick," wrote Connolly.

As the interview progressed, Janis became drunker and drunker as her band members looked on in disapproval.

"Nobody ever asks me about my singing," she told Connolly. "All anyone ever wants to know is about fellas and booze and sex. I want to be known as a singer."

She also revealed that her doctor had recently warned her that her liver had become swollen from too much drinking.

"Man," she declared, "I'd rather have ten years of superhypermost than live to be seventy sitting in some goddamn chair watching TV. And you know what I wanted most in the world? I wanted to be on the same bill with Otis Redding. It was all arranged, and then he was killed. He was my idol. I wanted him to tell me I was good."[6]

———

The afternoon of the show, writer Mark Williams of the underground newspaper *International Times* was at the Albert Hall to see Janis rehearse.

"She was obviously nervous," he later wrote, "dashing from one cat to another, laughing, shouting and gesticulating wildly."

Back in her dressing room, Janis knocked back tequila shots with American singer P. J. Proby while complaining about the lack of limes at her hotel.

"Janis announced that it was her private ambition to own a bar," wrote Williams, "where she could entertain her friends and make lots of new ones."

Then Janis invited everybody back to her hotel, so they could "freak out all those straights."[7]

At the show that night, Janis was in top form, bringing the six thousand fans to their feet with a dynamite set featuring: "Maybe," "The Combination of the Two," "Summertime," "Work Me Lord," and "Ball and Chain."

Eric Clapton watched from a box with photographer Bob Seidemann as Janis exhorted the audience to loosen up.

"I don't want to offend propriety or anything," she declared, "but if you want to dance then that's what it's all about."

Janis brought the house down after the last encore, leaving the audience on their feet screaming for more. A few minutes later, she held a press conference in her dressing room.

"We did it! We did it!" she shrieked triumphantly, "and a room of pressmen ain't going to bring me down."

Then she announced she had to leave. She had a party to go to.

"I'm not sitting here talking to you," she told the reporters. "I'm going out to have a ball. I'm so happy!"[8]

Back at her suite at the Royal Garden Hotel in Kensington, Janis held court with Clapton and other English musical celebrities.

"Eric Clapton was very complimentary," said Andrew. "We played a good gig that night so everybody was happy."

Someone at the party had heroin and discreetly led Janis and Sam Andrew into a bedroom to shoot up. Suddenly the lead guitarist turned blue, and Janis helped take him into the bathroom and put him in a cold-water bath to bring him around.

Several days later, Janis was invited to dinner at George Harrison's country house in Esher, Surrey. After the meal she cozied up to him.

"Hey, man," she told the Beatle, "I've been wanting to make it with you for years."[9]

— ◆ —

At the beginning of April, after several unsuccessful attempts to record their first album, Santana found the last piece of its musical jigsaw puzzle. Michael Carabello, who had rejoined the band, was jamming in Aquatic Park when he first saw Nicaraguan timbales player José "Chepito" Areas.

"It was, 'Oh my God,'" recalled Carabello, "'this guy plays his ass off.'"[10]

That night he brought Carlos Santana and Gregg Rolie to the Nite Life club, where Chepito was performing with his band, the Aliens. He was a Latin music virtuoso, also playing congas, trumpet, and drums.

"He was a complete firecracker of a player," recalled Michael Shrieve, "who just brought the house down, dressed in those big frilly shirts with the huge collars and greased-back hair."[11]

Carabello then introduced Chepito to Carlos, and they spoke to each other in Spanish, as Chepito's English was almost nonexistent at that time.

"And Santana came to see me play," said Chepito, "and he liked the sound of Latin rock. They said, 'We're going to record an album and we like this kind of sound that you've got. If you could teach us how to play Latin rock it would be good.'"[12]

The newly minted Santana was an extraordinary ethnic mix that should never have worked on paper in 1969, but did spectacularly. There was a Mexican, an African American, a Puerto Rican, a Nicaraguan, and two white boys from the suburbs.

"And we looked cool, you know," said Michael Shrieve. "We were really *the* American band, as opposed to Grand Funk Railroad or something like that."

When Chepito joined Santana, he was told to stop wearing fancy suits and ties. Such attire didn't fit in with the band's rough image.

"They looked like a lot of dirty hippies who needed shaves," explained Chepito. "They gave me blue jeans with holes and a shirt all ripped-up."

According to Shrieve, five-foot-tall Chepito was culturally like "a fish out of water," but an "incredible and natural" musician.

And once he started rehearsing with the band, that's when the unique Santana sound was born.

"The rehearsals started taking on a whole new vibe with the advent of the timbales and two conga players," explained Shrieve. "Between their new drummer, me, and their new percussionist, Chepito, the band . . . felt an incredible surge of new energy. Chepito's musicianship and sound had an incredible influence on the band."

In May, Santana went into the studio for their third attempt to record their first album. This time they recruited a friend named Brent Dangerfield, who did the sound at the Straight Theater in Haight-Ashbury, to produce the album. He had absolutely no previous studio experience.

"We were real prima donnas," explained Carlos Santana, "but we wanted a lot more freedom . . . we didn't want to be controlled."[13]

Bill Graham attended many of the recording sessions, pressing the band to become more radio-friendly and stop playing long jams. Chepito was a huge musical influence in the studio, adapting many of the songs to Latin rock.

"Carlos didn't know how to play that style," said Chepito. "They were starting to do 'Evil Ways,' 'Black Magic Woman,' and 'Oye Como Va.' I taught them to play the Latin rock."

During the recording, Santana played half a dozen Fillmore West shows, as well as a show with the Jimi Hendrix Experience at the Santa Clara County Fairgrounds. Somebody there dosed Chepito with LSD, and he would always suspect Carlos of doing it. The timbales player had such a bad trip that Carlos had to take him home and nurse him until he came down.

﹋

In early 1969, an ambitious young promoter named Michael Lang had joined forces with former Fillmore East employees John Morris and Chip Monck to organize a music festival in Woodstock, New York. During the next few months, Lang, who had staged the Miami Pop Festival a year earlier, booked the entire Fillmore East's summer schedule of groups for his upcoming Woodstock Festival. When Graham found out, he was furious. The event put attendance at all his summer shows in jeopardy.

"He threatened to pull [Woodstock]," said Lang. "He was afraid that we were going to wipe out his Spring and Summer, so he was trying to bully us. Bill had one of the great egos of our industry and [Woodstock] was going to put him in the shadow."

In May, Lang met Graham for breakfast at Rattner's to try to work something out. At the meeting, Lang agreed not to announce any of his Woodstock bands until after they had played the Fillmore East.

"We had a nice chat," said Lang. "I think we had six or seven acts in common. I invited him to come up on one of the days and he said he would. We left on friendly terms and his parting comment to me was, 'I guess we can't play god on the same day.'"[14]

Throughout the next few weeks, Graham lobbied Lang to book Santana for Woodstock, although they still did not have an album out. According to Graham, Lang was having problems booking the Grateful Dead and needed his help.

"I said they could use my name," said Graham, "in return for Santana being put on the show on Saturday night. During prime time. I didn't want them on at seven in the morning or three in the afternoon."[15]

﹋

On Sunday, April 13, Jefferson Airplane hosted a lavish wedding reception at their mansion for KSAN-FM radio boss Tom Donahue's wedding to Rachael Hamilton, a close friend of Grace Slick. The food and champagne punch had been spiked with LSD, and many of the guests, including plenty of San Francisco's social elite, were dosed.

KSAN DJ Dusty Street was at the reception and had a six-hour radio show that night.

"Now I didn't realize they had put acid in everything," she said, "and as my fiancé was driving me to the radio station, I turned to him and said, 'Gee, you know I think I'm coming onto acid.' And he said, 'Of course you are. There was acid in everything.'"

By the time Dusty went on the air she was flying.

"And I went to read the first commercial," she remembered, "and it was for Woodstock and the opening line was, 'How would you like to take a really far-out trip?' And I went off onto some tangent and [somehow] realized that I was out there somewhere in the cosmos. So I very quietly turned the microphone off and didn't talk again for another five and a half hours."

A few hours later, her boss, Tom Donahue, called her from the Biltmore Hotel, where he was spending his wedding night.

"Street, you're doing a great job, man," he told her.

"And I'm sitting here having figured out how to queue this thing up," she said, "and just dropping it on the album and hoping it hits the cut. Really free-form radio."[16]

Two weeks later, Jefferson Airplane went into Wally Heider's brand-new studio in San Francisco to record their next album, *Volunteers*. Now that Grace Slick and Paul Kantner were a couple, the band's whole dynamic had changed. It was during this time that Kantner started writing more overtly political songs, speaking out against the Vietnam War and Richard Nixon's drug policies.

"A lot of changes happened in the world," Kantner explained. "I mean for me it started off with the assassination of John Kennedy, which turned my focus around, and I think probably a lot of our generation, from relying on the government. And there's a lot of shit going on. And this is reflected in most of the songs that I wrote then."

The opening song on the album was Kantner's "We Should Be Together"—a call to arms for young people to "tear down the walls, motherfucker." It was the first use of the word "fuck" on an album, and the Airplane knew they would have to battle RCA to bring it out. Another controversial track was "Eskimo Blue Day," with Grace's music and lyrics cowritten with Kantner. The refrain: "Doesn't mean shit to a tree."

"People call us protest singers because of *Volunteers*," said Kantner, "but we weren't really protest singers, so much as just mentioning what's going on in the world. And here's something you should think about and maybe come to your own conclusions, rather than us telling people what to do. And we got away with it."

Paul Kantner still resented Spencer Dryden for firing Bill Graham, believing it had been a big mistake.

"I was never good friends with him since," said Kantner. "I'm still pissed off with him for getting rid of Bill Graham so superficially. Because that was a big downturn from my point of view."[17]

After his split from Grace, Dryden's days in the band were numbered.

The first weekend of April, the Chambers Brothers played the Fillmore East with the Hello People and Elephants Memory. In a subsequent *New York Times* review, critic Mike Jahn applauded the band's "exciting musical fusion," but criticized the "rough" Fillmore East audience.

"Friday night the house seemed filled with the type of people who go to stock car races hoping for accidents," wrote Jahn. "They booed and otherwise interrupted a beautiful, sensitive intertwining of jazz rock and mime by the Hello People, a New York City group."[18]

Two days after the review came out, a fuming Bill Graham wrote to the *New York Times*'s music editor, Raymond Ericson, demanding to know Jahn's musical qualifications to review his shows.

"I am infuriated by the slanderous remarks he leveled at one recent artist," wrote Graham. "May I have the courtesy of hearing from you at your earliest convenience."

Ericson replied by return of mail.

Dear Mr. Graham:

The New York Times always satisfies itself regarding the qualifications of its writers before engaging them. This was true in the case of Mike Jahn, and I believe that that should be a sufficient guarantee for you.

Yours truly,
Raymond Ericson
Music Editor

A couple of weeks later, Bill Graham ran both his and Ericson's letters in his Fillmore East program.

"This was prompted by our feelings of frustration at the hands of one critic whose background we attempted to question," he explained.[19]

Mike Jahn would continue to review Fillmore East shows for the *New York Times* until its close.

⌒⌒

In mid-April, Bill Graham finally persuaded The Band to play Winterland, followed by more dates at the Fillmore East a month later. The deal Graham signed with The Band's manager, Albert Grossman, paid them $20,000 ($127,400) for the three West Coast shows.

On Wednesday, the day before the first sold-out show, Robbie Robertson came down with a high fever and was too sick to attend the soundcheck. When Winterland opened for the show the following night, the lead guitarist was sick in bed and could hardly move.

"We were giving him all the shots and vitamins we could," said Bill Graham. "By the late afternoon, Albert started wondering if hypnosis might work, so I got the yellow pages and found a 24-hour hypnotist."

As the Ace of Cups opened, a hypnotist arrived and put Robertson into a deep trance, telling him he was feeling great and could play that night.

And when The Band took the stage, the hypnotist was in the wings to offer encouragement. As they started their set, Robertson could barely stand, leaning against Garth Hudson's organ for support, while the hypnotist kept shouting, "Grow! Grow!"

After just seven songs The Band left the stage to boos and did not return. When Bill Graham came out to try to pacify the crowd, they turned on him.

"Well, there must be a lot of tourists here tonight," Graham told them, "because San Francisco people just don't act this way."[20]

By the next night, Robertson had fully recovered and The Band played a great show to thunderous applause, with rock critic Greil Marcus calling their encore of the old blues song "Slippin' and Slidin'," one of the "great moments in the history of rock 'n' roll."

On Friday, May 9, The Band made their East Coat debut at the Fillmore East. There was great excitement about the four sold-out shows, and usher Allan Arkush got his NYU Film teacher Martin Scorsese tickets for Saturday's late show.

"He was crazy about The Band," recalled Arkush, "and we had to get him really good seats."

The Band took the stage, playing most of their hit album *Music from Big Pink*, which they called "mountain music." They performed an hour-long set with three encores.

"In their first set Friday," wrote Mike Jahn, "it took them two or three songs to really warm up, but when they did they played with great freshness and ease. The members of The Band are coolly professional. They appeared onstage wearing suits (of all things) and worked into a rocking fever of an intensity seen only occasionally."[21]

⁓

The last week of April, Led Zeppelin played four nights at the Fillmore West on their second US tour. Bill Graham paid the band a flat fee of $10,000 ($64,000) for two forty-five-minute shows each night, payable in full before the first show. Bill Graham grossed a total of $72,441 ($462,000) for the performances.

Things got off to a bad start when Led Zeppelin arrived at the Fillmore West for a soundcheck to find Bill Graham shooting hoops on the stage with some of his staff. When a Led Zeppelin roadie politely asked if they could start setting up equipment, Bill Graham lashed out.

"Who the hell are you speaking to, fella?" he yelled, waving his index finger at the astonished members of the band and their manager, Peter Grant. "When I'm ready to talk to you, I'll talk to you. Can't you see I'm right in the middle of something."[22]

Then Led Zeppelin patiently waited for Graham to finish the game before setting up and doing the soundcheck.

—◦—

Bill Graham was determined to keep the Fillmore West from being demolished. He had been mobilized by a *San Francisco Chronicle* editorial that applauded him for bringing the city to "the front of the national rock scene." A month after receiving his marching papers, Graham vowed to fight, describing his landlord's order to vacate as "a solid right cross to the jaw. I been down before but this time I ain't coming off the floor too quick."

He told *Rolling Stone* in May that he had not considered an alternative venue and would probably close down if he had to move. Asked if he would still keep the Fillmore East open if that happened, Graham threw a tirade.

"New York is gutter warfare," he shouted. "Industrial psychology. There's no salt and pepper for me . . . but this is where I'm from, I would keep this operation going."

The reporter then asked about a rumor that he was planning to open up a Fillmore in Los Angeles.

"Never, ever, ever, ever will I go to Los Angeles," he barked. "I hate that fucking place so bad."

He then calmed down, saying he was fed up with the music business and dreamed of just sailing away on a big sailboat.

When the reporter questioned why he did not, as he could easily afford to, Graham exploded.

"Look," he snarled, "when circumstances put you on top of the mountain and you got a whole industry—a whole fucking industry—trying to pull you off . . . well, no motherfucker is gonna do that to me."[23]

—◦—

In mid-May, Jefferson Airplane went back on the road for a short three-city tour. In Chicago they played a huge free concert in front of fifty thousand dancing fans in Grant Park. During the show, Grace Slick told the fans to "buy acid with the $5 you would have had to spend for this concert."

At their next stop in New Orleans, cops burst into their hotel room, busting Jack Casady and Bill Thompson for two suspect cigarettes.

"Louisiana is a very uptight state," Thompson told *Rolling Stone*. "If you sell grass to someone under eighteen, it's punishable by death."

At the final stop at an outdoor concert in Miami, the police turned the power off at eleven o'clock in the middle of the Airplane's set, causing a near riot.

"Wait 'til we burn down your society," Paul Kantner told a cop, before promptly being arrested for disturbing the peace.

On Friday, May 16, The Who premiered Pete Townshend's new Rock Opera *Tommy* at the Fillmore East, the day before its US release.

"On the opening night I was more excited than usual," recalled Townshend, "and we were bullish that we'd have a good show."[24]

To get in the mood, each band member had a bottle of brandy backstage, as well as another on Keith Moon's drumhead for refreshments during the performance.

Toward the end of their first show, somebody hurled a Molotov cocktail into the Lion Supermarket that shared a wall with the Fillmore East. As firefighters arrived to put out the three-alarm blaze, fire chiefs reassured Bill Graham there was no imminent danger to his audience. So he decided to wait until the end of *Tommy* before evacuating the theater.

Fillmore East usher Allan Arkush smelled smoke and then looked outside to see flashing lights and firemen all over Second Avenue.

"And the smoke got thicker," he recalled, "and Pete was singing 'Listening to you, I get the music.' The focus in the theater was on them and the energy of it [was] lifting everyone."

Suddenly a plain-clothed tactical force detective appeared from the wings at the right of the stage and tried to grab the microphone out of

Roger Daltrey's hands, yelling, "Give me the mike!" Without missing a beat, Townshend lined up a kick to the detective's testicles with his Doc Martens.

"He came from nowhere," said Arkush, "and Townshend kicked him in the balls. Somebody from the stage crew grabbed him and dragged him off and the entire audience jumped to its feet. It was positively a Roman spectacle."

As more police raced toward the stage, The Who carried on playing as if nothing was happening. The audience thought the thickening smoke inside the theater was all part of the show.

"But the adrenaline level was beyond," said Arkush. "The blood pressure level was huge. And they finished *Tommy* with that fantastic note, and the audience went crazy. Then The Who just counted off and lit into 'Summertime Blues.' Just like that."

Finally, Bill Graham managed to get Townshend's attention and went onstage to tell him about the fire next door.

"And I could see them whispering," said Arkush, "and The Who kind of brought it way down. It was like a rocket ship turning off its boosters and the audience is standing there panting. What's going on. Then Graham went to the microphone and was so cool. He said, 'We have a little problem.'"[25]

He announced that the ushers were going to clear the theater until it was safe to return, and then The Who would finish the set.

"That building was empty within three minutes," said Arkush. "And of course there was no late show, as the smoke was really too thick in the theater."[26]

Later that night, Townshend was charged with assaulting a police officer, and a warrant was sworn out for his arrest. The next morning he turned himself in, spending a few hours in the tank until Bill Graham bailed him out.

On Saturday and Sunday nights, The Who were back at the Fillmore East, playing four more sensational shows.

In the next edition of the *Village Voice*, Annie Fisher reported the fire in her "Riffs" column, calling Bill Graham "Field Marshall Von Fillmore," and labeling the Fillmore East as a "fascist state."[27]

When Graham read the piece he went crazy, calling Fisher "a fucking vicious ratfink scumbag," and complaining that her paper was even worse than "those crumbs" at *Rolling Stone.*

A couple of weeks later, a New York City court fined Townshend $75 for a misdemeanor.

On June 17, The Who played the first of three nights at the Fillmore West. This time Pete Townshend told Bill Graham they would play only one show a night instead of two.

"But he was intractable," said Townshend. "We made our first set very short as a challenge to his so-called 'authority,' so he had a disgruntled audience on his side, too."[28]

Finally, Graham backed down, and The Who never played more than one show a night for him again.

—⟡—

The first weekend in June, the Grateful Dead played four shows at the Fillmore West. One night backstage, the Dead's Psychedelic Hit Squad dosed all the apple juice with extra-strong Owsley LSD.

"[This] may have been the first occasion since the Trips Festival in '66 that so many people were dosed so hard for so long," wrote Dead bassist Phil Lesh in his autobiography, *Searching for the Sound.*

Hanging out in the dressing room that night was Janis Joplin and her sax player, Snooky Flowers, who drank some of the LSD. He ended up in the hospital, with Janis holding his hand for six hours until he came down.

Janis was furious, later attacking the acid king Owsley Stanley, putting him up against a wall and yelling, "You motherfucker! You killed my bass player!"[29]

On June 16, Janis and her band went into Columbia studios in Hollywood to record an album. Since their European trip, Janis and Sam Andrew had become strung out on heroin, and their shows had lost their spark.

"It was the non-returning phenomenon," said road manager John Cooke. "It wasn't something that could be replicated once we were back in America."[30]

During the ten days of recording, producer Gabriel Mekler wrote a song for it called, "I Got Dem Ol' Kozmic Blues Again Mama!"

"All of a sudden they just grabbed hold of that phrase 'Kozmic Blues,'" said Cooke. "And then the band became the Kozmic Blues Band."[31]

Janis wanted to record the Bee Gees hit "To Love Somebody," which she had been performing at shows. So she called up writer Robin Gibb for permission.

"We got a phone call," recalled Gibb, "and it was Janis, who said she loved the song. And she was very complimentary about it and wanted to know if she had our sanctification. We said, 'Yeah, go ahead.' She did [it] unlike anybody's ever done and I was surprised. She had the ability to put her stamp on a song."[32]

One night in Los Angeles, Janis summoned Sam Andrew to her room at the Landmark Hotel in West Hollywood. Then and there, she fired him.

"She offered me some heroin," said Andrew, "so we literally were shooting heroin while this was happening. We were kind of numb, but yeah, it was devastating."

When Janis asked if he wanted to know why she was firing him, he said no because he already did.

"We were going to write a lot of songs together," he explained, "and we didn't because we were stoned. That particular time was deadly."

Soon after, Janis took Sam Andrew to bed for a one-night stand to commiserate.

"After she fired me," he said. "I let myself have a romantic thing with her. It was just one night."[33]

On Friday, June 20, Santana headlined the Fillmore West while the Grateful Dead rocked the Fillmore East. As usual the backstage area was awash with LSD, and most of the Fillmore East crew would be dosed over the two nights of shows.

"One night we turned off all the lights in the theater," said Allan Arkush, "and just had the light show screen. And then the ushers turned on their flashlights and aimed them at the Grateful Dead. They would play those first notes of 'Dark Star,' and there would be a cheer, and then [the Dead] would settle in. That's how you ended up with thirty-minute-long 'Dark Stars.'"[34]

At another Dead show during the run, lighting technician Candace Brightman was so high she turned off all the spotlights, plunging the stage into darkness. The Grateful Dead loved it, immediately hiring her to be their lighting designer.

The Grateful Dead finished playing at three o'clock on Sunday morning. Then the Fillmore East stage crew moved all their equipment uptown to the Great Lawn in Central Park, where Bill Graham had arranged a free concert for them and Jefferson Airplane that afternoon. After the show, Graham donated dozens of trash cans, as well as his Fillmore East staff, to clean up the Great Lawn.

Bill Graham takes a break at the Fillmore Auditorium in June 1966.

Grace Slick takes a break between Jefferson Airplane sets in Bill Graham's Fillmore Auditorium office on December 30, 1966. Graham had started managing the Airplane several months earlier.

Janis Joplin took the stage to join Grace Slick in a song during Jefferson Airplane's 1967/1968 New Year's show at Winterland in San Francisco.

The Joshua Light Show mesmerized audiences for almost two years at the Fillmore East. (L–R) William Schwarzbach, Cecily Hoyt, Thomas Shoesmith, Jane Rixman, Ken Richman, Joshua White.
PHOTO BY JOE SIA / © WOLFGANGSVAULT.COM

The Joshua Light Show team posing on the stage of the Fillmore East (L–R) Eugene Theil, Amalie R. Rothschild, Ken Richman, Jane Rixman, William Schwarzbach, Joshua White, and Cecily Hoyt.
PHOTO BY AMALIE ROTHSCHILD / © JOSHUA WHITE

Bill Graham and Joshua White at the Fillmore East in 1968.
PHOTO BY AMALIE ROTHSCHILD / © JOSHUA WHITE

Janis Joplin and Big Brother and the Holding Company launched the Fillmore
East on March 8, 1968.

Janis Joplin backstage at an East Coast show in 1968.

Proud father Bill Graham with his baby son, David. Graham first saw David's photograph projected on the screen at the Fillmore East, just hours after his birth in San Francisco.
© BONNIE MACLEAN

Bill Graham ran a tight ship at his Fillmore East. Here he is making a last-minute inspection before Jimi Hendrix's 1969/1970 New Year's Eve show at the Fillmore East.
PHOTO BY JOE SIA / © WOLFGANGSVAULT.COM

Jimi Hendrix's 1969/1970 New Year's Eve show, which later became a best-selling live album, was legendary.
PHOTO BY JOE SIA / © WOLFGANGSVAULT .COM

After Jimi Hendrix's first 1969/1970 New Year's Eve set, Bill Graham critiqued his performance, complaining that he was playing to the crowd with his visual pyrotechnics. Hendrix took his advice and concentrated on the music for the second set. Then he let loose for the encore.

PHOTO BY JOE SIA / © WOLFGANGSVAULT.COM

Grace Slick performing with Jefferson Airplane during an East Coast run of shows in March 1970. By this time the Airplane had fired Bill Graham as manager but had become the de facto house band at his Fillmore East.

PHOTO BY JOE SIA / © WOLFGANGSVAULT.COM

Crosby, Stills, Nash & Young insisted on bringing in their own sound equipment and lighting during their run of shows in June 1970.

PHOTO BY GENE ANTHONY / © WOLFGANGSVAULT.COM

The Joshua Light Show made history by mixing live video of Janis Joplin performing at the Fillmore East into the light show in 1970.
PHOTO BY AMALIE ROTHSCHILD / © JOSHUA WHITE

Janis Joplin performing at the Fillmore East with the innovative Joshua Light Show.
PHOTO BY AMALIE ROTHSCHILD / © JOSHUA WHITE

Bill Graham took his wife, Bonnie, on a rare vacation to Geneva, Switzerland, in 1970 to visit his sister, Evelyn Udry. Also pictured is Evelyn's husband, Jean-Pierre Udry, and their daughter, Cathy.
© BONNIE MACLEAN

Bill Graham discovered Carlos Santana during an audition at the Fillmore West and nurtured his rise to rock superstardom. This shot of Carlos performing at the Capitol Theatre, Port Chester, New York, was taken on October 14, 1970.
PHOTO BY JOE SIA / © WOLFGANGS VAULT.COM

John Lennon and Yoko Ono spontaneously took the stage to perform an encore with Frank Zappa on June 5, 1971, stunning the Fillmore East audience.
PHOTO BY JOE SIA / © WOLFGANGS VAULT.COM

Bill Graham takes the stage to introduce the Allman Brothers Band at one of the final Fillmore East shows on June 25, 1971.
PHOTO BY JOE SIA / © WOLFGANGSVAULT.COM

The Allman Brothers Band closed the Fillmore East with a legendary set on June 27, 1971.
PHOTO BY JOE SIA / © WOLFGANGSVAULT.COM

CHAPTER NINETEEN

Three Days of Peace, Love, and Music

July to September, 1969

One afternoon in early July 1969, Grace Slick strolled into the stately British Motor Cars showroom in San Francisco. A huge fan of the James Bond movies, Grace had fallen in love with the Aston Martin DB5. Agent 007 had driven it in *Goldfinger*. So she zeroed in on the $18,000 gleaming blue sports car on display at the dealership.

"Wow, what's *that?*" she asked a salesman. Not recognizing her and thinking she was hippie, in her sandals and scruffy hair, he was dismissive, saying it was an Aston Martin DB5 with an automatic shift, but she probably could not afford it.

"Far out," Grace replied. "That's just what I want. I'll take it."

She then walked out of the showroom and straight to her bank, reappearing an hour later with $18,000 in cash. After handing it to the bewildered salesman, she got in the Aston Martin and drove away.

"James Bond yeah," said Grace, "that's why I got it. I don't have any of the spikes, the machine guns, or the ejector seat in the front or anything, but it's a good car."[1]

Soon after Grace bought the DB5, she souped it up to make it even faster.

"She had the engine taken out and put a Chevrolet engine in it," said Jorma Kaukonen, who had just bought himself a Lotus Elan. "I mean that's something you don't see every day."[2]

In early July, Bill Graham stepped up his operation, opening the Fillmore West six nights a week for most of the summer. He also announced a "Fillmore Night at Tanglewood," as part of the Berkshire Music Center's prestigious summer music series. His program for August 12, designed to capture the atmosphere of the Fillmore East, starred The Who, Jefferson Airplane, and B.B. King. It would break all previous attendance records for the annual summer music series.

At the beginning of July, Bill Graham had given an interview to Howard Smith for his WPLJ-FM Sunday radio show, describing himself as "a volunteer madman."

"You live in an eat or be eaten society," he told Smith. "It's the ugliest business I've ever known. I don't know if any business has more shady characters in it. Maybe the underworld?"

Asked if money had changed him at all, Graham reminisced about his early days running the Fillmore with Bonnie at his side. He painted a picture of an idyllic relationship, even though his marriage was now falling apart because of his infidelity.

"At that time Bonnie was working in the office with me," he told Smith, "and now she's with the baby. On some obscure Wednesday night I'll get through at nine o'clock and I'll call her. I'd say, 'All right put on some slacks and we'll take a ride to Mill Valley and have dinner.' And if we go to the country and we have some wine and we have a fillet. If the waiter comes back and says, 'Mr. Graham, I'm sorry there are only two fillets left but they are two specials that we've saved for the last nine hundred years and they'll cost you $10,000.' I'll say, 'Bring it.' That's luxury."

He also discussed his love of Latin music, which he was now channeling into Santana.

"I was one of the authentic Latin American mambo freaks of New York City," he declared. "And when my old lady isn't home I have to admit to dancing in front of the mirror sometimes. I get very freaky."

Then Smith asked for Graham's reaction to accusations that he was "exploiting the lifestyle," and ripping off the music fans with high prices.

"Isn't it ironic that Bill Graham is knocked for making all this money," he replied. "Is it ever questioned what Joe Superstar makes. Does anyone say, 'Hey, Jim Morrison, why don't you give me some of your money?' 'Hey,

Jimi Hendrix.' 'Hey, Rascals.' 'Hey, Simon and Garfunkel.' They make a lot of money. They're entitled to it for a very simple reason. Why should the promoter get it all?"[3]

Everything was about to change in the concert promotion business, with the balance of power shifting from the promoter to the artist. The new rock festivals had started drawing thousands of fans as well as the biggest concert names. Last summer's Newport Pop Festival in California, with Jefferson Airplane and the Grateful Dead, had pulled in an estimated 140,000 fans. And the previous December's Miami Pop Festival with the Jimi Hendrix Experience had drawn 50,000 people.

Eager to jump on the bandwagon, ambitious young promoters like Michael Lang were now lining up an array of festivals in Atlanta, Denver, Toronto, and Atlantic City. These were all a direct threat to Bill Graham, who could see the writing on the walls of both his Fillmores.

After The Doors had snubbed the Fillmore East in favor of Madison Square Garden, Jimi Hendrix had followed and Janis Joplin would not be far behind.

There was also what had happened after Memorial Day weekend, when Led Zeppelin had played three sold-out shows at the Fillmore East with Woody Herman and Delaney and Bonnie opening. Graham had also booked the band for the Rose Palace, Pasadena, during the West Coast leg of that tour, several weeks after playing another four shows at the Fillmore West.

But in late July, Graham discovered that Led Zeppelin planned to play Carnegie Hall on their next tour that fall, bypassing the Fillmore East.

He immediately fired off a letter of protest to Zeppelin manager Peter Grant in London. It was dated July 31, 1969—just two weeks before the Woodstock Festival.

Dear Peter:

During a conversation today with Frank Barsalona, I learned of your intention of putting Led Zeppelin into Carnegie Hall in New York sometime in October.

Needless to say, I have no right to tell a manager what to do with his artists. However, I do have a right to speak my piece; which is what I intend to do now. I never cease to be amazed at the lack of ethics of this wonderful business that you and I are involved in. You, Peter, asked me for the extra money regarding the Rose Palace engagement, and you got it. But more important than anything else, you needed and used the Fillmores to build Led Zeppelin to a headline attraction, and now you honestly can feel that there is nothing wrong in not giving the act back to us; now that you no longer need us. Supposedly.

Tell me, if every manager takes your point of view, when the Fillmores are there to expose the new Led Zeppelins of our business to the mass audience, shouldn't the star Led Zeppelins continue to play the Fillmores so that we will be there to expose these new groups—the Led Zeppelins of tomorrow? Even if I wasn't the producer here, I would wonder why Hendricks [sic] and The Doors play the Garden, where the sound is abominable. And why would you prefer to play Carnegie Hall. Is it really so disgraceful to play the Fillmore for two nights and earn a mere pittance of $25,000?

Don't you think the Fillmores should be supported?

The reason I put this directly to you is because I find myself falling into a very dangerous position now. We are building acts to a level of great notoriety and then they go on and play the big money houses. There was a time in this business when the top price was around $10,000 a night. In our houses you can make that kind of money, but you get more than that. You get quality production and I wonder if that still means anything to you, Peter. If nothing else, wouldn't it be proper that, regardless of the huge coliseums you would play all over the country, that Led Zeppelin does continue to support the two or three places that were there when Led Zeppelin needed them, i.e. the Fillmores, the Kinetic Playground, etc.?

And I'm not just talking about Led Zeppelin. I'm talking about Hendricks [sic], The Doors and all the other giants of this ethical business we are in.

I should like an answer to this letter from you at your earliest convenience. I will reiterate that no one can tell you how to run your show, but in my opinion, it is this kind of inconsideration on the part *of managers that would help to put places like the Fillmores out of circulation. And then where would you be in America?*

   Cheers,

   Bill Graham[4]

On August 19, Peter Grant replied via a Western Union telegram.

DEAR BILL:

   THANKS FOR YOUR LETTER OF JULY 31. THIS IS PROBABLY NOT GOING TO BE GRAMATICALLY CORRECT AS IT IS COMING STRAIGHT FROM THE TOP OF MY HEAD AS IT COMES, SO HERE GOES. OF COURSE THERE IS NO QUESTION OF THE FILLMORE'S BEING THE BEST RUN HOUSES IN THE STATES WITH SUPERIOR SOUND AND LIGHTING. THAT IS FOR OPENERS. AS FOR BEING ETHICAL AND FAIR HOW ABOUT WHEN JEFF BECK HEADLINED THE FILLMORE EAST FOR $5000 FLAT AND SELLING OUT FOUR SHOWS. AS A THANK YOU TO YOURSELF FOR BEING THE FIRST TO BOOK HIM IN THE STATES. WHAT ABOUT LED ZEPPELIN THE SECOND TIME IN SAN FRANCISCO WHEN WE WORKED OUT A PERCENTAGE AFTER WE FINISHED THE DATE. WERE NOT THOSE FAIR TO YOU? BUT WAS IT FAIR TO THE LED ZEPPELIN AT THE ROSE PALACE WHEN YOU RENEGGED ON THE DEAL? I DID NOT ASK YOU FOR EXTRA MONEY I ONLY ASKED YOU FOR WHAT THE ACT WAS ENTITLED TO ON THE ORIGINAL DEAL WE MADE AND WHO SAID LED ZEPPELIN WOULD NOT PLAY THE FILLMORE ANYMORE? COMMUNICATION BREAKDOWN, MY FRIEND. WE TRIED VERY HARD TO WORK OUT A DATE ON THE COAST THIS SUMMER. AS FOR THE MONEY QUESTION WHEN YOU WERE MANAGING JEFFERSON AIRPLANE YOU WERE NOT TOO BASHFUL TO ACCEPT $15,000 A NIGHT FROM PROMOTERS. HOW ABOUT THE FORTUNE YOU MADE FROM

THE KIDS WITH THE SALE OF YOUR POSTERS. WHEN LED ZEPPELIN ARE OFFERED MORE IN A GUARANTEE FOR TWO NIGHTS AT THE PAVILION, ONE SHOW PER NIGHT THAN THEY CAN MAKE ON FOUR SELL OUTS FOR YOU AM I SUPPOSED TO TURN THAT DOWN? HOW ABOUT THE FACT THAT JIMMY PAGE SUPPORTED THE REST OF THE GROUP FOR THE FIRST SIX MONTHS. HE NEVER HAD A DIME OUT OF THE GROUP FOR THIS PERIOD EXCEPT FROM HIS RECORD EARNINGS. LET ME TELL YOU BLEW A LOT TO ME WHEN YOU TRIED TO WELSH ON THE ROSE PALACE DEAL AND TOLD FRANK BARSALONA TO TELL ME TO DROP [THE] DEAL AND NOW YOU SEEM JUST AS BRAVE AT THE TOP OF THE TYPEWRITER AS YOU DO BY PHONE AND YOU WILL NEVER STOP SENDING COPIES OF YOUR LET-TER TO AARON RUSSO, DON LAW, FRANK BARSALONA, UNCLE TOM COBBLY AND ALL. I DID NOT KNOW YOU COULD STOOP SO LOW TO TRY AND ATTEMPT TO PUT ME DOWN.
    PETER GRANT[5]

Soon afterward, Bill Graham inserted a clause into all his contracts excluding bands from playing Madison Square Garden if they wished to play his Fillmores.

Although Bill Graham liked to project the image of the happily married family man, he was still seeing Diane LaChambre. Their relationship was a tempestuous one, and he was obsessed with his beautiful young mistress.

"She didn't wear underwear," said Chris Brooks, "and she would flash him and do all sorts of things to get his motor running. He was just being a man. We felt sorry for him because she was using him . . . and apparently he was paying her rent."

Once, Graham discovered Diane with a musician in a dressing room at the Fillmore West.

"I remember Bill standing outside the door of the dressing room," said Brooks, "while she was inside screwing somebody from some band. Just standing there with his arms folded and his face red. Then she came out and she turned red, and Bill gave her this look, turned on his heel and walked away."[6]

Over the summer, LaChambre made two suicide attempts after Graham tried to break up the relationship. Then she became pregnant and he paid for an abortion.

After one bitter argument, she had blackmailed him for a large sum of money, threatening to go public with their relationship. After Graham paid up, she bought some expensive clothes and then threw the rest of the money off the Golden Gate Bridge.[7]

By all accounts, things had slowed down for Bill Graham financially. His boom years were between 1965 and 1968, and by 1969 an economic recession had cut into his profits. The Fillmore audiences had changed, too, graduating from marijuana and acid to speed, downers, and heroin.

As the San Francisco scene began to collapse, Graham became *the* scapegoat. All the hostility against him finally surfaced with the great San Francisco Lightshow strike. After Graham refused to pay the San Francisco light shows $900 a weekend with equal billing with bands, they picketed a Grateful Dead concert.

"There was a virtual fistfight," said Chet Helms. "The Dead are a pretty physical bunch of people and there were a couple of punches thrown. Jerry Garcia showed up while this was erupting and we both managed to calm things down and persuade the leaders to go across the street to the beach and talk."[8]

Garcia, Helms, and a delegation of strikers then crowded into the back of the Grateful Dead equipment van to discuss the matter. A meeting was then arranged for the following Tuesday at the Family Dog hall.

Bill Graham was among the three hundred people at the meeting, as the light show members were threating to picket the Fillmore West that night.

"You do not tell me what to do," Graham yelled, jabbing his finger at them. "Where the fuck does the artist come to say, 'you the businessman must support *us*,' when I personally think the light shows are not producing an income for me?

"The only way you can do this is to kill me and step over me. I will never have anyone tell me . . . what I must pay a light show."

The self-appointed leader of the light show union, Stephen Gaskin, then cast himself as Graham's prosecutor in some kind of weird courtroom scene.

"When you started," declared Gaskin, "you had to make a choice between love and money. You've got our money, so you can't have our love."

Trembling with emotion, Graham stood up and defended himself, recounting his days in the Holocaust and his struggle to survive in the Bronx and how he started his own business.

Then Gaskin accused Graham of being a fraud, saying had just quoted a speech verbatim from an Eli Wallach movie.

"I apologize, motherfucker, that I'm a human being," yelled Graham with tears in his eyes. "I fucking apologize. Emotional—you're fucking right. You think I'm an actor? You're full of shit, man. I have more fucking balls than you'll ever see. You want to challenge me in any way about emotions? You slimy little man . . . you slimy little man."

Graham then stormed out, trailed by an astonished *Time* magazine writer who was writing a profile on him.

On his way out, someone tried to calm him down. Seething with anger Graham hissed, "Don't get peaceful with me."

His publicist, Chris Brooks, who was at the meeting, said she was shocked to see everyone turn on Graham.

"Bill had tears in his eyes. He hurt," said Brooks. "He sat there while they called him a capitalist pig and kept attacking him. He kept trying to explain his position. He's a businessman. He's not a hippie."[9]

The next day, Graham announced he was leaving San Francisco forever.

"This town has never stopped rapping an honest businessman for four fucking years," he told *Rolling Stone*. "I leave here very sad. I may be copping out but your attitudes have driven me to my decision."

On Friday, August 1, Santana debuted at the Fillmore East, third on the bill to Canned Heat and Three Dog Night.

"They were very humble when they came," recalled Allan Arkush, "and I remember getting them a lot of food, because I realized this was going to be their main meal of the day. They were great and beloved among the staff."[10]

That weekend's Fillmore East playbill had a double-page advertisement for the upcoming Woodstock Music and Arts Fair, with the Grateful Dead, Janis Joplin, and Santana billed for Saturday, August 16. The Jefferson Airplane, who would headline Saturday night, were missing from the advertisement, as they were playing the Fillmore East the following weekend.

The Atlantic City Pop Festival—held the first weekend of August—had an almost identical bill to Woodstock's two weeks later. The Friday-night headliners would be Crosby, Stills & Nash, Joni Mitchell, Johnny Winter, and Santana Blues Band, as the poster mistakenly read. Jefferson Airplane and Creedence Clearwater Revival topped the bill on Saturday, with Janis Joplin closing the festival Sunday, where she would sing a duet with Little Richard.

A couple of weeks earlier, Sam Andrew had played his last show with Janis at the Forest Hills Music Festival. He then flew back to San Francisco, as Janis made her first appearance on the *Dick Cavett Show*. Wearing a red crushed velvet shirt, a large gold necklace, and a faraway look, Janis seemed subdued. When the genial Cavett asked what she had done "to kill time" since they had last met, Janis said she had been working.

"We went to Europe," she said. "Scared them to death, I think."

"Did you have fun?" asked Cavett.

"No," Janis replied, "I had a terrible time. Nobody really gets loose and nobody rocks over there. They're all so cerebral."

Then Cavett asked if it were still possible to sing the blues if you were making several hundred thousand dollars a year.

"It doesn't have anything to do with money," she said, "or it really shouldn't. Playing's just about feeling. Playing isn't necessarily about misery. Playing isn't necessarily about happiness. But it's just about letting yourself feel all those things that you have already inside you, but you're all the time trying to push them aside because they don't make for polite conversation."

———

All the hard drinking and drugging were beginning to take their toll on Janis, and her performances were suffering.

"[Those] Kosmic Blues years," said John Cooke. "That's the only time that Janis's drug use affected her performances. It wasn't any fun anymore."[11]

At the end of July, John Morris invited Janis to stay at his house in the Virgin Islands so she could clean up her act for Woodstock.[12]

Before leaving, Janis called Albert Grossman and swore she would sober up in the Caribbean. But nine days later, when Myra Friedman collected her from the airport, she immediately noticed that Janis was the same ghostly pale as she had been before leaving.

"It rained every day," Janis explained.[13]

———

Jefferson Airplane rocked the Fillmore East the weekend of August 8 and 9, the band's fourth appearance there. On Friday night the Airplane's second set went on well past four o'clock, and Saturday's finished even later.

After the final set, the Airplane had played two encores and the crowd were still applauding and screaming for more. Then Bill Graham came out onstage, suggesting they remain silent for a minute. He then went backstage and offered to carry Spencer Dryden out on piggyback. The drummer got on his back and Graham brought him out and placed him on his drum stool for the Airplane's third encore.

It was at these shows that Jorma Kaukonen and Jack Casady unveiled their new offshoot band called Hot Tuna.

"The Hot Tuna thing just evolved," Kaukonen explained. "We've known each other for a long time, and we've been playing together in hotel rooms and just sort of fooling around. Hot Tuna didn't really exist and then at the Fillmore East someone said, 'Why don't you guys play a couple of songs?' I think we might have played 'Embryonic Journey' and 'Hesitation Blues.' And then we got back with the band and played and the crowd liked it. So in a way Jefferson Airplane introduced what was to become Hot Tuna to the world and allowed us to do that."[14]

Paul Kantner says that he suggested Hot Tuna open for the Airplane that night.

"Yeah, I encouraged that," he said. "And it probably led to the breakup of the band eventually."[15]

On Sunday, Jefferson Airplane headlined another Graham-organized free concert at the Sheep Meadow in Central Park. Santana opened the show and were joined onstage by Jorma Kaukonen and Jack Casady to play for a couple of blues numbers.

Later, in a review in the "Riffs" column in the *Village Voice*, Don Heckman wrote that Grace Slick had not been at her best at the Fillmore East shows.

"Unfortunately, the pressures of non-stop flying are taking their toll," he wrote. "The Airplane is beginning to look and sound tired. Grace Slick sang more consistently out of tune than I have ever heard, and Spencer Dryden seems to be wearing himself out."

The Fillmore East now closed down for a month as the staff moved up to Lenox, Massachusetts, to stage a special show at the Tanglewood Festival the weekend before the Woodstock festival. Presented by Bill Graham, the bill consisted of Jefferson Airplane, The Who, and B.B. King.

Joshua White videotaped all the performances for a potential television special, but unfortunately Graham had failed to secure clearances from the bands, and the project was eventually shelved.

~ ~

After Tanglewood, many of the Fillmore East staff headed to Bethel, New York, for the Woodstock festival. After getting fired by Graham, John Morris had gone to work with Michael Lang to organize Woodstock, recruiting many of his old Fillmore staff to help.

"Bill started putting Woodstock down from the very first minute," said Morris. "Bill thought Woodstock was taking a bunch of kids and putting them in a field [and] hated the idea. Bill looked at festivals and outdoor shows as uncontrollable and unsafe to the audience. You can't hear as well. You can't see the music."[16]

Agent Frank Barsalona sold many of the Woodstock acts to John Morris for prices that would skyrocket after the festival and the resulting hit movie and best-selling double album.

Headliner Jimi Hendrix received $30,000; The Band, Janis Joplin, and Jefferson Airplane were paid $15,000; Sly and the Family Stone, The Who, and Crosby, Stills, Nash & Young all got $12,500; Joan Baez and Creedence Clearwater Revival each received $10,000; The Grateful Dead got $7,500; Ten Years After got $6,500; and Joe Cocker and Santana received only $2,500. By the purchasing power of the 2010s, the range is approximately $191,000 for Hendrix to $16,000 for Santana.

The only reason Bill Graham went to Woodstock was to see his protégés Santana perform. Bonnie had flown in to accompany him there, and they would be staying at Grossinger's Resort, where he had once waited tables.

"We were able to stay in a nice hotel and went in on the helicopter," said Bonnie. "He only really went because of Santana and that was it."[17]

———

Several days before Woodstock, many of the musicians playing the festival met for a late dinner at El Quijote restaurant, next door to the Chelsea Hotel. Grace Slick and the Jefferson Airplane shared a table with Country Joe and the Fish, and Jimi Hendrix sat nearby with a ravishing blonde woman.

Patti Smith wandered in that night looking for friends before being amazed to see most of her musical heroes there eating dinner and discussing the upcoming festival.

"They were here for the Woodstock Festival," said Smith. "Grace Slick got up and brushed past me. She was wearing a floor-length tie-dyed dress and had dark violet eyes like Liz Taylor.

"'Hello,' I said, noticing I was taller.

"'Hello yourself,' she said."[18]

———

On the afternoon of Thursday, August 14, Jefferson Airplane arrived at the Holiday Inn in Liberty, New York, where most of the bands were staying. Various members of the Airplane and The Who had bonded during the previous weekend in Tanglewood.

"We partied with Keith Moon," recalled Bill Thompson. "He was our good friend and we'd stay up the whole night with him."[19]

When Janis Joplin turned up at the Holiday Inn with her girlfriend Peggy Caserta, she sought out her old boyfriend Country Joe McDonald.

"Janis and I talked and then she asked me to come to her room," recalled McDonald. "When we got there she decided I needed to have sex. She gave me a blow job, much to my surprise."

After they had sex, Janis got out her works to shoot up some heroin.

"It was all quite casual and natural for her," said McDonald. "It wasn't for me. I could not stand needles and watching someone shoot up was sure not my idea of fun."

He told Janis he was leaving, but she begged him to stay and watch her shoot up.

"I told her . . . I was not going to watch her kill herself," he said. "I left her room and did not see her for the rest of the festival."[20]

———

On Friday morning—the first day of Woodstock—Bill Graham attempted to upstage the organizers. His office issued a press release proudly announcing that his recent "Fillmore Night at Tanglewood" had broken all attendance in the venue's thirty-two-year history. To celebrate, read the release, Bill Graham would donate a thousand dollars to establish a Fillmore scholarship to send a young musician to the Berkshire Music Center.

———

On Saturday morning, the Jefferson Airplane helicoptered into the festival, flying in directly behind Janis Joplin and her Kozmic Blues Band. Backstage, Bill Thompson then organized a meeting of all the managers of the main bands. Thompson told everyone that the bands should be paid first to make sure they were not ripped off. A deputation of managers then met with Michael Lang and his partner, Artie Kornfeld, demanding their money by that night, or they would go home without performing.

"Now that kind of freaked him out," said Thompson. "It was Saturday and the banks were not open. But we scared him enough that they talked to the banks about opening up."[21]

Late morning, Lang and Kornfeld arrived with cashier's checks and the bands were paid in full.

A few hours earlier at their hotel, Santana and Barry Imhoff, a staffer from Bill Graham's management office, heard radio reports that all the roads to the festival were closed. So, they flew to the Bethel festival site.

"That's why we had to take a helicopter in," said Michael Shrieve. "There was no other way to access the site. Flying over the crowd was like a revelation. Nobody had ever seen that many people together, and this was for a rock concert."

Carlos Santana, who had recently celebrated his twenty-second birthday, was thrilled when he saw the half-million people below.

"We weren't afraid," he said. "All I could see was an ocean of flesh and hair and teeth."[22]

Backstage, Santana was greeted by Bill Graham, who had arrived earlier to see them play. He had helicoptered in with Bonnie and Kip Cohen, who took one look at the huge crowd and left.

"I wanted nothing to do with it," said Cohen, "anymore than Bill did. But our whole stage staff had agreed to go up there and get it set up. I became actually disgusted by the sight of what was going on, as Bill was. I got back in the helicopter . . . and drove back to New York."[23]

When Michael Lang ran into Graham backstage, he invited him to go onstage and announce some of the bands.

"He said, 'No, no, no. It's your party,'" recalled Lang.[24]

Most of the time he was there, Graham sat on a bench backstage, critiquing the organizers and picking faults. To the obsessive control freak, it was anathema to see the festival veer out of control and become a free one.

"And you've got to understand," said Jack Casady, "if Bill was brought into something and he's told he can't run it—then why do it."[25]

Backstage, Bill Graham caught Jefferson Airplane's Paul Kantner and road manager Bill Laudner trying to dose the main water supply with pink tablets of LSD.

"They were busted by Bill Graham," said Grateful Dead bassist Phil Lesh. "[He] excoriated them mercilessly. However, it was agreed that the tablets would be given out by hand, individually."[26]

Most of the bands dropped acid backstage while the bad weather caused big delays in the program.

"I remember sitting on the stage on acid in the afternoon," said Paul Kantner. "And the stage apparently was a little rocky because of the rain."

When Chip Monck, who would become known as the voice of Woodstock, tried to clear the stage when it became too dangerous, he encountered a spaced-out Paul Kantner.

"He wanted me to get off the stage," said Kantner, "and I was sitting there on acid. My internal being was going deep into the heart of the earth and I could not move to save my life. I told him that. He thought I was just being a rock star . . . but it wasn't that. I was the only one on the stage eventually, as everyone else had gone off worried that the stage was going to collapse. And I was just not in a position to really want to move, much less [being able to]."[27]

Santana had been told they would not be playing until Saturday night, and despite his confidence in the helicopter on the way to the festival, Carlos seemed nervous. So Jerry Garcia told him to relax and gave him some LSD, saying he had hours before he had to play. But at around two o'clock in the afternoon, just as the drug took hold, Santana were summoned to the stage, as Country Joe and the Fish finished playing.

"Everybody was getting high," said Carlos. "At the peak of whatever I was getting high with, people are saying you've got to go on right now."[28]

According to Chip Monck, Carlos initially refused to go on, and John Morris had to force him.

"He held Carlos by the neck with his feet against the trailer," remembered Monck, "and said, 'You're going to go on now! It's now or never!'"[29]

Carlos later remembered going onstage spinning and trying to clear his head enough to play.

"Damn! Why did I take LSD before I went on?" he later asked. "Like a drunk [I wanted to] find a telephone pole that I can hang onto. And so my telephone pole was saying, 'God, please help me stay in time and in tune. That's all I ask. I promise I'll never touch this stuff again.'"[30]

From the very first notes of "Waiting," Santana's forty-five-minute set was a triumph, and the audience went wild. They got up and danced to the pulsating Latin rhythms and Carlos's inimitable guitar solos, which many were hearing for the first time.

"The guitar neck . . . was literally like an electric snake," said Carlos. "I'm making faces to try and keep it from slithering too much."

The high point of the set came during Michael Shrieve's drum solo in "Soul Sacrifice," when Bill Graham crept onstage and sat behind an amplifier, playing his cowbell.

"It was one of the highlights of my life," said Shrieve in 2013. "So many people just know me for that. . . . It was all improvised."[31]

Grateful Dead drummer Mickey Hart watched his drum solo in awe.

"Michael Shrieve was playing like a god," he said, "and the percussion section was snapping. Carlos was driven [and] I could see what he was doing to this crowd. They just had this incredible energy that was golden. It was like a heavenly clockwork."[32]

Santana's new timbales player, José "Chepito" Areas, had a religious experience playing Woodstock.

"I went all the way to the sky," he said. "I was looking at Jesus's face when I played in front of all those people. And I was the only one that was straight."[33]

Jefferson Airplane watched the Santana set from backstage in total admiration.

"We'd never heard anything like it before," said Jorma Kaukonen. "Knock out."[34]

Also watching closely was Clive Davis, who was just weeks away from releasing the first Santana album.

"And Clive saw [500,000] people going crazy and what Santana could do live," said record producer David Rubinson. "It rocked his world and he realized what he had in his hands. Then he turned the marketing and promotion forces of Columbia Records full on."

As soon as Santana came offstage at 2:45 p.m., Bill Graham demanded a helicopter to take him and Bonnie back to Grossinger's Resort. When they arrived at the helicopter pad, they found a long line of musicians and music executives waiting to leave. He went straight to the front of the line, ordering Frank Fava, who was in charge of security, to get him on the next helicopter.

"And he said, 'Hi, I'm Bill Graham and I gotta get a helicopter out of here,'" Fava remembered. "I said, 'I can't get you a helicopter right now. I got all these people ahead of you.'"

Graham kept insisting he had to leave, threatening to have him fired.

"Right now, I'm the authority here," Fava told him. "You want a helicopter? You get in the line. You keep it up, you don't get out."

Then a furious Graham vowed that Fava would never work in the music business again, as he took his place at the end of the line.[35]

— ⁓ —

Before he left, Bill Graham was interviewed for a documentary film of the festival. He was asked how he felt about the crowds climbing over the fences and turning Woodstock into a free event.

"So you have to find a control point at the beginning of the highways," he replied, "and those with tickets are allowed in and those without tickets are not. And you have to have some control.

"You know, when you have the man-eating Marabunta ants coming over the hill in South America, if they want to cut 'em off and then stop 'em from coming, they make a ditch and they make a flame. Now I'm not saying they should put up flames to stop the people. There has to be some way to some to stop the influx of humanity."[36]

— ⁓ —

As Bill Graham was leaving, Janis Joplin arrived with Peggy Caserta. They had never seen so many people and couldn't stop laughing.

"We were hysterical," recalled Caserta. "We were so happy because it was just seas and seas of people. We knew . . . the exposure was going to be tremendous."[37]

Janis was desperate for a fix of heroin. So she and Caserta found a backstage porta-potty to shoot up in.

"We got in there and it was gut-wrenchingly awful," said Caserta. "And she goes, 'Shut up and fix!' So we did."

By the time she was due to take the stage with the Kozmic Blues Band, Janis was so out of it that her performance had to be postponed for eight hours while she sobered up. Later, she hung out backstage with Grace Slick, drinking expensive champagne from paper cups. The two Queens of Rock were photographed together by *Time* magazine.

"I remember Janis had a girlfriend with her that was a knockout," said Mountain lead guitarist Leslie West, who played Saturday evening. "It took me a while to realize she was a lesbian. That was entertaining. My first lesbian duo and their stuff backstage."[38]

When Janis eventually took the stage at two o'clock Sunday morning, she could barely stand up.

"How are you out there?" she drawled. "Are you okay?"

It was the first gig for Kozmic Blues Band's new guitarist John Till, who had replaced Sam Andrew, and everybody was nervous. Then Janis struggled through the hourlong set, a performance that would go down as far from her best.

The Who were waiting to go on next when Janis finished her encore of "Ball and Chain."

"She had been amazing at Monterey," said Pete Townshend, "but tonight she wasn't at her best, due probably to the long delay, and probably, too, to the amount of booze and heroin she's consumed while she waited. But even Janis on an off-night was incredible."[39]

The sun was coming up when Jefferson Airplane finally took the Woodstock stage after The Who. They should have gone on at midnight, but everything was so backed up that they spent more than six hours sitting behind the stage waiting.

"We didn't go on until six o'clock in the morning," said Bill Thompson. "Of course [Grace] had taken just about every drug known to man, but the show turned out pretty good."[40]

Grace's chief complaint was that there were no bathrooms. Her overall assessment was that Woodstock was badly organized.

"I was part of a congregation of musicians from the tribes of a temporary divided state," she later wrote in her autobiography, *Somebody to Love.* "No bathrooms—my body, seemingly obeying a higher order, shut down and I had no need. We partook from each other's stash of fruit, cheese, wine, marijuana, coke, acid, water and conversation."

Glenn McKay's Headlights, who had brought all their equipment from San Francisco, had all been set up and ready to go for hours. But by the time Jefferson Airplane came on it was bright sunshine, making a light show redundant.

Although she had been up partying all night, Grace looked beautiful in a plain white laced top and her long black hair in a perm.

"All right friends," she told the crowd squinting into the sun, "you have seen the heavy groups. Now you will see morning maniac music. Believe me, yeah, it's a new dawn."

Then the Airplane launched into "The Other Side of This Life" for a sensational ninety-minute set.

～❦～

After playing, Jefferson Airplane flew to New York City for the *Dick Cavett Show* on Monday night. After being introduced as "San Francisco's greatest export," Grace shouted out cheekily, "Hi Jim," to Cavett, who replied, "Good Morning, Grace."

Then with a swirling light show behind them, Jefferson Airplane performed a blistering version of "We Can Be Together" from the new *Volunteers* album, complete with the refrain, "Up Against the Wall, Motherfucker!" It made history as being the first time the word "fuck" had been broadcast on American television.

"You were wonderful," Cavett told Grace after they finished. "Boy, is the old lady upstairs going to be sore."

Then the genial talk show host sat cross-legged on the floor in a circle with the Jefferson Airplane, Joni Mitchell, David Crosby, and Stephen Stills to chat.

Cavett asked Grace what she had done during her "off-hours" at the Woodstock festival?

"Listen Jim," replied Grace, to howls of audience laughter, "I wish I could tell you."

"You've got to learn my name Miss Joplin," Cavett replied, to Grace's applause. "Calling me Jim like that. Didn't they teach you nothing at Finch?" [41]

A few days after Woodstock, Columbia Records released the first eponymous Santana album. The record company took out half-page advertisements in all the music papers with the iconic cover, adapted from a Fillmore West poster.

"It makes you sweat," read the ad. "Pulsating African Rhythms, Hot Latin Soul, Wild, Restless, Primitive. Santana. For your body as well as your mind."

Santana was an instant hit, peaking at number 4 on the *Billboard* chart. Then Clive Davis released "Jingo" as a single, which failed to chart. But the next single, "Evil Ways," made it straight into the *Billboard Top Ten.*

Surprisingly, the album was panned in *Rolling Stone.* Then, speculation surfaced that the band's work was a victim of the ongoing feud between *Rolling Stone* publisher Jann Wenner and Bill Graham.

"Maybe its just a coincidence that Santana and speed became popular at the same time," read the review. "Maybe not. At any rate their 'long awaited' album is definitely a speed freak's delight—fast, pounding, frantic music with no real content."

The reviewer also found fault with Carlos Santana's lead guitar.

"Carlos has stumbled upon a tired and mechanical guitar lick which he likes so well that he plays it in virtually every song. It's even possible that it was recorded only once and then overdubbed wherever the engineers thought it would fit. You'll know it when you hear it."

It forecast that although the album might sell, people would forget about it after a week and "file it away under 'S.'" [42]

Thirty-four years later, *Rolling Stone* would rank it as one of the five hundred greatest albums of all time.

After Woodstock, and under the guidance of Bill Graham, Santana went into high gear. At the end of August, he got them on the bill of the Texas International Pop Festival with Janis Joplin, Led Zeppelin, and Sly and the Family Stone.

"Bill called me and asked me to put Santana on," said festival organizer Alex Cooley. "He was very forceful. The lineup was full but he did a number on me and I put Santana on."[43]

On Friday, September 19, Crosby, Stills, Nash & Young debuted at the Fillmore East for the first of two nights. The new supergroup wanted to use their own sound system and play in a garden setting. None of it went down well with the Fillmore East staff, who took an instant dislike to CSN&Y.

"We were under the impression that we had the best there was," said Allan Arkush, "and now they wanted to tear it all out and bring in their own. Also they demanded a lot of food which they never ate, which was good for us because we ended up with it."[44]

Nonetheless, CSN&Y were a huge hit with the Fillmore East audiences. Neil Young and Stephen Stills trading guitar riffs on Young's "Down by the River" was a highlight of the shows.

"Their sets at the Fillmore East last weekend," wrote Joanna Schier in the *Village Voice*'s "Riffs" column, "created some of the most genuinely sympathetic rapport between performers and audience that I've ever seen. It all looked so easy."

The following weekend, the Grateful Dead and Country Joe and the Fish played the Fillmore East. On Saturday, Country Joe and Jerry Garcia tossed a coin to decide who would close the second show that night.

"We won the toss," said Fish lead guitarist, Barry Melton, "or at least we'd thought we'd won the toss."

Closing the early show, the Grateful Dead had to be asked to stop playing by Bill Graham so the house could be turned over. Then the Dead opened the second show and played for five hours, finally coming off at around four o'clock in the morning.

"By the time we got on there was about ten people left in the audience," recalled Melton, "and whoever was there was completely and totally exhausted. We never flipped that coin again."[45]

CHAPTER TWENTY

Running on Ego

October to December, 1969

On October 2, 1969, Janis Joplin and Santana played four shows at the Fillmore West, with Santana receiving $7,500 ($48,000) for the run. One night after a show, Janis seduced Santana's five-foot-tall timbales player, José "Chepito" Areas, back at her hotel.

"Oh yeah, she kind of raped me," he recalled. "She grabbed me and threw me on the bed and then started attacking me. She was scratching my body and she destroyed me. She was wild."[1]

Perhaps Janis's temperament was a result of her long-awaited first solo album—*Kozmic Blues*—being released to mixed reviews just a few days prior. *Rolling Stone* hedged its bets by running two reviews side by side.

In the first review Ed Leimbacher called *Kozmic Blues* a "fine and solid" album that almost justified all the hype.

"But for all that," he wrote, "I'll play *Kozmic Blues* a few times, then file it away. But I no longer can hear what it was that turned me on at Monterey. The good's gone."

Underneath, reviewer John Burks found Janis's new band to be the main problem with the album.

"She sounds great," he wrote. "Just great. It's simply a matter of reaching the point where you are able to shut out the band—entirely—and listen to this woman sing. An odd strategy, admittedly, but guaranteed worth it."[2]

Always thin-skinned, Janis was deeply hurt by the reviews. She told a reporter for *Time* magazine that she was taking six months off "to clear my head."[3]

The first week of October, John Cooke quit as road manager, fed up with seeing Janis destroy herself. Janis had also told him she was disbanding the Kozmic Blues Band at the end of the year to start a new band.

"It wasn't any fun anymore," Cooke explained, "and I didn't want to see her go downhill. They made the decision that we're no longer going to try and fix this."[4]

Janis spent the next two months in New York, where it was easy to cop heroin. She started frequenting Nobody's Bar on Bleecker Street in the West Village, where she met Dave Davies of The Kinks, who were playing the Fillmore East in mid-October.

"Janis Joplin was always there," he recalled. "She'd talk 'till the cows come home and was like one of the guys. She could outtalk anyone."[5]

In late October, The Who performed an entire week of *Tommy* shows at the Fillmore East. It was the first time the English band had performed the opera live in its entirety.

Tommy had now gone gold in America, selling a million copies, and Bill Graham was determined to do something really special for the six sold-out nights. So he appointed a special production staff with a $5,000 budget to work on it, headed by Joshua White and Chris Langhart.

"It was absolutely brilliant and Bill put it all together," said White. "That was just an over-the-top thing. You could not get a ticket. From the get-go it was super-sold-out."[6]

The Who and its management were totally behind the special week, and there would be one show a night with a fifteen-minute intermission.

It must have been music to Bill Graham's ears when Pete Townshend told the *New Yorker* how The Who much preferred playing the Fillmore East to Madison Square Garden.

"We could have played Madison Square Garden instead of the Fillmore, and made more money in one night than we'll get for the whole week," explained Townshend. "But we're willing to turn down huge offers for the chance to reach an audience. The problem with a place like the Garden is that the audience can't see you wince. They can't see you smile.

And that's important to us, because to us a rock concert is so much a theatrical performance as a musical one."[7]

For the show, Joshua White commissioned a special twenty-foot-high wraparound cinemascope-sized screen. The middle of the screen would be closer to the audience and the edges farther away.

Chris Langhart then constructed it with his NYU theater students.

"We had to build a curved screen frame for it to be laced into," said Langhart. "And that required a lot of the things that I taught at NYU. The kids rallied round it."[8]

Photographer Amalie Rothschild, who was now also working for the Joshua Light Show, was given $500 to produce *Tommy* film sequences. These included filming special visuals for the "Acid Queen" number, featuring her light show colleague Cecily Hoyt walking naked back and forth across the Fillmore East stage. It was filmed multiple times, using different lenses, camera angles, and speeds, before being meshed together to produce "a wild psychedelic job."

"It was fabulous," said Rothschild. "That was what was so enlightened about Bill Graham. As much as he was a businessman he also cared about giving his audiences their money's worth and doing a good show.[9]

Even the *Tommy* playbills were collectables, with a stunning cover design by artist David Byrd. Inside was the story of *Tommy* with its complete lyrics. The cover read:

Bill Graham Presents In New York
THE WHO
PERFORMING THEIR ENTIRE ROCK-OPERA

TOMMY
PRESENTED BY SPECIAL ARRANGEMENT WITH HER MAJESTY
QUEEN ELIZABETH II

"*Tommy* was a real highlight," recalled Allan Arkush. "Once again it was Bill striving to do more. He appreciated and really loved The Who."

For the "Overture" and the first four numbers, it was decided to have The Who play without a light show. And the stage crew soon discovered that they could stand directly behind drummer Keith Moon's shoulder without being seen by the audience. It was like being onstage with The Who, and crew members took turns onstage that week to experience the amazing rush.

"They'd count down and then kick off," said Arkush, "and the stage would shake and you'd feel like you were on a rocket. And you're looking at the faces of all these kids pinned to their seats from the scale of the music. It was unbelievable."

It was at these *Tommy* shows that the Fillmore East staff invented its ten Klieg light salute, honoring a band that had delivered a transcendent set, by lighting up the audience.

"We would raise the screen and shine white light on the audience," Arkush explained. "So The Who would be silhouetted in this incredible white light. And it became a tribute that if a band succeeded in being so good that they transcended, someone would call for raising the screen for their last number. And they'd shine all the lights on the audience. It was like breaking the fourth wall and the whole place became one celebratory moment. We only did it maybe five or six times. You had to earn it."[10]

Among the select groups that the stage crew did this for would be Jimi Hendrix, the Grateful Dead, the Allman Brothers, and Leon Russell.

❦

Jefferson Airplane's new album *Volunteers* was finally released in late October. It had been delayed for months while the band battled with RCA over the words "motherfucker" and "shit to a tree." The record company also objected to the use of the American flag on the cover and the original title, *Volunteers of Amerika*. The differences were finally sorted out with the title being abbreviated to just *Volunteers*, and although the two objectionable words stayed in the final sound mix, "motherfucker" was changed to "fred" in the enclosed lyrics sheet.

Inside the double cover—which opened up to become a peanut butter and jelly sandwich—was a spoof newspaper called the *Paz Progress*, dated August 1, 1939. It contained a cartoon ridiculing President Richard Nixon and the recent moon landing.

It was mostly the work of Grace Slick and Paul Kantner. Spencer Dryden, who had been responsible for all previous covers, had nothing to do with this one.

"I personally hated that cover," said Marty Balin. "I had no idea why they would put a peanut butter and jelly sandwich on there. I guess they thought it was funny."[11]

Many viewed *Volunteers* as the band's public protest against the Vietnam War and the Nixon administration. Arguably, it was the band's last great album, and it sold well, reaching number 13 on the *Billboard* chart. The title track, "Volunteers," was released as a single but flopped.

"*Volunteers* is when [they] come to a peak," said music critic Robert Christgau. "After that their music falls off a cliff."[12]

⌒

Several weeks before the release of *Volunteers*, popular television host Art Linkletter's twenty-year-old daughter Diane jumped out of a sixth-floor window in West Hollywood and died. The next day, Linkletter held a press conference, blaming Grace Slick and claiming his daughter had been on LSD when she had jumped. A subsequent autopsy found no drugs in her system at the time of her death, but Linkletter insisted it must have been a flashback.

Grace Slick was watching television in a New York hotel room when she saw Linkletter attack her.

"He said Grace Slick . . . is responsible for my daughter's death," said Grace. "And I rolled around to the TV and [said] 'what the hell is he talking about?' And I called the TV station [to complain] but I couldn't get through."[13]

⌒

In mid-November, Janis Joplin was arrested for screaming obscenities at police after a concert in Tampa, Florida. She had lost her temper with the cops, who were trying to stop her fans from dancing. Four months later, she would be fined $200 for the offense.

Around this time Janis had attempted to explain how she was now coping with success, and how it had changed her.

"The whole success thing has been weird," she told Michael Lydon of the *New York Times*. "I look around after all the violent changes I've been through in the last year, and I see how surreal it's gotten. Flying around in airplanes, kids screaming, a lot of money and people buying me drinks."

She said she loved being Janis "the star," and especially all the money and other trappings that came with it.

"That fur coat . . . know how I got that?" she asked Lydon. "Southern Comfort! Far out! I had the chick in my manager's office Photostat every goddam clipping that ever had me mentioning Southern Comfort, and I sent them to the company, and they sent me a whole lotta money. How could anybody in their right mind want me for their image? Oh, man, that was the best hustle I ever pulled—can you imagine getting paid for passing out for two years?"[14]

—◆—

That Halloween, Mountain played the Fillmore East for the first time. The three-piece hard-rock band, with Leslie West on lead guitar, Felix Pappalardi on bass, and Corky Laing on drums, would soon establish themselves as a firm Fillmore East favorite. But eighteen months earlier, West had had a serious run-in with Bill Graham at Winterland, when his previous band, the Vagrants, opened for The Who.

"We used to smash the guitars," said West, "and use flash pods and smoke. Bill was sitting on the stage when we were doing our opening act, and I smashed my guitar right in front of him. He then wrote a letter to our agency, 'I never want to see the Vagrants here again! Especially that three-hundred-pound psychedelic canary Lesley West.'"

When the guitar virtuoso first arrived at the Fillmore East for a soundcheck, he was worried about how Bill Graham would receive him.

"Bill walks over," said West, "and I think, 'Oh shit, he's going to say something to me.' And he sticks out his hand, and says, 'I guess you've grown up since then.'"[15]

—◆—

At the beginning of November, Bill Graham used his influence to have Santana booked on three of America's most popular TV shows—the *Ed*

Sullivan Show, the *Tonight Show Starring Johnny Carson*, and the *Dick Cavett Show.*

And Carlos Santana's sudden fame was now being felt in the San Francisco Mission District, where he still lived.

"Santana changed the whole attitude of people's lives in the Mission," said percussionist Richard Segovia, who lived a few block away from Carlos and knew him. "Everybody wanted to be a conga player. Everyone wanted to be a timbales player. Instead of the battle of the barrios it became the battle of the bands, and instead of fighting they did it musically."[16]

On November 7 and 8, Santana headlined the Fillmore East for the first time, with the Butterfield Blues Band and Humble Pie opening.

"Santana had them standing on the seats," wrote the *Village Voice's* "Riffs" column. "I haven't seen that kind of sheer physical response since the Chambers Brothers were last around Second Avenue."

But critic Mike Jahn was far less enthusiastic about Santana.

"The group's long drum passages become boring after a while," he wrote, "particularly in a theater where the audience can't move around. Latin music is created for dancing, and Santana's super-charged Latin especially so."

On Sunday, November 9, Bill Graham presented the Rolling Stones at the Oakland Coliseum as part of the group's 1969 tour. There had been much tension between Graham and the Stones after they had turned down his pitch to present the entire US tour. Graham had even asked Mick Jagger to intercede, but he refused.

"He'd done the Fillmores and now he wanted to do the '69 Stones' Tour," said the Stones' business manager Ronnie Schneider. "Mick [Jagger] called me and said, 'We don't want him doing the tour.' I felt bad I had to tell him no, so I gave him a couple of shows."[17]

During the first Oakland Coliseum show, thousands of people rushed the stage in the middle of "Satisfaction," knocking over Graham's closed-circuit cameras.

"Graham jumped onto the stage and began bouncing around like a man trying to stamp out a nest of snakes, pushing kids away and giving orders," wrote *Rolling Stone* reviewer Jerry Hopkins. "Sam Cutler [the Stones' tour manager] asked Graham to leave the stage. Graham told Cutler to get the hell off *his* stage. Then Graham grabbed Cutler—and Cutler, having a fuse only millimeters longer than Graham's, grabbed back. They were going to kill each other. Five feet away the Stones were still playing 'Satisfaction.'"[18]

Then a raging Graham went backstage to sulk. Soon afterward, when the Rolling Stones came offstage and went back to their dressing room, they found someone had put up several huge posters of Bill Graham flipping them the bird.

"There were all these posters up in our dressing room of [Graham]," recalled Bill Wyman. "And we just threw cakes at them and all that sort of stuff. He kind of underestimated us and he was a bit arrogant with us. We couldn't give a damn who this guy was."[19]

Outside the dressing room, Graham confronted Ronnie Schneider, accusing the Stones of disrespecting him by throwing food everywhere.

"And we started screwing with each other," recalled Schneider. "Then he poked me in the chest with his finger, and I hit him in the nuts with my briefcase, as we say sweetly. He got ready to take a swing at me but these big security guys had heard us screaming and grabbed him. Then Keith [Richards] grabbed me and pulled me back into the dressing room and told me to calm down."[20]

A furious Graham then marched into Mick Jagger's dressing room, where the frontman was putting on makeup. Graham was going to tell Jagger that he was canceling the late show.

"Didn't I speak to you on the phone once?" Jagger inquired. "You were rude to me. I can't stand people who shout on the phone. It shows the most appalling manners."[21]

The singer then turned back to his mirror to finish making up, leaving Bill Graham lost for words.

❧

That Thanksgiving weekend, Jefferson Airplane were back at the Fillmore East for the sixth time. On the first night of the run of sold-out shows, Grace Slick dressed up as Adolf Hitler in full Nazi regalia, complete with a stick-on mustache and her hair slicked back. Later in their set, Rip Torn walked out disguised as Richard Nixon, to the boos of the audience.

"Grace liked a bit of the theater," said Jack Casady, "so we never quite knew what she was going to do."[22]

On Thanksgiving Day, Bill Graham again laid on a lavish feast in the theater lobby for the performers and the Fillmore East staff. Among the guests were Janis Joplin and Ike and Tina Turner, who were opening for the Rolling Stones that night at Madison Square Garden.

Before the catered meal, Airplane manager Bill Thompson was sitting in the back of the theater talking to Graham when Ike and Tina Turner walked in.

"Ike looked like a pimp," remembered Thompson, "and Tina was wearing a miniskirt that was above the waist. They went past us and Bill and I are kind of mesmerized looking at Tina. And he looked to me and said, 'That ain't chopped liver.'"[23]

At the Thanksgiving meal, Bill Graham sat at a table with Grace Slick, Janis Joplin, and Tina Turner.

"Janis and Grace Slick were the two queens of rock 'n' roll in the Sixties," said Graham. "Dual royalty on the feminine side."[24]

During the meal, Janis sipped champagne but hardly ate, constantly leaving the table to go to a nearby stairway and talk to a friend. There was also some tension between Janis and Graham, as she was booked for a single show at Madison Square Garden in mid-December instead of her usual four at the Fillmore East. Graham spent most of the meal talking to Tina Turner.

"And we had a long, long rap," said Graham, "when Ike was off with the musicians somewhere. She was telling me about the old days of her one-nighters. Tina away from business is very ladylike and very calm. She saves her energy for the stage."

That night the Fillmore East was closed, so many of the staff headed to Madison Square Garden to see the Rolling Stones play.

"We all had gotten tickets," said Allan Arkush. "We went up to see them play the set that would eventually become the album *Get Yer Ya Ya's Out*."

During Ike and Tina Turner's opening performance, Tina noticed Janis Joplin watching and invited her onstage to sing a number. The two rock goddesses were then photographed singing together by Amalie Rothschild.

"For me, time stopped," said Amalie. "I think it was the only time these two extraordinary rock divas ever sang onstage together."[25]

Later backstage, Janis was the worse for wear after many hours of drinking and drugging. She was drinking Southern Comfort with Jimi Hendrix and a few others in the Stones' dressing room when Sam Cutler ordered everybody to leave, as the Stones were going on in fifteen minutes.

"Only Janis made a fuss," said Cutler. "Janis wobbled unsteadily on her feet and breathed fumes of Southern Comfort into my face. 'You know who I am, man?' she mumbled."

When Cutler said he did, she took another swig and started at him blankly. The road manager then asked her not to be difficult. The Stones just needed some privacy, he explained.

"Janis swiveled around to face Keith," said Cutler, "who was sitting behind her. 'Hey, man,' she whined, 'Your dude is trying to throw me out of your dressing room.'"

Keith Richards merely smiled, saying the band needed to tune up and collect themselves before taking the stage. Janis sat down next to him, and it was obvious she was not going anywhere.

Then Cutler asked her if she wanted a couple of thick lines of high-grade Peruvian cocaine.

"Chop 'em up, big boy," Janis drawled.

Cutler explained they needed to go somewhere more private, as there were too many press around to snort up in the dressing room.

"Well, I guess I'll see you boys later," Janis announced as she stood up. "I gotta see a man about a dog."[26]

—◆—

The next day Janis Joplin flew to Florida to play the Miami Pop Festival with the Rolling Stones, Jefferson Airplane, and Johnny Winter. The red-hot albino blues guitarist had grown up in Beaumont, Texas, where Janis had gone to college. It was their ever first meeting backstage in Miami, and they immediately hit it off.

"I ended up jammin' with her, and doin' vocals and drinking Southern Comfort," Winter later remembered.

That first night, Winter drank so much Southern Comfort that he threw up on Janis in the helicopter on the way back to the hotel.

"She was alright with it," he said. "She called me up later on and asked me for another date."[27]

During the next few weeks, the two Texans would occasionally meet up in New York for one-night stands, but the relationship never became too serious.

———

The first week of December, Bill Graham recruited Herbie Herbert to become Santana's road manager. And on Saturday, December 6, the twenty-one-year-old found himself working his first show with Santana, who were playing the soon-to-be infamous free concert at the Altamont Speedway in California.

"And that was my first day on the job," said Herbert. "The stage was maybe eighteen inches high, and across the front was the wall of Hells Angels' motorcycles."

As Michael Carabello was tightening up his congas, a six-foot five-inch Hells Angel with a big beard and long greasy hair came over with a stein of beer and a large mason's jar of downers.

"He offers the beer and big jar of pills to Carabello, who says no," said Herbert. "He then turns around and faces the audience, rears his head back and pours the bottle of pills into his mouth. And then washes down an impossible mouthful of pills in one swallow. And I look at Carabello, who looks wide-eyed back at me, and say, 'It's going to be a long day.'"[28]

As Santana opened the show, fights were starting to break out in the audience. At one point Santana stopped briefly when a Hells Angel ran across the stage to beat up someone.

By the time Jefferson Airplane took the stage, things were getting really ugly. Spencer Dryden had been against playing Altamont and was only there under duress. All through the red-eye flight back to San Francisco from the Miami Pop Festival, the drummer had argued with the other members of the band, saying the Altamont vibes were wrong. Finally, Bill Thompson told him to shut up and just do it.

It was late afternoon when a nervous-looking Grace Slick took the stage. As they began "We Can Be Together," the drunken Hells Angels were beating people up indiscriminately. During the second number, "The Other Side of This Life," Grace saw a fight break out below the stage and stopped the band.

"Easy," she said calmly. "Easy, easy, easy."

Then, there was a scream and Marty Balin jumped into the crowd to tackle a massive Hells Angel called Animal, who was beating up a young man with a pool cue.

"Marty unfortunately said, 'fuck you!' to him, which is something you don't do to a Hells Angel," recalled Paul Kantner. "In life I generally don't fuck with nuns, cops or Hells Angels with good reason. But Marty did and the guy just decked him."

Kantner stood on the side of the stage observing the goings-on.

"I'm looking up at this eight-foot-tall Hells Angel," he recalled, "with a big animal thing on his head. And I'm giving him a look like a principal in high school, 'What the fuck are you doing?' And to his credit he's going, 'I'm sorry, man.' So I got away with that without dying."[29]

Grace Slick, who was short-sighted and didn't have her contact lenses in, had to ask Dryden what was happening.

"He said, 'The Hells Angels are beating up Marty,'" Grace remembered. "Apparently the Hells Angels were beating up somebody else and Marty said, 'Don't do that, fuck you.'"

Grace then tried to calm down the Hells Angels, preaching a "Make Love Not War" doctrine.

"No! Stop it!" she yelled. "That's really stupid. You've got to keep your bodies off each other unless you intend love."

Later, after the Airplane completed their set and left the stage, Balin was helped over to the band's equipment truck to recover.

"Marty was just waking up in the back of the truck," said Kantner, "and a Hells Angel came to apologize. He said, 'I'm sorry man. You shouldn't say 'fuck you.'" Marty looks up at him and says, 'Fuck you!' and so the guy gives it to him again. Maximum. I don't know if he ever recovered, to be honest."[30]

After the rest of the band left, Grace and Paul Kantner watched the rest of the nightmare concert unfold from the side of the stage.

Later Grace would claim that she had advised using the Hells Angels for security, as the Airplane were friendly with them and had used them before.

"Paul and I went over to London to talk to Jagger about putting on Altamont," explained Grace, "and it was our fault. You don't mix speed and alcohol on people with chains and knives. It's not a good move."[31]

The Grateful Dead, who were due on next, wisely decided not to play. Then after brief, uncomfortable sets by the Flying Burrito Brothers and Crosby, Stills, Nash & Young, the Rolling Stones took the stage.

In the middle of their set, as the Maysles Brothers's cameras were rolling for a documentary on the Stones US tour, a young black man named Meredith Hunter was stabbed to death by a Hells Angel. At a later murder trial, witnesses testified Hunter had been waving a gun, and the Angel was acquitted.

After the tragedy, Bill Graham accused Mick Jagger of being responsible and mocking Uncle Sam.

He offered Jagger $50,000 to debate him on live television or radio.

"He's in his home country now," said Graham. "What did he leave behind throughout this country? Every gig, he was late. Every fucking gig, he made the promoter and the people bleed. What right does this god have to descend on this country this way? It will give me great pleasure to tell the public that Mick Jagger is not God, Junior."

Calling Altamont a "Holocaust," Graham blamed the police.

"They should have taken Mister Jagger," he railed, "twisted his fucking arms behind his back, put him in front of the radio and said, 'Mister Jagger, if we have to break your arms, call it off.'"

Bill Wyman believes Graham's challenge was a publicity stunt.

"I think he used people to promote himself," said the former Rolling Stone. "We thought he was more interested in extending his ego to his best advantage, as opposed to doing his job and being a promoter."[32]

***

Two weeks later, Janis Joplin played Madison Square Garden, her final concert with the Kozmic Blues Band. After her wild behavior at

Thanksgiving, a worried Albert Grossman had sent her to endocrinologist Dr. Ed Rothschild of Manhattan's Sloan-Kettering Hospital for treatment. Janis denied having any problems with alcohol or drugs, saying she had no idea why her manager was getting so upset. She told the doctor that being stoned was the best thing in the world, although she did admit to six heroin overdoses.

Dr. Rothschild later described Janis as "brilliant," saying her problems arose from possessing an advanced intellect with "childlike and uncontrollable emotions."

He put her on a ten-day withdrawal treatment of the heroin substitute Dolophine.[33]

Three days earlier, Janis had guested on the top-rated *Tom Jones Show*, singing a blistering duet of "Raise Your Hand" with the Welsh singer.

"She was a wild person," said Jones, "but she was very real and she didn't take any bullshit. I did the duet with her and when we finished it she said, 'Wow, you can really sing, you know.' And to me it was a scream-up, but to her that was really singing."[34]

Janis spent the week before the Madison Square Garden show in New York with Bobby Neuwirth and Michael J. Pollard. One night they went to the Bachelors III nightclub on Lexington Avenue, which was owned by New York Jet Superbowl III MVP Joe Namath. As soon as she arrived, Janis introduced herself to Broadway Joe and immediately propositioned him. Later, she would proudly boast that she had seduced Namath with a bottle of Tequila in his apartment upstairs.

The next morning she tipped off *Rolling Stone* magazine's Random Notes column with the exclusive that she and Joe Namath had "gotten together."

"Joe, Joe, where are you?" Janis cooed into the microphone at Madison Square Garden on December 19 after dedicating the concert to Joe Willie and the Jets. That night Janis was electrifying and had everyone on their feet dancing.

"What are you doing in your seats?" she screamed. "This is a rock 'n' roll concert!"

At the end of the show, she called Johnny Winter and Paul Butterfield to the stage to join her for a couple of songs.

"It was her last night with the [Kozmic Blues Band]," said Winter. "I never was crazy about that band."

Winter says Janis was shooting heroin that night but warned him to stay away from the drug.[35]

After the show, Clive Davis and his wife threw Janis a party at his apartment on Central Park West. Among the guests were Bob Dylan, Miles Davis, and Tony Bennett.

"I wanted to make it a truly extraordinary night for her," remembered Davis. "Janis arrived at 1:00, and though she was clearly high, she was in good cheer and made a vibrant entrance. By the end of the night, Janis had tears in her eyes as she thanked . . . me for creating this evening for her. All of us were deeply moved."[36]

Back in San Francisco, Janis moved into a new home in Larkspur, Marin County, a short walk away from Jerry Garcia's house. She decorated it in Rococo Bordello style, buying two Samoyed puppies and a Siamese fighting fish, who lived in a wine bottle. To celebrate, Janis held a big housewarming/Christmas party and invited all her friends.

"She bought the house because of *Cheap Thrills*," said her friend David Cohen, who had now left Country Joe and the Fish. "I went to the party and she dragged me out. She looked up at the house and said, 'One fucking record for the house and the car!'"[37]

At the end of 1969, Bill Graham's trusted right-hand man at the Fillmore West, Paul Baratta, staged a coup to unseat his mentor as the king of San Francisco rock. The former actor cut a deal with the owners of Winterland to jump ship and run concerts at the larger venue, which Graham had been using for years. On hearing the news, Graham acted fast and met with the owners of Winterland. He managed to wrestle Winterland away from Baratta by guaranteeing $60,000 in rentals for the rest of the year in return for exclusive use.

Only three weeks after quitting the Fillmore, Baratta had been effectively neutralized and was safely back in the Graham fold, heading up its new Southern California operation, aptly named Shady Management. . . .

The day after Christmas, a new Southern band arrived in New York in an old battered Winnebago camper to play their first gig at the Fillmore East. The Allman Brothers Band, whose first album, *Idlewild South,* would be released in January, were third on the bill behind Appaloosa and Blood, Sweat and Tears. In the lobby of the Fillmore, someone had pinned up a poster of the band bathing naked in a creek, looking like a bunch of rednecks.

"All we knew about them was that album cover in the lobby," said Allan Arkush, who now headed up the stage crew. "Now you've got these hipster New Yorkers looking at the Southern guys naked in the stream, and immediate opinions were formed as to what kind of inbred weirdoes they were."

It didn't help when the band arrived several hours late for the sound-check. The stage crew then helped unload their old rundown equipment, and they were appalled.

"It was all these Marshall amps held together with gaffer tape," said Arkush. "This was not the equipment of a successful band."[38]

But as soon as Duane Allman launched into the opening bars of "Statesboro Blues" at the soundcheck, something magical happened at the Fillmore East.

"Wow!" said Arkush. "And within about ten seconds you stopped what you were doing. Doors were opening throughout the theater and people were stepping out to see who was making this music."[39]

Dan Opatoshu of the stage crew called that soundcheck a revelation.

"We had said, 'Who the hell are these sheep-fuckers from who knows where?' Until they started playing,'" said Opatoshu. "Then we were, 'This is something amazing.'"[40]

After the soundcheck, Allan Arkush headed straight to their dressing room to meet them.

"I said, 'What would you guys like to eat?'" he remembered. "And they were so astonished that they were being brought food for free."

Arkush sent out for pizza and wine, and it was the beginning of a close bond between the Allman Brothers Band and the Fillmore East stage crew. Over the three nights, the Allman Brothers made themselves at home at the Fillmore East, hanging out in the audience hunting for groupies.

"Blood, Sweat and Tears were furious at them," said Opatoshu, "because the Allman Brothers would not leave the audience after their set, trying to get girls' names and phone numbers. There was this brouhaha going on with Blood, Sweat and Tears, who wanted to play."[41]

On the final night, Blood, Sweat and Tears' guitarist Steve Katz's mother arrived from Queens to see her son play, and she was horrified by the Allmans' backstage antics.

"She complained," said Allan Arkush, "about all these guys running around half-naked."[42]

That New Year's Eve—as the Sixties morphed into the Seventies—Bill Graham's Fillmore empire reigned supreme. In New York he presented Jimi Hendrix's Band of Gypsys at the Fillmore East, while in San Francisco he had Santana playing the Fillmore West and Jefferson Airplane and the Quicksilver Messenger Service at Winterland.

"Hendrix was preparing for the Band of Gypsys' shows," said Allan Arkush, "and he would rehearse sometimes in the afternoons at the Fillmore. I'd come in and set up for a show and get to see Hendrix jamming with the Band of Gypsys, which is pretty impressive. You just put your feet up on the chairs watching him jam."[43]

On New Year's Eve, as the audience arrived at the Fillmore East, they were escorted to their seats by an eighteen-year-old usher named Ken Mednick, who had just been hired.

"The first day I showed up for work was the night Jimi Hendrix was playing," he said. "And it was absolutely mind-boggling. I was a huge Hendrix fan and I was flabbergasted."[44]

The final playbill for 1969 contained several New Year's greetings from several musicians. "All the hangups of 1969—kiss my behind," wrote Hendrix. "It's a groovy thing to look forward to the future and hope that things'll be better," said Roger McGuinn of The Byrds. Bill Graham's was, "And my hope for the new decade—may the dove rest."

The Voices of East Harlem opened the Fillmore East New Year's show with a short film by Amalie Rothschild, showing the young children's choir preparing for it in Harlem.

"I went uptown," said Amalie. "I filmed them getting ready, coming out of their homes and taking the subway."

The film, projected onto the Joshua Light Show screen, then showed the children running out of the Astor Street subway and onto Second Avenue, where they turned left to the Fillmore East and went inside.

"Then they came down the aisle," said Amalie, "climbed up onto the stage and launched into their first number."

After playing the first show, Jimi Hendrix came into Graham's office and asked what he had thought.

"So I ask Kip and the others to leave the office," said Graham. "And I said, 'Jimi, you're the best guitar player I know, and tonight for an hour and a half you were a shuck. You were a disgrace to what you are.'"

Hendrix looked hurt and asked if Graham had heard the audience going crazy and demanding more.

"'You know what you did?'" Graham remembered explaining. "'You made the same mistake too many of the other great ones make. You subconsciously play what they want, you sock it to them. You did an hour and a half of shuck and grind and bullshit, that you can do with your eyes closed lying down somewhere. But you forgot one thing. You forgot to play. And it's tragic for you because you can play better than anyone I know.'

"Well, the guy fell apart. 'Why are you telling me that?' 'BECAUSE YOU ASKED ME!' And we had a bad scene, pushing the furniture around, yelling. And Jimi's a quiet guy.

"And I said to Jimi, 'If I were you, and I'm dreaming, but if I could, one of the great ways to educate the public, to let them know that they've fallen into your shit, is to come out and say, 'Did I sock it to you?' 'Yeah!' 'Boogie Woogie?' 'Did you dig it?' 'Yeah!' 'You're all full of shit, I apologize. Don't let me do that to you.'

"And Jimi said, 'You're right, you're right. I'm sorry.' And then we went down for egg creams, settled down. And what happened next is one of the warmest things that ever happened to me."

For the second show, Hendrix took Graham's advice to heart, delivering one of the greatest sets of his career, which was immortalized on his *Band of Gypsys (Live)* album.

Recalled Graham, "What followed, with respect to Carlos and Eric and all those others, was the most brilliant, emotional display of virtuoso electric guitar playing I have ever heard. I don't expect ever to hear such sustained brilliance in an hour and fifteen minutes. He just stood there, did nothing, just played and played and played.

"He comes off the stage afterwards, a wet rag, and says to me . . . 'Alright?' I said, 'Jimi, it was great.' And I hugged him and got all wet, and I asked him if he would do an encore. 'Yeah.' He goes out and does every conceivable corny bullshit thing he can do."[45]

CHAPTER TWENTY-ONE

A New Decade

January to March, 1970

On January 2, 1970, the Grateful Dead played the first of two nights at the Fillmore East, supporting their new album *Live Dead*. The Hells Angels, who had their New York City headquarters a couple of blocks away on Third Street, were there in force.

"By this time the Dead were very popular in New York," said Allan Arkush, "and a lot of Hells Angels were coming to visit them. So you always had this incredible mix of people backstage at a Dead show."

The Angels had also brought along a canister of nitrous oxide, which they carried into the Grateful Dead's dressing room.

"So you were basically living a [Robert] Crumb cartoon," said Arkush.

Bill Graham had instructed his sound screw to play the theme from *2001: A Space Odyssey*, "Thus Spoke Zarathustra," before he came onstage to introduce the Dead.

"This was a great idea," said Arkush, "but no one had told the Grateful Dead. So they are all in the dressing room on nitrous oxide and laughing. We took them down and they were giggling, and Garcia practically fell down the steps getting on the stage."

After plugging in their equipment and tuning up, the Grateful Dead waited onstage in the dark as the Zarathustra music began. Then Bill walked up to the microphone for his introduction—"Ladies and Gentlemen, the Seventh Samurai of Rock—the Grateful Dead."

"Then the big chord came up and the light show started," said Arkush. "And the Dead just stand there giggling. Then the giggling turned into

Jerry noodling on 'China Cat Sunflower' with the chords. And it sounds like he's laughing on the guitar, so to speak. Then the band kicks into 'China Cat Sunflower' and we're off and running—a three-hour night."[1]

— ⁓ —

After Woodstock, musicians suddenly realized their new clout and began to demand a bigger slice of the profits from promoters.

"Woodstock was when everybody realized it was real," said Albert Grossman's assistant, Vinnie Fusco. "It was both the beginning and the end. That's when we asked, 'Why did 400,000 people come?' Woodstock just told everybody, 'Maybe it's not Bill Graham the promoter, it's our acts.' And then eventually the artists assumed, 'It's me.'"[2]

Bill Graham viewed Woodstock as nothing less than the destruction of the rock industry.

"It was a tragedy," he said. "Groups recognized that they could go into larger cattle markets, play less time and make more dollars." But although the top rock stars were now raking in millions while preaching hippie values, audiences still viewed Graham as the capitalist bogeymen of rock 'n' roll. And as bands forced up ticket prices, he would always be blamed.

Jazz & Pop magazine columnist Patricia Kennealy observed that while "it may be quite fashionable in certain circles to damn Bill Graham as a capitalist," he had given more to the music business than anyone.

"It is all too easy to take a gratuitous swipe at Graham," she wrote.

Kennealy noted how some bands who played for "hamburger and beer money" a couple of years ago now demanded $50,000 for a forty-five-minute set, plus a percentage of the gross.

"When the promoter who has to pay the band and cover overhead costs," she wrote, "gets *blamed* for all this, then I think change is due."[3]

Joshua White also noticed the change in many musicians' attitudes after Woodstock.

"We all knew the Fillmore was doomed," said White. All the managers figured their bands could play arenas and stadiums and eventually that's where they went. It was very hard to get the Airplane and the Dead on a bill together after Woodstock because they wanted to play those giant venues."[4]

Pete Townshend pointed out that it was impossible for The Who to play the Fillmores and make a profit.

"We've always been fond of Bill and have tried to be fair to him," Townshend said. "So we used to go there for a third of what we can make on the road . . . and for a man who's close to becoming a millionaire, it's a bit of a hard-luck story."[5]

As the musicians wielded their power, a new arrogance set in. In a September 1969 editorial, *Variety* condemned the increasing number of acts who failed to show for performances, noting their "shorter tempers and longer lists of demands." Comparing it to industrial wildcat strikes, *Variety* pointed the finger at Diana Ross for canceling a show after her pet dog died and Jimi Hendrix for storming offstage after breaking a guitar string. It also singled out Jefferson Airplane as the group most feared by promoters for their bad attitude and frequent cancellations.[6]

Jefferson Airplane manager Bill Thompson said that came down to Grace Slick's heavy drinking.

"Every time we went on a tour we missed about one out of every six or seven dates because she was getting drunk," he said. "We would cancel the show [and] it cost us a lot of money."[7]

On Monday, January 26, 1970, Grace Slick was the maid of honor at Spencer Dryden's wedding to Sally Mann. Held at the Jefferson Airplane Mansion in front of three hundred guests, with Paul Kantner as the best man, the ceremony was performed by the Rev. Scott Beach, a director of the Committee Theater and a minister in the American Humanist Institute.

"Miss Grace Slick, the Airplane's glacial contralto was radiant as maid of honor," observed *Rolling Stone* in its next issue. "Some fifty friends and relatives attended, including many of the San Francisco rock and roll world's most prominent swells, and they were radiant too. Refreshments were freely served, and in some quantity. The former Miss Mann, it will be recalled, was featured in the *Rolling Stone* special issue on The Groupies."[8]

Grace graciously handed the newlyweds a thousand dollars in cash before Jerry Slick drove her back to the Sausalito house they now shared.

At the reception, Paul Kantner came downstairs with a silver tray that was loaded with lines of cocaine laced with Orange Sunshine acid next to a hundred-dollar bill. He snorted up the powerful drug mixture with the newly married couple, who then went upstairs to their room.

Some time later, a very stoned Paul Kantner was looking for Grace. After being told she had already left, he became upset. Finally, Sally Mann called Grace in Sausalito and asked her to return and take care of him. Grace drove straight back, and that night Paul Kantner fell in love with her.

———

Within weeks, Spencer Dryden was fired from Jefferson Airplane. Since his split from Grace, he no longer exerted any power in the band, and Paul Kantner, who had never liked him anyway, got rid of him.

"Basically I fired him after he broke up with Grace," said Kantner. "He was out of the picture at that point."[9]

Dryden, who then joined the New Riders of the Purple Sage, was immediately replaced by Joey Covington, who had recently moved into the Airplane mansion and had been waiting in the wings.

———

By the dawn of the new decade, Janis Joplin had become a fashion icon, with thousands of young girls across America imitating her gypsy style. In early January, the *New York Times* ran a feature about what the cutting-edge Manhattan fashionistas had been wearing at Janis's recent Madison Square Garden show.

"I call [it] poverty fashion," a young Australian rock writer named Lillian Roxon told the *New York Times*. "The idea is to try and get a rich look with very little money."

Roxon said that fashions started with rock stars like Janis Joplin, who then passed it on to the fans. It was then picked up by the Seventh Avenue designers, who mass-produced it for the rest of the country.

"Janis gave us fringes and long, bushy hair," explained Roxon. "Cher gave us bell-bottoms [and] Jim Morrison popularized leather."

She cited tie-dye clothes as the latest fashion innovation, pointing out that Janis now slept in tie-dye satin sheets.

By February, Bonnie Graham had finally had enough of her husband's philandering and filed for divorce. She moved into an apartment with their son, David, and sought full custody of the boy.

"[His] gallivanting was difficult," explained Bonnie, "and what a rounder he was. He was going with every woman that came along. And for me that was the end. I didn't hang around long after that."[10]

Looking back, she believes Bill Graham's traumatic childhood rendered him incapable of loving another human being.

"I think he got obsessed about something that didn't last very long," she said. "I don't know what it was about me that he liked. He never really told me. I can only imagine that it had to do with that I'm just a pretty straight person [which is] maybe an antidote to his own being, his own personality. But it didn't take too long to wear off."[11]

In early February, Janis Joplin flew to Rio for the Carnival, and to clean up from drugs. A month earlier she had disbanded the Kozmic Blues Band, and Albert Grossman was now busy recruiting for her next group. Janis took her friend Linda Gravenites along, and they rented a luxury apartment on the beach and attended the various Carnival balls.

One morning, while walking on the beach in a white bikini, Janis met a young teacher named David Niehaus, who was traveling around the world. She fell in love.

"He's just fantastic," Janis breathlessly told Myra Friedman in a phone call from Rio, "and he's gorgeous."[12]

Janis moved Niehaus into her rented apartment, and she stayed clean. She even held a press conference, and for the rest of the trip she was trailed around the city by reporters and photographers.

"It's vicious, man," she told *Rolling Stone*, referring to the Brazilian police. "If you've got long hair they can drag you off and never let you out."

She and Niehaus then headed up the coast to Salvador, looking for action.

"There was nothing there," she said, "No entertainment."

So Janis and her new boyfriend spent three nights drinking at a whorehouse, where she sang with the house band.[13]

At the beginning of March, Janis returned to San Francisco alone, with Niehaus planning to join her as soon as he got the necessary visas.

When he arrived at her Larkspur house a few weeks later, Janis was back on heroin and he hardly recognized her. After trying unsuccessfully to get her to quit drugs and finding her in bed naked with Peggy Caserta, he packed up his suitcase and left.[14]

Soon afterward, Janis's friend Lyndall Erb, who was a clothes maker, moved into the house as Janis's new roommate.

On January 15, the Allman Brothers Band debuted at the Fillmore West, third on the bill to Buddy Guy and B.B. King. They received just $1,500 for two shows a night during the four-night run.

"That was really something," wrote Gregg Allman in his autobiography, *My Cross to Bear*. "My brother and I got to meet B.B. when we opened for him. Between the two of us, we had worn out three of his records—played those LPs until they turned white."[15]

The Fillmore West audience gave the Allmans a good reception. But it wouldn't compare to the one they received at the Fillmore East a month later when they opened for Love and the Grateful Dead.

That late show on the Friday of the Presidents' Day weekend was memorable. The Grateful Dead's hit squad dosed the backstage water cooler with Owsley acid, and almost everybody tripped out.

"That was a legendary show," recalled Allan Arkush. "Someone had put acid in the water, so we were all under the influence."[16]

His stage crew colleague Dan Opatoshu said that getting spiked with acid was an occupational hazard whenever the Dead played the Fillmore East.

"They would dose everybody," he said. "And we would fall one by one like soldiers in the field of battle. You'd just say, 'Ah, ah. They got me. I'm outta here. Goodbye.'"[17]

It was the first time the Allman Brothers had played on the same bill as the Grateful Dead, and Gregg Allman asked his brother Duane what he thought of the Dead's music.

"He didn't hesitate," wrote Gregg. "'This is shit. You see them jugs that they're passing out?' he said, referring to the cases of Gatorade that they would electrify backstage and then pass out to the crowd. And then I knew what he was talking about. One tiny sip of that shit and it would be raining fire, man, so no wonder everyone was grooving on that music—anything would sound good like that."[18]

At the end of the Grateful Dead set, at around four o'clock in the morning, Jerry Garcia invited the Allman Brothers out onstage to join them in "Dark Star" and "Turn on Your Love Light."

"It was a total cluster-fuck," recalled Allman Brothers' drummer Butch Trucks. "There was every member of the Grateful Dead, every member of the Allman Brothers, and Peter Green and Mick Fleetwood from Fleetwood Mac onstage jamming. I guarantee it was total cacophony."[19]

Grateful Dead bassist Phil Lesh remembers the long jam being "a surprisingly coherent free-for-all, with five guitarists, four drummers, organ and Pigpen rolling over it all."[20]

It was already daylight when they finally finished playing, and it was snowing.

"And when the doors opened," said Arkush, "and you got all this smoke in the air and shafts of light, there was Sixth Street covered in virgin snow, as the audience wandered out."[21]

<hr />

Soon after Grace Slick and Paul Kantner became a couple, they started collaborating on songs together. Kantner, who was a science fiction buff, wrote a song called "Have You Seen the Saucers?" about space aliens. And in response to President Nixon's newly initiated Operation Intercept, to stop the flow of Mexican marijuana into the United States by spraying it with paraquat, Grace wrote "Mexico."

By the time the Jefferson Airplane went into the studio to record the new tracks, which would be released as a double "A" single, the band was falling apart.

"Jack came in and took five days to do a bass part," said Stephen Barncard, who worked as an engineer on the sessions. "Then Jorma came in and did his part. Paul was pretty much running the show and Grace was hanging out and grossing everyone out."[22]

—◦—

On Friday, March 6, the Miles Davis Quintet played the Fillmore East, opening for the Steve Miller Blues Band and Neil Young and Crazy Horse. His new album *Bitches Brew* had just been released on Columbia Records, and Clive Davis ordered him to play the Fillmore for exposure to white audiences.

"He went nuts," recalled Davis. "He told me he had no interest in playing for 'those fucking long-haired white kids.' [Bill] Graham would only rip him off."[23]

After Miles threatened to leave Columbia Records, Davis eventually calmed him down, and the jazz great reluctantly agreed to play the Fillmore East. He signed a contract for a single one-hour show for payment of $5,000, with $1,000 due on signing.

The day after he signed the contract, Davis's agent Jack Whittemore sent Graham a tersely worded telegram announcing that Miles Davis had pulled out of the gig.

"Terribly sorry," wrote Whittemore, "but I have no control over this situation."

Nonetheless, Miles Davis did relent and play the Fillmore East at the beginning of May, deliberately arriving late for the first show to spite Bill Graham.

"You could see them bristling at each other," wrote *New York Post* music columnist Al Aronowitz. "Miles walking in through the stage door in his long, white furry coat and Bill pacing back and forth in his shirt-sleeves. They hardly spoke a word and yet they also hardly let a moment pass when they weren't in each other's sight. You kept finding them just off the wings backstage, Miles ignoring his dressing room, Bill ignoring his office, each ignoring the other."[24]

Miles, whose formidable band included Chick Corea on electric piano and Wayne Shorter on saxophone, had no respect for the rock acts on the bill and tried to sabotage them.

"I was opening for this sorry-ass cat named Steve Miller," he wrote in his autobiography. "Steve Miller didn't have shit going for him, so I'm pissed because I got to open for this non-playing motherfucker, just because he had two sorry-ass records out. So I would come late and he would have to go on first."[25]

On the last night, when Davis was late again, Bill Graham was waiting for him at the Sixth Street artist's entrance.

"Bill is madder than a motherfucker," recalled Davis. "He's standing *outside* the Fillmore. He starts to cut into me with this bullshit about 'disrespecting Steve.' So I just look at him, cool as a motherfucker, and say to him, 'Hey, baby, just like the other nights and you know they worked out just fine, right?' So he couldn't say nothing to that because we had torn the place down."

Reviewing the final show of the run, Mike Jahn noted Davis's "short, aggressive set" met with "restrained curiosity" from the Fillmore East audience.

"To one raised on the Beatles," wrote Jahn, "the name Miles Davis rings like a legend, to be revered if not understood."[26]

A month later, in April 1970, Miles Davis played four nights at the Fillmore West, opening for the Grateful Dead. During the run, Bill Graham introduced Miles to Jerry Garcia.

"[We] hit it off great," said Davis, "talking about music . . . and I think we all learned something, grew some. Jerry Garcia loved jazz, and I found out that he loved my music and had been listening to it for a long time."[27]

The Grateful Dead deeply respected Miles Davis, and they were intimidated by having to follow him onstage.

"As I listened, leaning over the amps with my jaw hanging agape," said Phil Lesh, "I was thinking, 'What's the use? How can we possibly play after this? We should just go home and try to digest this unbelievable shit.'"[28]

⌁

On March 8, the Fillmore East celebrated its second anniversary with the Joshua Light Show "Movie Orgy." The seven-hour show, created by future movie director Joe Dante and Jon Davison, who coordinated cartoons and movie snippets for the Fillmore East, included "singing cowboys, neurotic werewolves and maladjusted Indians."

Throughout the two years they had worked there, many of the Fillmore East staff saw themselves as a family, with Bill Graham as their often intimidating father figure.

"He was the father that you loved and hated but listened to," said his Fillmore East personal assistant, Lee Blumer. "He punished you."[29]

Jane Bernstein, who was the official Fillmore East Candy Chick, working the concessions, remembers Graham's siege mentality.

"He would gather us together to give us a talk about something," she said. "A lot of his metaphors were kind of war metaphors [and] military allusions. He was a little scary."[30]

Graham also kept morale high at the Fillmore West by holding similar monthly "family meetings," where employees could raise any problems.

"We felt part of his family and he was like the father," remembered Fillmore West publicist Chris Brooks. "We'd all sit there and Bill would talk and then ask for suggestions. [One day] I was feeling weepy and very upset. He put his arm round me and said, 'Don't worry, you're in good hands with a Jew.'"[31]

On March 26, the *Woodstock* movie was released. Without Bill Graham's knowledge, the producers had included his interview comparing the Woodstock audience to "man-eating Marabunta ants," and saying fire was the only way to control them.

At the premiere, Graham's original Fillmore East manager, John Morris, who had worked on the film's production and knew exactly where the speech was, deliberately watched Graham's reaction.

"He was critiquing the *Woodstock* movie," said Morris, "and taking notes on the whole film with a little pad and a pencil. When his speech about the ants came up he snapped the pencil in half. And it shot out and hit somebody in the audience."[32]

CHAPTER TWENTY-TWO

Dosing Richard Nixon

April to May, 1970

Since Janis Joplin had left the band, Big Brother and the Holding Company had been busy touring with their new singer, Nick Gravenites. In early April 1970, they played the Fillmore West, calling Janis onstage to sing a few songs. The delighted crowd rose to their feet when she came out and sang her song "Ego Rock" with Gravenites, as well as a couple of other numbers.

"She jammed with us when we played the Fillmore West," said Peter Albin. "It was fun and very cordial and warm."[1]

After Janis left the stage and Nick Gravenites ran through some new Big Brother songs, the crowd screamed for Janis. And she came back.

"We're really dredging up the past for ya, folks," she told the audience.[2]

Janis then sung "Piece of My Heart" and "Ball and Chain" to wild applause.

A week later, Janis joined Big Brother onstage again at Winterland. Backstage, Sam Andrew spoke to her for the first time since she had fired him a year earlier.

"She looked real puffy the way alcoholics do," he said, "and she was repeating herself onstage. It was kind of embarrassing."

That night, Andrew had a premonition that something bad was going to happen to Janis, and he told her so.

"I was real worried for her," he said. "We were alone and she said, 'I'm not going to die. My ancestors are pioneer stock and we're real strong. And it's in my genes and I'm going to survive.'"

"And I just thought, 'I wish she wouldn't have said that.' I got a chill up my spine."[3]

———

Two weeks after the *Woodstock* movie was released, Santana played a three-night run at the Fillmore East for $20,000 ($120,000), with It's a Beautiful Day opening. Before the first show on Friday, the band went to see the movie that would launch them into megastardom.

"We waited in line with all the other folks for the early show," said Michael Shrieve. "It was the first time we had ever seen it. When I saw the drum solo, and myself split on the screen like that, I didn't know if I should stand up in the theater and yell, 'That's me!' or sink down low in the seat."[4]

Billboard magazine reviewed one of Santana's Fillmore East shows, calling it a mini-Woodstock.

"There is very little that can be said about their set except that it was perfect," it read. "Santana made every other rock group look as if it ought to go home and practice."[5]

Road manager Herbie Herbert said that the band played some of their best shows at the Fillmore East.

"We loved the Fillmore West but the Fillmore East was in another league," he said. "It was the most professional gig in the business and it was done in a full theatrical manner. And they had a serious theatrical crew of stagehands and would pretty much get everything right."[6]

———

That spring, Janis Joplin cleaned up her act and kicked heroin. She concentrated on finding a new band, getting back on the road, and recording an album. From the Kozmic Blues Band, she retained John Till on guitar and Brad Campbell on bass. Then she drafted pianist Richard Bell, organist Ken Pearson, and drummer Clark Pierson, whom she found playing at the Galaxy Topless Bar in San Francisco.

John Cooke, who rejoined Janis as road manager, had never seen her so focused and motivated.

"Janis's level of professionalism had increased by a quantum leap," said Cooke. "She had figured out how to be the band leader. She was just tickled pink."[7]

When Janis started rehearsing the new band at her Larkspur home in mid-April, everything came together.

"I'm super-gassed," she told a reporter. "They're fuckin' professionals. I've got my head back."

But she was soon diverted when her old friends Michael J. Pollard, Bobby Neuwirth, and country singer Kris Kristofferson suddenly turned up without warning at four o'clock one morning. It was the beginning of a mad three-week tequila bender around Marin County. They breakfasted on piña coladas, lunched on screwdrivers, and then headed off to the Trident Bar in Sausalito for cocktail hour.

Jefferson Airplane manager Bill Thompson ran into Janis at the Trident late one afternoon. A few weeks earlier, Janis's good friend Nancy Gurley had died from a heroin overdose, and her husband, James, Big Brother's lead guitarist, had been charged with murder after injecting her with it. He would eventually be sentenced to probation.

"I told her about it," said Thompson. "I knew that she was probably still floating around with heroin, but I thought maybe that would scare her into quitting."[8]

During the marathon tequila binge, Janis had an intense affair with Kris Kristofferson, who would write the song "Me and Bobby McGee" for her.

"Yeah, we made love a lot," said Kristofferson. "She had a real sexy bed. She had silk sheets and it was pretty fancy stuff for a guy of my limited experience."

During their time together, Kristofferson got to see the real Janis, and her problems with stardom.

"I never met anybody like Janis," said Kristofferson. "Janis was a vulnerable character in a rock 'n' roll situation where dreams come true—partially."[9]

One afternoon, Janis drove across the Golden Gate Bridge into downtown San Francisco, going to Lyle Tuttle's tattoo shop on Seventh Street. She had him tattoo her wrist with a simple Florentine bracelet of hearts and flowers in green, red, and yellow. Her inspiration was a bracelet she had bought in South America. He also tattooed a small heart on her breast.

"I wanted some decoration," she explained. "See, the one on my wrist is for everybody. The one on my tit is for me and my friends—just a little treat for the boys, like icing on the cake."[10]

Janis was so pleased with her tattoos that three days later she threw a big party for Tuttle in her Larkspur home, where he tattooed eighteen guests. Michael J. Pollard had his wife's name tattooed on his shoulder, and one of Janis's girlfriends had the words "Property of Janis Joplin" tattooed over one of her breasts.

At the party, Janis met a handsome young Berkeley student named Seth Morgan, who was paying his way through college selling cocaine, and took him to bed. Within weeks they would get engaged.

———

On Friday, April 24, Grace Slick went to the White House to dose President Richard Nixon with Orange Sunshine LSD. She had been invited to a tea party by the president's daughter Tricia, who had organized it for all her Finch College alumnae. The invitation had been sent to Grace Wing, and apparently no one at the White House realized she was now the notorious Grace Slick of Jefferson Airplane.

Grace then invited radical Yippie leader Abbie Hoffman along as her date and bought six hundred micrograms of powdered LSD. Hoffman, who had been a defendant in the Chicago Seven Trial two years earlier, duly shaved off his beard, slicked back his long curly hair, and put on a conservative suit. Grace opted for the preppy look: a camel hair coat over a miniskirt and boots.

Her year at Finch College had taught Grace all about formal teas, so she devised a plan to surreptitiously slip acid into Richard Nixon's cup and be long gone before it took effect.

"You have two urns at either side of a long table," she explained, "and you stand—you don't sit—and since I'm an entertainer, I gesture a lot. And I was going to gesture across Nixon's tea and in about a half an hour, he would have been out of his mind and nobody would've known why."

Grace then planned to thank Tricia Nixon for the tea, telling her she would really enjoy the rest of the afternoon.

The day of the tea party, Paul Kantner drove Grace and Hoffman to the White House gates and dropped them off.

"Grace took about seven thousand micrograms of Orange Sunshine into the White House," said Kantner. "But they figured out who she was."[11]

After putting the powdered acid under a long fingernail she used to snort cocaine, Grace put her hands in her pockets and walked up to the White House gates with Abbie Hoffman.

"And the security guard comes up to me and says, 'I'm sorry you can't go in. You're a security risk,'" said Grace. "And I go, 'What?' And he says, 'You're on the FBI list.' And I go 'What?' And I found out that the members of Jefferson Airplane were on a list because of 'suspect lyrics.' They didn't know why I was a security risk, but they were right."[12]

The next morning's *New York Times* reported that Abbie Hoffman had told White House security that he was "Miss Slick's bodyguard and escort," and they had been denied entry.

"Mr. Hoffman brought out a black flag emblazoned with a multi-colored marijuana leaf and hung it on the White House gate," read the story. "It was quickly removed. The singer and Mr. Hoffman ran across the street and were driven away by a member of the Jefferson Airplane."[13]

"That would have been amusing if that had occurred," said the getaway driver Paul Kantner. "She was a definite untouchable."

———

At the end of April, Joshua White disbanded his Joshua Light Show and quit the Fillmore East to start his own pioneering television company. He was also angry at the way hard drugs had now permeated into the Fillmore East and West managements.

Most of the key executives in Bill Graham's organization were often high at work. But the drugs of choice had changed from marijuana and LSD to cocaine and heroin.

"The fish stinks from the head down," said White. "Instead of getting stoned and getting mellow, they got stoned and mean. A lot of high-level management at the Fillmore were taking cocaine, which didn't have evil connotations at that time. In the Joshua Light Show I was dealing with people

I loved but they were making me crazy. When they smoked they would just get silly and mellow, but then when they started taking cocaine they weren't silly and mellow anymore. I had to get out of the Fillmore because I was just scared of those people. I thought everybody was getting crazy here."

White says that cocaine was one of the main reasons he left the music business to move into television production.

"The thing about coke is that you think you're being terribly organized," said White. "You have meetings and everything goes real fast and you just feel like you can rule the world. And for a time you can. But when you crash you lose it all."[14]

As hard drugs penetrated deeper into both Fillmores, the audiences also moved to cocaine, downers, and alcohol, and even worse. At one show, a smartly dressed, short-haired twenty-one-year-old man died at the Fillmore East after inhaling Freon gas and freezing his lungs.

"I was giving him artificial respiration in the balcony of the Fillmore," said Bill Graham's personal assistant, Bonnie Garner. "And that kid dying just threw me. I thought, 'I'm done. I'm done.'"[15]

The next day, she handed in her notice.

The first week of May, Jefferson Airplane were back in New York for a run at the Fillmore East. Two days before their first show, four Kent State University students were shot dead by National Guardsmen during a peaceful anti-Vietnam protest in Ohio.

The shootings came in the wake of the United States invasion of Cambodia and President Nixon's announcement that he was sending 150,000 more troops off to the war.

Bill Graham had scheduled the Airplane to play a free concert on Sunday afternoon, after the Wednesday- and Thursday-night shows at the Fillmore East. But after the Kent State Massacre, some Yale students tried to convince the band to come to New Haven instead to take part in a student strike.

"Reportedly, this request caused some consternation in the band," recalled Robert Christgau, "with Grace and Marty tempted and the others reluctant."

Ultimately, the Airplane went ahead with the Central Park show, arriving at the Naumberg Bandshell by limo. And inexplicably during her performance Grace berated the audience for being there instead of protesting in New Haven.

During their four shows at the Fillmore East that week, the Jefferson Airplane—with new drummer Joey Covington—seemed reenergized. Just before they went on every night, a photo of Grace and Abbie Hoffman outside the White House was projected onto the light show screen. Its caption read: "What's a nice girl like you doing in a place like this?"

Backstage at the Airplane shows, cocaine was rampant. And the band was very generous with its high-grade marching powder.

"I will say the Airplane had the best coke I've ever had," said Dan Opatoshu of the stage crew, "so I was happy to partake. But I wasn't that happy with the set. Again, it's a personal thing and some people love the grumpy Airplane shows [best]."[16]

Robert Christgau covered the late Thursday show for the *Village Voice*. The performance would become legendary.

"Grace was wearing one of her bitch costumes," he wrote, "short black skirt, see-through top, black squares covering her breasts, black hair teased and splayed in a crown around her head—and looked like a cross between Jean Shrimpton and the Wicked Witch of the North. She was high on coke, apparently—and as she explained later, menstruating."[17]

After the first couple of songs, Grace launched a verbal attack on the audience.

"How can you live like men," she demanded to know, "if you're stacked like rats in a cage?"

Then she told them how she could not wait to go back to California. And after observing that "New York chicks don't fart" and that Paul [Kantner] never smiles because he's German, the band struck up the first notes of "Somebody to Love."

Then in the middle of the song, a coked-up Grace started taunting the audience again.

"You paid $3.50 to come in here and you probably don't have it, man, but we do," she told them. "We can ride in cars that are all closed up and nobody sees us . . . [We] can smoke all this dope and nobody gives you any shit. But they give *you* shit because you don't have a Cadillac. We do. You know the people you're rising up against? They're right up here on this stage. They're also in the White House but they're also right here. Because you had to pay to get in here. It wasn't free. You're paying our asses so I can stand up and have a shrimp salad and all that shit—and I'm a jerk because I love it. I love that shrimp shit."

Grace's take on being a modern Marie Antoinette would go down in Jefferson Airplane folklore as the "shrimp shit rap."

"She was doing coke that night, right," said Robert Christgau in 2012. "It never helps as far as your regression level is concerned. To me it doesn't seem hard to understand at all. It happens in May 1970 at the moment when the Airplane in particular, and a lot of the bands, were at their most explicitly political.

"There was political change going on and it involved conflict not persuasion. But it wasn't all just going to flower into something else. That became extreme clear [after] Kent State."[18]

Back in the hotel after the show, Grace went to Paul Kantner's room. Then, as they were about to make love, she announced that she wanted to have his child.

"And I said, 'Okay,'" said Kantner, "'that's flattering in some way. This could be interesting.'"[19]

Several days later, Bill Graham complained about Grace's recent behavior to his Fillmore West staff at one of their regular meetings.

"And he was particularly upset," said Chris Brooks. "Grace was as high as a kite and had said something very rude onstage. She had apologized to the audience for her behavior by saying, 'Excuse me for my behavior but I'm on the rag.' And the people in the audience whooped it up. You know, 'ho, ho, ho.' Bill found it particularly offensive as we all did."[20]

But Bill Graham would never dare confront Grace about her offensive behavior, as Jefferson Airplane were still his biggest draw.

At the beginning of April, Santana flew to London to play the Royal Albert Hall. Although the *Woodstock* movie and soundtrack were a huge hit in America, they were still three months away from release in Europe. When they returned to San Francisco, Santana went straight into the studio to start recording their second album, *Abraxus*.

There was a lot of pressure on the band to match the huge success of their first album, and they would more than rise to the occasion. When Gregg Rolie suggested covering Fleetwood Mac's "Black Magic Woman" on the new album, the others were against it. But the organist insisted and it would eventually become their biggest hit single, peaking at number 4 on the *Billboard* chart.

The other huge hit on *Abraxus* would be Tito Puente's "Oye Como Va," which Bill Graham had first suggested they record months earlier. Again, some of the band did not want to, but this time Carlos fought hard.

"So the band go, 'That's not rock 'n' roll,'" said Carlos. "And so I say, 'Well I don't care. These songs are going to be on the record. And if you don't [like it] get another guitar player.'"[21]

Tito Puente, meanwhile, did not want a rock band to tinker around with his music and protested to Bill Graham. But after it became a huge hit, he changed his tune.[22]

One of the lynchpins of *Abraxus* is José "Chepito" Areas, whose Latin musical influences were integral to the Santana sound. Areas, an expert in Latin music from his years of playing in the Mission, believes Carlos Santana never properly acknowledged his contribution to the Santana sound.

"I created the Latin rock," he said. "I taught Gregg Rolie and Carlos, but I didn't get [any] credit. Then we did "Black Magic Woman" and "Oye Como Va," and boom—all over the world."[23]

While they were recording *Abraxas*, a fifteen-year-old guitar prodigy named Neal Schon was hanging out at the studio. Gregg Rolie and Michael Shrieve had first seen him play with his band Old Davis at a Palo Alto club called the Poppycock.

"We'd been hearing about Neal so we went to hear him play," said Michael Shrieve. "And he was amazing in that English rock 'n' roll blues style of Eric Clapton. He was really a prodigy."[24]

After jamming with him for hours, Shrieve and Rolie were so impressed that that they invited him to the *Abraxus* sessions.

For the next few weeks, Schon was a constant presence in the studio, even playing on Rolie's "Mother's Daughter" track.[25]

Although Rolie wanted the more rock-orientated Schon to join Santana, he knew it would be bad politics to ask Carlos to add another guitar and lessen his role in the band. So he waited until Carlos could play with him and see how good he was.

"Carlos had to bring it up," said Rolie, "and he did after playing with him. He asked me, 'what do you think about having another guitar player in the band?'"[26]

Abraxus begins with Michael Carabello's "Singing Winds, Crying Beasts," an aural personification of cocaine, which the band were now freely indulging in.

Road manager Herbie Herbert was in Wally Heider's studio during the recording, and he and producer Fred Catero wondered how Santana kept going without apparently needing any rest.

"It'd be six, seven in the morning," said Herbert, "and the band would be, 'Let's cut this!' We're dead on our feet. It's fucking daylight outside. Where's this crazy energy coming from?"

Finally, Herbert asked Carabello what was going on.

"Michael says, 'Oh! We're doing blow,'" recalled Herbert. "'You guys ought to try a bump.'"

The band then came into the control room and laid out a few lines of blow for them to try.

"Me and Fred didn't feel a thing at first until we got the buzz," said Herbert. "Then [we] looked at each other, 'Holy fuck, I'm lit up like a Christmas tree.' We were whack."[27]

The huge amounts of cocaine and other drugs that Santana were now ingesting, along with all the acclaim they were receiving, were starting to affect the whole band. For the first time in their lives, they had real money and the power that it brought.

After Woodstock, Bill Graham had warned Carlos about the dangers of instant superstardom, urging him to keep his feet firmly on the ground.

"Bill Graham had told us . . . it's going to fuck you up," Carlos recalled. "Your egos are gonna get so big you're gonna need a shoehorn to come into a room. We said, 'No. No,' and sure enough, that's exactly what happened."[28]

On Friday, May 22, Janis Joplin unveiled her new band, now being billed as Main Squeeze, at a Hells Angels benefit in San Rafael, Marin County. Albert Grossman flew in for the show, and Big Brother and the Holding Company were the opening act. Janis joined them onstage for a couple of songs.

The show was awash with alcohol, and the local Southern Comfort distributer had donated several cases of Janis's favorite drink. During Big Brother's set, a drunken couple stripped naked and began making love as the audience applauded. Grossman stood silently at the back of the ballroom, looking uncomfortable.

When Janis took the stage, all hell broke loose after a Hells Angel tried to take a swig from her bottle of Southern Comfort. When she refused to give it to him, he hit her in the face.

"She wound up getting punched by some Hells Angel," said Mike Wilhelm, who also played with Loose Gravel. "She was drunk and out of hand. She was running around being a really obnoxious drunk, and he slapped her around. Then she burst into tears and went back into the dressing room."[29]

A couple of days later, Bobby Neuwirth was at a band rehearsal when he suddenly shouted out, "Is everybody ready for a full-tilt Boogie?"

Janis Joplin immediately latched on to the expression "Full Tilt Boogie," christening her new band with it on the spot.

At the end of May, Janis and the Full Tilt Boogie Band opened in Gainesville, Florida, before moving on to Jacksonville, Miami, Columbus, and Indianapolis.

The mini-tour had been badly handled by local promoters and some of the shows were only half full, with several being canceled. All this pressure was getting to Janis, who was drinking herself into a stupor.

She was also worried that Albert Grossman planned to drop her, even sending him a cable pleading with him not to do so.

"I know I'm not The Band or Dylan," it read, "but care about me too."

Grossman, who had no intention of dropping Janis, was so alarmed he insisted she seek further medical treatment for her drinking, which she did.

During the tour, she became obsessed with Nancy Milford's new biography of F. Scott Fitzgerald's tragic alcoholic wife Zelda, whom Janis had always related to.

"Well I've been an F. Scott Fitzerald freak for years," she would explain. "I read that he sort of destroyed her. I don't believe it's true. We destroy ourselves."[30]

— ❦ —

Soon after inviting Paul Kantner to father her baby, Grace Slick became pregnant. She decided to abstain from LSD until after her baby was born.

"If a drug makes me feel bad," she said, "then it would make my baby feel bad. I didn't take any acid because it didn't feel right for me."[31]

But during her pregnancy, Grace barely slowed down with regard to her performances. She and the band played the Bath Festival in England, followed by the Kralingen festival in Rotterdam. Then, the Jefferson Airplane took a short hiatus from each other.

Jorma Kaukonen and Jack Casady flew to Jamaica to try to record a Hot Tuna live album, while Grace and Paul Kantner moved into a four-bedroom beach house together in Bolinas, Marin County, to prepare for their new arrival.

They settled down in as domestic a lifestyle as either had enjoyed in a long time, writing songs for what would become the first Jefferson Starship album, *Blows Against the Empire*.

CHAPTER TWENTY-THREE

The Festival Express

June to July, 1970

At the beginning of June, Crosby, Stills, Nash & Young played a week of shows at the Fillmore East. On the day tickets went on sale a month earlier, there were lines four-deep around the block—hours before the box office opened. Many people had camped outside all night.

When house photographer Amalie Rothschild arrived that unusually hot May morning, she was amazed to see the crowds lining up for tickets.

"It was a revelation," she recalled, "and I thought I've got to be up high [and take a photograph]."[1]

So the resourceful young photographer started knocking on doors in an apartment block across the street, talking her way onto the roof. From her vantage point there, she photographed the hundreds of fans swarming around the Fillmore East.

Prior to the first show a month later, right before Crosby, Stills, Nash & Young arrived for the soundcheck, Bill Graham called a staff meeting. Referring to the band as "the American Beatles," he ordered his staff to give CSN&Y everything they wanted.

Soon afterward, the band's crew arrived in a fleet of trucks, carrying tons of sound and lighting equipment. Once again, they insisted on using their own gear rather than the Fillmore East's superior equipment. They also announced that they wouldn't be needing the theater's new Joe's Light Show, requesting a black curtain instead.

"There was a lot of ego going on," explained Allan Arkush. "These guys were acting like they owned the world."[2]

Arkush also sensed how arrogant the supergroup had become since they had first played the Fillmore East the previous August after Woodstock.

"They saw themselves as stars," he said, "and had a different attitude."[3]

The final straw came when the band's road manager demanded a Persian rug for them to play on. After finding one that had been used by Ravi Shankar, the road manager declared it too dirty.

Furious, stagehand John Ford Noonan, who hated CSN&Y's attitude, decided to make a point. He grabbed an industrial vacuum cleaner and got down on his hands and knees, vacuuming every inch of the rug as if his life depended on it.

"We're going to do this for the Crosby, Stills, Nash! We're going to do this for the Crosby, Stills, Nash!" he kept repeating.

Finally, when he had finished, he walked up to band, who had been watching him, telling them, "You know, even if you guys were good, this would be too much work."

At that point, Bill Graham announced he had a phone call and rushed back to his office so he wouldn't have to face the angry band members.

"Basically," said Dan Opatoshu, "it was the clash of two entities with huge egos. The Fillmore staff versus the supergroup of all time."[4]

A few minutes later, as the soundcheck began, everything changed. Neil Young played his moving new song "Ohio," his emotional response to the Kent State Massacre. One by one the Fillmore East staff came over to thank him for writing the song, which perfectly summed up everybody's feelings about Richard Nixon and the senseless violence seemingly everywhere.

All the Fillmore East shows were being recorded for a live album, and they were some of the best shows CSN&Y would ever play. On the second night—Tuesday—Bob Dylan was quietly smuggled in through a side entrance to watch the group.

"We used to sneak Dylan in so he could sit upstairs in one of the light booths and watch shows that he wanted," recalled Bonnie Garner. "This was back when we didn't have cell phones, so Al Aronowitz [who was a close friend of Dylan] would call the office and say that Dylan wanted to see the show tonight. Someone would be at the back door waiting for him and then sneak him upstairs."[5]

The first half of the show was played acoustically, with each member of the band playing two songs solo before taking an intermission and coming back electric.

"We would do little solo sets," said Graham Nash. "I'd do two, David would do two, Stephen would do two and Neil would do two. And this night, because Dylan was there, Stephen did five songs. And that pissed me off righteously, because I knew why he was doing it. We all could have done that. We all wanted to impress Dylan, but he did it. We were so infuriated."

During intermission, the other band members rounded on Stills, angry about his blatant grandstanding to impress Dylan.

"He's holding a Budweiser can in his hand," said Nash, "and he's slowly gripping it and crushing the can. [He] crushed it flat, so that it was frothing all over the carpet . . . with this maniacal energy. And then we went out and played the greatest set we ever played. Go figure."[6]

On the final night of the run, after several encores, the audience was still screaming for more.

"Bill Graham came and knocked on the door," said Nash, "and he said, 'They're not leaving. Can you come back and do some more?' And we go, 'Look, we've just done three hours. Come on, give us a break.'

"So, I think it was Crosby who said, 'We want money.' And Bill Graham starts to feed hundred dollar [bills] under the door. And when he got to eight, Neil said, 'Okay, We'll do one more song.'"

That same day—Sunday, June 7—Bill Graham also presented The Who's final two performances of *Tommy* at New York's Metropolitan Opera House. It was Graham's most prestigious show to date, and he saw it as the beginning of a new phase of his career.

"Rock music may have reached its all-time peak," wrote Albert Goldman in *Life* magazine. "A great leap across the gaps of generation, class and culture, the performance installed rock as a maturely rounded art in the shrine of the great European classics."[7]

Almost eight thousand people jammed into the stately opera hall in Lincoln Center, paying up to a record $7.50 to see a matinee or evening performance of *Tommy*, billed as the last time The Who would ever play it. The Met had never seen anything like it.

"Helium balloons bobbed from the orchestra," reported the *New York Post*, "the kids shouted from the Family Circle to the Grand Tier, waved to each other, smoked pot when the ushers weren't looking . . . in a delightful display of irreverence."[8]

Ironically, just a few hours before he would slip hundred-dollar bills to bring Crosby, Stills, Nash & Young back for an encore, Graham found The Who far more difficult to bring back.

After the 8:00 p.m. *Tommy* show, the crowd were on their feet for fifteen minutes, screaming for an encore. Bill Graham then knocked on The Who's dressing-room door and ordered them to go back out and play some more. Townshend was still angry about the May 16, 1969, fire at the Fillmore East, when he'd been arrested.

"I asked him to tell the audience to go home," recalled Pete Townshend in his autobiography. "He refused, so I did it myself. When the crowd realized what I was saying they started to jeer. I threw my mike stand into the pit and stalked off."

Walking past Graham in the hallway, Townshend fixed him in the eye and said, "It's easy to bring us on, Bill. It's much harder to get us off."

A week later, Bill Graham restaged *Tommy* at the Berkeley Community Theater and tried to mend fences with The Who. On the second night, he arranged to have three klieg lights turned onto the audience in a Fillmore East–style salute. Then after the show, Graham gave the valuable lights to The Who, who were delighted.

"Bill Graham had redeemed himself," said Townshend.

———

On Wednesday, June 17, Laura Nyro played three nights at the Fillmore East, with Miles Davis as her special guest. Davis's new L.P. *Bitches Brew* had just gone gold, selling half a million albums to become his bestselling record to date. Bill Graham had started booking the jazz legend's shows through his Millard Agency, and the two of them quickly came to blows.

"We had our disagreements," said Davis, "because Bill is a tough motherfucking businessman, and I don't take no shit."[9]

On Friday morning at 8:22 a.m., the furious trumpeter sent a telegram to Graham, back in San Francisco, calling an upcoming San Diego gig an insult. Davis wrote:

I REFUSE TO BELIEVE THAT A PROMOTER COULD BE SO DUMB AND CHEAP. I AM NOT A $2500.00 PERFORMER. THE PROMOTER KNOWS THAT OUR BAND WILL ENHANCE ANY MUSICAL CONCERT IN THE WORLD AND WE'RE NOT ABOUT TO ENHANCE IT FOR $2500.00. WE DON'T NEED THAT KIND OF MONEY. YOU KNOW OUR VALUE. IN OTHER WORDS BILL I WON'T PLAY A $2500.00 CONCERT EVEN THOUGH I KNOW YOU'RE HUSTLING FOR US.
 RIGHT ON FOR YOU BILL FOR WORKING SO HARD. WE LOVE YOU SWASTIKA AND ALL MILES.

Ten days later, the furious trumpeter sent Graham another telegram after a conversation with Laura Nyro's manager, David Geffen:

DAVID GEFFEN CLAIMS THAT HE WAS TO MATCH YOUR SALARY FOR ME FOR THE ENGAGEMENT WITH LAURA NYRO AT FILLMORE. I CAN'T BELIEVE THAT A MAN WHO WANTS TO HANDLE MY AFFAIRS RESPECTS MY MUSIC SO MUCH MEANING TWO AND TWO THAT'S WHORES MONEY. MILES.

The next morning, Miles fired off another telegram after Bill Graham had presumably called to find out what was wrong.

THIS IS WHAT'S BUGGING ME. DAVID GEFFEN SAID THAT LAURA SAID 'I WANT MILES TO PLAY WITH ME AT THE FILLMORE NO MATTER WHAT HIS PRICE IS.' DAVID GEFFEN TOLD ME THAT LAURA SAID SHE WOULDN'T PLAY WITHOUT ME AT THE FILLMORE NO MATTER WHAT MY PRICE AND SHE'D PAY HALF.

YOU THEN CALL BACK AND TOLD HER PEOPLE THAT MY PRICE WAS 4,000 DOLLARS. SHE THEN PAID 2,000 DOLLARS AND YOU PAID 2,000 DOLLARS. SHE MADE 23,000 DOLLARS. YOU MADE 23,000 DOLLARS. BLACK MILES MADE 4,000 DOLLARS. YOU ASKED ME TO DO IT FOR THE EXPOSURE. WHICH IS A DISGUISE TO MAKE MONEY—IF YOUR [sic] GOING TO BE A PRO-MOTER UNDER THE DISGUISE OF EXPOSURE AND SELL ME TO YOURSELF FOR NOTHING AND MAKE ALL THE PROFIT AND I GET NO PERCENTAGE OR FRONT MONEY—(NOW I NEED 10,000 DOLLARS FOR THE GOV-ERNMENT. WHO DO I TURN TO YOU OR LAURA NYRO OR JACK WITTEMORE [Whittemore] OR SANTANA OR D.S.T'S AND ETC.?)

THIS MAKES ME SO SICK UNTIL I CAN'T SPEAK OF IT ON THE PHONE. BUT IT'S BUGGING ME UNTIL I CAN'T SLEEP. SOMETHING IN ME SAYS HERE'S A GOOD MAN—BUT WHEN IT COMES TO MONEY ALL GOOD MEN LIKE ALL BAD MEN TAKE CARE OF THEMSELVES FIRST. I KNOW YOUR AGENCY NEEDS ME, BUT SINCE YOU'RE GOING TO PLAY THAT WAY WHY NOT GIVE ME A PERCENTAGE OF THE AGENCY AND LET ME RETURN SOME OF THE SUPER MONEY THAT YOU WILL EARN FROM ME.

MY SECOND SENSE KEEPS ME FROM BEING A COM-PLETE FOOL. BILL, I'M SURE THERE ARE OTHER WAYS TO MAKE MONEY, BUT DON'T USE ME.

P.S. THIS TELEGRAM IS FOR YOU TO LOOK AT AND STARE AT AND REMEMBER AND DO SOMETHING ABOUT.

MILES DAVIS.

Bill Graham replied by return mail, copying Davis's agent Jack Whittemore. He was particularly hurt to be called a racist.

My first reaction to your telegram is disappointment in you that you could make such insinuations relating to my integrity in the handling of Miles Davis, the musician. Your telegram to me is unrealistic, unfair and without foundation. It does not take into consideration what I have tried to do for you, Miles Davis, the creative musician. Not as a black man or a white man, but as one man to another. For you to imply that I have taken advantage of black Miles is for you to also suggest that I am not worthy of representing you. If that be the case, then so be it. But be sure of one thing, I try never to take advantage of any man without justification.

From the first day that I became involved in your representation, it has been my feeling that, being a great artist, you should be exposed to a bigger and more varied audience than you had been in the past. To some extent, we all have tried to "play the game."

Your earnings at Fillmore East may have seemed like short money to you; but the gig did land for you a feature story with photos in the New York Times, a feature story in the Village Voice and, last month, a feature article in Time Magazine.

Don't ever misunderstand me, Mr. Davis; it is your ability as a musician that has brought you the recognition you are receiving. But don't ever dare underestimate the necessity of exposure. It is the combination of your ability and the exposure I have helped to get for you that has made it possible for you, for the very first time, to have a record high on the charts. The result of it all will be a higher income for you and, admittedly, for me. Based on your telegram, you do not believe that my having gotten involved with you had anything to do with potential earnings for you

My books for your date in New York are open to you for you to see what my profits were when you played there with Laura. I need not defend my actions to you or anybody. My record stands for itself; but I do think it is important for you to know who I am. I give you 48 hours to decide whether to trust me or not. Should I not hear from you, I will assume that it is the latter and I will continue to finish whatever projects I have started for you. After that, you'll be on your own and I sincerely wish you the best. This is not a threat, Mr. Davis, but I will never work with a man who does not trust me. Your opinion of me as a producer and manager is based on a short relationship. Check me out, Mr. Davis; I've been a man for 40 years.[10]

Within a couple of days, Miles Davis had made up with Bill Graham and was booked on the same bill as Santana for the summer's Fillmore East at Tanglewood concerts.

On Wednesday, June 24, Janis Joplin attended the glitzy New York premiere of *Myra Breckenridge*, taking along Johnny Winter as her date. She sported an ostrich-tail headpiece, complete with pink and green feather boas, and a cape.

Janis drew up in front of the movie theater on 49th Street and Broadway in a stretch limo with the albino guitarist. It was a mob scene, with police holding back the crowd who had come to see Racquel Welch and the other stars walk the red carpet.

After the movie and reception, Winter went back to Janis's hotel at One Fifth Avenue, where they reminisced about growing up in the Texas panhandle.

"Janis was a real sweetheart," said Winter, "but she was drinking too much and taking too much dope."

The next day Janis made her second appearance on the *Dick Cavett Show*, where she introduced the Full Tilt Boogie Band. Janis was in high spirits, wearing a feather-boa headdress and a two-piece purple velvet suit inlaid with embroidered silver.

After singing "Move Over," running around the stage like a whirling dervish, with the Full Tilt Boogie Band solidly behind her, an out-of-breath Janis sat down to be interviewed by Cavett.

"Janis," he told her, "it's a shame you couldn't do an up-tune for us."

Then Cavett asked her about the song she had just sung.

"I wrote the one we just did," she replied. "It's about me. Did you ever see those mule carts? There's a dumb mule up there right, and they have a long stick with a string and carrot, which they hang over the mule's nose and he runs after it all day long."

"Who's the man in this parable?" asked Cavett. "The mule or the person holding the carrot?"

"No, the woman is the mule," replied Janis, "chasing something that somebody's always teasing her with."

"Constantly chasing a man and it always eludes her?" he asked.

"Well, they just always hold up something more than they're prepared to give."

"I have to defend my entire sex, ladies and gentlemen."

"Go right ahead," Janis replied, to audience applause.

Then Cavett asked if she sat down every morning to write a song.

"You just make it up," replied Janis. "I don't write songs. I make them up. Sometimes I write down the words, so I don't forget them."

Cavett then asked what she thought about when she was singing.

"I'm not really thinking much," said Janis. "You just sort of try not to feel."

"Do you ever get back to Port Arthur, Texas?" Cavett suddenly asked.

"No, but I'm going back in August, man," said Janis, suddenly brightening up, "and guess what I'm doing? I'm going to my tenth annual high school reunion. Hey, would you like to go with me?"

"Well I don't have many friends in your high school class," quipped Cavett.

"I don't either, believe me. That's why I'm going."

He then asked if she thought she'd have a lot to say at the reunion, and whether she had many friends at school.

"They laughed me out of class, out of town, and out of the state," she replied with a wry smile. "So I'm going home."

In the second half of the show, *Myra Breckenridge* star Racquel Welch came on to promote her new movie.

"It's a full-on smash," declared the sex symbol, "and I'm really happy. Janis was there."

"You were looking good," Janis told her, "but the movie's too choppy . . . not that I know anything about movies, but I couldn't understand it. It kept changing all the time."[11]

"Yeah, well. It's about change," replied Welch angrily.

"I'll drink to that," said Janis, lighting a cigarette in a long white holder as the audience applauded.

Years later, Dick Cavett would discuss that poignant moment, when Janis announced she was attending her high school reunion.

"I think there were two Janises," he said. "There was the high school girl who desperately wanted acceptance, and that character she created, which was the tough-talking, tough-drugging, drinking rock 'n' roll star."[12]

~~~

Three days after the *Dick Cavett Show*, Janis joined the Festival Express for a five-day musical train trip across Canada, stopping off at various cities to perform concerts. Also along for the ride were the Grateful Dead, the New Riders of the Purple Sage, Mountain, Delaney and Bonnie, Rick Danko of The Band, and Buddy Guy.

The twelve-coach train departed in Toronto and wound its way west through Saskatoon and Winnipeg to the final show in Calgary. It was a nonstop party, and the performers drank the bar car dry several times. There was also a dope shortage, as no one wanted to risk taking marijuana over the border. So, some of the roadies were sent off to score.

"It was like Woodstock on wheels," said John Cooke. "We had a great deal of fun . . . but the train was special because we were with all these other musicians."[13]

Janis loved all the attention, and her new Kris Kristofferson song, "Me and Bobby McGee," became the unofficial theme of the Festival Express.

"Janis was the hot shit on the train," recalled Mountain lead guitarist Leslie West. "We would stop in certain cities, and in between the cars Janis would go and wave to her fans."

As a joke, West asked his New York stripper girlfriend, Geri Miller, whom he had brought along, to stand between the cars ahead of Janis and take off her top when the train arrived at the next town.

"All of a sudden the kids were going, 'Wow!' said West, "and Janis is screaming, 'Where's all my people?'"[14]

Janis had a great time during the train trip, proudly boasting of getting Jerry Garcia totally drunk.

"Janis was the presiding spirit of this journey," reported *Rolling Stone*, "the bacchanalian Little Red Riding Hood with her bag full of tequila and lemons, lurching from car to car like some tropical bird with stream-ing feathers.[15]

~

On June 27, Bill Graham took out a full-page advertisement in *Billboard* magazine announcing that both his Fillmores were fighting for survival. The ad warned that managers, agents, and rock bands were pricing them-selves out of the theater concert business.

"Economics have taken the music from the clubs," stated Graham, "from the clubs, ballrooms and concert halls to the larger coliseums and festivals."

And he warned that his twin temples of rock were in imminent dan-ger, as there were not enough major acts to replace the ones now playing the bigger venues like Madison Square Garden.

"Once one got to the Seventies," said Kip Cohen, "there was a big shift and things got harder and uglier. There was a change. A change in the music. A change in the audience. A change in the attitude."[16]

Cohen said that the Fillmores could no longer compete with the bigger venues that paid the artists far more money and satisfied their increasingly inflated egos.

"We had something to sell for three years," he said, "and then it was not something that we could sell anymore. Could we sell it to the audi-ence? Yes. But not to the artist."[17]

~

On Saturday, July 4, Janis Joplin stopped off in Seattle on her way back to San Francisco. She ran into an old friend named Eddie West and spent the night drinking and setting off firecrackers from her hotel balcony.

Janis boasted to him of her sexual exploits on the Festival Express, complaining that she had gotten laid only 65 times, when there had been 365 people aboard.

At one point, West asked her what she thought she'd be doing at thirty.

"I'll never see thirty," replied Janis.[18]

Bill Graham's shows that summer of 1970 were becoming more and more adventurous. On July 7, he staged the first of three Fillmore East at Tanglewood shows with The Who, Jethro Tull, and It's a Beautiful Day. Two weeks later Joe Cocker would star in the second one, with Santana and Miles Davis booked for the third in mid-August.

On July 9, he presented "Dead At Midnight," a run of four shows beginning at midnight, with the New Riders of the Purple Sage opening for the Grateful Dead. These would be classic Dead shows, often finishing well after the sun came up the next morning.

"The thing about the Fillmore East," said Mickey Hart, "was that we could play all night. There were no curfews on the East Coast. In most other halls there were always curfews."[19]

At the end of July, Hot Tuna headlined a weekend at the Fillmore East, the first time they had played there without Jefferson Airplane. Leon Russell was the opening act. The first eponymous-named Hot Tuna album had just been released, and it was a sure sign that the Airplane was now splitting into different factions.

"Jorma and I were working on material that didn't quite fit into the format of Jefferson Airplane," explained Jack Casady. "So the Fillmore East was a great opportunity for us to start putting out this other kind of music."[20]

"Hot Tuna, a subsidiary of the Jefferson Airplane, the San Francisco band," wrote Mike Jahn in the *New York Times*, "played as quiet a concert as has ever been heard at the Fillmore East."[21]

That summer Bill Graham hired Gary L. Jackson to run the Fillmore West. The twenty-five-year-old was already a veteran on the San Francisco music scene, having co-owned the Matrix nightclub, where Jefferson Airplane had started out. He was also a trained accountant.

Jackson had asked Graham to stage a benefit for a friend of his running for Congress. And when he took some flyers over to the Fillmore West, Graham offered him the job on the spot.

"We got along famously," said Jackson, "and he basically gave me everything I asked for."

Jackson says there was a healthy rivalry between the Fillmore East and West.

"We kind of looked at ourselves as the leader," he said. "I went to the Fillmore East just to check it out. It was a nice venue but it's not in the greatest neighborhood in town."

Santana drummer Michael Shrieve said playing the Fillmore East was a totally different experience from playing the Fillmore West.

"It was New York City," he said. "It was a different feeling. It was edgier down in the East Village. The difference was we were on the road when we were playing there, and it was exciting."

Shrieve said Santana always looked forward to playing the Fillmore East, and it never disappointed.

"The hippies in New York were different than the hippies in San Francisco," he said. "And they were very welcoming of the band and really enjoyed it."[22]

The Allman Brothers Band drummer Butch Trucks said that the Fillmore West was far looser than its eastern sibling.

"Bill [Graham] would allow us to do a lot more jamming at the Fillmore West," he said. "I don't remember doing much jamming at the Fillmore East until right toward the end. And Bill ran it much more like a theater."

Jorma Kaukonen agreed that playing the Fillmore East was a far difference experience.

"The Fillmore West was a ballroom," he explained, "and it didn't have the same theater ambience that the Fillmore East did. And the other thing was the audiences. There is a quality to the New York tri-state audiences that is theirs and theirs alone. . . . I mean there's just nothing like them. And so to be able to get a positive response from the New York audience was a big deal. When they loved you, they loved you. If they didn't, they didn't."[23]

CHAPTER TWENTY-FOUR

"Somewhere Near Salinas"

August to October 11, 1970

In August 1970, Grace Sick, now three months pregnant, toured the East Coast with Jefferson Airplane. Since the band's return from England, Marty Balin had become more and more withdrawn, even growing a full Charles Manson–type beard.

The band resembled a bloated corporation, employing a secretary, a gardener, an art director, and even a fan club president. And on tour they traveled with an entourage of at least fifteen people, with everyone going first class.[1]

"Everybody was living the high hog," said Marty Balin. "They all had their own entourages and fifty people hanging around each guy. Me. I've got nobody. Everybody thought I was a dork. I wasn't into the drugs, I just drank in those days. Everybody was on coke so I just got bored by it."[2]

Jack Casady believes that the founder of the Jefferson Airplane now found himself completely overshadowed by Grace and Paul Kantner.

"[Marty's] personality isn't pushy like that," said Casady. "Paul has a very strong dynamic personality and so does Grace. Marty, I think, pulled back for a period of time with all of them."[3]

The Airplane were now one of the most bankable bands in America, earning at least $17,500 ($105,000) per concert. A year later, Paul Kantner would boast that he regularly wrote off all his drugs as a business expense.[4]

At the end of the tour, the band found themselves stuck in Toronto because of an airline strike, so Paul Kantner chartered a Lear jet to fly them back to San Francisco. During the flight everybody got high and drank champagne, and Kantner asked the pilot to put the plane into barrel rolls, curious to see the effects of centrifugal force on the champagne glasses.

"Yeah," said Kantner. "Just buckle your seat and then flip over. The amusing thing is when they do these flips you'd have a glass of champagne on the table and it wouldn't move."[5]

After a few barrel rolls, Kantner asked the pilot to go into freefall before firing up the engines and heading home.

On Friday, July 31, Janis Joplin checked into the Chelsea Hotel for a couple of weeks while working around the New York area. Aware of the temptations that New York held for Janis, Albert Grossman enlisted Emmett Grogan, the founder of the anarchist group the Diggers, to make sure she stayed clean.

"And you talk about a cat guarding the henhouse," said Barry Melton. "Albert had hired Emmett as Janis's bodyguard and to watch over her because he thought she had a drug problem. It was a total absurdity."[6] (Five years later Grogan would die of a heroin overdose on an F train in the New York Subway system.)

On Saturday night, Janis and the Full Tilt Boogie Band were booked to play the Forest Hills Festival in Queens. All twelve thousand tickets for the open-air concert had been sold, and soon after she came onstage there was a heavy thunderstorm.

The organizers then cleared the stage and canceled the show, declaring the conditions to be too dangerous.

"The people, refusing to leave, began to boo," recalled Patti Smith, who was standing at the side of the stage with Bobby Neuwirth. "Janis was distraught. 'They're booing me, man,' she cried to Bobby. 'They're not booing you, darling,' he said. 'They're booing the rain.'"[7]

Later that night, Grossman invited Janis to dinner at a restaurant called Remington's in the West Village. Among the others there were actress Tuesday Weld and Michael J. Pollard. Janis promptly got extremely drunk and propositioned Albert Grossman, who politely declined her offer.

Then she told Tuesday Weld that she may be a big star but she couldn't get laid. When no one paid her any attention, she stumbled over to the bartender and asked where she might find "all the pretty young boys."[8]

On Sunday, Janis played a rain date at the Forest Hill tennis stadium. It was a triumph.

"Janis Joplin and Her New Group Give Rousing Forest Hills Show," was the *New York Times* headline over Mike Jahn's rave review.

"Janis Joplin finally has a backup band worthy of her," it began. "Miss Joplin is a tremendously exciting blues/rock shouter, one who has had trouble finding musicians able to weather her storm. Her first group, Big Brother and the Holding Company, was exciting but imprecise, sometimes embarrassingly so. Her second band, which went unnamed, was precise enough but lacking in the energy department.

"Full Tilt Boogie, as the name implies, has the emotion and drive needed to back Miss Joplin, and is also composed of fine musicians."

The next night, Janis Joplin taped her third appearance on the *Dick Cavett Show*. After performing "Fill Me Like a Mountain," she looked unsteady as she walked back to Dick Cavett, spilling coffee over her hand. Her eyes, never fully engaging with Cavett or his other guests, Gloria Swanson and Margot Kidder, were glazed.

"She was a little off," remembered Cavett, "and by that I of course mean a little drugged."[9]

During the break, Janis brought out a bottle of Southern Comfort and was swigging it in full view of the audience. When Gloria Swanson, the silent movie star who had just made a big comeback in *Sunset Boulevard*, came out things became a little uneasy. After she started flattering Cavett, handing him a series of humorous calling cards, Janis called out, "You silver-tongued devil, you."

"I beg your pardon," snapped Swanson. "What did you say?"

"I said you were a silver-tongued devil," repeated Janis.

Later on, Swanson discussed her 1922 silent movie *Queen Kelly*, which had been heavily censored after director Erich von Stroheim had added explicit brothel scenes.

"I was in Germany when boys were dressing like girls," said Swanson. "So I have seen everything, but a lot of what's going on today [is] a bad imitation."

"But it shouldn't be illegal," Janis interjected, "just because somebody up there doesn't like it. Well back then you couldn't drink because they didn't like it, right. Now you can't smoke grass. Back then you couldn't be a flapper, because they didn't like it. Now you can't play rock 'n' roll. That seems to me you get the people that went through all that Prohibition and flappers . . . should realize that young people are always crazy, you know. And they'll leave us alone."[10]

After the show, Dick Cavett took Janis out for dinner and asked her if she was using heroin.

"And she said, 'If I were, who would care?'" said Cavett. "And I was so stopped by that I couldn't even do the obvious, which is to say, 'I would.' It just seemed to be such an admission of . . . it's over."[11]

On Monday, August 10, as *Abraxus* neared release, Santana played three nights at the Fillmore East. It was their fifth appearance, and in the year since their Woodstock triumph the band had changed radically. With all the sudden fame and fortune, Carlos Santana and the rest of the band were now living the high life, indulging their every whim.

"You're going from a Mission District kid with nothing to having everything," Carlos would explain later. "You're Number One. Too much drugs, everything to excess."[12]

Although Carlos was heavily into such psychedelics as LSD, mescaline, ayahuasca, and peyote, other band members preferred cocaine and heroin. During this period, Carlos had a recurring nightmare that he would be at a show in no condition to play.

"Bill Graham is screaming at me," said Carlos. "'You're nothing, you're unprofessional, you're a piece of shit.'"[13]

Michael Shrieve says that the insanity began after the *Woodstock* movie became a worldwide blockbuster.

"And it just blew up internationally," he explained. "So from there it was gravy. We played all over the world. I mean the first album came out and the second album was even bigger. There were drugs, cocaine specifically, that entered the scene for us. We were young and misguided. We didn't have the abilities or the maturity . . . to know how to deal with that kind of success and everything that goes with it at such a young age. In some ways it was the typical story."[14]

Organist Gregg Rolie believes that Santana was ill-equipped for all the sudden success.

"It's almost like too much, too soon," he said. "You had the world at your feet, you could do anything you want. And during those days you really could do anything you want."[15]

Road manager Herbie Herbert went along on Santana's roller-coaster ride.

"I always say they went to cocaine heaven," he said. "They were just a little too high and everyone was coming off nonexistent walls."

Janis Joplin came to one of the Santana shows at the Fillmore East after a very drunken dinner. On the way there, Myra Friedman asked her why she didn't play the Fillmores anymore. Janis replied that there was just not enough money in them anymore, while conceding it would be nice to play for a "hip" audience again.

When they arrived at the Fillmore East, a drunken Janis sat down by the stairs to compose herself.

"That being against the fire laws," said Friedman, "she got an usher frantic. 'You've *got* to move,' he pleaded. 'Even if you *are* Janis Joplin, you're not allowed to sit here!'

"'Honey,'" she said sweetly, "'you're doing a wonderful job and I want you to keep it up—but I ain't movin'.'"

Then Janis turned to Friedman and said that although she liked being treated like anybody else, she still wasn't going to move.[16]

A week later Bill Graham presented Santana, Miles Davis, and the Voices of East Harlem at a special Fillmore East night in the open-air amphitheater in Tanglewood, in the Berkshires. Miles was still feuding with Graham and once again deliberately arrived late.

"The Voices of East Harlem had already performed," recalled Herbie Herbert, "and Miles Davis's greatest band were onstage opening for Santana, with no sign of Miles showing up. Bill Graham was pacing up and down, 'That motherfucker, Miles; I'm gonna break his fucking neck.'"

All of a sudden, there's a screeching sound and a Maserati convertible careened to a halt by the stage, with Miles, wearing a patched leather vest, and his trumpet in the passenger seat.

"[He] jumps out of the car, straight onstage and just hits it," said Herbert. "Bill and I watched this go down with our mouths hanging open."[17]

After Miles's set, Santana came out and played with Bill Graham sitting behind an amplifier banging his cowbell. It was recorded by Joshua White's new television company for what Graham planned as the first made-for-television rock special.

"We played at Tanglewood next to Miles Davis," said José 'Chepito' Areas. "That was a beautiful concert."[18]

After the show, Graham threw a celebratory party for Santana in a trailer at the back of the stage.

"We were just happy," said Graham. "[They said] 'Bill, you're the greatest.'"

That night Carlos Santana and Miles Davis bonded musically and soon became major influences on each other. After seeing Santana, Davis introduced a percussion section to his band. And the next time Santana played the Fillmore East, Davis would be there for every show.

<hr>

Two days after Tanglewood, Santana had a band meeting and decided to fire Bill Graham.

"We didn't like him," said José Areas. "He wanted to manage Santana and he was after the money, because he knew we would make millions."[19]

Stan Marcum then telephoned Graham at his Fillmore East office and left the message that Santana had decided to "do its own thing" and no longer needed his services. When his secretary told him, Graham was furious, feeling deeply betrayed.

A few hours later, when he landed at San Francisco airport, he headed straight to Santana's Paisley Penguin rehearsal space to have it out with them.

"Bill Graham smashed the door open and comes walking in," said Herbie Herbert. "'Where are they?' he shouted. I go, 'Bill, you can hear them. They're in the back rehearsing.'"

As soon as Graham walked into the rehearsal studio, the music stopped. Then he began yelling at Stan Marcum for daring to fire him after everything he had done for Santana.

"It was ugly," recalled Herbert, who was listening outside. "I'm a non-confrontational hippie from Berkeley. I don't do fighting, and I was about to go across the street and get a milk shake."

As Herbert was walking out, Gregg Rolie ordered him back to fire Bill Graham. Herbert explained he was only a roadie and that was not his job. But the organist insisted, saying his job with Santana was on the line if he didn't.

Then Herbert went in the rehearsal room and stood between Graham and the band. He told Graham that they just could not afford to pay commissions to two managers, and Stan Marcum, who had been there from the very beginning, would be manager. But he said Graham could continue to present and book Santana shows.

"And here I am firing the guy that got me the job," said Herbert. "He's my mentor. My best friend. My second father, and now I've got to go in and fire him. But I did. And I did a very efficient and thorough job of it, and explained it to him. And when I was done Bill went, 'Okay,' and walked out and left."[20]

❦

On Wednesday, August 12, Janis Joplin almost caused a riot when she played in front of forty thousand screaming fans at the Harvard Stadium in Cambridge, Massachusetts. Half of them had tickets and the rest had climbed over the walls to get in for free. Before taking the stage, Janis told *Cambridge Phoenix* music writer Jon Landau, "My music ain't supposed to make you want to riot! My music's supposed to make you want to fuck!"[21]

Janis was on fire, delivering a great performance. It was the last one she would ever give.

The next day she flew to Port Arthur for her tenth high school reunion, taking along John Cooke, Bob Neuwirth, and her New York limo driver, John Fischer, for moral support. Before leaving, she told a reporter that she was going to the reunion "just to jam it up their asses" and "see all those kids who are still working in gas stations and driving dry cleaning trucks while I'm making $50,000 a year."[22]

"She wanted to go home with all her finery," said Cooke, "and her reputation and her well-earned fame and strut for Port Arthur."[23]

When they landed at the Golden Triangle Airport after a stopover in Houston, Janis and her entourage checked into a Port Arthur hotel. Her parents had skipped town for a couple of days to avoid any embarrassment their daughter might cause.

The next day Janis arrived at the stately Goodhue Hotel on Proctor Street, where the Thomas Jefferson High School Reunion was being held. She swept into the Petroleum Room, wearing purple and pink feathers, silver slippers, and sunglasses, with an assortment of bracelets and necklaces.

Then she gave a press conference for reporters and a local TV station, as many of her old high school classmates looked on.

"What have you been doing since 1960?" asked a reporter.

"Oooooh, hangin' out," Janis replied, sipping a cocktail. "You know just hangin' out. Havin' a good time. Tryin' to get laid, stay stoned—no, don't say that. That doesn't work in Port Arthur."

Suddenly, Janis's demeanor seemed to change and she went on the defensive, becoming the vulnerable high school girl again.

"You can really see her retreat from that 'I want to rub it in your face' stuff," said Cooke. "And she became really vulnerable like this wasn't a great idea to come be a jerk."[24]

Janis spent the evening ensconced with her entourage and pointedly ignoring her old classmates.

"Her peers spent the evening gawking at her," noted a reporter from *Texas Monthly*, "or making catty comments out of her earshot. Several asked for autographs. At least one of them, who had never been close to the singer, assured Janis that she'd given the media the wrong impression about Port Arthur's treatment of her. 'Janis, we liked you!' she insisted. Janis did not respond."[25]

After leaving the reunion, Janis had John Fischer drive across the river into Louisiana so she could show them the Texas Pelican, where she had her first drink.

That night, Jerry Lee Lewis was playing and Janis went backstage during a break to introduce her younger sister Laura to him. When the Killer quipped that Laura might be good looking if she didn't try to look like her sister, Janis hit him. Then Lewis punched her square in the face, saying that if she was going to act like a man, he was going to treat her like one. Janis burst into tears and had to be led away to the bar to regroup.

After more drinking, she took her three friends back to her parents' home to crash.

A few hours later, Seth and Dorothy Joplin, who had watched Janis's press conference on TV aghast, arrived home. They found Bob Neuwirth collapsed in a car outside with its engine running, John Fischer asleep on the living-room floor, and Janis upstairs in the bedroom.[26]

A huge argument ensued, and Dorothy told Janis she wished she had never been born.[27]

<hr>

That fall, a grim-faced Bill Graham gathered his young Fillmore West staff together for a family meeting. He told them that the future of the Fillmore West was uncertain.

"We are paying dearly for having provided the city of San Francisco with fine entertainment for the past five years," he said. "The public is spoiled rotten."

He then accused the San Francisco musicians of disloyalty for snubbing the Fillmore to make more money in bigger venues.

"When they were unknown," said Graham, "we hired them. When they were busted, we were there. We were always there. When the time came to stand up and be counted, I always thought we would be on the same team. I was wrong."

Graham also reminded them that the Fillmore West was still under a death threat from Howard Johnson's, and it would eventually be torn down.

"Running a ballroom," he told his staff, "is like a weekly invasion of Normandy, and there are already too many casualties."[28]

<hr>

On Thursday, September 10, Santana started a three-night run at the Fillmore West—the first time they had played a Bill Graham venue since they had fired him. At Santana's request, Graham had booked Dr. John as opening act. The morning of the first show, Graham messengered a letter to Stan Marcum, pleading with him for Santana to play two sets a night instead of the contracted one, because of the high demand.

> *Dear Stan:*
>
> *Have not been able to reach you by phone. Request for tickets for this weekend is tremendous. Please, please ask the group if they could not possibly do two sets for me Thursday and Sunday evenings also. Have gone out of my way to get Dr. John for you and the light show you requested. I would consider it a personal favor if you would relay this request to the group and get back to me some time today. My sincere thanks for their consideration.*
>
> *Best*
> *Bill Graham.*[29]

Soon after jettisoning Graham, Stan Marcum opened an office by the San Francisco waterfront. Santana's manager now rarely arrived at work before dinner, and he used his safe to house the band's cocaine stash. Drugs were rampant in the office, and Herbie Herbert had once found Marcum's personal secretary crying because she had snorted too much coke.

Marcum hired a lawyer named Herb Resner, who renegotiated Santana's contract with Columbia, obtaining a $1 million check in royalties. Bill Graham then had a stormy meeting with Resner, demanding $650,000 in fees. At the meeting, Graham produced an itemized list of everything he claimed to have accomplished for Santana, going through it point by point.

"We got very heated," said Graham, "and he started calling me some names and I lunged at him."

In mid-September, Santana's second album, *Abraxas*, was released. To tie in with it, *Time* magazine ran a story about the group, which had been originally pitched by Bill Graham publicity chief Chris Brooks.

"It had taken months to get them a story in *Time* magazine," she said, "with Bill pulling in some favors. They were all drugged out at the time, including their manager Stan Marcum. I had explained everything to him, like what time the band had to be there [for the interview]. And I knew something was wrong when after the discussion Stan looked at me and said, 'Now, what time are they supposed to be there?'"[30]

Only a couple of band members even bothered to turn up for the interview, which made just three paragraphs.

"There is nothing simple about Santana's music," it read. "The group's second recording, *Abraxas*, released this week by Columbia Records, shows less propulsive violence than the first, *Santana*. What it offers instead is a rare poetic delicacy."

But the final line carried a real sting to Bill Graham.

"From the beginning, the group has been managed by a music-struck local barber named Stan Marcum."

Rolling Stone also hailed the new album, which would later be ranked number 205 on its list of the greatest albums of all time.

"Carlos Santana is a Chicano," read the review, "and he loves the guitar, which has always been used heavily in Mexican music. He has perfected a style associated with blues and cool jazz and crossed it with Latin music. It works well because the band is one of the tightest units ever to walk into a recording studio."[31]

Soon after *Abraxas* was released, José "Chepito" Areas was flying back to Nicaragua, carrying a stack of new albums wrapped up in brown paper for his family. Just before takeoff, a stewardess told him that the large brown package would have to go in an overhead compartment.

The timbales player said he didn't want to put it up there, as it was "dynamite." Thinking it was a bomb, the stewardess told the pilot, who then abandoned the takeoff and alerted the FBI. Areas, who spoke little English, was then dragged off the plane while protesting his innocence.

Finally, Bill Graham had to call the FBI and explain that it was a mistake, and that Areas had been trying to say that it was a "dynamite recording."[32]

On Sunday, September 27, Pink Floyd made their debut at the Fillmore East, playing their new concept album *Atom Heart Mother*. Bill Graham did not believe the psychedelic English band, who were on their first tour of America, could sell out the Fillmore East.

"So instead of promoting the show himself," said Floyd drummer Nick Mason, "he rented the theater out to us for $3,000. We sold out."

For their performance of *Atom Heart Mother*, Floyd brought in all their own sound and lighting equipment, as well as ten horn players, a conductor, and a twenty-piece choir onstage to augment them.

"They were doing quadrophonic sound," said spotlight operator Ken Mednick. "It was totally revolutionary and quite mind-boggling."[33]

It was also the first time that Pink Floyd met the Fillmore East lighting director Arthur Shafransky, who would soon take over all the band's lighting, renaming himself Arthur Max.

During the intermission, a couple of scruffy-looking individuals came into the dressing room and made themselves at home.

"We had [them] ejected," said Mason, "only to discover later they were members of The Band. This was particularly embarrassing for us, since *Music from Big Pink* was a favored album in all our record collections."[34]

———

Bill Graham still could not bring himself to end his relationship with Diane LaChambre. Since Bonnie had moved out with his son, David, and filed for divorce, Graham underwent therapy to try to sort out his tangled personal life. The therapist had advised him to finish the relationship, but he just was unable to do so.

When Diane became pregnant again and wanted to marry him and settle down, Graham insisted she have an abortion, which she did reluctantly.[35]

Graham was also having problems on the business side, and his attempts to move into the Los Angeles and Southern California concert market had collapsed. Police harassment pulled the plug on many shows, and the Musicians Union began to investigate him after complaints from Little Richard, Country Joe and the Fish, and Roger McGuinn. Many music industry observers saw Bill Graham on the ropes, desperately fighting to keep his empire together.

Later Graham admitted that the two Fillmores alone had run him ragged, bringing him to the edge of a nervous breakdown.

"The economics got so it was madness," he later explained. "They'd become a 52-week job and they were 3,000 miles apart and driving me mad because it was becoming more and more difficult to operate very small halls."[36]

Now believing Graham to be vulnerable, Paul Baratta staged a second coup for Winterland. This time he was in a much stronger position than his first attempt nine months earlier, as Graham had failed to pay his $60,000 guarantee. The owners decided to back Baratta, giving him sole rights to stage all future Winterland concerts.

Baratta immediately signed Jefferson Airplane and the Grateful Dead for his first show there. For the San Francisco bands, even though they owed part of their success to Graham, it would be an ideal opportunity to start a bidding war among the promoters, and thus drive their prices up.

"I think Bill's in for a fight," Baratta told *Rolling Stone*, vowing to become the number-one promoter in San Francisco. "Graham has never had any real competition. I know how to package a show as well as Bill. Winterland is the biggest hall in town and I know the market well enough to put the shows together so the people will come to see them."[37]

Baratta then attacked his former boss, calling him a heartless moneymaking machine.

"I broke with Bill because of a growing disenchantment," he said. "At first what Bill did was good. He had heart. Then it began to seem like the bankbook was pumping blood through his veins. We just went our separate ways." Watching from the sidelines, *Rolling Stone* reported the action with the gravity of a world championship boxing match, forecasting that the seasoned pro could be expected to "fight a hard battle" against the young challenger.

Siding with Baratta, *Rolling Stone* had this warning for the hard-nosed promoter: "You meet the same people on the way down as you did on the way up.

"Graham has made many enemies over the years. Now, at least some of them are happy to see him get some real competition and will do all they can, including playing the Winterland affairs, to reduce Graham's overwhelming totalitarian position in the entertainment world."

After her high school reunion, and as a tribute to one of her greatest influences, Janis Joplin had purchased a headstone to be placed above Bessie Smith's grave. She also became engaged to Seth Morgan, whom she had met at her tattoo party. Independently wealthy, Morgan claimed to be the famous banker J. P. Morgan's grandson, but was in fact the son of an obscure poet named Frederick Morgan.

Janis invited him to move in with her, and within days she told friends he was *the* love of her life and they were getting married. Many were suspicious of his true intentions.

The first week of September, Janis Joplin moved into Room 105 at the Landmark Hotel in West Hollywood to start recording her new album. During the next couple of days the rest of the Full Tilt Boogie Band also checked into the hotel. Seth Morgan remained in Larkspur, flying in on weekends to see Janis.

Soon after arriving in Los Angeles, Janis reconnected with her old girlfriend Peggy Caserta, who was staying at a nearby hotel. And it wasn't long before Janis, who had been clean for six months, was back on heroin.

Throughout the last few months, Janis had started referring to herself as "Pearl," personifying the tough, hard-drinking, seen-it-all good-time girl whose image she liked to project. This would be the name of her last, and arguably her best, album.

Ironically, it would be produced by Paul Rothchild, who three years earlier had tried to lure her away from Big Brother and the Holding Company to become a star. The early sessions were a strain, with Janis listening to hours of tapes looking for new songs.

She was now working eight to ten hours a day recording in the studio, while at night she partied hard.

"To the band she always presented [herself as] this very up, very happy, very ready-to-rock, ready-to-play and make the music," said Full

Tilt Boogie guitarist, John Till. "That was the side of her we saw [and] we didn't really see the other side."[38]

While she was in Los Angeles, Janis met her old lover Kris Kristofferson and writer J. Marks for a drink at a seedy little bar on Santa Monica Boulevard.

"Her personal life was very lonesome," recalled Kristofferson, "and it was overwhelming to her."[39]

After spending a couple of hours with Janis, Marks walked her back to the Landmark Hotel.

"She crashed almost as soon as she hit the bed," said Marks. "I remember I was frightened by her massive fatigue. 'Are you all right?' I asked. She half opened her eyes and smiled bitterly. 'Sure,' she muttered, 'I'm just working on this tune,' she mumbled in her rusty voice. 'I'm gonna call it something like this: 'I just made love to 25,000 People, But I'm goin' Home Alone.' Then she went to sleep."[40]

On Friday, September 18, Jimi Hendrix overdosed in London, choking to death at the age of twenty-seven. After hearing the sad news in the studio, Janis became obsessed with her own mortality. She asked bassist Brad Campbell if he thought she would get as much publicity as Hendrix if she died. She also told her fiancé, "I can't go out the same year because he's a bigger star."

The following Thursday, producer Paul Rothchild called Nick Gravenites and asked him to write a couple of new songs to complete the album. Four days later Gravenities arrived in Los Angeles and headed straight to the Landmark Hotel, where he played Janis a new unfinished song called "Buried Alive in the Blues."

In her hotel room, Janis told Gravenites that she was really happy and looking forward to marrying Seth Morgan.

"She was telling me everything about her new old man," said Gravenites, "and how there were wedding bells in the air. She finally dug an old man she could relate to . . . and she was so happy with her band."[41]

Janis loved the new song, and the next day Gravenites finished it and brought it into the studio for the band to learn. Other tracks that had already been recorded included Kristofferson's "Me and Bobby McGee" and a quirky campfire song called "Mercedes Benz," which Janis had written with Bobby Neuwirth and poet Michael McClure and sang a cappella.

By the end of September, after almost a month in the studio, the album was 80 percent finished, and everybody was excited at how well it was going.

On Wednesday, September 30, Janis Joplin did a short telephone interview with Howard Smith to air on his Sunday show on the New York rock station WPLJ. Smith would have interviewed Janis months earlier, but she had been so upset about a negative review in *Rolling Stone* that she had canceled.

"Are you still upset when you get put down in any articles?" he asked her.

"I should be able to get past that," Janis replied, "but it's like most people, especially girls . . . want to be reassured. I know that [they] are just assholes but in my insides it's really hurtful if somebody doesn't like me. That was a pretty heavy time for me. I was leaving Big Brother and it was really important whether the people were going to accept me or not."

Then Smith asked how the recording of her new album was going.

"It's really going good," she told him. "We've got enough now for the record but we're still putting down some more tunes."

Smith then asked how she felt about the Women Libbers, who had recently complained that she was too sexually upfront for the movement.

"That's their problem not mine," she replied. "How can they attack me? I'm representing everything they said they want. I mean you're only as much as you settle for, and if they settle for being somebody's dishwasher, that's their own fucking problem. How can they attack me? I'm just doing what I wanted to do and what feels right and not settling for bullshit and it worked. How can they be mad at that?"

Finally, Smith inquired how her voice was holding out after her demanding stage shows.

"I'm not losing my voice," said Janis. "It's in better shape than it ever has been. It's stronger than ever . . . so long as I only have to work three nights a week I can last forever."

"Okay, good luck," said Smith, "and maybe when you're in New York we'll get together."

Then, apparently concerned about her comments regarding the Women's Liberation movement, Janis asked him to run it past Myra Friedman before it aired.

"Tell her what I said," said Janis, "in case she thinks I said something wrong, so maybe she won't let you use it."

"Don't worry about it," Smith reassured her. "Really, don't worry."[42]

"Oh, I don't want to offend people," Janis explained. "It's just like I have a certain set of things I try and live under. Like all this repressive upbringing and things. I have it too. You don't think I have a repressive upbringing in Port Arthur, Texas, you know? It's just that it drove me crazy and I kept fighting against it. You know, I don't think you can talk anybody into fighting against it if they don't have it in themselves to need more. You know what I mean?

"But hey, would you do that and talk to [Myra] in case I said anything wrong."[43]

———

The next day, Janis made a new will, splitting her estate four ways between her parents and her brother and sister. She also approved a premarital agreement her attorney Robert Gordon had drafted for Seth Morgan to sign.

"She seemed very happy," recalled Gordon. "She told me she was thinking of getting married. She was also very happy about her album. She said she 'felt like a woman.'"[44]

After leaving his office, Janis stopped off at a beauty parlor and got her hair streaked. She had also been on a diet, telling friends she planned to wed Morgan on a Mexican cruise ship.

Later that day, during her last telephone conversation with Clive Davis, Janis seemed positive and upbeat about the new record, playing him a few of the new songs.

"She seemed so thrilled about the record she was making," he said. "She couldn't have seemed happier."[45]

On Saturday, October 3, Janis didn't have to be in the studio until late afternoon, so she hung out at the Landmark Hotel. She tried to call San Francisco City Hall to inquire about marriage licenses, but it was closed on weekends. By the afternoon, Janis felt bored and edgy. She called her dealer, reaching him on her third attempt. They arranged for a heroin delivery.

When she called Seth Morgan, who was at her house in Larkspur, they argued after he told her he couldn't come to Los Angeles that day as planned. But he agreed to meet her at the Landmark early Sunday morning so they could have a three-way with Peggy Caserta.[46]

After her dealer arrived at the hotel, Janis shot up some old heroin she had in the room before driving her Porsche to the studio, arriving at around 5:30 p.m.

She walked in to find her band working on their arrangements for the new song "Buried Alive in the Blues," for which Janis would record the vocals the next day.

"She was really liking the song," said John Till. "She really felt good about what was going on and she told us many times, 'I just love that.'"

After laying down the instrumental track, Janis took a couple of the band members to Barney's Beanery, where she drank two vodkas before driving back to the Landmark Hotel with her organist, Ken Pearson.

"She had two drinks," said John Cooke, "which for Janis was like very little."[47]

Back at the hotel, Janis went into her room and waited for Seth Morgan and Peggy Caserta. When they didn't show she tried to call them but was unable to reach either. Upset at being stood up, Janis shot some of the almost pure heroin that she had scored earlier.

At about one o'clock in the morning, waiting for the drug to take effect, she left her room to get change for a $5 bill for the cigarette machine. After chatting with the desk clerk, she put fifty cents into the machine for a pack of Marlboros.

Janis then returned to Room 105, put the cigarettes on the bed, and undressed down to her blouse and panties. Suddenly the full force of the pure heroin hit her like a lightning bolt. It knocked her to the ground with such force she broke her nose and was dead instantly.

And there she lay, between the bed and a chair, for the next eighteen hours.

—~—

At six o'clock Sunday evening, after Janis failed to arrive at the studio, producer Paul Rothchild asked John Cooke to check on her.

"Janis was most punctual," said Cooke. "She had missed her time and wasn't at the studio, so I set out to look for her with two of our equipment men."[48]

It was dusk when Cook pulled into the Landmark Hotel on Franklin Avenue and observed Janis's distinctively painted Porsche parked outside. He also noticed that the lights were on in her ground-floor room. After getting her room key from the manager, he let himself in.

"And there was Janis," said Cooke, "except that Janis wasn't there. I put a finger on the flesh and the spirit was long gone. And there was no question, Janis was dead on the floor of her hotel room."

—~—

As the coroner arrived to transport Janis Joplin's body to the mortuary for autopsy, three thousand miles away, Howard Smith broadcast the interview he'd done with her four days earlier.

"It was a five-hour live show on WPLJ," he recalled, "and it was going to end with her interview and then a couple of her songs."

Smith was packing up to go home when the 1:00 a.m. news bulletin came on announcing that Janis Joplin had just been found dead in Los Angeles. It sent shivers up his spine.

"And I'm trying to be quiet," said Smith, "because it's a live mike and the assistants and engineer all go, 'oooohhh.' We draw our breaths in because of the weird coincidence of what's just happened."

—~—

Back in San Francisco, the Grateful Dead, Jefferson Airplane, and Quicksilver Messenger Service were playing Paul Baratta's first show at

Winterland. It was being broadcast live on San Francisco public television, as well as in quadrophonic sound on two radio stations.

During the Grateful Dead's set, word reached backstage that Janis had died, which was soon confirmed by a phone call to UPI. Baratta deliberately withheld the news from Jefferson Airplane and Quicksilver Messenger Service, who had yet to play.

"I think we heard just before we went onstage," recalled Paul Kantner. "Marty [Balin] was devastated. I know he went offstage and I don't remember if he came back or not."[49]

Baratta said that Grace Slick was visibly upset by the news.

"I think she felt a kinship with Janis," he said. "It was a guys' world. Grace was probably somewhat threatened by all the other ones that had gone down, but this was too close to home."[50]

Jorma Kaukonen said Janis's death was a huge shock to everybody.

"When you're in your twenties you don't expect one of your friends to die," he said. "Janis was the first death of one of my contempories that was close to me."[51]

Later that night, the members of Big Brother and the Holding Company gathered at David Getz's home in San Francisco.

"We held a small wake for her," said Sam Andrew, "and talked about her. We were all kind of numb [and] everybody was pretty high at that time. Pretty stoned. It's just amazing it was her instead of us."[52]

Peter Albin said he had not been surprised by Janis's death.

"She was burning the candle at three ends," he explained. "She was holding a match to the middle here as things were burning on the ends. She was just doing so much stuff and trying to work at the same time."[53]

On Monday night, Jefferson Airplane and the Grateful Dead were back at Winterland. Marty Balin was still too traumatized to play, and a fifty-five-year-old black fiddler named Papa John Creach played his first show with the Airplane. Asked later why he had not shown up to play, Balin replied he had been "attending a funeral."

Bill Thompson said that although the whole band was upset about Janis's death, only Balin bailed that night.

"I always thought that maybe Marty had a thing with Janis," said Thompson, "but he would never tell me about it."[54]

Backstage, Jerry Garcia told a reporter that it was probably the best time for Janis to die.

"If you know any people who passed that point into decline," he said, "you know, really getting messed up, old, senile, done in. But going up, it's like a skyrocket, and Janis was a skyrocket chick."

When Grace Slick was asked if she had a comment on Janis's death, she replied: "Well, not really. Why print all that stuff about someone who's dead? She's gone, it's done. I mean, I'm sorry she's dead, but . . . you know. If I come up with any jewels I'll send them to you, OK?"[55]

Years later, Grace spoke about her friend's tragic death on a television show.

"It's like a Russian roulette," she said, "and you have to know that when you start it. Janis had a new record coming out. A new boyfriend at that time. A new producer [and] everything was looking good. She just decided to have a little more, because if this feels good one more is going to feel great. Two more may have worked last week, but it didn't work this week."[56]

———

The day after Janis's death, Kris Kristofferson went to the studio to hear her recording of the song he wrote for her, "Me and Bobby McGee," for the first time.

"It was like a very intense experience for me to hear her singing," he recalled, "and it's still very emotional for me because the song is associated with her. That line, 'Somewhere near Salinas I let her slip away.' You can't help but feel you let somebody down. I'm sure that there's not a person that really was close to her that doesn't feel that way."[57]

———

On Monday, October 5, Los Angeles County Coroner, Dr. Thomas Noguchi, held a press conference and confirmed that Janis Joplin had died of an accidental heroin overdose. He told reporters that a hypodermic needle had been found in her hotel room, along with a red balloon containing white powder in a trash can. Some marijuana had also been found. The autopsy had also revealed numerous needle marks on her arms and an enlarged liver from drinking alcohol.

"We have excluded the possibility of homicide," said Dr. Noguchi. "Suicide? There is nothing to indicate at this time it was a death by suicidal attempt."[58]

That same day Janis was cremated at a private service for her immediate family. Her parents had wanted to transport her body back to Port Arthur for burial, but they later agreed to abide by Janis's wishes to have her ashes scattered at sea, off Stinson Beach, north of San Francisco.

"God what a year this is turning out to be," wrote Don Heckman in the *New York Times*. "As if the mass violence at Kent State weren't enough, we now seem to be caught in an almost hypnotic string of personal violence. Three weeks ago, Jimi Hendrix, and now Janis Joplin. The king and queen of the gloriously self-expressive music that came surging out of the late sixties are dead, the victims, directly or indirectly, of the very real physical excesses that were part of the world that surrounded them.

"But I don't think Janis Joplin would want anyone to sing sad songs for her. Whatever her problems, she dealt in the currency of life, of right—here—and—now—do—it—baby—before—it's—too—late. And how she did it all right, oh how she did it."[59]

CHAPTER TWENTY-FIVE

"The Show Must Go On"

October 12 to December, 1970

On Columbus Day, Bill Graham held a Rock Relics Auction Show at the Fillmore East to raise money for peace candidates at the next election. It would be *the* first rock memorabilia auction ever, setting the stage for a multimillion-dollar industry.

Janis Joplin's fur hat was to have been auctioned off, but the item was withdrawn so that it wouldn't look like anyone was capitalizing on her recent death.

Among the items auctioned off from the Fillmore East stage were Joni Mitchell's spiral notebook, containing handwritten drafts of all the songs for *Song to a Seagull*, which had a suggested starting bid of $200 but sold for just $90; Carlos Santana's switchblade, marked "Not in working order, given up for peace," which sold for $20.30; and a vial of dried rose petals thrown from the Madison Square Garden stage by Mick Jagger, which fetched just $20.

Other items on the block included: drumsticks belonging to Keith Moon, going for $10; a shard of a guitar Pete Townshend had smashed in action at the Fillmore East, verified by Kip Cohen as authentic, which sold for $75, Leonard Cohen's tuxedo, $25; Miles Davis's trumpet with his name engraved on it, $270; and a brassiere tossed to Jerry Garcia at a recent Fillmore East show, which fetched $15.[1]

"It's the first auction of our generation's future memorabilia," said auctioneer John B. Thomas "Why, buying a Fillmore poster today is like buying a Currier and Ives print a hundred years ago."

On October 30, 1970, Grace Slick turned thirty. Two weeks earlier, Grace and Paul Kantner's much anticipated *Blows Against the Empire* had been released to a cool reception. Ironically, as the couple had used all their new material for the album, RCA was forced to release a best-of compilation, entitled *The Worst of Jefferson Airplane*.

The *Blows Against the Empire* album, credited to Paul Kantner and Jefferson Starship, featured a who's who of guest appearances by Jerry Garcia, David Crosby, and Graham Nash.

The album was divided into songs about revolutionary politics, Kantner's obsession with science fiction, and the couple's imminent new baby. Their collaborative song "A Child Is Coming" told how Grace had broken the news to Kantner on an "electric Sunday morning," saying, 'I've got a surprise for you. A child is coming.'"

The week of its release, Jefferson Airplane was profiled by the *New York Times*, with Grace singled out as its undisputed star.

"Grace is a beautiful girl," wrote *Times* journalist Calvin Kentfield. "She plays the guitar, the piano, the Hammond organ, what have you. She's thirty years old now, the oldest of the group. She clearly takes her work seriously, is self-critical, intelligent, loathes hypocrisy and puts people on mercilessly; in fact, even those close to her are not always certain if they're being had."

In the lengthy feature, Grace proudly recounted her unsuccessful attempt to dose President Nixon with LSD.

"Their concerts are invariably sold out," read the article, "and young people with sleeping bags habitually line up the night before at the Fillmore East box office in New York in order not to miss getting tickets at $10 top."

The profile also said that unlike many other top bands, Jefferson Airplane won't play the larger venues like Madison Square Garden because of the bad acoustics.

"So they refuse to play just anyplace," it said. "In New York, for instance, they play at the relatively small Fillmore East because it's a beautifully set up place with great sound, and they decline to perform in Madison Square Garden where they would draw many more people, the acoustics are terrible."

The profile also reported a recent late-night recording session, revealing the personality conflicts splitting the band apart.

"Ego were rampant," wrote Kentfield, "everybody was mad at everybody else, every time they tried another tape each one tried to outdo the other. It sounded terrible.

"Marty: 'Play it smooth and gentle, none of your cocaine jumps.'

"Paul: 'You don't like the way I play, you can get yourself another guitarist.'

"Grace went home disgusted."[2]

On Monday, October 26, San Francisco's rock elite gathered at the Lion's Share in San Anselmo, California, for a special wake for Janis Joplin. She had set aside $2,500 in her will "so my friends can have a ball after I'm gone."

The Grateful Dead played at the "Drinks Are on Pearl" party, and then jammed with other Bay Area musicians for the all-night bash. One of the moving highlights was Country Joe McDonald playing "Janis," the love song he had written for her three years earlier.

"People were coming out of the backroom going, 'I think I just saw Janis,' recalled Peter Albin. "I said, 'Oh, man. You're stoned. Crazy.'"[3]

Bill Graham brought along his Fillmore West personal assistant, Vicki Cunningham, and ended up seducing her that night and starting an affair. She would be the first of a long line of employees he would become romantically involved with during the next few years.

Kip Cohen said his boss spent so much time working, it was natural he would gravitate toward young women in his office.

"There was usually a crossover between the romantic relationship and that," Cohen explained. "There were a lot of people who were staff but were also involved with him romantically."[4]

Still several years away from the finalization of their divorce, Bonnie Graham was well aware of Bill's behavior.

"And I know he had many secretaries," she said. "[That] was how he had relationships. I couldn't look at them and feel comfortable. It made me so sad."[5]

Graham was still seeing his troubled girlfriend Diane LaChambre, who called his house one day and Cunningham answered the phone. When she told the teenager she was now Graham's girlfriend, Diane arrived at the office the next morning in a fury. She then physically attacked Bill Graham, kicking and scratching. After ordering Cunningham out of his office, he wrestled Diane to the floor and tied her arms together with his belt to restrain her.

A few minutes later, Diane stormed out of his office and finally out of his life.

On November 12, a twenty-three-year-old English singer-songwriter called Elton John opened for The Kinks at the Fillmore West. Three months earlier, Elton had played the Troubadour in Los Angeles and received ecstatic reviews. Bill Graham had been in the audience, immediately booking him for four nights at the Fillmore West, followed by another two at the Fillmore East a week later.

"Big talent," recalled Graham. "I overheard [him] and called and booked it. He's the first artist that I can recollect that I liked that I booked him second [on the bill] into the Fillmore East 'right off.'"

The Fillmore East staff were already prejudiced against the unfamiliar English musician because he had insisted on coming in early to try out the Steinway grand piano that had been especially brought in for the show.

"[We thought] this is pretentious," said Dan Opatoshu of the stage crew. "Who the hell is he, Van Cliburn? So he comes in and sits down at the piano and goes through his entire repertoire. It was everything from the first two albums. And just everybody stopped. We'd never heard these songs before, and could he play piano."[6]

Bob Dylan was sitting in the light booth during Elton's last night at the Fillmore East to check him out. The four shows were a triumph, really launching Elton John in America.

"Elton John, a British singer-songwriter who is the current 'most talked-about' pop music arrival," wrote Mike Jahn, "made his New York concert debut at the Fillmore East this weekend and proved the rumors were true. [He] is a writer of unusual force and imagination."[7]

In mid-November, Santana were rehearsing in Wally Heider's Studio on their third album when Eric Clapton arrived to check out the fifteen-year-old guitar prodigy everyone was talking about. Neal Schon now regularly hung out with Santana, hoping to be asked to join the band on second guitar.

"We were in the studio messing around on some new material," said Schon. "And Clapton stopped by because he was in town with Derek and the Dominoes. And we ended up jamming that night."

In the middle of the jam, Carlos Santana arrived at the studio but was too stoned to play.[8]

"I felt really bad because I wanted to play," he said later. "I'd just taken LSD. I used to take a lot of LSD in those days."

The next day, Schon arrived at the studio to find Clapton had left him a note at the front desk. It was an invitation to come to the Berkeley Community Center that night, where Derek and the Dominoes were playing a show for Bill Graham.

As soon as Schon arrived, he was taken backstage to meet Clapton and the rest of the band, who were all zonked out on heroin.

"I got there ten minutes before they went on," Schon recalled, "and everyone was asleep. They were kind of out [of it] backstage and I was like, 'different.'"

But they soon woke up and played a great show.

"And [Clapton] pulled me up onstage," Schon recalled, "and I played a good portion of the set with him."

After the show, Clapton invited the teenager to move to England and join Derek and the Dominoes.

"It was kind of crazy," said Schon, "because I felt like I was just about to get asked to join the Santana band. I had been hanging out with those guys for months and to have two offers like that. I was fifteen and I was like, 'Oh, this is insane. Two great offers. Amazing offers.'"

Although he was tempted to join Eric Clapton, when Santana made him a firm offer the very next day, he accepted.

"I didn't feel I was ready to move all the way to England away from my family," he explained. "I had also become very close to the Santana guys. Carlos had taken me under his wing like a little brother."[9]

The young teenager soon found himself traveling the world with Santana and being treated like rock royalty. He was also exposed to the band's hedonistic lifestyle of unlimited drugs and sex.

"When Neal came out on the road he'd room with me," recalled Michael Carabello. "We hung out and I taught him some bad habits. Drugs were free-flow back then."[10]

Schon held back for a while before he joined in the nonstop Santana party.

"Well it was an eye-opener," he said. "These guys were all very wild and crazy. And it was that period in life in the music industry where everything went. I mean it didn't matter what it was."[11]

Carlos Santana would later say that the band started falling apart during the recording of the third album.

"Success was getting to be too much," he explained. "We were trying to make *Santana 3*, but overindulgence in everything available to a successful rock 'n' roller was becoming a problem. I started catching my friends shooting up in the bathroom. Nobody, apart from Bill Graham, kept a level head."[12]

José Areas says that Carlos would dose the band's drinks with acid before they went onstage.

"One time Gregg Rolie got mad and threw Carlos in the pool," said Areas, "because he [dosed us] with acid before we were going to play this concert. Carlos was putting stuff in our drinks and he destroyed the group because of doing that shit. I cannot play with drugs, I play nutso, but Carlos had to have acid."[13]

Carlos was now secretly battling his own demons, mentally going back to being molested as a young boy, which had him questioning his sexuality. He still felt guilty about what had happened, and it would be many years before he sought help.

"I was really at war with myself," he said later. "When you fight yourself you start blaming that wall and this lamp, and then this amplifier. I wasn't ready to forgive the person who molested me. I wasn't ready to do the inner-work to be liberated from my own demons. I became really, really short-tempered and quick to anger."[14]

Carlos would come to realize that all his unresolved issues combined with drugs was destroying the band.

"I'm sure I made hell for the original guys in the band," he said, "because I didn't have a way to express it and crystallize and heal it."[15]

The same night that Bill Graham presented Eric Clapton at the Berkley Community Center, he also had Country Joe and the Fish at Winterland; Leon Russell and Captain Beefheart playing his new Marin County venue, Pepperland; and Black Sabbath, Love, and the James Gang at the Fillmore West.

Rolling Stone sent reporter Andrew Moss to the Fillmore West to see how the audiences had changed over the years. He found that about two-thirds of the audience were in high school, making them too young to remember the early days of the Grateful Dead and Jefferson Airplane.

"For most of the high school audience," wrote Moss, "the 1966 San Francisco scene served as a kind of primeval origin myth. Unfortunately it doesn't seem to be the Dead setting their musical style now. It's Led Zeppelin and (of course) Grand Funk Railroad."

Moss found that dope was rampant at the Fillmore West, with at least thirty dealers selling every kind of drug, including heroin.

"The waiting line is like a dope supermarket," wrote Moss. "One of the dope dealers ran the market down to me: 'What kind of a night am I having? Fair. About 50 bucks so far and I should do 75. You used to be able to do $300 to $500 a night, but there are too many dealers here now.'"

Moss calculated that the average Fillmore patron spent around $1.50 a night on dope, which would buy a hit of acid, six downers, or two joints.

"That's how it is at the Fillmore West this year," he wrote. "It's a downer. It's fucked."

Fillmore West manager Gary L. Jackson claims to have had the situation well under control, with five security guards spread out around the ballroom.

"They'd bring the dealers into my office," he said. "I busted them and took all their drugs and then I'd throw them out."

Jackson would confiscate their drugs and any cash he found on them, which he later donated to a local Catholic church.

"The drugs," he said. "We never resold them and put them in a pile and destroyed them. If you don't police it yourself the police are going to come in and do it."

But when it came to the bands and drugs, the Fillmore management took a different approach.

"Obviously we turned the other cheek," Jackson explained. "Backstage you get treated another way. What would you do if you were managing the Fillmore and David Crosby says I'm not going on unless you get me some grass. The show must go on."[16]

In mid-November, Grace Slick was the subject of a coveted *Rolling Stone* interview, joining the likes of John Lennon, Bob Dylan, Mick Jagger, and Phil Spector. The lengthy interview by Ben Fong-Torres, which was recorded shortly before Janis Joplin's death, was accompanied by photographs by Annie Leibovitz of Grace and Paul Kantner relaxing at their new home in Bolinas

"Would you like to be photographed with a very large stomach?" Leibovitz asked Grace. "No," she replied. "For some reason I don't . . . it's not the large stomach, it's the posing I don't like. I hated modeling."

At one point, Fong-Torres asked about their ex-manager Bill Graham, and if he was receptive to their idea of setting aside nights at the Fillmore for people to come and hang out.

"He's got it too well down," replied Kantner, "so it's becoming like a TV show—the same thing every week."

"How are you getting along with Bill?" asked Fong-Torres.

"Fine," replied Kantner. "It's always been cordial. He's trying to help us go to South Vietnam and North Vietnam. But the government doesn't like the idea . . . it's the long hair and the dope. We'd probably tell people that anybody who didn't want to fight could put down their guns and split."[17]

That Thanksgiving, Jefferson Airplane once again played at the Fillmore East, with eight-months-pregnant Grace Slick wearing a white maternity dress. A few weeks earlier she had to pull out of a Fillmore East show with the Grateful Dead because of her pregnancy, but she had soldiered through the rest of their winter tour.

"I went on two tours when I had a big stomach out to here," she said later. "Never threw up. Never got sick. It just went fine."[18]

Once again Bill Graham laid on his traditional Thanksgiving Dinner, but this year things were different. The band members were hardly talking to one another, and Marty Balin was deeply depressed and drinking heavily.

"Everybody was dying in 1970," he recalled, "and things were getting very dark. And then cocaine came in and cocaine ruined the music. I didn't like the people in the band anymore. I didn't like their attitude. I didn't like the way they treated me. The Airplane was so important to me, but it wasn't important to the other people in the Airplane."[19]

On Thanksgiving night, Grace returned to her hotel room to find a stranger waiting for her, claiming to be the father of her baby.

"Grace is about eight months pregnant," said Bill Thompson, "and she gets to her hotel room and there's some hippie in her room. He goes, 'I've been waiting for you to come home, dear.' He thought he was the father of her child."[20]

After the last show on November 28, the Airplane flew back to San Francisco for the holidays, with Grace and Paul preparing for their new baby. It would be the last time that Jefferson Airplane would ever play the Fillmore East.

—⁘—

By mid-December, Bill Graham had recaptured Winterland, leaving Paul Baratta out in the cold. Using all his business cunning, the wily promoter now had exclusive use of Winterland for 1971, with options on the next two years.

Taking aim at his critics, Graham told England's *Melody Maker*, "After a time I get sick of being called a capitalist pig, the big rip-off, being talked about as though I were some kind of leper. In San Francisco they say I have a monopoly. Man, there are four to five halls in that city waiting for someone to make it happen. Isn't it just possible that someone is better than the rest at making it happen?" [21]

On Thursday, December 31, Bill Graham presented the Grateful Dead at Winterland, Cold Blood at the Fillmore West, and Mountain at the Fillmore East. With their new album *Nantucket Sleigh Ride* just released, Mountain sold out all six of their shows that week, climaxing in the New Year's Eve one.

"Mountain played there for a week at Christmas," said Johnny Ramone. "I went about four times."[22]

After Jimi Hendrix's death, *Rolling Stone* observed that many of his fans had been won over by the hard-rock sound of Mountain. It was Mountain's fourth appearance at the Fillmore East, and at one of the Christmas shows, guitarist Leslie West recognized an old schoolmate in the audience, someone who used to tease him about his weight.

"I recognized his voice," recalled West. "It was George Pressman. He yelled out, 'Hey fat boy!' And so I couldn't resist. I said, 'How much did you pay for your ticket? Well fuck you. I'm up here and you're not.' I never forgot that."

That night Bill Graham hired Nathan's to come to the Fillmore East and serve hot dogs to everyone as a New Year's Eve treat.

"And it was my idea to have the party," said West, who weighed in at near three hundred pounds. "What kind of catering? We had Nathan's pushcarts with frankfurters and knishes onstage afterwards. Everybody seemed to love it."[23]

CHAPTER TWENTY-SIX

The Last Hurrah

January to March, 1971

On New Year's Day, 1971, Santana played the Diamond Head Crater festival in Hawaii, marking Neal Schon's first appearance as a member of the band. During the trip, Santana partied hard with a full bowl of cocaine in their rented mansion. Carlos had even brought along his new personal astrologer, Dr. Stars, who joined in all the fun.

Abraxus had now reached number 1 on the *Billboard* charts. It would go on to sell more than four million copies, remaining in the charts for eighteen months.

"They beat the sophomore jinx," said Herbie Herbert. "And so Santana was one of those rare artists that actually takes a leap forward."[1]

On January 6—two days before he turned forty—Bill Graham reached out to Carlos Santana, writing him an eight-page letter expressing his deep feelings of betrayal by his protégé. He said he didn't question Santana's right to fire him, only the manner in which it was done. And he wrote how the breakdown in their relationship had hurt him personally.

"What am I trying to tell you, Carlos?" he wrote. "I'm trying to tell you that I felt very sad and depressed that our relationship had come to this point. That the relationship that once was has crumbled to this level of degradation. I ask you to please ask yourself whether you think that my work for you warrants this type of treatment; if all that I have tried to do for Santana over the years can be blurred out by the immediacy of your tremendous success. Can success block out truth, reality, ethics, wisdom— the right way?"

He then appealed to Carlos to search his conscience and fairly compensate him for all his work to make Santana so successful.

"There is no hope on my part for a reconciliation of our relationship in business," he wrote. "I'm not asking for that. Your decision to go your own way was accepted by me immediately. However, it is the proper settlement of our previous business relationship that I'm concerned about. And that, Carlos, is what I'm asking you to look into at this time."

Finally, he asked Carlos to imagine how demeaning it had been for him to read about his firing in the press.

"I ask you to think about how I might feel," he wrote, "when I read of these accounts in a magazine like the *Rolling Stone* that isn't good enough to be used by you as toilet paper. And yet, a magazine such as that tells the world that Santana has dropped Bill Graham as though he was some dried, decaying prune."

<hr>

Also two days before his fortieth birthday, Bill Graham predicted the death of rock 'n' roll in a major interview in *Variety*.

"Right now there is a struggle going on between rock's essence and its decadent alter ego," warned Graham. "Five years ago when the current phase of rock began, the majority of promoters were young kids who dug rock. That was the beginning. It was a $100 business. Then it became a $1,000 business and some young people had to get knowledgeable about what they had to do to run dances. But then rock became a million-dollar business and then a multi-billion-dollar business.

"The entire monetary structure of rock has greatly changed, meaning that many groups can play a few large arenas and pocket enough money to live in luxury. It is not uncommon to find a 22-year-old earning up to $1 million a year. This emphasis on playing the big halls, taking your money and running has had a bad effect on rock. Many groups have priced themselves out of the medium-sized concert market and lost respect for the audience."

Graham said that as a concert promoter he had certain responsibilities to the public, like providing a good sound system, good lighting, and security. He then drew his favorite analogy of himself as the maitre d' of the Fillmores.

"We are in theater," he wrote. "You put a steak on a paper plate and it tastes all right, but you take the same steak and put it on china and it tastes different."

He then warned bands against underestimating audiences by playing in huge arenas with no personal contact.

"Three quarters of the groups around today are lousy," he wrote. "They just get out there and bang away to make a quick killing. The groups today know they don't have to be good, just gimmicky—give 'em what they want. I book the bad ones into the Fillmores because of economics—an overhead of $30,000 a week—not including talent. We bring in the best groups we can and then the best of the worst."[2]

On January 15, 1971, Electric Hot Tuna headlined the Fillmore East for the first time, with Taj Mahal and Brethren opening. With Grace Slick due to give birth at any time back in California, Jefferson Airplane were now on an indefinite hiatus.

Ten days later, on Monday, January 25, Grace was with Paul Kantner and some friends at their Bolinas home when she suddenly went into labor.

"And I said, 'Okay. That's it. Into San Francisco,'" Grace recalled. "[Paul] took me into the hospital and then promptly went to sleep through the entire thing."

Grace gave birth to a seven-pound baby girl at the French Hospital in San Francisco. It was a natural birth, but the anesthetist didn't show up until two minutes before the baby was born.

"It hurt," said Grace, "but that's approximately what I thought it was going to be like. So it was all as smooth as silk."[3]

A couple of weeks earlier, *Rolling Stone* had claimed that the "aristocratic couple," who still did not know the sex of their unborn baby, would name their son "god" with a lower case *g*.[4] After the baby was born, *San Francisco Chronicle* columnist Herb Caen ran an item suggesting that Grace had given a name to her daughter, and indeed the name was "god." It was picked up by newspapers all over the world.

On January 30, the new mother and baby were photographed by the Associated Press while leaving the hospital.

"Grace Slick . . . took her newborn daughter home from the hospital," wrote the *San Francisco Examiner*, "declaring that baby 'god' would be reared in the world of rock concerts and recording sessions.

"Its real name is god with a small 'g,'" she said, cuddling the child at the French Hospital. 'It's a small 'g' because with a name like that you have to show some humility.'"

After refuting any suggestion of being the "Queen of Rock," Grace told the reporter she had abstained from dropping LSD during her pregnancy.[5]

Time magazine also duly commemorated the royal rock birth in its "Milestones" column, getting Grace's age wrong.

> *Born. To Grace Slick, 31, acid-voiced rock singer, and Paul Kantner, 29, guitarist, both of Jefferson Airplane fame: a daughter; in San Francisco.*
>
> *Name: "god" (a small g). No plans for marriage: god will have no surname.*
>
> *Said Grace: "Art Linkletter and Al Capp will be disappointed to learn that she is very healthy, in spite of what they say about drug-crazed hippies."[6]*

Later, Grace would claim that she had only been joking about naming her daughter "god," and one of the hospital nurses had tipped off Caen, who ran with it.

"I was just sort of dicking around with the nurse," Grace maintained. "I had no intention of calling her god."[7]

Soon afterward, she announced that her daughter would be known as China Wing Kantner.

In mid-January, Janis Joplin's final album, *Pearl*, was released to rave reviews. It went straight to number 1 on the *Billboard* charts, staying there for nine weeks.

"Fortunately *Pearl* is a good record," wrote *Rolling Stone* reviewer Jack Shadoian, "and Janis is often magnificent. The voice cut off was clearly in its prime. There is every indication that Janis was working toward a new maturity and confidence."

On February 6, *NBC's First Tuesday* news magazine broadcast a program entitled, "The Bitter Sweet Legacy of Janis Joplin." It examined how Janis had already become a legend in the three months since she had overdosed.

"She was a product of a subculture that thrives on drugs," said show producer Anthony Potter, "but her appeal extended beyond those boundaries."

Janis's parents were both interviewed, as well as Clive Davis.

"Janis had had an enormous public while she was alive," said Davis. "She will sell very, very well with this album."

Also interviewed was a Philadelphia lady who did "big business" selling Janis posters, as well as Harry Essex, who claimed he owned the movie rights to her life story.

"The Joplin mystique left a lucrative market to exploit," said Potter. "She may well make more money dead than alive."[8]

In February, just days before Santana were due to leave for shows in Africa and Europe, José "Chepito" Areas had a brain hemorrhage and nearly died. Santana were rehearsing for the upcoming tour, and when Areas didn't show up, Neal Schon and bassist David Brown went to his house. They arrived to find Areas lying unconscious in his bedroom in a pool of blood. He was then taken to Franklin Hospital, where a Catholic priest performed the last rites.

"I had a stroke," said Areas. "I was five days in a coma and they pronounced me dead. And then I woke up. I don't remember anything."[9]

While Areas lay in a coma near death, Carlos Santana refused to cancel the tour, although many in the band thought they should do so out of loyalty to their fallen bandmate.

"We had a meeting," said Michael Carabello, "because Carlos was getting restless, just sitting around and waiting. He wanted a gig. His head got about as big as Humpty Dumpty!"

Carabello told Carlos it was wrong to play without Chepito, as he was part of the band. He then threatened to quit if Carlos replaced him with another musician.

"And that just showed me a little greed on [Carlos's] part," said Carabello. "He should have been more concerned about his so-called brother."[10]

Finally, Santana flew to Accra, Ghana, drafting Willie Bobo to replace Areas. But the veteran percussionist was also taken ill after they performed, and by the time they had reached London for the European leg of the tour, he had been replaced by Coke Escovedo.

In Europe, the newly hired percussionist befriended Carlos Santana, sharing hotel rooms with him. He soon cozied up to the insecure young guitarist, telling him *he* was really Santana and no one else was as important to the band.

"The wrong people were whispering in Carlos's ear," said Herbie Herbert. "'This is you, buddy. It is your name. This is your band.' As a matter of fact the idea of calling it Santana was Carabello's."[11]

<hr>

The first week of March, Aretha Franklin played three consecutive nights at the Fillmore West, receiving $20,000 ($115,600). Bill Graham paid the Queen of Soul half on signing and the rest in cash before she even sang a note. As part of her four-page rider, Graham would provide her with a brand-new Cadillac limousine with chauffeur to transport her to and from San Francisco Airport.

These shows were a milestone in Aretha's career, resulting in the classic album *Aretha Live at Fillmore West*. They also exposed her to a new white audience for the first time, turning her into a superstar. Aretha's amazing band during the run included King Curtis on sax, Billy Preston on organ, and Cornell Dupree on guitar.

A beaming Bill Graham walked onstage to introduce her, saying: "For all of us here at the Fillmore West, it's a long-awaited privilege and a great pleasure to bring out the number-one lady—Miss Aretha Franklin."

On the final night, Ray Charles joined Aretha onstage, giving Bill Graham a career highlight.

"It was one of the magnificent moments of my life," he later said. "For the first time, an egg cream, a fifty-fifty audience, black and white. And at the end of the night, Ray and Aretha are hand in hand, King Curtis is playing, all the house lights are turned up, and I'm looking out into that sweating, swaying, dancing audience . . . you can't buy that. That's why I'm in the business."[12]

The next morning, *San Francisco Chronicle* columnist John L. Wasserman applauded Bill Graham for "hustling, haranguing, conning and cajoling" Aretha to record her live album at the Fillmore West.

"After five years of enjoying the best rock music available anywhere," he wrote, "we tend to take Fillmore West for granted. On the basis of quality and quantity of acts, the unequalled production of Bill Graham, attendance and ticket prices, Fillmore West is simply the world's greatest rock and roll music hall."[13]

Four days later, the Allman Brothers played a three-night run at the Fillmore East, recording their legendary live double album *Live at the Fillmore East*. Incredibly, top billing for the shows went to Johnny Winter and the Elvin Bishop Group, with the Allman Brothers Band listed as a special added attraction.

On Thursday afternoon, as the Allman Brothers arrived, a large truck with a mobile recording studio was parked outside on Sixth Street to record the shows in quadrophonic sound. At the soundcheck, head roadie Red Dog gave the Fillmore's assistant stage manager Dan Opatoshu the band's orders for various drugs. He then passed the info on to lighting engineer Jene Youtt, who went out to score.

"I was selling drugs to the bands," recalled Youtt. "I was into cocaine and I would sell that to the bands—user/dealer. It paid for my use. When they cut the album *Live at the Fillmore East*, I'd sell them cocaine for each show. And then Duane [Allman] needed heroin to come down afterward."[14]

Drummer Butch Trucks said that Bill Graham had no problem with the band getting high, as long as they delivered a great show.

"Bill understood the nature of sex, drugs and rock 'n' roll," explained Trucks. "But at the Fillmore East, rock 'n' roll came first. Then you could do the sex and drugs."[15]

On a previous occasion there, Gregg Allman had gotten too wasted to play.

"Gregg was really kind of a mess," said Trucks, "and Bill didn't really go into him because he understood the nature of the sickness. But he just told him, 'Gregg, if you continue to play at the Fillmore you can't do that anymore. You just can't. If that's what you want to do, then you're going to have to play somewhere else, because I'm not going to have that happening in my venue.'"

Whenever the Allman Brothers played the Fillmore East, there were so many available groupies that Red Dog had special T-shirts made up that read "No head. No backstage pass."

"So if you were a female you had to suck some dick," said Trucks, "and if you were a male you had to bring some cocaine. Oh man! I got my dick sucked in every corner of that building. It was a great place to do anything you wanted to do, as long as when it was your time to play you got on the stage and played *the* best show you could."

On the first night, the Allman Brothers Band opened and Johnny Winter closed the show.

"When we finished our first set," said Trucks, "half the audience got up and left. And so Johnny Winter's manager went to Bill Graham and said, 'I guess Johnny can't go on after the Allman Brothers anymore.' So we switched and we got to close the show. If that hadn't have happened, we wouldn't have had time to do all that stretching out and do a damn near fifteen minute 'Whipping Post.'"[16]

That weekend, the Allman Brothers were transcendent, and every night after they came offstage they went back to Atlantic Studios with producer Tom Dowd to listen to the tapes.

"When we listened to them," said Dowd, "we knew what we had nailed and what we might have to work on. And we started editing, 'We don't need to do this song tomorrow. Let's change the set.'"[17]

The resulting *Live at the Fillmore East* album featured "Whipping Post," "In Memory of Elizabeth Reed," and "Statesboro Blues" from the last two nights. Other classic tracks, such as the thirty-four-minute "Mountain Jam," would surface on the following year's *Eat a Peach* double album.

Allman Brothers drummer Jai Johanny Johanson had first played there in Otis Redding's band in 1966, when it was the Village Theater. He believes the building is haunted by generations of jazz musicians, whose spirits helped the Allman Brothers scale new musical heights.

"You know their spirits are hanging there," he said, "waiting for somebody to come in that's got the ability, so they can play a little bit better. They're what we call 'wandering spirits,' and they're just lying there waiting to have a ball."[18]

These classic shows were recorded just seven months before Duane Allman's untimely death in a motorcycle accident. His brother Gregg says that in hindsight this made their performances far more poignant.

"Those concerts were so special," he explained. "It was almost like somebody knew what was gonna happen; it was kind of eerie."[19]

The iconic album cover, showing the band and roadies surrounded by all their equipment, was actually taken weeks later in Macon, Georgia, as the band were too busy to fly back and pose in front of the Fillmore East. Somebody suggested stenciling the words "The Allman Brothers Band at Fillmore East" on the equipment cases and stacked them up against a brick wall.

"It was a great idea," said Gregg Allman, "so you would think we were in New York, but we were really in Macon, Georgia."

Live at the Fillmore East was released in July 1971 and eventually went platinum, reaching number 13 on the *Billboard* album charts. It is listed at number 49 in *Rolling Stone*'s 500 greatest albums of all time, with many considering it the finest live rock album ever made.

CHAPTER TWENTY-SEVEN

"The Flowers Wilted"

April to June 6, 1971

When Santana headlined the Fillmore East the first weekend of April 1971, the band was falling apart. After their return from Europe, they had gone straight back into the studio to work on the third album, but it wasn't coming together. Everybody had their own ideas about musical direction, and there were constant arguments.

"Things were coming unglued," said Herbie Herbert. "They just kind of imploded on themselves and lost themselves really. Disparate egos and personalities."[1]

Opening for Santana at the Fillmore East were Rahsaan Roland Kirk and the Tower of Power, whom Bill Graham had booked at Santana's request. Since Graham's January 6 aggrieved letter to Carlos, there was an uneasy truce between them, and Graham still booked the band for his venues. Santana's two Fillmore East shows those April nights were among their best ever and the audience loved them.

But they were musical spikes in a downward trajectory for the band. Michael Shrieve believes that ultimately cocaine was responsible for the demise of Santana.

"I think [that when] cocaine entered into the scene for us," he said, "it kind of closed [us] down. I can see it in the band on film. We were still playing well, but our hearts and minds had closed down to each other."[2]

Dan Opatoshu said he was shocked to see the state of Santana in their dressing room before they went on to play. He believes heroin might have also ruined the band.

"You had to peel them off the floor to get them onstage," he recalled. "I don't know that Carlos was on smack, but some of those other guys certainly were. When people go into a nod it's rather [easy] to see what they're doing."[3]

Then Santana hit the road, playing a string of dates in the United States. In Detroit, there was so much tension that the band took a communal acid trip to try to smooth things out.

"We tried to change the spiral by dosing them with liquid Owsley," recalled Herbie Herbert. "It was Gregg's first acid trip. We took the drops, too, to stay on the same page. It was the most electrifying show . . . and Carlos was wondering what was going on."[4]

After the American tour, Santana flew back to Europe, where they played nine countries, culminating in their second appearance at the Montreux Jazz Festival. While they were in Europe, José Areas, now fully recovered from his stroke, rejoined the band, playing alongside his replacement, Coke Escovedo. But bassist David Brown, who had a severe heroin problem, was replaced by Doug Rauch from the Voices of East Harlem.

While they toured the world, Coke Escovedo once again pressured Carlos to make changes in the band.

"And a lot of political bullshit went on," said David Rubinson, "with Carlos and Coke being bosom buddies against somebody else, and then this one against that one."[5]

Finally, Escovedo encouraged Carlos to get rid of manager Stan Marcum, who had a serious heroin problem himself, and start asking him exactly where all the money was going. Later it would emerge that there had been financial irregularities, which even Marcum was not aware of.

"Marcum lost his controls when I came into the band," said Escovedo. "We started finding out things he should have told us. It got to the point where no one knew what was happening."[6]

❦

That April, as Bill Graham jousted with Sol Hurok over booking the Metropolitan Opera House, he fell into a deep depression, questioning the price of his success.

"I wasn't happy," he said. "I was married in 1967. My work became my mistress. The marriage broke up simply because my love and adulation went to the work. I found myself in 1971, looking at the audience and looking at the stars and saying, 'This year I made thirty-nine trips to New York and back.'"[7]

Although the Fillmore East could make him a healthy $15,000 ($90,000) profit during a good weekend, the Fillmore West was losing money because of the high overheads. Graham had also tied himself up in knots by becoming involved in many conflicting areas of the music business. Not only was he a promoter, he was now a theater owner, manager, agent, and recording company executive.

"Graham almost single-handedly ran a music industry within the music industry," claimed *Rolling Stone* during an investigation into his business operations. "Because the various positions he assumed were by tradition adversary in relation to one another—an agent *negotiates* with a promoter; a manager deals with a record executive—he was in constant conflict with himself. And everyone else, or so it seemed."[8]

Graham now realized that to survive into the Seventies, he must eat his words and promote the mega rock 'n' roll concerts he claimed to detest so much. But his true reasons for closing the Fillmores were not for public consumption. He would always maintain that the straw that broke his camel's back was The Band's refusal to accept "a lousy fifty grand" for six shows.

In April, Marty Balin quit Jefferson Airplane, walking away with a $30,000 compensation package from the band he had founded. He also surrendered any rights to the name Jefferson Airplane.

He finally made the break as the band started rehearsing for their new album. It was the first under the band's lucrative new contract with RCA, which gave them their own record label they christened "Grunt."

Manager Bill Thompson said no one wanted Marty Balin to leave, but he stopped attending band rehearsals and meetings.

"A lot of times we would knock on his door to get Marty to come to our meeting," said Thompson, "and he would go, 'Oh gee. I had to disappear,' and the door closed."

After he missed a whole week of rehearsals, Thompson asked him why. Balin replied that he had come to the rehearsal and then somebody had told him to drive his car to Stinson Beach, where Janis Joplin's ashes had been scattered.

"And it happened for the whole week," said Thompson. "Fine, we didn't go back. So we used to tell people that Marty didn't quit the band, his car did."[9]

According to Balin, it was the other way around, and it was his band-mates who refused to work with him.

"I got disgusted with all the ego trips," he would later explain, "and the band were so stoned out I couldn't even talk to them. Everybody was in their little shell and had private rooms in the mansion. It was like, 'Hey, I got a song. Does anybody want to help me with it?' In the studio [I was told], 'Oh, man do it yourself, I can't be bothered to help you out. I can't play the bass for you. I can't play the guitar for you.'"[10]

Bill Graham went public with his decision to close the Fillmores during a sold-out five-night run by the Grateful Dead at the Fillmore East. The Dead's breakthrough studio album *American Beauty* had just been released, and all the shows were being recorded.

On Monday night, during the late show, Duane Allman walked onstage to jam with the band, trading licks with Jerry Garcia. The next night, Bob Dylan was smuggled into the light booth to see the Grateful Dead, with whom he would tour sixteen years later.

Bill Graham, who was there that night, had decided to try to persuade Dylan to join the Dead onstage for a couple of songs. Halfway through the late show, the Beach Boys came onstage to the audience's delight. They harmonized with Pigpen on "Searchin'" before playing "Riot in Cell Block No. Nine" with the Dead.

Allan Arkush, now working with Joe's Light Show, was putting up slides of the various guests as they were announced. In the event that Bob Dylan did decide to play that night, a special slide with his name was there waiting.

"And then word went out through the headsets that Dylan was there," said Arkush, "and Dylan was thinking of going onstage. Of course we had a Bob Dylan slide that we never used, but was there just in case it ever happened. And I put it in the projector and when the [Beach Boys] finished, by mistake I hit the wrong slide and Bob Dylan's name went up. And the audience went crazy because they though Bob Dylan was coming down to play."

As soon as Dylan saw his name flash up on the screen, he left through the back door.

"I did something really, really stupid," said Arkush, "and Bill [Graham] got really, really mad at me. Obviously his biggest get at the Fillmore was to have Bob Dylan play. I imagine Dylan was deciding when he saw that and left. Bill was pretty pissed off."[11]

⁓

A few hours after Bob Dylan stormed out of the Fillmore East, Bill Graham held a press conference and announced he was closing both Fillmores and retiring from the music business. Perched on the edge of the Fillmore East stage clad in a V-neck sweater and rolled up sleeves and wearing his trademark two-faced watch, he sent shock waves through the music industry with the news that the Fillmore East would close on June 27. The Fillmore West would close later that summer, to make room for "a four-hundred-room Howard Johnson's."

During the ninety-minute press conference, which was catered by Rattner's, Graham held court, rambling on about greedy bands, unscrupulous promoters, and Madison Square Garden. He sadly declared that the "flowers had wilted and the scene had changed."

"What's going to happen to the Fillmore East?" asked one reporter, "this structure that's housed so many livelihoods."

"The frightening aspect is, I don't know," Graham replied.

Another reporter then asked how he saw the future of rock music.

"What is happening to rock is that it's joining America," he replied. "It is General Motors, it is Pacific Gas and Electric. I'll play for forty thousand people, OK. Sure. Make sure it's against 60 percent [of the gross]."

Bill Graham told reporters about one Fillmore East show when he had pulled a practical joke on the audience. He had announced from the stage that on New Year's Eve he was staging the Azores Pop Festival, which would be *the* biggest rock event in history.

"By the end of the night," said Graham, "the kids were going out of this theater and saying, 'Dig it! I hear the Beatles and the Stones and Dylan are making it, man. I gotta go. How much?'"

The next afternoon, Graham walked into his office to find Sha Na Na's manager, Ed Goodgold, waiting for him.

"Kip [Cohen] was sitting behind his desk and I just winked at him," said Graham. "And I said to Kip, 'Wouldn't you know it, Bob and the Beatles both want to go on at midnight. Now, how the hell are we going to do that?'"

Goodgold then demanded that Sha Na Na must be booked for the Azores Pop Festival at any cost. Graham replied that would be "a million-to-one shot," advising him to get his agent on it immediately.

Several days later, back in San Francisco, Graham got a call from Sha Na Na's agent, who sounded nervous. He said the group was definitely in for the festival and wanted to know all about it.

"And I said, 'Well I can't,'" said Graham. "And he says, 'Well the biggest problem we have is the Azores is out in the middle of nowhere, and we don't know whose territory it is.' This one manager became a mental case until we finally told him that it wasn't happening."

Graham said that he and Kip Cohen had then worked out two possible scenarios for the imaginary festival in the middle of the Atlantic. One had the public on the island, with the bands playing forty-five-minute sets from a tugboat circling it. The other reversed things, with the bands playing on the island, while the audience sailed around in tugs.

"That was our idea of the ultimate festival," Graham told reporters. "And then we were going to blow up the island, let it sink, cover it up and start all over again."

◆━━◆

After the press conference, Bill Graham handed reporters a seven-point indictment of the music business, which he and Kip Cohen had been working on for several weeks. It would be printed verbatim in the next Fillmore East program and the next issue of the *Village Voice*.

"Two years ago I warned that the Woodstock Festival syndrome would be the beginning of the end," he wrote. "I am sorry to say that I was right."

He accused many rock bands of hypocrisy and selling out, saying that although they had "long hair and play guitars" they had become "large corporations." He also attacked the audiences for their lack of musical sophistication.

"Now," he wrote, "there are too may screams for 'More' with total disregard for whether or no there was any musical quality."

Throughout, he portrayed himself as the aggrieved party, a victim of greedy bands, unscrupulous managers and agents. The timbre and nuances of the charges and the embittered reprimands of each and every part of the music business were pure Bill Graham.

"For six years, I have endured the abuse of many members of the public, and press," he wrote, "The role of 'anti-christ of the underground' has obviously never appealed to me."[12]

⸻

Following his announcement, Bill Graham was interviewed by almost every major magazine and newspaper. He appeared on many late-night talk shows, explaining his decision and discussing the future of rock 'n' roll. He loved the spotlight, coming across well as an articulate and witty elder statesman of rock.

Life magazine also ran a large spread about the imminent closings under the headline, "Goodbye to Rock." It compared the closing of the Fillmores to the recent breakup of the Beatles.

"His decision was another violent blow to the rock era," it read. "Graham's two concert halls, the Fillmore East and West, in New York and San Francisco, were the showcases from which the entire rock music scene had sprung. They had meant as much to the rock explosion as the Birdlands, the Palladiums and the Peppermint Lounges had meant to other music in other times."[13]

Kip Cohen told *Rolling Stone* he was glad they were was closing.

"Let's put it this way," he said, "amputation while it's still possible can save the rest of the body from picking up the disease."[14]

That spring, Grace Slick and Paul Kantner began work on the next Jefferson Airplane album, *Bark*. They each wrote three songs for it, with Jorma Kaukonen and Joey Covington penning the rest. Grace's contributions were as idiosyncratic as ever. "Never Argue with a German if You're Tired, or European Song," was written in her invented phonetic German. "Sticken in mine haken, sticken in mine haut," it began.

Her second song, "Law Man," warns officers that her old man has a gun and she'd hate to shoot them with it. Her third, "Crazy Miranda," was an all-out attack on young women who buy into what the fashion media tells them to be.

Jorma Kaukonen's contribution, "Third Week in The Chelsea," recounted the breakup of Jefferson Airplane as its members began to believe what *Rolling Stone* wrote about them.

"That's pretty much how I felt at the time," he said in 2013, "for whatever reason. I mean here I am in New York City for three weeks and I'm complaining about it. What a baby. But it made sense at the time."[15]

Grace Slick viewed Jorma's revealing song as a clear message to the band that he had had enough of Jefferson Airplane.

"[He's] letting us know he wants to be free," she said, "the feeling of being trapped by that group."[16]

At around four in the morning on Thursday, May 13, after an all-night recording session with much drinking, Grace and Jorma went drag racing at full speed toward the Golden Gate Bridge. Three months after giving birth to China, Grace had reportedly started occasionally sleeping with Jorma.

"Grace did certainly sleep with me a couple of times," said Kaukonen. "The first time involved Jack Daniel's and Tuinol [downers], which is not exactly a heightening of perceptions."[17]

As they raced through the empty streets of San Francisco at more than one hundred mph, Grace lost control of her Mercedes sports car and hit a wall, wrecking her new car and nearly killing herself. The force of the crash threw her across the car into the passenger side.

"I was there," said Kaukonen, "and I was able to pull her out of the car until the ambulance came. And thank goodness she wasn't seriously injured. Now when I called my ex-wife [Margaretta] at six in the morning to tell her what was going on, her first comment wasn't, 'Oh, I'm so glad you're all right.' The comment was, 'What were you doing with Grace at six in the morning.'"[18]

In June, Santana flew to Lima, Peru, to play their first concert in South America. They were already big stars there after the *Woodstock* movie, and "Black Magic Woman" was constantly on the radio. Soon after arriving, Santana were told that the concert had been banned by the ruling military regime and they had to leave immediately.

"Peru opened my eyes toward reality," Carlos later told Ben Fong-Torres of *Rolling Stone*. "That was really a slap. I used to get a lot of slaps from acid and mescaline and drugs. But when reality itself is slapping your face."

When the band flew back to San Francisco to resume recording the third album, things became even crazier.

"Well, we show up at CBS Studios," recalled Herbie Herbert, "and I'm all set up with the gear and the band shows up in all their fancy cars and motorcycles, and just terrorize that place. Chepito has stolen all the lightbulbs, all the toilet paper, all the soap. Everything. They rode their motorcycles—Harleys—all the way through the building. They sat in this brand-new studio on the couch and put their feet up on the walls and left black marks. The studio manager wants to kill me."[19]

Carlos Santana compared getting the band into the studio together to pulling wisdom teeth.

"And when [we] do get in the studio," he said, "we have an attitude. You either show up late or you're too over-the-top with drugs to play. But nevertheless, I think that when we put our egos and illusions aside, there's incredible beauty."[20]

Gregg Rolie believes that it was exactly this raging fire in Santana that made their music so great.

"The band was built with passion and it fell apart with passion," he said. "And if that kind of animal attack on music hadn't been there, it would never have happened."[21]

That Memorial Day weekend, the Grateful Dead played at Bill Graham's Winterland to sold-out audiences. On Saturday night, at the first intermission, there was a stage announcement: "Those of you who are going to get some liquid refreshment, pass it on so your neighbor can have some." Then several containers of apple juice, heavily dosed with Owsley acid, were passed into the audience.

By midnight, more than fifty young fans were in the crisis unit of Mount Zion Hospital suffering from bad trips. Seven others were arrested by police outside Winterland, including a naked young man covered in blood, screaming, "There's LSD in the water!"

"You had to be really careful with the Dead," said Fillmore West manager Gary L. Jackson, "because you never know what's going to happen, especially when Owsley's there."[22]

On Monday morning, it made the front page of the *San Francisco Chronicle*, along with the headline, "Bad Trips at Rock Hall—Report of Spiked Drinks."

The story said the mass-dosing recalled the early days of the "acid tests."

"About 1,000 persons," read the article, "most of them between 12 and 18, got unexpectedly stoned after drinking 'liquid refreshment' passed around at a Grateful Dead concert, according to police."

A young fan named Alison McDonald told a *Chronicle* reporter that she'd drank some of the apple juice after the stage announcement.

"It seemed like a friendly thing," she said. "I took a sip because I was very thirsty."

About forty-five minutes later, when she started coming up on the acid, she took another sip.

"It was okay acid," she said, "but I feel sorry for anyone who took more than two sips. Pretty soon everybody got going. It was like a revival meeting—a religious experience almost."

Bill Graham, who had been at the concert, said he was unaware of any stage announcement about "liquid refreshments."

"I'm very sorry about this, if it did happen," he told the *Chronicle*. "The overuse of heavy drugs and the need to escape by young people is one of the reasons I'm backing away from this business."[23]

Within hours of the *San Francisco Chronicle* story, a furious Graham told his Fillmore West manager he was moving up the date of the closing.

"That's what triggered it," said Jackson. "After we hit the front page of the *Chronicle*, Bill Graham just said, 'That's it. We're closing.' And then for the next month we were planning the closings of the East and West."[24]

The next morning, San Francisco's Police Chief Alfred J. Nelder demanded that Bill Graham's license to run Winterland be revoked, saying he was lucky nobody had died. Chief Nelder said he had received numerous calls from worried parents whose children had accidentally taken the LSD at the Grateful Dead show, and his narcotics detail was now investigating.

Two days later, Graham called a press conference to defend himself. He attacked the *Chronicle*'s coverage of the story, disputing that a thousand people had taken the LSD. He claimed it was closer to fifty.

"In the last six years we've given something like twelve hundred concerts," Graham told reporters. "We've had four million customers, not counting Fillmore East. In all that time, we've had less than ten arrests for drugs."

He then lashed out at the police for daring to insult him.

"What am I?" he railed. "Some fly-by-night operator trying to rip off the kids . . . being blasted for something I didn't do."

Graham said that as a parent himself, he was concerned about drugs.

"What can you do?" he asked. "LSD is a chemical that's impossible to detect. It can be carried on the pinkle [*sic*] of your hand or a hip pocket and put in a tub of water. But you don't close down the whole railroad because there's one wreck."[25]

On Thursday, June 10, Bill Graham called a Fillmore West staff meeting in the ballroom's dining room, announcing it would close at the end of the month. The thirty-some staff were shocked, as they thought the meeting was to discuss a July 4 employee party.

"The executioner is here," he told them. "The end of the month we're gonna close this place."[26]

Then he mournfully spoke of his years of "voluntary slavery" that had cost him "a lot of personal happiness."

"I started to become robotized," he said. "I tried to do too much and I failed. I never really wanted it to end this way."[27]

But within days, Graham had abandoned his original plan to close with a single concert. Realizing the potential gold mine, he announced that the Fillmore West would now close with a week of shows, which would be recorded for an album and filmed for a major motion picture.

———

The first weekend in June, the Fillmore East had one of its greatest nights when John Lennon took the stage to jam with Frank Zappa and the Mothers of Invention. Lennon's impromptu appearance was engineered by Howard Smith, who had spent Sunday interviewing him and Yoko Ono for his WPLJ-FM show.

At the end of their conversation, Smith said he was leaving to interview Frank Zappa, who was playing the Fillmore East that night. Lennon suddenly lit up, saying he was a big fan of Zappa and would love to meet him.

"And that's when the idea hit me," said Smith. "I asked John and Yoko to come along to the interview in Frank's hotel room and meet him. But I had also decided to get John and Yoko onstage with Zappa that night."[28]

Lennon and Zappa found an immediate rapport during the interview, and when Smith suggested they play together that night they agreed.

"So Zappa said, 'Oh, that'll be great, are you up for it?'" recalled Smith. "John looked at Yoko and they were both quite scared. At that point John hadn't played live in a while. So I kind of talked everybody into it."

The plan was for John and Yoko to take the stage during the first encore of the last show. So after finishing his live radio show an hour early, Smith took them to the Fillmore East. An employee was there at the side door to meet them and brought them up to the lighting booth.

"And on the way down there," said Smith, "John and Yoko said, 'We can't do this without coke. Can you get us some really good cocaine?'"

At the Fillmore, they were soon hooked up with assistant stage manager Dan Opatoshu, who would later describe dealing coke to John Lennon as one of the great thrills of his time at the Fillmore East.[29]

"They did their coke," said Smith. "It wasn't so much they needed to wake up, it's more they needed that kind of confidence that coke gives you."

Then about two in the morning, just before the end of Frank Zappa's set, a Fillmore staffer arrived to bring John and Yoko backstage. But first they swapped shirts for good luck, leaving Howard Smith in the light booth.

"The audience were screaming and yelling for Frank Zappa to come back," said Smith. "Then the lights came on and there was John and Yoko standing there."

The audience went crazy as Lennon and the Mothers of Invention, who had not been told what was going to happen, tuned up.

"I'd just like to say, 'Hello,'" John Lennon told the Fillmore audience, "It's wonderful to be here. This is a song that I used to sing when I was in the Cavern at Liverpool. I haven't done it since so . . ."[30]

For the next twenty-five minutes, John, Yoko, and Zappa played wild, improvised versions of, "I Love You Baby, Please Don't Go" and "Scumbag." At one point two of the Mothers of Invention covered Yoko in a huge burlap bag, as she wailed away inside on a microphone.[31]

CHAPTER TWENTY-EIGHT

"Thank You and Farewell"

June 7 to July 4, 1971

In mid-June of 1971, the yellow invitations to the final Fillmore East show went out to the crème de la crème of the music industry. The shows would be headlined by the Allman Brothers Band, with the J. Geils Band and Albert King playing second and third on the bill. Tickets to the Friday and Saturday shows were on sale to the public, but the final night on Sunday, June 27, was by invitation only and would be simulcast live on New York City radio stations WNEW and WPLJ.

Jefferson Airplane, who had become the Fillmore East's unofficial house band over the last three years, were also breaking up at this time. While they no longer jibed as a band, they felt an affinity with the Fillmores.

"It was the end of an era, the end of a time," said Paul Kantner. "I was just disappointed. I could understand what [Bill] was doing."

Jorma Kaukonen said he had been surprised by Graham's decision.

"We'd come to take for granted how much we love it," he said. "It definitely took a destination away from us."[1]

Jack Casady said the rock experience both venues gave fans would never be repeated.

"It was a great deal," he said. "And don't forget the ticket prices were $3.50 to see three major acts. But you're not going to have nineteen cents for a gallon of gas again, so that's the way it goes."[2]

When the fans arrived for the final Fillmore East shows, the marquee now read, "Thank You and Farewell." Inside, each patron was handed a special playbill, looking more like a funeral program with its cover bearing the dates "March 8, 1968—June 27, 1971." The playbill's interior was bursting with glowing tributes to Bill Graham and the Fillmore East from all the major record labels and some of the biggest names in the music business.

"To Bill Graham and the entire Fillmore staff: a standing ovation and an encore, we hope, very soon," was the message from RCA. A&M Records took out an advertisement, reading: "There is no debating that the Fillmore has presented the finest rock music available with greater reliability than any other venue on the planet."

Jac Holzman of Elektra Records wrote: "Even after the Fillmores have closed their doors, and even after the last chords have echoed into the night, even after the final curtain has come down and the last light has been extinguished, the silence and the darkness will be alive forever with those unforgettable ghosts of music that for five years filled the silence and lit the darkness. An era has passed—our twin meccas of music will be missed. We offer our thanks to you, Bill, and to your Fillmore staffs, for having been midwives to the music."

The playbill also had photographs of every Fillmore East staff member, a full discography of all the live albums recorded there, and a personal message from Bill Graham himself.

"Time will tell what we've shared," he wrote. "I do know that I am proud to have been here, with you, with the artists, and with the staff—peace, good health, and joy in life. Cheers, Bill Graham."[3]

Patrons could also buy limited-edition original Fillmore concert posters from the upstairs and downstairs concession stands for just $1.

As Saturday night bled into Sunday morning, after Albert King—who had helped open the Fillmore East—and the J. Geils Band played, the Allman Brothers Band took the stage at about 2:30 a.m. And for the next five hours they held the audience spellbound, playing some of the finest music ever heard at the Fillmore East.

"It was probably the greatest show we have ever played," said Butch Trucks. "And it was just magic. It was absolutely what music is all about.

It was one of those nights where you couldn't make a mistake. No matter what I did, two or three other guys in the band were already there. No matter how far out we would [go], we all went to the same place, and the crowd was right there with us all night long. It was just unbelievable."[4]

When the band came offstage at around 5:00 a.m. after several encores, they did not want to stop.

"And Duane looked at me backstage and said, 'Gee Bill, I'll play more,'" recalled Bill Graham. "And they went back onstage . . . and he was in heaven."[5]

As the band started "Mountain Jam," all the lights in the theater were turned off and a single spotlight was aimed at an ancient mirrorball hanging from the ceiling.

"We never used it," said Allan Arkush. "But we said, 'Let's hit the mirrorball [for] "Mountain Jam."' And they're noodling in the dark and then when they hit the big riff the spotlights hit the mirrorball, and the dots of light went from the stage to the walls of the theater. And it was so beautiful as they're playing that theme. Phenomenal"[6]

There was also a slide of a bird, reflected off a pliable mirror onto the walls. So it looked like a bird flying around the theater, flapping its wings along with Duane Allman's majestic guitar solos.

It was past seven in the morning when the Allman Brothers Band finally finished playing. There was no applause. Just silence.

"Nobody even clapped," said Butch Trucks. "Everybody just sat there with a smile on their face. Then somebody got up and opened the doors and the sun came pouring it. And the audience are just sitting there looking at us, and we're standing there looking at them. And then little by little people started standing up and filing out quietly.

"And I remember Duane walking in front of me, dragging his guitar, going, 'Goddamn, it's like leaving church.'"[7]

———

At Sunday night's invitation-only show, Bill Graham's guests arrived to find a red rose and a commemorative poster on every seat. There were rumors that John Lennon, Paul McCartney, Bob Dylan, and Eric Clapton might jam together onstage. Unfortunately, earlier in the day there had been several bomb threats, as well as a minor riot on Second Avenue when some kids had tried to storm the Fillmore East.

"It was as chaotic as the opening," remembered Kip Cohen, "with the same kind of crush to be there. And a very sad, very soulful experience."[8]

As the guests arrived for the private party, WNEW DJ Alison Steele described the action to the thousands of listeners at home.

"It reminds me of a Broadway opening rather than a closing," she said. "Everybody's kind of hanging out in the lobby and it's all very social. It's just a tremendous picture of excitement."

Among the stars who turned out were John Lennon and Yoko Ono, Stephen Stills, Neil Young, and Laura Nyro. Running a few minutes late, Bill Graham and Kip Cohen walked onstage to a standing ovation. Behind them was a giant banner, saying "Graduation 1971."

"Good evening," said Graham, wearing a baggy white shirt with a red rose in a buttonhole and jeans. "It's very gratifying to get that kind of response in New York City. It's a rather delicious feeling. Now if I can just put it in little jars and put it on my shelf I'd be very happy."

Then he announced Albert King, who had opened the Fillmore East three and a quarter years earlier. King played a moving forty-minute set, receiving great applause for his unique electric blues.

While everyone waited for the J. Geils Band to come onstage, WPLJ DJ Alex Bennett discussed how the previous night's audience had vandalized the theater, slashing seats and stealing pieces of furniture as mementos.

"They were trying to get a piece of the Fillmore," said Bennett. "As Kip [Cohen] put it, it kind of justified the closing."

Dave Herman of WPLJ said the whole counterculture had changed into something dark.

"The scene that went down in the Fillmore East last night," said Herman, "one of real aggressiveness, vandalism, and hostility."

Bennett then said you only had to walk out on Second Avenue at four in the morning, to see the junkies trying to score.

"Well obviously the Fillmores were built out of flower power," said Herman, "and saw their way into cocaine karma. What started out as kind of a gay romp through the woods is now turning into somewhat of a nightmare."[9]

After the J. Geils Band played a rousing set, Bill Graham came back onstage to introduce Mountain.

"He uttered a few forgettable words," wrote rock critic Robert Christgau, "before some guy in the balcony yelled . . . 'Fuck you!' Graham glanced up and continued briefly, but soon someone in another part of the balcony began to shout. That stopped him. Graham looked in the direction of his first tormentor. 'I'm not going to say much more,' he said. 'It only takes one guy like you to ruin it for [everyone].'

"I must admit I felt a bolt of sympathy for Bill. The poor fucker packs the house, admission by fucking invitation only, and a couple of ringers sneak in to haunt him."[10]

After Mountain's set, the Beach Boys arrived backstage and unloaded their gear. Their road manager then informed Bill Graham that the Beach Boys would be closing the show.

"And Bill didn't even look at him," said Butch Trucks. "He just said, 'Well, you can go ahead and pack up your shit and get out of here. I've got my closing act.'"

The Beach Boys then went on, playing songs from their new album *Surf's Up*, which received a cool reception from the audience. It wasn't until they played a medley of their old hits that they connected.

At around 3:00 a.m., the Allman Brothers Band were waiting backstage to go on and close the Fillmore East.

"Bill came running across the stage and grabbed me by the neck," said Trucks, "and I had never met him up to that point. He started yelling, 'You're the big man!' I mean he was squeezing my neck. And he said, 'Butch, all these years of all this bullshit I've had to put up with to run this. I'll never forget last night. If I had my way when you guys finished playing at seven or eight in the morning, I would have been sealed up in my bubble and gone off to wherever I'm going.' And that was the beginning of my very close friendship with Bill."[11]

Then Graham strode out onto the Fillmore East stage to make his final introduction.

"Over the years that we've been doing this," he began, "the introductions are usually very short, and this one's going to be . . . a little longer than usual. In the past year or so we've had them on both coasts a number of times. In all that time I've never heard the kind of music that this group plays.

"And last night we had the good fortune of having them get onstage at about 2:30—three o'clock and they walked out of here at seven o'clock in the morning. And it's not just that they played quantity, and for my amateur ears in all my life I've never heard the kind of music that this group plays. The finest contemporary music. We're going to round it off with the best of them all—the Allman Brothers."

"And that was special," said Gregg Allman. "I'd heard a rumor before that Bill had said of all the bands he'd ever worked with, we were his favorites, but I hadn't believed it. So when I heard him say that with my own two ears, I was elated."[12]

After another inspired set by the Allman Brothers, Bill Graham led his entire Fillmore East staff onto the stage to take a final bow with him.

"Take a good look at these people," said Graham, wiping a tear from his eye, "because when you pass them on the street some day, I want you to know that they've been your friends for a long time. Thank you very much for coming."

❦

The next morning, Bill Graham announced the lineup for the closing week of the Fillmore West, and the tickets went on sale. Billed as "the bands that built the Fillmore," the Wednesday to Sunday closing week headliners would be Cold Blood, Boz Scaggs, the Grateful Dead, Quicksilver Messenger Service, and Electric Hot Tuna, with Santana playing the final night on July 4.

At the last minute, Keeva Kristal had persuaded Bill Graham to commission a fly-on-the-wall documentary film to be made about the closing week at the Fillmore West.

"The film was put together in the last few days without warning to anyone," said Graham. "There was no time to talk about contracts, money or negotiations. The basic deal was, 'Let these people film it. I give you my word if you don't like your footage . . . you don't have to be in it.'"

Eli Bleich, a twenty-eight-year-old filmmaker who worked for a political consulting firm, was brought in to direct, although he knew little about rock music.

"I was contemporary with the rock 'n' roll age," he explained. "I didn't know who Jerry Garcia was, but I learned very quickly."

From the beginning there was no question that the star of the movie would be Bill Graham, who would put on an Oscar-worthy performance.

"Bill knows how to turn it on and turn it off for the cameras," said Bleich. "He commanded the room and the subject. When he began to talk or do stuff everybody was quiet. He was very opinionated and knew what he wanted."[13]

Graham soon became obsessed with the film. It was as if he were finally appeasing the ghosts of his failed acting career and becoming a movie star.

"It was insane," said his record company partner, David Rubinson. "Bill really, really loved being on camera and he loved playing the part of Bill Graham. So he took over my office. Took over the studio. We were working full-time on that."[14]

When the resulting movie *Fillmore* was released the following May, it would carry an "R" rating because of Graham's foul language. Through shouting, screaming, and cursing through the one-hour, forty-five-minute film, Bill Graham delivered his finest character performance—playing himself. Although it was a documentary, Graham was hailed by England's *Melody Maker* film critic for being "as riveting as Bogart or Cagney."

For a large part of the movie, Graham lambastes, browbeats, and argues with stars, such as Boz Scaggs and Carlos Santana, as he micro-manages the final Fillmore West shows.

A high point of the movie comes after former Charlatan Mike Wilhelm asks Graham to book his new band for the closing shows. When the promoter refuses, a frustrated Wilhelm tells him, "Well, I'd just like to say, 'Fuck you and thanks for the memories, man.'"

Bill Graham then unleashes a torrent of abuse as he marches Wilhelm out of the door, raging, "The next time you say 'Fuck you' to me, I hope it's out there somewhere with no camera around. I'll take your teeth out of your mouth and shove 'em through your nose. . . . Fucking animal."

The camera then follows Wilhelm down the stairs and out of the building, trailed by a further stream of abuse from Graham.

"He certainly didn't stay angry with me," said Wilhelm. "I got a call from him saying 'That thing you pulled on me is the most exciting thing in the movie.' Bill wanted me to sign a release for them to use it, which I did, and I got royalties."[15]

—

The final week of the Fillmore West began with a Tuesday night in-house basketball game between the Fillmore Fingers and FM Productions. Bill Graham was as competitive as ever as he "dribbled, coached and hollered" up and down the brightly lit Fillmore West onstage basketball court. It was a close game, and in the final five minutes the referee was threatened and fists flew, with a player being knocked to the ground.

"Get out of the fucking building!" yelled Graham at a spectator who had dared to criticize one of his plays. Then Graham briefly left the game to frog-march the offender out of the building before coming back to finish the contest, which the Fingers won 60–58.

"It was an action-packed week," said Fillmore West manager Gary L. Jackson. "We're making a movie. Everything is being recorded for a Fillmore album. It was an eighty-hour week for me, but I was having the time of my life."[16]

On Friday, July 2, the Grateful Dead played their final show at the Fillmore West. Before the show, an excited Bill Graham called Jackson, who captained his Fillmore Football team, into his office.

"Bill said, 'We're challenging the Grateful Dead after the show,'" recalled Jackson. "It was their last concert [there] and Bill named it the 'Toilet Bowl.'"

At 11:15 p.m., Bill Graham introduced the Grateful Dead, telling the audience, "After all the shit that's gone down over the years, I'm very grateful to them and consider them friends . . . the Grateful Dead."[17]

The Dead then played a classic three-hour set, interrupted by one intermission, ending with "Not Fade Away" and "Johnny B. Goode."

After the audience had left, Bill Graham led them outside to a football sandbox for the Toilet Bowl.

"We started playing at maybe 2:30 a.m.," said Jackson. "Jerry Garcia's there and the rest of them and the crew. Bobby Weir was the most athletic of them."

The Grateful Dead's team managed to beat Graham's team, and Jackson found a toilet bowl for the official trophy presentation.

"So Bill brought out the oak toilet bowl with roses on it and gave it to Garcia," said Jackson. "The game was that competitive but we had fun doing it."[18]

⌁

The next morning, Jim Morrison of The Doors died in his bath in Paris at just twenty-seven years old—the exact same age at which Janis Joplin and Jimi Hendrix had died. Paul Kantner, who knew them all, viewed their deaths as unfortunate accidents.

"They were just experimenting with all the drugs that be," he said. "I never liked needles from the beginning, when I was three years old in the doctor's office. I still have trouble getting a blood test. So that kept me away from heroin. I don't like downers generally anyway. I've done a lot of acid, which was my favorite [drug] because it would take you out and up and search out adventures."

Kantner believes that a lot of musicians did heroin to better relate to the great blues and jazz musicians of the past.

"Yeah, a lot of musicians thought they had to be ultimately cool, particularly blues musicians," he explained. "That they had to do heroin like the famous blues and jazz musicians did, otherwise they won't be definitive or something. I lamented that on one level, but no, I never thought of doing it myself. I didn't even start drinking until I was in my fifties. Grace was the big drinker. Janis was a big drinker."[19]

On Saturday night, Electric Hot Tuna played a smoking three-hour set, opening for Quicksilver Messenger Service.

"Once again we were the stars of the moment," recalled Jorma Kaukonen. "We probably felt pretty important. I couldn't give you any specifics, but I'm sure we were really pleased with ourselves."[20]

On Sunday night, the Fillmore West had its grand finale, just one day short of its third anniversary. As it had been in New York, it was by invitation only and would be broadcast live by KSAN and KSFX in quadrophonic FM, each radio station carrying two channels of sound.

"This is going to be the greatest motherfucking evening of our lives," announced Bill Graham, as he came onstage to a standing ovation to start the show. "And now, a bitch of a band from the East Bay—Tower of Power."

361

Next up was Creedence Clearwater Revival, playing as a trio for the first time since John Fogerty had fired his brother Tom. Santana road manager Herbie Herbert was in the artist's dressing room talking to DJ Tom Donahue when John Fogerty walked in with an Elvis Presley pompadour and a perfectly tailored turquoise suit with matching boots.

"I couldn't believe the spectacle," said Herbert. "And I just said to Tom Donahue, 'Who the fuck is that? It looks like Elvis.' He said, 'You won't believe it. That is John Fogerty.' I went 'bullshit!' The guy was *the* squarest motherfucker on the face of the earth by hippie standards.

"They went out that night as a trio and played the best I ever heard Creedence Clearwater Revival. Wow. And they set the stage for Santana to deliver one of their most classic landmark performances."[21]

By now the album *Santana III* was finished, but still months away from being released. Just before they went on to close the show, Carlos Santana told Herbert they were going to play the new album for the first time that night. When Herbert pleaded with them not to do so, since the show was being broadcast live and would certainly be bootlegged, the band ordered him to make sure it didn't hit the airwaves.

"They were nothing but a fucking street gang," said Herbert, "and I knew because I was part of that gang I would have to go and do something."

So Herbert took out a Cub Scout hatchet from the band's toolbox. He then went over to the side of the stage where a small radio mixing device was attached to the dedicated phone lines taped to the floor and going out to the radio stations.

"And just before Bill Graham came out to introduce them, I hatcheted and the lines went dead. Dusty Street from KSAN jumped on my back, and tried to claw both of my eyeballs out. So I had to knock her out. And we performed the show with the new material but it didn't go out on the radio."[22]

That night would be the last time the original Santana lineup that had played Woodstock would ever perform together. They started with "Incident at Neshabur," off the new album, finishing with Carlos Santana's moving arrangement of Miles Davis's "In a Silent Way." The set signaled Santana's change in musical direction.

"We wanted to come off as a little more progressive," said Michael Shrieve, "as we felt that it would represent us at the given time when the Fillmore closed. We were sort of transformed as a band and that's why we chose to do the Miles Davis tune . . . and have our kind of groove to it. That was really important to us."[23]

At the end of their set, Bill Graham came onstage and brought out Van Morrison, Mike Bloomfield, Lydia Pense, Sam Andrew, Jack Casady, and many others for a final jam session.

"The music was terrible," wrote David Felton in *Rolling Stone.* "At one point, Van Morrison insisted they all stop and try something else. But the show was great."[24]

Then Bill Graham brought his staff onstage to throw gifts at the audience, including champagne, beer, and ice cubes.

The final show ended at around 5:00 a.m., when "Greensleeves" was played through the P.A. system. Fans lined up to shake Bill Graham's hand and personally thank him.

—⁓—

Before the show, *Rolling Stone* writer David Felton had been puzzled by a glass-encased bulletin board for coming attractions, in which Graham had constructed an eerie shrine, apparently for the Fillmores.

"At the top he pinned his May press release," wrote Felton, "underneath that, a small, upside down American flag and two flowers; at the bottom, a drawing of a thick, wooden cross. On each arm of the cross was nailed a hand—nailed right through the palm—one hand pointing downward, hands pointed to each side, and a hand pointing upward, giving the finger—to what? God? The flag? The Fillmore? Who knows?"[25]

CODA

After closing the two Fillmores, Bill Graham hardly retired from the music business. By December 1971, he had made his peace with Madison Square Garden, where he presented the Grateful Dead—his first New York show after closing the Fillmore East.

In January 1972, his divorce became final, but it was followed by an acrimonious child custody battle with Bonnie, who eventually won control of their young son, David. In June, the documentary on the last days of the Fillmore West was released and flopped. *Time* magazine called Graham the undisputed star of the movie.

"He gives quite a performance," wrote *Time* reviewer Richard Heffron, "by turns nasty, cajoling and funny."[1]

During the next few years, Graham concentrated on producing mega-arena rock tours, working with Bob Dylan, the Rolling Stones, Crosby, Stills, Nash & Young, and George Harrison. In July 1973, he surpassed the attendance at Woodstock with the Watkins Glen Festival in upstate New York. Featuring the Grateful Dead, the Allman Brothers Band, and The Band, it drew an estimated 600,000 people and is still listed in the *Guinness Book of Records* as the biggest festival crowd in history.

On Thanksgiving 1978, he brilliantly staged The Band's farewell show at Winterland, which Martin Scorsese filmed as *The Last Waltz*.

In January 1980, Bill Graham turned fifty. He was now grossing $100 million a year, and was showing no signs of slowing down. He had become an icon of rock, and in September 1984, San Francisco Mayor Dianne Feinstein issued a proclamation declaring it "Bill Graham Day."

A year later, he staged the American half of *Live Aid*, although he hated the new MTV generation.

"There was no television until I was seventeen," he complained. "Today with twenty-four channels and cable and video stores, people have become much more isolated. There's much less communal entertainment and communal joy."[2]

But Graham's personal life failed to match up to his astonishing business success. He tore through relationship after relationship, without ever finding a lasting one. He would call these his "hate-fucks."

He proposed and then ended a relationship with Marcia Sult, who bore him his second son, Alex. Then he had a turbulent on-off four-year relationship with his beautiful receptionist, Regina Cartright. In December 1988, she gave birth to a baby girl she named Caitlin, claiming Bill Graham was the father. DNA tests would later prove he was not.

After leaving the Fillmores, Bill Graham started using drugs, getting heavily into cocaine, ecstasy, and marijuana cookies. At one point he became addicted to Halcyon and sought treatment.

On October 25, 1991, Bill Graham died while coming back to his Mill Valley home from a Huey Lewis concert, when his helicopter hit a high voltage electrical tower just west of Vallejo, California, and exploded. Also killed were his fiancée, Melissa Gold, and friend and pilot Steve "Killer" Kahn.

A week later, more than 300,000 fans flocked to a free memorial concert in Golden Gate Park to celebrate him. The Grateful Dead, Santana, and Crosby, Stills & Nash played, and a tearful Carlos Santana delivered a moving eulogy to his "best friend and brother."

He told the audience how Graham had called him the night before he died, saying, "Stay well, my friend."

"Just the way he said it," Santana told the audience. "Maybe his mind didn't know, but something inside him did."

In 1992, Bill Graham was inducted into the Rock and Roll Hall of Fame in the nonperformer category by Carlos Santana and John Fogerty.

⚬⌒⚬

In October 1971, *Santana III* was released and became another huge hit, staying at number 1 for five weeks. In early 1972, Santana started recording their follow-up, *Caravanserai*, which would be a turning point for the group, taking their music into jazz fusion. Clive Davis was furious, warning Carlos he was committing "career suicide."[3]

Gregg Rolie and Neal Schon also felt the band was veering in the wrong direction, but Carlos stood his ground. Eventually the band split up with Carlos and Michael Shrieve carrying on with Santana, while Gregg Rolie and Neal Schon started the immensely successful rock band Journey, under Herbie Herbert's management.

In 1972, Carlos Santana met his first wife, Deborah, at a Tower of Power concert. He also gave up drugs and found religion, becoming a disciple of Sri Chimnoy, who gave him the name "Devadip." He then recorded an acclaimed album with another Sri Chimnoy devotee, John McLaughlin.

Santana soldiered on with changing personnel but never found the huge success and album sales of the original band.

In 1998, Carlos Santana, now fifty-five, was inducted into the Rock and Roll Hall of Fame by John Popper, whose band Blues Traveler was discovered by Bill Graham's son, David.

Then a year later, Clive Davis, now running Arista Records, suggested Carlos record a collaborative album with some of the recording industry's biggest stars. The result was *Supernatural*, which put Carlos back on top, selling twenty-five million albums and winning nine Grammys, the first he had ever won. The single "Smooth" with Rob Thomas spent twelve weeks at number 1 on the *Billboard* chart.

It was around this time, while in psychiatric counseling, that Carlos finally confronted being molested more than forty years earlier. He also went public with it, bravely telling *60 Minutes'* Charlie Rose how it had torn him apart.

"It made me realize I was thinking wrong, like a victim," said Carlos. "It's a very, as children say, icky part of your life. By the grace of the holiest of holiest, I am free from feeling guilt, shame, fear."[4]

In December 2013, Carlos Santana received the nation's highest honor when he was awarded a Kennedy Center Award for influencing American culture through the arts. President Barack Obama welcomed the new honoree, saying: "Before Carlos Santana took the stage at Woodstock, few people outside his hometown of San Francisco knew who he was and the feeling was mutual: Carlos was in such a, shall we say, 'altered state of mind,' that he remembers almost nothing about the performance."

After Grace Slick's drag-racing accident, which almost killed her, her behavior became even more bizarre. In late August 1972, while at the Rubber Bowl in Akron, Ohio, a drunken Grace and Paul Kantner were both arrested and landed in jail after she grabbed a cop by his police whistle and took a swing at him.

After Bill Thompson bailed them out, they took a private plane to a show in Chicago.

"So the show is starting and Grace is drunk," said Thompson, "and what does she do? Somebody says 'Take it off!' And Grace pulled up her dress and she had no underwear on. A good shot. It was kind of like the end of the Airplane."[5]

A month later, on September 22, Jefferson Airplane played their final concert at Winterland.

In January 1974, Grace released her first solo album, *Manhole*, which was conceived as a soundtrack for a movie that never materialized. Soon afterward, she and Paul Kantner formed a new band called Jefferson Starship, which would achieve even bigger success than Jefferson Airplane.

During the first Jefferson Starship tour, Grace, now thirty-five, fell in love with Skip Johnson, the band's twenty-year-old lighting engineer. When Paul Kantner found out, he was furious. Eventually Grace split up with Paul and married Johnson in Hawaii. She and Paul would continue to share custody of China, who spent most of her time being brought up by a nanny.

Ironically, it was only after Marty Balin joined Jefferson Starship that they broke big, with their album *Red Octopus* hitting number 1.

In early 1978, Grace outdid herself as a celebrity judge in a charity takeoff of *The Gong Show*. After getting drunk, she began abusing contestants, fellow judges, and audience members and had to be dragged offstage. The audience cheered.

A few hours later she was arrested for DWI by the California Highway Patrol, but the charges were later dropped on the condition that she join Alcoholics Anonymous.

"I'm a periodic alcoholic," she explained in 2012. "I don't drink every day. Never did. I was sober all during the Eighties. I'll go for ten years without drinking and it's all self-will. And a lot of that comes out of the ethos of the Sixties. We just did pretty much what we wanted to do."[6]

In 1985 Grace finally hit number 1 on the *Billboard* singles chart with "We Built This City," in which she dueted with Mickey Thomas.

A year later, Starship, as the band was now called, hit the number 1 spot again with "Sara," although Grace only sang backup vocals.

During her years touring, her daughter, China, rarely saw her parents, and she resented them for it.

"China felt abandoned," said Grace, "because both her mother and her father would take off at the same time for months. So I can understand that."

Grace quit Starship in 1988. A month later she reunited with the original members of Jefferson Airplane, with the exception of Spencer Dryden, for a twenty-five-date tour and album. It flopped. She also divorced Skip Johnson after discovering he was having an affair with a woman half her age.

On September 30, 1989, at the age of fifty, Grace retired from singing after the final Jefferson Airplane show in Golden Gate Park, San Francisco.

"There is something painful, something sad, about seeing people of my age performing with a rock band," she told Charles Laurence of the *Daily Telegraph*. "I watch Mick Jagger singing 'Satisfaction,' and think: 'Boy, if you still can't find satisfaction, with all your money and at your age, there really is something wrong!'"[7]

Grace did give one other public performance, however, at Hollywood's House of Blues in 1995, making a guest appearance with Jefferson Starship during a tribute to Papa John Creach, who had died two years before.

A year later, she was inducted into the Rock and Roll Hall of Fame with Jefferson Airplane, but she didn't bother to attend the ceremony. During their acceptance speeches, Marty Balin and Paul Kantner both thanked Bill Graham.

"Very few if any people ever came to the Fillmore to see a band, if you know what I mean," said Kantner, as the audience laughed. "As Grace said, she liked being in the band because it was the least crowded place of the party. She sends you her love and wishes and says, 'What are these old fuckers all doing over here? A bunch of doddering, goddamn old people.'"

In retirement, Grace let her hair turn snow white and started a new career as a commercial artist, specializing in painting white rabbits and other characters from *Alice in Wonderland*. As of this writing, she is seventy-five and lives with her daughter, China, and her husband, Seth, in Malibu, California.

"I can draw a white rabbit blindfolded by now," she told *Vanity Fair* in 2012. "The whole thing about rabbits has just continued all through my life. It's not exclusive; it's just part of my deal. I've done pictures of rock-and-roll people, obviously. Woodstock, Monterey Pop . . . a lot of stuff that is known to me."[8]

———

In the forty-four years since Janis Joplin's untimely death, her star now burns brighter than ever. New generations have discovered her music, and she remains a fashion icon.

In 1995, Melissa Etheridge inducted Janis into the Rock and Roll Hall of Fame, hailing her as an inspiration for men and women everywhere.

"I feel like what she did in her life at that time," said Etheridge, "enabled me when I was a young girl in 1976 growing up, not to feel so strange about wanting to do the things I wanted to do. She gave me power in my life, we didn't have to be secretaries or housewives, we could be rock stars."

On January 19, 2008, on what would have been her sixty-fifth birthday, the town of Port Arthur placed a historical marker outside her childhood home.

"She was a very popular figure in the Sixties," said Yvonne Sutherlin of the Jefferson County Historical Commission. "We just want people to know she's from here."

Eighteen months later, Janis's life and music were celebrated during the Fourteenth Annual American Music Masters series.

"I am touched, as is the rest of the family," said her younger sister, Laura, "that Janis's musical and social power continue to inspire and remain important in the lives of so many."

A Broadway musical entitled *A Night with Janis Joplin*, starring Mary Bridget Davies, who toured with Big Brother and the Holding Company in late 1990s, opened in 2013, receiving positive reviews.

On November 4, 2013, Janis received her own star on the Hollywood Walk of Fame at a moving ceremony attended by Kris Kristofferson and Clive Davis.

"There has never been an artist like Janis," said Davis. "This contradictory chick from Texas was on top of the rock world. She was unapologetically herself. She helped change what we perceive star quality to be. I'm so glad she's here on the Walk of Fame. She'd be drinking Southern Comfort and having a good time."[9]

After Bill Graham closed the Fillmore East, it lay empty for three and a half years until it was reopened by a promoter named Barry Stein as the NFE Theater, standing for New Fillmore East. In 1975, it changed its name to the Village East after Bill Graham objected to the Fillmore name being used.

In September 1980, after a $4 million renovation, it became The Saint, one of the most popular gay nightclubs in New York. It lasted until 1988, when it closed at the start of the AIDS epidemic.

In the early 1990s, the stretch of street outside the onetime Fillmore East was officially renamed "Bill Graham's Way" by Mayor Rudolph Giuliani. But the sign was soon stolen.

Today, the building houses the Emigrant Bank, which has some pictures of the original Fillmore East in its entrance, the only trace remaining of the legendary rock theater.

After the Fillmore West closed its doors, Howard Johnson's abandoned plans to raze it to the ground and build a hotel. Instead, the 50,000-square-foot building reverted back to being a Honda car dealership, which it remains as of this writing. Recently, the San Francisco planning authorities approved plans to demolish it and build a tower of luxury high-rise apartments.

ACKNOWLEDGMENTS

This book has been a true labor of love and the result of more than twenty years of research. My first book, *Rage & Roll: Bill Graham and the Selling of Rock*, was published in 1993 and chronicled how Bill Graham almost single-handedly invented the music business.

Since then I have written more than twenty books on a wide variety of subjects, but I've always wanted to revisit the rock music I grew up with and still love so much. And nothing crystalizes it more than Bill Graham, who bottled rock 'n' roll lightning at the Fillmore East and the Fillmore West.

On March 8, 1968, he launched the Fillmore East on New York's Lower East Side. Two months later he opened the Fillmore West, three-thousand miles away in San Francisco. In just three transcendent years, these two legendary venues would change rock music forever.

Like a rock 'n' roll colossus standing astride the East and West Coasts, they became meccas for a generation of devoted music fans who treasure their precious memories to this day. Every major rock act of the time played the Fillmores, performing classic shows that entered rock mythology. Jimi Hendrix, the Grateful Dead, Santana, Jefferson Airplane, Led Zeppelin, Cream, and the Allman Brothers; the list is endless.

There are so many people to thank, but first and foremost I owe a huge debt to Joshua White, whose legendary Joshua Light Show shared equal billing with all the rock stars on the marquee of the Fillmore East. I want to thank Josh for his friendship and his guidance throughout the writing of this book. I am also indebted to Bill Graham's ex-wife Bonnie MacLean for her generosity and help. She was with Bill in the trenches at the beginning, helping him build the foundations of his Fillmore empire.

I am especially indebted to Paul Kantner, who gave me his insight into Bill Graham and the Jefferson Airplane early one Saturday morning outside his favorite coffeehouse in North Beach, San Francisco.

I would also like to thank all those who were interviewed for the book: Peter Albin, Sam Andrew, José "Chepito" Areas, Allan Arkush, Marty Balin, Bruce Barthol, Jane Bernstein, Eli Bleich, Lee Blumer, Chris "Sunshine" Brooks, Arthur Brown, David Bustamonte, Jack Casady, Robert Christgau, Bobby Cohen, David Bennett Cohen, Kip Cohen, Richard Cole, John Byrne Cooke, Robbin Cullinen, Alex Cooley, Dave Davies, Vinnie Fusco, Bonnie Garner, Dave Getz, Bob Grossweiner, Bill Hanley, Jim Haynie, Chet Helms, Herbie Herbert, Gary L. Jackson, Jai Johanny Johanson (Jaimoe), Jorma Kaukonen, Dennis Keefe, Alton Kelley, Bill King, Michael Lang, Chris Langhart, Bill Laudner, Ken Mednick, Barry Melton, Chip Monck, John Morris, Dan Opatoshu, Lydia Pense, Hugh Romney (Wavy Gravy), Amalie R. Rothschild, David Rubinson, Marc Rubinstein, Ron Schneider, Neal Schon, Bob See, Richard Segovia, Michael Shrieve, Howard Smith, Dusty Street, Derek Taylor, Bill Thompson, Butch Trucks, Leslie West, Mike Wilhelm, Bill Wyman, and Jene Youtt.

I would also like to thank Bill Sagan and Grant Feichtmeir of Wolfgang's Vault for all their help with the book, and for allowing me free access to Bill Graham's personal papers and correspondence.

I also owe a huge debt to my editor, Keith Wallman, for all his help and guidance, and to my literary agents, Jane Dystel and Miriam Goderich, who first came up with the idea for this book, for their help and encouragement throughout.

Thanks is also due to Jennie Thompson and Dianna Ford of the Rock and Roll Hall of Fame Library and Archives, Marta Sanchez, Karen Rogers, Shandi Vanore, Danny Trachtenberg, Larry Cancro, Adrian Areas, George Eichen, Cash Edwards, Annette Witheridge, Roger Hitts, Onnie MacIntyre, Debbie, Doug and Taylor Baldwin, and Emily and Jerry Freund.

NOTES

PROLOGUE

1   Interview with Allan Arkush, January 20, 2013.
2   Transcript of Bill Graham's April 17, 1971, staff meeting.
3   Transcript of Bill Graham's Fillmore East press conference, April 28, 1971.

PART ONE

CHAPTER ONE: THE REFUGEE

1   *The Escort Notes*, September 26, 1941.
2   *Details* magazine, October 1991.
3   Detail from his temporary passport issued by the American Friends Service Committee, August 10, 1941.
4   *Performance Magazine*, December 22, 1989.
5   The Foster Home Bureau Files and Escort Notes, September 26, 1941.
6   Letter from the Foster Home Bureau's Director of Placements, Lotte Marcuse, to her superior, Elsie L. Heller.
7   Letter from Lotte Marcuse to Robert Lang, executive director of the US Committee for the Care of European Children.
8   *Chabad Journal*, 1983.
9   The Foster Home Bureau Supervisory Reports, March 5, 1943, and June 29, 1943.
10   *Bill Graham Presents*, Graham and Greenfield, 31.
11   *Details* magazine, October 1991.
12   Ibid.
13   USNA Report Summary, January 4, 1949.
14   Foster Home Bureau Report, January 30, 1950.
15   *Details* magazine, October 1991.
16   Ibid.
17   Ibid.
18   Graham's business résumé would claim he attended City College from 1953 to 1955 and graduated with a BA in business administration.
19   Interview with Jack Levin, February 8, 1992.
20   *Rolling Stone*, December 12, 1991.
21   Interview with Irving Cohen, February 8, 1992.
22   *Details* magazine, October 1990.
23   Ibid.

CHAPTER TWO: CARLOS

1   *Soul Sacrifice*, Simon Leng.
2   *Billboard*, December 7, 1996.
3   Ibid.
4   *Voices of Latin Rock*, McCarthy.
5   *Angels & Demons*, BBC TV, 2004.
6   Ibid.
7   *Angels & Demons*, BBC 4, 2011.
8   *Billboard*, December 7, 1996.
9   *Soul Sacrifice*, Simon Leng.
10   *Billboard*, December 7, 1996.
11   *Soul Sacrifice*, Simon Leng.

CHAPTER THREE: FINDING DIRECTION

1   Interview with Bonnie MacLean, October 14, 2012.
2   Ibid.
3   Interview with Peter Coyote, May 7, 1992.
4   Interview with Jim Haynie, March 24, 1992.
5   Interview with Chet Helms, March 23, 1992.

CHAPTER FOUR: GRACE

1   *Don't You Want Somebody to Love*, Slick, 11.
2   *Religion Matters*, cable TV show, September 16, 2012.
3   *Got a Revolution*, Tamarkin, 97.
4   *New York Times*, October 18, 1998.
5   *Religion Matters*, cable TV show, September 16, 2012.
6   Ibid.
7   Ibid.
8   *Religion Matters*, cable TV show, September 16, 2012.
9   *Interview* magazine, 2007.
10   *Don't You Want Somebody to Love*, Slick, 17.
11   *Vanity Fair* blog, June 15, 2012.
12   *Wall Street Journal*, April 29, 2011.
13   *Got a Revolution*, Tamarkin, 100.
14   *Time Out Chicago*, 2008.
15   *Oui* magazine, February 1977.
16   Ibid.
17   Ibid.
18   *Rolling Stone*, November 12, 1970.
19   *Oui* magazine, February 1977.
20   *Got a Revolution*, Tamarkin, 103.
21   *Don't You Want Somebody to Love*, Slick, 34.
22   *Rolling Stone*, November 12, 1970.

23   *Fly, Jefferson Airplane*, DVD, 2004.
24   *Don't You Want Somebody to Love*, Slick, 47.

CHAPTER FIVE: THE RIGHT TIME AT THE RIGHT PLACE

1   Interview with Alton Kelley, March 19, 1992.
2   Ibid.
3   Interview with Bonnie MacLean, October 14, 2012.
4   *Bill Graham–Day at Night*, PBS Radio, 1974.
5   *San Francisco Chronicle/Examiner*, December 8, 1991.
6   *Jefferson Airplane and the San Francisco Sound*, Gleason.
7   Interview with Jorma Kaukonen, April 3, 2013.
8   Interview with Ronnie Davis, January 10, 1992.
9   Interview with Mary Travers, June, 8, 1975.
10   *Summer of Love*, Selvin, 45.
11   Interview with Bonnie MacLean, October 14, 2012.
12   Interview with San Andrew, March 26, 1992.
13   Interview with Jim Haynie, March 24, 1992.
14   *Don't You Want Somebody to Love*, Slick, 78
15   *Vanity Fair*, July 2012.
16   *Wall Street Journal*, April 29, 2011.
17   *Up Close: Jefferson Airplane*, radiow show, 1989.
18   *Don't You Want Somebody to Love*, Slick, 68.
19   Ibid.
20   *Oui* magazine, February 1977.
21   Ibid.

CHAPTER SIX: THE SALOON KEEPER

1   Interview with Chet Helms, March 25, 1992.
2   Ibid.
3   Ibid.
4   Interview with Alton Kelley, June 14, 1992.
5   Interview with Jim Haynie, March 24, 1992.
6   *Buried Alive*, Friedman, 74.

CHAPTER SEVEN: JANIS

1   BBC Radio 2, Janis Joplin documentary, January 19, 2011.
2   *Love Janis*, Joplin, 29.
3   *Texas Monthly*, October 1, 1992.
4   *Buried Alive*, Friedman, 17.
5   *Texas Monthly*, October 1, 1992.
6   BBC Radio 2, Janis Joplin documentary, January 19, 2011.
7   Ibid.
8   *Time*, August 9, 1968.

9 Biography Channel, January 13, 2000.

10 *New York Times*, February 23, 1969.

11 *Janis Joplin: Final 24*, TV documentary, 2007.

12 BBC Radio 2, Janis Joplin documentary, January 19, 2011.

13 *Buried Alive*, Friedman, 27.

14 Interview with Peter Albin, summer 1970.

15 *Rolling Stone*, October 29, 1970.

16 *Ramparts* magazine, August 1, 1968.

17 Interview with Chet Helms, March 23, 1992.

18 BBC Radio 2, Janis Joplin documentary, January 19, 2011.

19 *Texas Monthly*, October 1, 1992.

20 Interview with Chet Helms, March 23, 1992.

21 *Little Girl Blue*, BBC 6 Music, October 4, 2010.

22 *Texas Monthly*, October 1, 1992.

23 Interview with Chet Helms, March 23, 1992.

24 Ibid.

25 Interview with Jorma Kaukonen, April 3, 2013.

26 *Texas Monthly*, October 1, 1992.

27 *Buried Alive*, Friedman, 48.

28 Interview with Bobby Cohen, March 27, 1992.

29 Interview with Chet Helms, March 23, 1992.

30 BBC Radio 2, Janis Joplin documentary, January 19, 2011.

31 Interview with Chet Helms, March 23, 1992.

32 Ibid.

33 *Janis Joplin: Final 24*, TV documentary, 2007.

CHAPTER EIGHT: THE PIECES COME TOGETHER

1 *Don't You Want Somebody to Love*, Slick, 97.

2 Interview with Jim Haynie, June 21, 1992.

3 Interview with Bonnie MacLean, October 14, 2012.

4 Ibid.

5 *Voices of Latin Rock*, McCarthy, 29.

6 *Rolling Stone*, December 7, 1972.

7 *Angels & Demons*, BBC 4, 2011.

8 Ibid.

9 *Billboard*, December 7, 1996.

10 Interview with Richard Segovia, May 13, 2012.

11 PBS Radio Documentary on Carlos Santana, 1996.

12 Interview with Marty Balin, October 4, 1992.

13 *Don't You Want Somebody to Love*, Slick, 114.

14 Interview with Peter Albin, December 14, 2012.

15 www.countryjoe.com.

16 *Rolling Stone*, October 29, 1970.

17 Interview with Peter Albin, December 14, 2012.

18	*Up-Tight: The Velvet Underground Story*, Bockris and Malanga, 47.
19	*Seeing the Light*, Jovanovic, 86.
20	*Up-Tight: The Velvet Underground Story*, Bockris and Malanga, 47, 48.

CHAPTER NINE: MOVING UP

1	Interview with Jorma Kaukonen, April 3, 2013.
2	*Fly, Jefferson Airplane*, DVD, 2004.
3	Interview with Jack Casady, March 22, 2013.
4	*Got a Revolution*, Jeff Tamarkin, 113.
5	*Relix* magazine, April 1993.
6	Interview with Bill Thompson, January 28, 2013.
7	Interview with David Getz, March 26, 1992.
8	Interview with Nick Gravenites, April 16, 1992.
9	Ibid.
10	Interview with Bonnie MacLean, October 14, 2012.
11	Ibid.
12	Interview with Jack Casady, March 22, 2012.
13	Ibid.
14	Interview with Paul Kantner, May 18, 2013.
15	Interview with Jorma Kaukonen, April 3, 2013.
16	Interview with Paul Kantner, May 18, 2013.
17	*Jefferson Airplane and the San Francisco Sound*, Gleason. 283.
18	House of Rock BlogSpot interview, July 31, 2009.
19	David Gans interview with Bill Graham, 1984.
20	*Vanity Fair*, July 2012.
21	*Bill Graham: My Life Inside Rock*, PBS Radio.

CHAPTER TEN: 1967

1	Interview with Jim Haynie, March 24, 1992.
2	Interview with Joe Smith, 1988.
3	Interview with Bill Thompson, January 28, 2013.
4	Interview with Jorma Kaukonen, April 3, 2013.
5	*Relix* magazine, April 1993.
6	Interview with Jim Haynie, May 23, 2013.
7	Interview with Bonnie MacLean, June 5, 2012.
8	Ibid.
9	Interview with Jim Haynie, May 23, 2013.
10	*Rolling Stone*, December 7, 1972.
11	*New York Times*, October 18, 1998.
12	Interview with Jim Haynie, May, 23, 2013.
13	Interview with Bill Thompson, May 13, 2013.
14	*Summer of Love*, Selvin, 125.
15	Ibid., 118.

16   Interview with Sam Andrew, December 14, 2012.
17   www.countryjoe.com, 2004.
18   Interview with David Cohen, January 15, 2013.
19   *Vanity Fair*, July 2012.
20   Interview with Bruce Barthol, January 22, 2013.
21   PBS Radio documentary on Carlos Santana, 1996.
22   *Rolling Stone*, March 16, 2000.
23   Interview with Paul Kantner, May 18, 2103.
24   Interview with Bonnie MacLean, October 14, 2012.
25   Interview with Bill Thompson, May 13, 2013.

CHAPTER ELEVEN: MONTEREY

1   Interview with Derek Taylor, August 14, 1992.
2   Interview with Robert Christgau, November 28, 2012, and *Any Old Way You Choose It*, Christgau, 24.
3   *Soundtrack of My Life*, Davis. 146.
4   *Janis Documentary*, BBC Radio 2, January 19, 2011.
5   Grace Slick interview by Ed Bernstein, June 2008.
6   Interview with Bill Thompson, May 13, 2013.
7   *Religion Matters*, cable TV show, September 16, 2012.
8   *Voices of Latin Rock*, McCarthy, 31.
9   Interview with Jim Haynie, May 23, 2013.
10   Jorma Kaukonen Collection at the Rock and Roll Hall of Fame.
11   Interview with John Morris, July 15, 1992.
12   Interview with Joshua White, July 4, 1992.
13   *Telegram*, August 1, 1967.
14   Interview with Joshua White, July 4, 1992.
15   Interview with John Morris, July 15, 1992.
16   Interview with John Morris, January 26, 2013.
17   Interview with John Morris, July 15, 1992.
18   Bill Graham interview with KSAN Radio, 1972.
19   Interview with Arthur Brown, September 5, 2013.
20   Interview with Chris Brooks, July 15, 1992.
21   Interview with Chip Monck, December 21, 2013.

CHAPTER TWELVE: HIRING AND FIRING

1   Interview with John Morris, January 26, 2013.
2   Interview with Peter Albin, December 14, 2012.
3   Interview with Pat Thomas, April 1993.
4   *Got a Revolution*, Tamarkin, 142.
5   Interview with Jorma Kaukonen, April 3, 2013.
6   Interview with John Morris, January 26, 2013.
7   *New York Times*, October 22, 1967.

8   *Fly, Jefferson Airplane*, DVD, 2004.
9   Interview with Bill Thompson, May 13, 2013.
10   *New York Times*, December 15, 1968.
11   Interview with John Cooke, November 2, 2012.
12   *A Tribute to the Fillmore*, 79.
13   Interview with Jack Casady, March 22, 2013.
14   Interview with Paul Kantner, May 18, 2013.
15   Interview with Bill Thompson, May 13, 2013.
16   Interview with Paul Kantner, May 18, 2013.
17   Interview with Bill Thompson, May 13, 2013.

PART TWO

CHAPTER THIRTEEN: BIRTH OF THE FILLMORE EAST

1   Interview with Nick Gravenites, April 16, 1992.
2   *Buried Alive*, Friedman, 95.
3   Interview with Sam Andrew, December, 14, 2012.
4   Interview with Jack Casady, March 22, 2013.
5   Interview with Jorma Kaukonen, April 3, 2013.
6   *Pearl*, Amburn, 159.
7   Interview with Robbin Cullinen, February 23, 2013.
8   *New York Times*, February 23, 1969.
9   Interview with John Morris, July 15, 1992.
10   Ibid.
11   Interview with Bonnie MacLean, October 14, 2012.
12   Interview with Kip Cohen, December 19, 2012.
13   Interview with Josh White, July 4, 1992.
14   Interview with Allan Arkush, January 20, 2013.
15   Interview with Sam Andrew, December 14, 2012.
16   *Bill Graham Presents*, Graham and Greenfield, 228.
17   Ibid., 230.
18   *Clive: Inside the Record Business*, Davis and Willworth.
19   Interview with Howard Smith, February 22, 2013.
20   Interview with John Morris, July 15, 1992.
21   *Fillmore East Program*, December 26, 1969.
22   Interview with Chip Monck, December 21, 2012.
23   Interview with Bob See, February 5, 2013.
24   Interview with Chris Langhart, January 26, 2013.
25   Interview with Joshua White, July 4, 1992.
26   Interview with Kip Cohen, December 19, 2012.
27   Interview with Bill Hanley, January 17, 2013.
28   Interview with John Morris, January 26, 2013.

29   Ibid.
30   Interview with Bonnie MacLean, October 14, 2012.
31   Interview with Lee Blumer, July 21, 1992.
32   Interview with Peter Albin, June 9, 1992.
33   Interview with Sam Andrew, December 14, 2012.
34   *Just Kids*, Smith, 58.
35   Ibid.
36   Interview with Joshua White, December 8, 2012.
37   Interview with Chip Monck, December 21, 2012.
38   Interview with John Morris, January 26, 2013.
39   *Fillmore East Program*, December 26, 1969.
40   Interview with Vinnie Fusco, September 4, 1992.
41   Interview with Kip Cohen, December 19, 2012.
42   Interview with John Morris, January 26, 2013.
43   Interview with Howard Smith, February 28, 2013.
44   Interview with Sam Andrew, December 14, 2012.

CHAPTER FOURTEEN: UP AND RUNNING

1   Interview with John Morris, July 15, 1992.
2   *Rolling Stone*, December 19, 1985.
3   *Village Voice*, March 14, 1968.
4   *Just Kids*, Smith, 59.
5   Interview with Bill King, October 26, 2012.
6   Interview with Sam Andrew, December 14, 2012.
7   Ibid.
8   *Going Down with Janis*, Caserta, 66.
9   *Janis Joplin*, Biography Channel, January, 13, 2000.
10   Interview with John Morris, January 26, 2013.
11   Ibid.
12   Interview with Bill Laudner, January 14, 2013.
13   Interview with Bill Thompson, May 13, 2013.
14   Ibid.
15   Interview with Jorma Kaukonen, April 3, 2013.
16   Interview with Chip Monck, December 21, 2012.
17   Interview with Arthur Brown, September 5, 2013.
18   *New York Times*, May 4, 1968.
19   *Village Voice*, May 9, 1968.
20   *Fly, Jefferson Airplane*, DVD, 2004.
21   *Somebody to Love*, Slick, 170.
22   Ibid.
23   Interview with Bill Thompson, January 28, 2013.
24   Interview with John Morris, January 26, 2013.
25   Interview with Amalie Rothschild, July 29, 2013.
26   Interview with Robert Christgau, November 28, 2012.

27   *Village Voice*, May 16, 1968.
28   *Village Voice*, April 18, 1968.
29   Interview with Sam Andrew, December 14, 2012.
30   Interview with John Cooke, November 2, 2012.
31   Interview with Peter Albin, December 14, 2012.
32   *Soundtrack of My Life*, Davis. 146.
33   Interview with Arthur Brown, September 5, 2013.
34   *Summer of Love*, 170.
35   *Rolling Stone*, December 7, 1972.
36   *Billboard*, December 9, 1996.
37   Interview with Herbie Herbert, January 30, 2013.
38   Interview with Barry Melton, January 25, 2013.
39   Interview with Lee Blumer, July 21, 1992.
40   Interview with Allan Arkush, January 20, 2013.
41   *Details* magazine, October 1991.
42   Interview with Chris Langhart, January 26, 2013.

CHAPTER FIFTEEN: THE FILLMORE WEST

1   KSAN Radio interview, 1972.
2   Interview with Jim Haynie, March 24, 1992.
3   Ibid.
4   Interview with Barry Melton, January 25, 2013.
5   *Rolling Stone*, December 12, 1991.
6   BBC Radio 2, January 19, 2011.
7   Interview with Peter Albin, December 14, 2012.
8   *Rolling Stone*, August 24, 1968.
9   *Time*, August 9, 1968.
10   Interview with Joshua White, December 12, 2012.
11   Interview with Jorma Kaukonen, April 3, 2013.
12   Letter from Bill Graham's personal correspondence.
13   *Village Voice*, August 8, 1968.
14   *Buried Alive*, Friedman, 134.
15   Interview with Sam Andrew, December 14, 2012.
16   Bill Graham letter dated August 9, 1968, Bill Graham's personal papers.
17   *New York Times*, September 1, 1968.
18   Interview with Sam Andrew, December 14, 2013.
19   *Little Girl Blue*, BBC 6 Music, 2001.
20   Interview with Peter Albin, December 14, 2012.
21   *Rolling Stone*, September 28, 1968.
22   Ibid.
23   Interview with Sam Andrew, July 14, 2012.
24   Interview with Peter Albin, December 14, 2012.
25   Ibid.
26   Interview with Vinnie Fusco, September 4, 1992.

27   Ibid.
28   *The Summer of Love*, Selvin, 176–77.
29   Australian Radio interview, September 24, 2009.
30   *The Roseanne Show*, 1998.
31   Grace Slick Australian Radio interview, September 24, 2009.
32   Interview with Bill Thompson, January 28, 2013.
33   Bill Graham's personal papers.
34   Interview with Mike Wilhelm, March 25, 1992.
35   *Rolling Stone*, December 7, 1972.
36   Interview with Lee Blumer, February 6, 2013.
37   Interview with Bonnie MacLean, October 14, 2012.
38   Interview with Kip Cohen, December 19, 2012.
39   Interview with Lee Blumer, July 21, 1992.
40   *A Tribute to the Fillmore*, 36.
41   *Life* magazine, September 20, 1968.
42   Interview with Barry Melton, January 25, 2013.
43   Interview with Kip Cohen, December 19, 2012.
44   Interview with Bill Thompson, January 28, 2013.
45   Interview with John Morris, July 15, 1992.
46   *New York Times*, December 15, 1968.
47   Interview with John Morris, January 26, 1968.

CHAPTER SIXTEEN: CATCHING FIRE

1   *Ed Bernstein*, cable TV show, June 2008.
2   Terroscope.co.uk interview.
3   *Rolling Stone*, February 1, 1969.
4   Interview with Paul Kantner, May 18, 2013.
5   Interview with Bill Thompson, May 13, 2013.
6   Interview with Paul Kantnerm, May 18, 2013.
7   Interview with Howard Smith, *Smith Tapes*, June 1969.
8   Interview with Bob Grossweiner, February 19, 1992.
9   Interview with Joshua White, July 4, 1992.
10   *Rolling Stone*, December 19, 1985.
11   Interview with David Bennett Cohen, January 15, 2013.
12   The Local East Village/New York Times.com, April 11, 2013.
13   *Voices of Latin Rock*, McCarthy, 56.
14   Interview with Jack Casady, March 22, 2013.
15   Interview with Bill Laudner, January 14, 2013.
16   Interview with Jorma Kaukonen, April 3, 2013.
17   Ibid.
18   Interview with Joshua White, December 8, 2012.
19   *Going Down with Janis*, Caserta, 143.
20   *Summer of Love*, Selvin, 193.
21   *New York Times*, November 17, 1968.

22   Interview with Bill King, October 26, 2012.
23   Interview with Bill King, October 26, 2012.
24   Interview with Sam Andrew, December 14, 2012.
25   Interview with John Cooke, November 2, 2012.
26   Interview with Bill King, October 26, 2012.
27   *Rod: The Autobiography*, Stewart, 102.
28   *Little Girl Blue*, BBC 6 Music, October 4, 2010.
29   Allaboutjazz.com, October 10, 2009.
30   *Rolling Stone*, February 1, 1969.
31   Interview with Bill King, October 26, 2012.
32   *New York Times*, December 15, 1968.
33   *New York Times*, January 19, 1969.
34   Interview with Bonnie MacLean, October 14, 2012.
35   Ibid.
36   *Rolling Stone*, February 15, 1969.
37   *Details* magazine, October 1991.
38   Interview with Howard Smith, January 18, 2013.
39   Ibid.
40   Interview with Allan Arkush, January 20, 2013.
41   Interview with Bonnie MacLean, October 14, 2012.
42   Ibid.

CHAPTER SEVENTEEN: THE SUNSHINE MAKERS

1   Interview with Bonnie MacLean, October 14, 2012.
2   Interview with Richard Cole, October 14, 1992.
3   Interview with David Rubinson, February 5, 2013.
4   Interview with Herbie Herbert, January 30, 2013.
5   *Voices of Latin Rock*, McCarthy, 57.
6   *Angels & Demons*, BBC 4, 2011.
7   Interview with Michael Shrieve, February 25, 2013.
8   Ibid.
9   *Angels & Demons*, BBC 4, 2011.
10   *Little Girl Blue*, BBC 6 Music, October 4, 2010.
11   *New York Times*, February 23, 1969.
12   Interview with John Cooke, November 2, 2012.
13   *New York Times*, December 15, 1968.
14   Ibid.
15   *Smith Tapes*, June 1969.
16   Interview with Allan Arkush, January 20, 2013.
17   Interview with Kip Cohen, December 19, 2012.
18   *No One Gets Out Alive*, Hopkins and Sugarman, 216.
19   *Village Voice*, January 30, 1969.
20   Interview with John Morris, January 26, 2013.
21   Interview with Allan Arkush, January 20, 2013.

22   *Rolling Stone*, March 15, 1969.
23   *Got a Revolution*, Tamarkin, 186.
24   Interview with Lydia Pense, May 10, 2013.
25   *Fillmore East Program*, March 14–15, 1969.
26   Interview with Marty Balin, October 4, 1992.
27   *Rolling Stone*, February 16, 1969.
28   Interview with Chris Brooks, July 15, 1992.
29   *Rolling Stone*, March 15, 1969.
30   Ibid.
31   Ibid.
32   *Rolling Stone*, October 29, 1970.
33   *The New Yorker*, March 15, 1969.
34   *Buried Alive*, Friedman, 159.
35   *Rolling Stone*, March 15, 1969.
36   Bill Graham interview with KSAN-FM, 1972.
37   *San Francisco Chronicle*, March 24, 1969.
38   Terrascope.com.co.uk.

CHAPTER EIGHTEEN: GO RIDE THE MUSIC

1   *Fillmore East Program*, May 23–24, 1969.
2   *Rolling Stone*, April 19, 1969.
3   Interview with David Rubinson, February 5, 2013.
4   Interview with Sam Andrew, December 14, 2012.
5   Interview with John Cooke, November 2, 2012.
6   *Evening Standard*, April 1969.
7   *International Times*, May 9, 1969.
8   *New Musical Express*, May 3, 1969.
9   *Summer of Love*, Selvin, 218.
10   *Voices of Latin Rock*, McCarthy, 35.
11   Moonflowercafe.com, 2011.
12   Interview with José Areas, June 7, 2013.
13   *Angels & Demons*, BBC 4, 2011.
14   Interview with Michael Lang, September 29, 1992.
15   *Back to the Garden*, Fornatale, 121.
16   Interview with Dusty Street, March 28, 2013.
17   Interview with Paul Kantner, May 18, 2013.
18   *New York Times*, April 7, 1969.
19   *Fillmore East Program*, May 16–17, 1969.
20   *Across the Great Divide*, Hoskyns, 204.
21   *New York Times*, May 12, 1969.
22   *Stairway to Heaven*, Cole, 71.
23   *Rolling Stone*, May 3, 1969.
24   *Who I Am: A Memoir*, Townshend, 249.
25   Interview with Allan Arkush, January 20, 2013.

26 Ibid.
27 *Village Voice*, May 22, 1969, and July 17, 1969.
28 *Who I Am: A Memoir*, Townshend, 252.
29 *Searching for the Sound*, Lesh, 149.
30 Interview with John Cooke, November 2, 2012.
31 Ibid.
32 BBC Radio 2 documentary on Janis Joplin, 2010.
33 Interview with Sam Andrew, December 14, 2012.
34 Interview with Allan Arkush, January 20, 2013.

CHAPTER NINETEEN: THREE DAYS OF PEACE, LOVE, AND MUSIC

1 *Oui* magazine, February 1977.
2 *Rolling Stone*, July 12, 1969.
3 *Smith Tapes*, June 1969.
4 Bill Graham's personal papers, Wolfgang's Vault.
5 Ibid.
6 Interview with Chris Brooks, July 15, 1992.
7 *Summer of Love*, Selvin, 266.
8 Interview with Chet Helms, March 23, 1992.
9 Interview with Chris Brooks, July 15, 1992.
10 Interview with Allan Arkush, January 20, 1013.
11 Interview with John Cooke, November 2, 2012.
12 Interview with John Morris, January 26, 2013.
13 *Buried Alive*, Friedman, 168.
14 Interview with Jorma Kaukonen, April 3, 2013.
15 Interview with Paul Kantner, May 18, 2013.
16 Interview with John Morris, July 15, 1992.
17 Interview with Bonnie MacLean, October 14, 2012.
18 *Just Kids*, Smith, 106.
19 Interview with Bill Thompson, May, 13, 2013.
20 www.countryjoe.com.
21 Interview with Bill Thompson, May 13, 2013.
22 *American Sabor*, www.americansabor.org.
23 Interview with Kip Cohen, December 19, 2012.
24 Interview with Michael Lang, September 29, 1992.
25 Interview with Jack Casady, March 22, 2013.
26 *Searching for the Sound*, Lesh, 152.
27 Interview with Paul Kantner, May, 18, 2013.
28 *Bill Graham: My Life Inside Rock*, radio show.
29 Interview with Chip Monck, December 21, 2013.
30 *Angels & Demons*, BBC 4, 2011.
31 Interview with Michael Shrieve, February 25, 2013.
32 *Angels & Demons*, BBC 4, 2011.

33   Interview with José Areas, June 7, 2013.
34   Interview with Jorma Kaukonen, April 3, 2013.
35   *Woodstock: The Oral History*, Makower, 223.
36   *Woodstock*, documentary, 1970.
37   BBC 6 Music, October 4, 2010.
38   Interview with Leslie West, February 7, 2013.
39   *Who I Am*, Townshend, 261.
40   Interview with Bill Thompson, May 13, 2013.
41   *Dick Cavett Show*, August 19, 1968.
42   *Rolling Stone*, October 18, 1969.
43   Interview with Alex Cooley, June 11, 1992.
44   Interview with Allan Arkush, January 20, 2013.
45   Interview with Barry Melton, January 25, 2013.

CHAPTER TWENTY: RUNNING ON EGO

1   Interview with José "Chepito" Areas, June 6, 2013.
2   *Rolling Stone*, November 1, 1969.
3   *Time*, October 19, 1970.
4   Interview with John Cooke, November 2, 2012.
5   Interview with Dave Davies, October 24, 2013.
6   Interview with Joshua White, December 8, 2012.
7   *The New Yorker*, November 15, 1969.
8   Interview with Chris Langhart, January 26, 2013.
9   Interview with Amalie Rothschild, March 13, 2013.
10   Interview with Allan Arkush, January 20, 2013.
11   *Got a Revolution*, Tamarkin, 209.
12   Interview with Robert Christgau, November 28, 2012.
13   *Religion Matters*, cable TV show, September 16, 2012.
14   *New York Times*, February 23, 1969.
15   Interview with Leslie West, February 7, 2013.
16   Interview with Richard Segovia, May 13, 2013.
17   Interview with Ron Schneider, January 15, 2013.
18   *Rolling Stone*, December 13, 1969.
19   Interview with Bill Wyman, August 20, 1992.
20   Interview with Ron Schneider, January 15, 2013.
21   *Mick Jagger*, Norman, 372.
22   Interview with Jack Casady, March 22, 2013.
23   Interview with Bill Thompson, January 28, 2013.
24   *Rolling Stone*, December 19, 1985.
25   *Live at the Fillmore East*, 117.
26   *You Can't Always Get What You Want*, Cutler, 150–51.
27   *Raisin' Cain*, Sullivan, 119.
28   Interview with Herbie Herbert, January 30, 2013.
29   Interview with Paul Kantner, May 18, 2013.

30	Ibid.
31	Australian Radio interview, September 24, 2009.
32	Interview with Bill Wyman, August 20, 1992.
33	*Buried Alive*, Friedman, 181.
34	Janis Joplin documentary, Biography Channel, January 13, 2000.
35	*Raisin' Cain*, Sullivan,122.
36	*Soundtrack of My Life*, Davis, 210.
37	Interview with David Bennett Cohen, January 15, 2013.
38	Interview with Allan Arkush, January 20, 2013.
39	Ibid.
40	Interview with Dan Opatoshu, February 4, 2013.
41	Ibid.
42	Interview with Allan Arkush, January 20, 2013.
43	Ibid.
44	Interview with Ken Mednick, January 14, 2013.
45	*Pacific Sun*, June 26, 1975.

CHAPTER TWENTY-ONE: A NEW DECADE

1	Interview with Allan Arkush, January 20, 2013.
2	Interview with Vinnie Fusco, September 4, 1992.
3	*Jazz & Pop*, June 1970.
4	Interview with Joshua White, July 4, 1992.
5	*Melody Maker*, June 4, 1971.
6	*Variety*, September 17, 1969.
7	Interview with Bill Thompson, May 13, 2013.
8	*Rolling Stone*, February 21, 1970.
9	Interview with Paul Kantner, May 18, 2013.
10	Interview with Bonnie MacLean, October 14, 2012.
11	Ibid.
12	*Buried Alive*, Friedman, 192.
13	*Rolling Stone*, May 28, 1970.
14	Ibid.
15	*My Cross to Bear*, Allman, 186.
16	Interview with Allan Arkush, January 20, 2013.
17	Interview with Dan Opatoshu, February 4, 2013.
18	*My Cross to Bear*, Allman, 190.
19	Interview with Butch Trucks, January 18, 2013.
20	*Searching for the Sound*, Lesh. 176.
21	Interview with Allan Arkush, January 20, 2013.
22	*Got a Revolution*, Tamarkin, 216.
23	*The Soundtrack of My Life*, Davis. 189.
24	*New York Post*, March 19, 1970.
25	*Miles: The Autobiography*, Davis. 301.
26	*New York Times*, March 7, 1970.

27 *Miles: The Autobiography*, Davis. 302.
28 *Searching for the Sound*, Lesh, 177.
29 Interview with Lee Blumer, February 6, 2013.
30 Interview with Jane Bernstein, September 16, 2012.
31 Interview with Chris Brooks, July 15, 1992.
32 Interview with John Morris, July 21, 1992.

CHAPTER TWENTY-TWO: DOSING RICHARD NIXON

1 Interview with Peter Albin, December 14, 2012.
2 *Rolling Stone*, April 30, 1970.
3 BBC 6 Music, October 4, 2010.
4 Moonflowercafe.com, 2007.
5 *Bill Graham Presents* press release, 1970.
6 Interview with Herbie Herbert, January 30, 2013.
7 BBC Radio 2, January 19, 2011.
8 Interview with Bill Thompson, January 28, 2013.
9 *20/20 Downtown*, January 13, 2000.
10 *Rolling Stone*, October 1, 1970.
11 Interview with Paul Kantner, May 18, 2013.
12 *Time Out Chicago*, 2008.
13 *New York Times*, April 25, 1970.
14 Interview with Joshua White, July 4, 1992.
15 Interview with Bonnie Garner, January 8, 2013.
16 Interview with Dan Opatoshu, February 4, 2013.
17 *Any Old Way You Choose It*, Christgau.
18 Interview with Robert Christgau, November 28, 2012.
19 Interview with Paul Kantner, May 18, 2013.
20 Interview with Chris Brooks, July 15, 1992.
21 *Angels & Demons*, BBC 4, 2011.
22 *Voices of Latin Rock*, McCarthy, 65.
23 Interview with José Areas, June 7, 2013.
24 Interview with Michael Shrieve, February 25, 2013.
25 Interview with Neal Schon, July 12, 2013.
26 *Nightwatcher's House of Rock*, July 31, 2009.
27 *Voices of Latin Rock*, McCarthy, 64.
28 *Billboard*, December 7, 1996.
29 Interview with Mike Wilhelm, March 25, 1992.
30 *Dick Cavett Show*, June 25, 1970.
31 *San Francisco Examiner/Chronicle*, January 31, 1971.

CHAPTER TWENTY-THREE: THE FESTIVAL EXPRESS

1 Interview with Amalie Rothschild, July 29, 2013.
2 Interview with Allan Arkush, January 20, 2013.

3   Ibid.
4   Interview with Dan Opatoshu, February 4, 2013.
5   Interview with Bonnie Garner, January 8, 2013.
6   Joe Smith interview with Graham Nash, May 5, 1986.
7   *Life* magazine, June 1970.
8   *New York Post*, June 8, 1970.
9   *Miles: The Autobiography*, Davis, 301.
10   Bill Graham's personal papers.
11   *Dick Cavett Show*, June 25, 1970.
12   *20/20 Downtown*, January 13, 2000.
13   Interview with John Cooke, November 2, 2012.
14   Interview with Leslie West, February 7, 2012.
15   *Rolling Stone*, September 3, 1970.
16   Interview with Kip Cohen, December 19, 2012.
17   Ibid.
18   *Buried Alive*, Friedman, 239.
19   *Temples of Rock*, Travel Channel, 2003.
20   Interview with Jack Casady, March 22, 2013.
21   *New York Times*, July 26, 1970.
22   Interview with Michael Shrieve, February 22, 2013.
23   Interview with Jorma Kaukonen, April 3, 2013.

CHAPTER TWENTY-FOUR: "SOMEWHERE NEAR SALINAS"

1   *New York Times*, October 18, 1970.
2   Interview with Marty Balin, October 4, 1992.
3   Interview with Jack Casady, March 22, 2013.
4   *Rolling Stone*, September 30, 1971.
5   Interview with Paul Kantner, May 18, 2013.
6   Interview with Barry Melton, January 25, 2013.
7   *Just Kids*, Smith, 158.
8   *Buried Alive*, Friedman, 256–57.
9   *20/20 Downtown*, January 13, 2000.
10   *Dick Cavett Show*, August 3, 1970.
11   *20/20 Downtown*, January 13, 2000.
12   *Rolling Stone*, March 16, 2000.
13   Ibid.
14   Interview with Michael Shrieve, February 25, 2013.
15   *Angels & Demons*, BBC 4, 2011.
16   *Buried Alive*, Friedman, 290–91.
17   *Voices of Latin Rock*, McCarthy, 67.
18   Interview with José Areas, June 7, 2013.
19   Ibid.
20   Herbie Herbert interview, January 30, 2013.
21   *Buried Alive*, Friedman, 318.

22   *Texas Monthly*, October 1, 1992.

23   *Janis Joplin: Final 24*, TV documentary, 2007.

24   Ibid.

25   *Texas Monthly*, October 1, 1992.

26   *Buried Alive*, Friedman, 300.

27   *Janis Joplin*, Biography Channel, January 13, 2000.

28   *Life* magazine, May 14, 1971.

29   Bill Graham's personal papers, Wolfgang's Vault.

30   Interview with Chris Brooks, July 15, 1992.

31   *Rolling Stone*, December 24, 1970.

32   *Voices of Latin Rock*, McCarthy, 67.

33   Interview with Ken Mednick, January 14, 2013.

34   *Inside Out: A Personal History of Pink Floyd*, Mason, 152.

35   *Summer of Love*, Selvin, 295.

36   *Melody Maker*, January 5, 1974.

37   *Rolling Stone*, October 1, 1970.

38   Ibid.

39   *20/20 Downtown*, January 13, 2000.

40   *New York Times*, January 31, 1971.

41   *Rolling Stone*, October 29, 1970.

42   *Smith Tapes: Janis Joplin*, September 30, 1970.

43   Ibid.

44   *Rolling Stone*, October 29, 1970.

45   *The Soundtrack of My Life*, Davis, 212.

46   *20/20 Downtown*, January 13, 2000.

47   Interview with John Cooke, November 2, 2012.

48   Ibid.

49   Interview with Paul Kantner, May 18, 2013.

50   *Got a Revolution*, Tamarkin, 227.

51   Interview with Jorma Kaukonen, April 3, 2013.

52   *Little Girl Blue*, BBC 6 Music, 2001.

53   Interview with Peter Albin, December 14, 2012.

54   Interview with Bill Thompson, May 13, 2013.

55   *Rolling Stone*, October 29, 1970.

56   *People Are Talking*, TV show, 1984.

57   *20/20 Downtown*, January 13, 2000.

58   *New York Times*, October 6, 1970.

59   *New York Times*, October 11, 1970.

CHAPTER TWENTY-FIVE: "THE SHOW MUST GO ON"

1   *Fillmore East Program*, October 12, 1970.

2   *New York Times*, October 18, 1970.

3   Interview with Peter Albin, December 14, 2012.

4   Interview with Kip Cohen, December 19, 2012.

5   Interview with Bonnie MacLean, October 14, 2012.

6   Interview with Dan Opatoshu, February 4, 2013.
7   *New York Times*, November 22, 1970.
8   *Guitar World*, August 1999.
9   Interview with Neal Schon, July 12, 2013.
10   *Voices of Latin Rock*, McCarthy, 95.
11   Interview with Neal Schon, July 12, 2013.
12   *Voices of Latin Rock*, McCarthy, 95.
13   Interview with José Areas, June 7, 2013.
14   *Angels & Demons*, BBC 4, 2011.
15   *Rolling Stone*, May 16, 2000.
16   Interview with Gary L. Jackson, May 5, 2013.
17   *Rolling Stone*, November 12, 1970.
18   *Oui* magazine, February 1977.
19   *Mojo*, October 1994.
20   Interview with Bill Thompson, May 5, 2013.
21   *Melody Maker*, January 5, 1974.
22   *Temples of Rock*, Travel Channel, 2003.
23   Interview with Leslie West, February 7, 2013.

CHAPTER TWENTY-SIX: THE LAST HURRAH

1   Interview with Herbie Herbert, January 30, 2013.
2   *Variety*, January 6, 1971.
3   *Oui* magazine, February 1977.
4   *Rolling Stone*, January 7, 1971.
5   *San Francisco Examiner*, January 31, 1971.
6   *Time*, February 8, 1971.
7   Australian Radio interview, 2009.
8   *Afro American*, February 6, 1971.
9   Interview with José Areas, June 7, 2013.
10   *Rolling Stone*, December 7, 1972.
11   Interview with Herbie Herbert, January 30, 2013.
12   *A Tribute to Bill Graham Program*, September 29, 1984.
13   *San Francisco Chronicle*, March 8, 1971.
14   Interview with Jean Youtt, December 5, 2012.
15   Interview with Butch Trucks, January 18, 2013.
16   Ibid.
17   *Skydog: The Duane Allman Story*, Poe, 177.
18   Interview with Jai Johanny Johanson.
19   *My Cross to Bear*, Allman, 232.

CHAPTER TWENTY-SEVEN: "THE FLOWERS WILTED"

1   Interview with Herbie Herbert, January 30, 2012.
2   Interview with Michael Shrieve, March 6, 2013.
3   Interview with Dan Opatoshu, February 4, 2013.

4   *Voices of Latin Rock*, McCarthy, 86.
5   *Rolling Stone*, December 7, 1992.
6   Ibid.
7   *Day for Night*, PBS, 1974.
8   *Rolling Stone*, April 27, 1972.
9   Interview with Bill Thompson, May 13, 2013.
10   *Relix* magazine, April 1993.
11   Interview with Allan Arkush, January 2013.
12   Transcript of the April 28, 1971 press conference and seven-point press release.
13   *Life* magazine, May 14, 1971.
14   *Rolling Stone*, May 27, 1971.
15   Interview with Jorma Kaukonen, April 3, 2013.
16   *Got a Revolution*, Tamarkin, 241.
17   Ibid., 239.
18   Interview with Jorma Kaukonen, April 3, 2013.
19   *Angels & Demons*, BBC 4, 2011.
20   Ibid.
21   Ibid.
22   Interview with Gary L. Jackson, May 11, 2013.
23   *San Francisco Chronicle*, May 31, 1971.
24   Interview with Gary L. Jackson, May 11, 2013.
25   *San Francisco Chronicle*, June 4, 1971.
26   *San Francisco Chronicle*, June 11, 1971.
27   *San Francisco Chronicle*, June 14, 1971.
28   Interview with Howard Smith, February 22, 2013.
29   Interview with Dan Opatoshu, February 4, 2013.
30   Interview with Howard Smith, February 22, 2013.
31   *Village Voice*, June 10, 1971.

CHAPTER TWENTY-EIGHT: "THANK YOU AND FAREWELL"

1   Interview with Jorma Kaukonen, April 3, 2013.
2   Interview with Jack Casady, March 22, 2013.
3   *Fillmore East Program*, June 27, 1971.
4   Interview with Butch Trucks, January 18, 2013.
5   *Bill Graham: My Life Inside Rock*, radio show.
6   Interview with Allan Arkush, January 20, 2013.
7   Interview with Butch Trucks, January 18, 2013.
8   Interview with Kip Cohen, December 19, 2012.
9   Transcript of WNEW broadcast, June 27, 1971.
10   *Any Old Way You Choose It*, Christgau, 192.
11   Interview with Butch Trucks, January 18, 2013.
12   *My Cross to Bear*, Allman, 236.
13   Interview with Eli Bleich, January 23, 2012.

14   Interview with David Rubinson, February 5, 2013.
15   Interview with Mike Wilhelm, March 25, 1992.
16   Interview with Gary L. Jackson, May 11, 2013.
17   *San Francisco Chronicle*, July 5, 1971.
18   Ibid.
19   Interview with Paul Kantner, May 18, 2013.
20   Interview with Jorma Kaukonen, April 3, 2013.
21   Interview with Herbie Herbert, January 30, 2013.
22   Interview with Herbie Herbert, January 30, 2013.
23   Interview with Michael Shrieve, February 25, 2013.
24   *Rolling Stone*, August 5, 1971.
25   Ibid.

CODA

1   *Time*, July 24, 1972.
2   *Details* magazine, October 1991.
3   *Angels & Demons*, BBC 4, 2011.
4   *60 Minutes*, October 1998.
5   Interview with Bill Thompson, May 13, 2013.
6   *Religion Matters*, cable TV show, September 16, 2012.
7   *Daily Telegraph*, December 29, 1998.
8   *Vanity Fair*, June 15, 2012.
9   Transcript of Walk of Fame ceremony, November 19, 2013.

Selected Bibliography

ORIGINAL INTERVIEWS

Albin, Peter—June 9, 1992; December 14, 2012
Andrew, Sam—March 26, 1992; December 14, 2012
Arkush, Alan—January 20, 2013
Areas, José "Chepito"—June 7, 2013
Balin, Marty—October 4, 1992
Barthol, Bruce—January 22, 2013
Bernstein, Jane—September 16, 2012
Bleich, Eli—January 23, 2012
Blumer, Lee—July 21, 1992; February 6, 2013
Brooks, Chris—July 15, 1992
Brown, Arthur—September 5, 2013
Bustamonte, David—May 16, 2013
Casady, Jack—March 22, 2013
Christgau, Robert—November 28, 2012
Cohen, Bobby—March 27, 1992
Cohen, David Bennett—January 15, 2013
Cohen, Kip—December 19, 2012
Cole, Richard—December 14, 1992
Cooke, John Byrne—November 2, 2012
Cullinen, Robbin—February 23, 2013
Cooley, Alex—June 11, 1992
Davies, Dave—October 24, 2013
Fusco, Vinnie—September 4, 1992
Garner, Bonnie—January 8, 2013
Getz, Dave—March 26, 1992
Grossweiner, Bob—February 19, 1992
Hanley, Bill—January 17, 2013
Haynie, Jim—March 24, 1992; June 21, 1992; May 23, 2013
Helms, Chet—March 23, 1992
Herbert, Herbie—March 18, 1992; January 30, 2013
Jackson, Gary L.—January 18, 2013; May 11, 2013
Johanson, Jai Johanny (Jaimoe)—January 25, 2013
Kantner, Paul—May 18, 2013
Kaukonen, Jorma—April 3, 2013
Keefe, Dennis—May 12, 2013
Kelley, Alton—March 19, 1992; June 20, 1992
King, Bill—October 26, 2012
Lang, Michael—September 29, 1992
Langhart, Chris—January 26, 2013

Laudner, Bill—January 14, 2013
MacLean, Bonnie—October 14, 2012; June 5, 2013
Mednick, Ken—January 14, 2013
Melton, Barry—January 25, 2013
Monck, Chip—December 21, 2013
Morris, John—July 15, 1992; January 26, 2013
Opatoshu, Dan—February 4, 2013
Pense, Lydia—May 10, 2013
Romney, Hugh (Wavy Gravy)—March 19, 1992
Rothschild, Amalie R.—March 13, 2013; July 29, 2013
Rubinson, David—February 5, 2013
Rubinstein, Marc—October 23, 2012
Schneider, Ron—January 15, 2013
Schon, Neal—July 12, 2013
See, Bob—February 5, 2013
Segovia, Richard—May 13, 2013
Shrieve, Michael—February 25, 2013; March 6, 2013
Smith, Howard—January 18, 2013; January 28, 2013
Street, Dusty—March 28, 2013
Taylor, Derek—August 14, 1992
Thompson, Bill—January 28, 2013; May 13, 2013
Trucks, Butch—January 18, 2013
West, Leslie—February 7, 2013
White, Joshua—July 4, 1992; December 8, 2012
Wilhelm, Mike—March 25, 1992
Wyman, Bill—August 20, 1992
Youtt, Jene—December 5, 2012

BOOKS

Allman, Gregg, with Alan Light. *My Cross to Bear*. New York: William Morrow, 2012.
Amburn, Ellis. *Pearl: The Obsessions and Passions of Janis Joplin*. New York: Warner Books, 1992.
Anson, Robert Sam. *Gone Crazy and Back Again: The Rise and Fall of the Rolling Stone Generation*. New York:. Doubleday, 1981.
Bockris, Victor, and Gerard Malanga. *Up-Tight: The Velvet Underground Story*. London: Omnibus Press, 1983.
Browne, David. *Fire and Rain: The Beatles, Simon and Garfunkel, James Taylor, CSNY, and the Lost Story of 1970*. Philadelphia: Da Capo, 2011.
Caserta, Peggy, with Dan Knapp. *Going Down with Janis*. New York: Dell, 1974.
Christgau, Robert. *Any Old Way You Choose It: Rock and Other Pop Music, 1967–1973*. Baltimore: Penguin Books, 1973.
Cole, Richard. *Stairway to Heaven: Led Zeppelin Uncensored*. New York: Harper Collins, 1992.

Cooke, John Byrne. *Janis Joplin: A Performance Diary 1966–1970*. Petaluma, CA: Acid Test Productions, 1997.

Cutler, Sam. *You Can't Always Get What You Want: My Life with the Rolling Stones, the Grateful Dead and Other Wonderful Reprobates*. Ontario, Canada: ECW Press, 2010.

Dalton, David. *Piece of My Heart: A Portrait of Janis Joplin*. Philadelphia: DaCapo, 1985.

Davis, Clive, with Anthony DeCurtis. *Soundtrack of My Life*. New York: Simon & Schuster, 2013.

Davis, Clive, with James Willwerth. *Clive: Inside the Record Business*. New York: William Morrow, 1975.

Davis, Miles, with Quincy Troupe. *Miles: The Autobiography*. New York: Simon & Schuster, 1989.

Davis, R. G. *San Francisco Mime Troupe: The First Ten Years*. San Francisco: Ramparts Press, 1975.

Draper, Robert. *The Rolling Stone Story: The Magazine That Moved a Generation*. Edinburgh, Scotland: Mainstream Publishing, 1990.

Echols, Alice. *Scars of Sweet Paradise: The Life and Times of Janis Joplin*. New York: Metropolitan Books, 1999.

Fenton, Craig. *Take Me to a Circus Tent: The Jefferson Airplane Flight Manual*. West Conshohocken, PA: Infinity, 2006.

Fong-Torres, Ben. *Not Fade Away: A Backstage Pass to 20 Years of Rock & Roll*. San Francisco: Miller Freeman Books, 1999.

Fornatale, Pete. *Back to the Garden: The Story of Woodstock*. New York: Touchstone, 2009.

Friedman, Myra. *Buried Alive: The Biography of Janis Joplin*. New York: William Morrow & Company, 1973.

Gleason, Ralph. J. *Jefferson Airplane and the San Francisco Sound*. New York: Ballantine Books, 1969.

Goldman, Albert. *Freakshow: Misadventures in the Counterculture, 1959–1971*. New York: Cooper Square Press, 2001.

Graham, Bill, and Robert Greenfield. *Bill Graham Presents*. New York: Doubleday, 1993.

Grushkin, Paul. *Art of Rock: A Spectacular Visual and Oral History*. New York: Cross River Press, 1987.

Henderson, David. *Jimi Hendrix: Voodoo Child of the Aquarian Age*. New York: Doubleday, 1978.

Hopkins, Jerry, and Danny Sugerman. *No One Gets Out Alive*. New York: Warner Books, 1981.

Hoskyns, Barney. *Across the Great Divide: The Band and America*. New York: Hyperion, 1993.

Joplin, Laura. *Love, Janis*. New York: Villard Books, 1992.

Jovanovic, Rob. *Seeing the Light: Inside the Velvet Underground*. New York: St. Martin's Press, 2010.

Kostelanetz, Richard. *Fillmore East: Recollections of Rock Theater*. New York: Schirmer Books, 1994.

Krieger, Susan. *Hip Capitalism* (SAGE Library of Social Research). Thousand Oaks, CA: SAGE Publications, 1979.

Leng, Simon. *Soul Sacrifice: The Santana Story*. London: Firefly Publishing, 2000.

Lesh, Phil. *Searching for the Sound: My Life with the Grateful Dead*. New York: Little, Brown and Company, 2005.

Makower, Joel. *Woodstock: The Oral History*. New York: Excelsior, 2009.

Mason, Nick. *Inside Out: A Personal History of Pink Floyd*. London: Weidenfeld & Nicholson, 2004.

McCarthy, Jim, with Ron Sansoe. *Voices of Latin Rock: The People and Events That Created This Sound*. Milwaukee, WI: Hal Leonard, 2004.

McDonough, Jack. *San Francisco Rock: The Illustrated History of San Francisco Rock Music*. San Francisco: Chronicle Books, 1985.

Nash, Graham. *Wild Tales: A Rock & Roll Life*. New York: Crown Archetype, 2013.

Norman, Philip. *Elton John: The Biography*. New York: Harmony Books, 1991.

———. *Mick Jagger*. New York: Ecco, 2012.

Parish, Steve, and Joe Layden. *Home Before Daylight: My Life on the Road with the Grateful Dead*. New York: St. Martin's Press, 2003.

Perry, Charles. *The Haight-Ashbury: A History*. San Francisco: Rolling Stone Press, 1984.

Poe, Randy. *Skydog: The Duane Allman Story*. San Francisco: Backbeat Books, 2006.

Rothschild, Amalie R. *Live at the Fillmore East: A Photographic Memoir*. New York: Thunder's Mouth Press, 1999.

Selvin, Joel. *Summer of Love: The Inside Story of LSD, Rock & Roll, Free Love and High Times in the Wild West*. New York: Dutton, 1994.

Simmons, Sylvie. *I'm Your Man: The Life of Leonard Cohen*. New York: Harper Collins, 2012.

Shapiro, Marc. *Carlos Santana: Back on Top*. New York: St. Martin's Griffin, 2000.

Slick, Darby. *Don't You Want Somebody to Love: Reflections on the San Francisco Sound*. Berkeley, CA: SLG Books, 1996.

Slick, Grace, with Andrea Kagan. *Somebody to Love?: A Rock-and-Roll Memoir*. New York: Warner Books, 1998.

Smith, Joe. *Off the Record: An Oral History of Popular Music*. New York: Warner Books, 1990.

Smith, Patti. *Just Kids*. New York: Harper Collins, 2010.

Stewart, Rod. *Rod: The Autobiography*. New York: Crown Publishing, 2012.

Sullivan, Mary Lou. *Raisin' Cain: The Wild and Raucous Story of Johnny Winter*. San Francisco: Backbeat Books, 2010.

Tamarkin, Jeff. *Got a Revolution!: The Turbulent Flight of Jefferson Airplane*. New York: Atria Books, 2003.

Taylor, Derek. *It Was Twenty Years Ago Today*. London: Bantam Press, 1987.

Townshend, Pete. *Who I Am: A Memoir*. New York: Harper, 2012.

Walker, Michael. *What You Want Is in the Limo: On the Road with Led Zeppelin, Alice Cooper, and the Who in 1973, the Year the Sixties Died and the Modern Rock Star Was Born*. New York: Spiegel & Grau, 2013.

Willis, Ellen. *Beginning to See the Light: Pieces of a Decade*. New York: Alfred A. Knopf, 1981.

NEWSPAPERS

New York Times
San Francisco Chronicle
San Francisco Examiner
Wall Street Journal
Washington Post
New York Post
New York Daily News
Houston Chronicle
Daily Telegraph
Evening Standard
Village Voice
Daily Texan
Pacific Sun

MAGAZINES

Rolling Stone
Vanity Fair
Time
Life
Newsweek
Details
Billboard
Variety
Time Out Chicago
Counterpunch
Interview
Oui
Texas Monthly
Ramparts
Relix

OTHER PUBLICATIONS

New Musical Express
Melody Maker
Guitar World
Jazz & Pop
A Tribute to the Fillmore Collector's Issue
Fillmore East Programs—1968–1971
Mojo Navigator
International Times
Afro-American
Thrust
Chabad Journal

RADIO, TELEVISION, AND DOCUMENTARIES

KSAN-FM
KPIX-FM
WPLJ-FM
WNEW-FM
KFOG-FM
PBS Radio
BBC Radio 2
BBC 6 Music
Australian Radio
60 Minutes
BBC TV
KRON-TV
20/20 Downtown
The Travel Channel
The Tonight Show with Johnny Carson
The Smothers Brothers Show
The Dick Cavett Show
The Roseanne Show
Biography Channel
Religion Matters, Cable TV
Ed Bernstein Cable Show
The Smith Tapes
Fly, Jefferson Airplane DVD
Festival Express DVD
Final 24—Janis Joplin DVD

WEBSITES

Terrascope.com.co.uk
CountryJoe.com
Allaboutjazz.com
MoonflowerCafe.com
Americansabor.org
NightwatchersHouseofRock.blogspot.com

BILL GRAHAM'S PERSONAL PAPERS AND OTHER CORRESPONDENCE

Telegrams between Miles David and Bill Graham: The Wolfgang's Vault Bill Graham Collection.
Personal letters from Bill Graham to Carlos Santana: The Wolfgang's Vault Bill Graham Collection.
Telegrams between Led Zeppelin manager Peter Grant and Bill Graham: The Wolfgang's Vault Bill Graham Collection.

June 2, 1967, and July 14, 1967, letters from Bill Graham to Beatrice Kaukonen: The Jorma Kaukonen Collection at The Rock and Roll Hall of Fame.

Bill Graham's January 2, 1969, letter to Chuck Berry: The Wolfgang's Vault Bill Graham Collection.

The 1984 Mill Valley Film Festival Tribute to Bill Graham Program.

INDEX

Abraxus (album), 282, 283, 302,
    308–9, 331
AB Skhy, 173
acid, 99, 206, 237, 267, 269, 326,
    341, 349–50, 361
Acid Tests, 47–48
Adler, Lou, 98
Adler, Renata, 179
After Bathing at Baxter's
    (album), 91–92, 110, 111
Albin, Peter, 65, 67, 74, 76, 107,
    108, 118, 132, 148, 156,
    160, 161, 274
    feelings toward Joplin,
    161–62
    Joplin's death, 318, 323
Alice in Wonderland (Carroll),
    35, 36, 51, 369
Allman, Duane, 337, 339, 343
Allman, Gregg, 269–70,
    337–38, 339
Allman Brothers Band, 260–61,
    269–70, 337–39, 353,
    357, 358
    at Fillmore East, 269,
    354–55
    at Fillmore West, 269
    at Watkins Glen
    Festival, 364
Altamont concert, 255–57
American Bandstand (TV
    show), 97
American Beauty (album), 343
Anderson, Signe Toly, 42,
    73–74, 79
Anderson Theater, 116, 120–21,
    122–24
Andrew, Sam, 49, 67, 68, 75,
    93, 100, 117, 123, 132,
    156, 159, 160, 182, 184,
    187, 208
    drugs, 161, 220
    and Fillmore East
    opening, 134

at Fillmore West
    closing, 363
and Janis Joplin, 147–48,
    210, 221, 274–75, 318
and Peggy Caserta, 137–38
plays last show with Janis
    Joplin, 231–32
relationship with Big
    Brother, 161
writes new material with
    Joplin, 196
Appaloosa, 260
Areas, José "Chepito," 210–12,
    238, 245, 282, 304, 309,
    326, 335–36, 341, 348
Arista Records, 366
Arkush, Allan, xiii, 123,
    152, 253
    and Allman Brothers, 260
    and The Band, 216
    and Band of Gypsies, 261
    and Bob Dylan, 343–44
    and CSN&Y, 243, 286–87
    and Grateful Dead, 221,
    264, 269
    and Joshua Light Show, 198
    last Fillmore East
    concert, 355
    and Led Zeppelin, 199
    problems with
    Motherfuckers, 190
    and Santana, 231
    and *Tommy*, 218–19,
    247, 248
Aronowitz, Al, 168–69,
    271, 287
Atlantic City Pop Festival, 231
Atlantic Records, 131,
    193–94, 338
Avalon Ballroom, 54, 67, 69, 74,
    76, 80, 92, 183
Avedon, Richard, 148

Baez, Joan, 234
Baker, Ginger, 106

Balin, Marty, 17, 42, 74, 81, 91,
    102, 112, 179, 256
    and Bill Graham, 368
    drinking, 329
    and drugs, 95–96
    on Grace Slick joining
    Jefferson Airplane, 80
    and Jefferson Airplane, 89,
    342–43
    joins Jefferson Starship, 367
    Joplin's death, 318
    and *Volunteers* album, 249
    withdraws from Jefferson
    Airplane, 299
Ballet Afro-Haiti, 173
Band, The, xv–xvi, 185, 310
    and Bill Graham, 155–56
    farewell show, 364
    Festival Express, 295
    at Fillmore East, 215, 216
    Music from the Big Pink
    album, 155, 216
    at Watkins Glen
    Festival, 364
    at Winterland, 215–16
    at Woodstock, 234
Band of Gypsies, 261, 263
Baratta, Paul, 102, 163, 259,
    311–12, 329
Bark (album), 347
Bar-Kays, 186
Barncard, Stephen, 270–71
Barsalona, Frank, 131, 225, 234
Barthol, Bruce, 94
Batiz, Javier, 22–23, 27, 71
Beach, Scott, 266
Beach Boys, 343, 357
Beatles, 179–80, 187–88
Beck, Jeff, 152
Bell, Richard, 275
Bennett, Alex, 356
Bennett, Tony, 259
Bernstein, Jane, 273

ABOUT THE AUTHOR

John Glatt is an investigative journalist with more than thirty-five years' experience and has written twenty-three books. A native of London, England, Glatt left school at sixteen and worked in a variety of jobs—including tea boy and messenger for B. Feldman & Co. music publisher in SoHo, where he once met Albert Grossman and The Band when they came into the office.

He then joined a small weekly newspaper outside London, where he honed his keen news sense. Over the next few years, he freelanced for many national English newspapers, including the *Daily Express*, the *Sunday People*, the *Daily Mail*, and *Woman Magazine*.

In 1981 he moved to New York, working on staff for *News Limited*, as well as freelancing for *Newsweek*, *Omni*, the *New York Post*, the *Australian*, *Modern Business*, and other newspapers and magazines worldwide.

His first book, *Rage & Roll: Bill Graham and the Selling of Rock*, was published in 1993, and he has written an average of one book a year since then.

His website is www.johnglatt.com.